A Museum of Faiths

THE AMERICAN ACADEMY OF RELIGION
CLASSICS IN RELIGIOUS STUDIES

Terry Godlove, Editor
Hofstra University

The *Classics in Religious* series republishes important materials in religious studies that have become inaccessible. To facilitate classroom use, many volumes will include, in addition to the original text, a new introduction, and a section of new critical essays. When possible, the volumes will also include a selection of influential writings contemporaneous with the text's original publication. Now in preparation are titles in the following sub-series:

Classics in Islam
Classics in Women's Studies
Classics in Philosophy of Religion
Classics in Religion and the Human Sciences
Classics in History of Religion

Classics in Religious Studies, No. 9

A Museum of Faiths
Histories and Legacies of the 1893
World's Parliament of Religions

Edited by
Eric J. Ziolkowski

A MUSEUM OF FAITHS

Histories and Legacies of the 1893
World's Parliament of Religions

Edited by
Eric J. Ziolkowski

Scholars Press
Atlanta, Georgia

THE AMERICAN ACADEMY OF RELIGION
CLASSICS IN RELIGIOUS STUDIES

A Museum of Faiths

© 1993
The American Academy of Religion

The portraits on the front cover are as follows:
*(left column)*Prof. Thomas Dwight, M.D., Rt. Rev. Shaku Soyen,
Rev. Walter Elliott, C.S.P.; *(right column)* Rev. Frank Sewall, Pershotam B. Joshi,
Zenshiro Naguchi.

Library of Congress Cataloging-in-Publication Data
A museum of faiths: histories and legacies of the 1893 World's
Parliament of Religions/ edited by Eric J. Ziolkowski.
    p. cm. — (Classics in religious studies; no. 9)
    ISBN 1–55540–904–0. — ISBN 1–55540–905–9 (pbk.)
    1. World's Parliament of Religions (1893: Chicago, Ill.)
2. Religions. 3. Religions—Relations. 4. Religion. 5. Religions—
Study and teaching. 6. Religions (Proposed, universal, etc.)
7. Women and religion. I. Ziolkowski, Eric Jozef, 1958–   .
II. World's Parliament of Religions (1893: Chicago, Ill.)
III. Series.
BL21.W8M87   1993
200—dc20   93–33152
                                                                 CIP

Printed in the United States of America
on acid-free paper

In Memory of
Joseph Mitsuo Kitagawa

CONTENTS

✳✳✳

PART I: PROCEEDINGS, 1893

PART II: APPRAISAL, 1894

PART III: REASSESSMENT, 1983-93

Preface

In this time of resurgent tribalism, nationalism, and "ethnic cleansing," it is difficult to look back without wistfulness and perhaps a tinge of sardonicism upon the unrestrained optimism that surrounded the World's Parliament of Religions held in Chicago in connection with that city's Columbian Exposition a century ago. To many of its countless contemporary commentators in this country and abroad, the parliament signified a new pinnacle in human "evolution" and religious "progress," pointing toward a future of universal human harmony and good will. But from the parliament's time up to our own, if time might be construed geographically, expands a seemingly measureless space potted by sites of unspeakable horrors: Verdun, Auschwitz, Hiroshima, the Gulag-Archipelago, Bosnia-Herzegovina... So one is now entitled to ask on evolutionary grounds, as does Edward O. Wilson in his recent essay in *The New York Times Magazine* (May 30, 1993), "Is Humanity Suicidal?": "Darwin's dice have rolled badly for Earth. It was a misfortune for the living world in particular, many scientists believe, that a carnivorous primate and not some more benign form of animal made the breakthrough....We are tribal and aggressively territorial, intent on private space beyond minimal requirements."

That we are forced by the history of our century to view the 1893 parliament differently from the way its contemporaries did does not diminish the import or fascination of that event. As the theologian David Tracy and others have observed, a "classic" religious or literary text distinguishes itself by its capacity to retain its power through different readings and different interpretations over time. Like texts, important historical events can prove classics in their own right, inviting new and different assessments in different times and from different perspectives while never losing their potency to provoke and perhaps unsettle our thoughts. Accordingly, and consistent with the name of the AAR series in which this volume appears, the World's Parliament of Religions is to be viewed here as such an event.

There is an intended irony in the title of this book, as my Introduction should make clear. I am not the first to consider the parliament an ironic happening. In singling out the parliament as the initiatory event of modern American religious history, Martin E. Marty has characterized the whole first period of that history (1893-1919) in terms of "the irony of it all," deriving his specific use of the term from its definition in *The Oxford English Dictionary* as "a condition of affairs or events as if in mockery of the promise and fitness of things." I apply the term to the parliament in a similar sense, but with a Kierkegaardian bite. In his M.A. dissertation *The Concept of Irony* (1841), as translated by Howard and Edna Hong, Kierkegaard found irony to assert "contradistinction in all its various nuances"; in his more celebrated later writings, in turn, the principle of "contradiction" essential to irony is shown to be present in all stages of existence. There are many ironic contradictions about the Parliament of Religions, as the reader will see. The particular contradiction my title is meant to evoke lies between understanding the parliament in its etymological sense as a *parlement*, literally a "speaking," in this case a "speaking" among representatives of the world's religions, which is how most of its participants and the public viewed it; and understanding the parliament as a "museum" or "exhibit" of religious faiths, "displayed" as "specimens," which is how several of its promoters and a significant minority of contributing "scientists" of religion construed it.

To what extent did the parliament serve as a true colloquy of religious representatives? To what extent did it serve very differently as yet another "display," albeit a uniquely spiritual one, among the countless displays that made up the Columbian Exposition with which it was affiliated? Or, to what extent did these two models, the colloquy and the museum, actually become confused at the parliament? These questions broach an imposing problem for any scholarly interpreter of the event. It is from the perspective of the academic study of religion that most scholars today contemplate the 1893 parliament. But this perspective, in tracing certain roots of its own development back to the parliament, will find the distinction between "religious" and "scientific" (or "scholarly") representation to have become blurred there.

The contents of this volume were selected, in part, to allow for a reconsideration of that blurring. Some words are necessary about my editing of them.

Part I contains six papers on the "scientific" study of comparative religion that were read at the parliament. These papers originally appeared scattered throughout the two authoritative published editions of the parliament's proceedings: the one by the parliament's chairman, John Henry Barrows; the other by Walter R. Houghton. (See the table of "Abbreviations" above for complete references.) None of these six "scientific" papers is included in Richard Hughes Seager's recently published selection from those proceedings, *The Dawn of Religious Pluralism: Voices from the World's Parliament of Religions, 1893* (La Salle, Ill.: Open Court, 1993), where papers are arranged in accordance with the religious or denominational "delegations" to which their authors belonged.

In calling the original Barrows and Houghton editions "authoritative," I borrow the term from Seager's Preface. But the term must be qualified. While embodying invaluable treasure-troves of materials, both those editions are an editor's purgatory and an annotator's inferno, filled with such constant torments as typographic errors, misspellings, and spelling inconsistencies; placements of sometimes loose paraphrases within quotation marks; omissions of documenting references for quotations; and so forth. An explanation of my editorial treatment of each paper is provided in the note on sources at the bottom of the paper's first page. All footnotes to these papers are mine, having been added wherever possible to make up for the lack of documenting references in their original versions. In the paper by Eliza R. Sunderland, incidentally, it would seem that the textual circumstances eliciting my comments in footnotes 1, 11-13, and 18 reflect the reported fact that she delivered it at the parliament "without a note," and that the printed version came from a stenographic transcription of her address. Indeed, many of the errata in the original proceedings, especially the Houghton edition, are clearly the result of stenographic copying.

The two articles appraising the parliament's "results" and "significance" in part II were published in journals the year after the parliament. Both articles are reprinted here as they originally appeared, with the exception of the footnotes, all of which I have added for the same reasons I added those in part I. As in the papers of part I, the English transliterations of foreign terms and names have been left the same in these two, and such obsolete terms as "Mohammedanism" have been allowed to remain to preserve the articles' nineteenth-century air.

The eight contributions to part III, all of them written during the past ten years, reassess various aspects of the parliament from different perspectives. Five of these contributions have been published previously, while three were prepared specifically for this volume. For obvious reasons, I have treated all eight differently from the much older contents of parts I and II. In the interest of consistency, I have conformed the notes in these contributions to one standard format. Except for a couple of notes from which tangential excursuses have been cut, no substantive changes have been made. Also, except where otherwise indicated, I have conformed the transliterations of foreign names and terms, and the usage of diacritical marks, to the standards of the sixteen-volume *The Encyclopedia of Religion* edited by Mircea Eliade (New York: Macmillan, 1987). In cases where a name or term in question is not listed in the *Encyclopedia's* Index (vol. 16), the author's judgment has been deferred to.

A section of "Notes on the Authors," covering all the scholars whose writings appear in this volume, appears in the back.

A number of people are to be thanked for the realization of this volume. The list must begin with all the contributors to part III, and with the editors, presses, and institutions that permitted me to reprint in that part the five previously-published contributions. I am especially grateful to the three authors whose contributions have *not* been published before—Tessa Bartholomeusz, Ursula King, and Sunrit Mullick—for preparing them specifically for this volume at my request.

Terry Godlove, editor of the Classics in Religious Studies series, is to be credited for supporting this project from its conception with remarkable patience and humor, as is Dennis Ford, for his smoothly professional management of the volume's production, and Sarah Foster, for her scrupulous typesetting and assistance in the production.

Other persons, too, contributed in valued ways. Norman Girardot kindly and unsolicitedly provided me with his detailed notes on *The Chinese Recorder and Missionary Journal*. Gregory D. Alles, Robert L. Cohn, Martin Marty, Craig Prentiss, and Theodore J. Ziolkowski responded helpfully to specific questions concerning the annotation of parts I and II. I am also indebted to Yvonne E. Osmun for her clerical and computer expertise, and to Richard L. Everett and Betsy Jo Moore in the interlibrary loan office of Lafayette College's David Bishop Skillman Library, for their tireless and exemplary service in tracking down and procuring obscure and often hard-to-obtain documents.

The editor of *The Journal of American Culture* granted my request to derive a portion of my Introduction from an article I published in that *Journal's* winter 1990 issue. My discussion of the poem by Minnie Andrews Snell is based on remarks from another article of mine forthcoming in *The Eastern Buddhist*. The Introduction was given exacting, helpful readings by Terry Godlove and Lee Upton. Notwithstanding those efforts, however, and despite Terry Godlove's heroic assistance in proofreading with me the entire volume, I accept total responsibility for any errors or inadvertencies throughout the volume.

To the members of my newly-housed familial parliament, Lee and Theodora, I owe a debt that is ceaseless and immeasurable.

This volume is offered in humble homage to the memory of the man named in its dedication—as scholar, teacher, friend, and example.

Eric J. Ziolkowski
Easton, Pennsylvania
Summer 1993

ABBREVIATIONS

The following abbreviations on the left are used for the sources on the right throughout this volume:

NHP   *Neely's History of the Parliament of Religions and Religious Congresses at the World's Columbian Exposition, compiled from Original Manuscripts and Stenographic Reports.* 4th edition. Ed. Walter R. Houghton. Chicago: F. Tennyson Neely, 1894.

WFP   *The World's First Parliament of Religions: Its Christian Spirit, Historic Greatness and Manifold Results. A Brief Summary of Testimonies Gathered from Many Lands, Indicating What the World has Said of this Memorable Congress of the Creeds, of its Organizer and Chairman, John Henry Barrows, and of the Official Literature of the Parliament.* Ed. George S. Goodspeed. Chicago: Hill and Shuman, 1895.

WPR   *The World's Parliament of Religions: An Illustrated and Popular Story of the World's First Parliament of Religions, held in Chicago in Connection with the Columbian Exposition of 1893.* 2 vols. Ed. John Henry Barrows. Chicago: Parliament Publishing Company, 1893.

INTRODUCTION

Eric J. Ziolkowski

Centennials are strange affairs. Like their successive spawn, bi-, tri-, quadri-, quincentennials, and so on, they are contrived and accidental in nature. There can be something vulgarizing or trivializing about the sudden, sometimes feverish renewal of attention that sprouts up around the memory of important persons every hundred years after their births and deaths, or around the memory of famous events every hundred years after their occurrences.[1] Centennial observances and kindred events often reveal more about the celebrants than about the celebrated. For example, from the countless heated debates in both the academy and the popular news media last year over the character and legacy of the alleged "discoverer" of America, one could easily come away knowing something about the clash between Eurocentrism and political correctness in our own time, and not much at all about the Genoan explorer who sailed from Spain to the New World, and then back, five hundred years earlier.

The first World's Parliament of Religions which convened in Chicago a century ago this year cannot be disassociated from the artificial phenomenon of centennial celebrations. Within the two

---

[1] Thus, for example, in 1905, which witnessed incessant verbiage throughout the Spanish-speaking world honoring the three-hundredth anniversary of the first publication of Cervantes's novel *Don Quijote*, the Nicaraguan poet Rubén Darío opened a "Letanía" to the hero of that Hispanic classic by commiserating with him for having to endure such trivializing tercentenary rituals as "elogios, memorias, discursos" (*Obras poéticas completas*, rev. ed. [Madrid: Aguilar, 1945], p. 755).

decades that preceded it, the hundredth anniversaries of the American and French revolutions had occasioned two highly successful world's fairs in Philadelphia (1876) and Paris (1889). For the city of Chicago, the four-hundredth anniversary of Columbus's voyage provided the excuse to try to outdo those events by staging its own Columbian Exposition (one year late) in 1893, and the Parliament of Religions came into being through affiliation with that fair. Yet, unlike Columbus's voyage, which has proved an eminently safe bet over the centuries to be perpetually remembered and discussed by the American public, whether favorably or unfavorably, and with or without such a bombastic quadricentennial celebration as the Chicago World's Fair, the parliament could strike Joseph M. Kitagawa as "all but forgotten" a decade ago in the land where it took place. In this country, the anticipation of the parliament's centennial largely accounts for the considerable retrospective attention which the original event has recently attracted—attention manifest in the proliferation of scholarly studies and conference panels on the subject; in the 1989 establishment of the Council for a Parliament of the World's Religions to be held in Chicago, August 1993; and, earlier this year, in the publication of a selection of speeches drawn from the voluminous proceedings of the original parliament.[2]

Reflecting on the 1893 parliament the year after it was held, F. Max Müller of Oxford, the renowned pioneer of the "science of religion," acknowledged the difficulty of trying "to measure correctly the importance of events of which we ourselves have been the witnesses." That same year George S. Goodspeed, then associate professor of comparative religion and ancient history at the fledgling University of Chicago, observed: "When the Parliament was past, it really only then began to live....In fact, the farther we are removed in time from the Parliament, the more extraordinary and significant its character becomes. Even those who took part in it, hardly realized its meaning."[3] These words proved augural. Although the parliament would be

---

[2] *The Dawn of Religious Pluralism: Voices from the World's Parliament of Religions, 1893*, ed. Richard Hughes Seager, with assistance of Ronald R. Kidd and "Foreword" by Diana L. Eck, published in association with the Council for a Parliament of the World's Religions (La Salle, Ill.: Open Court, 1993); cited hereafter as *DRP*. See the list of "Abbreviations" above for complete references to the two standard editions of the original proceedings by John Henry Barrows and Walter R. Houghton, to be cited throughout as *WPR* and *NHP*.

[3] George S. Goodspeed, "Introduction" to *WFP*, p. 5. (See "Abbreviations" above for complete reference.) The words of Müller are from his article in the present volume.

virtually forgotten in the West a dozen years later, and remain so for the greater part of this century, the event began to be retrieved from obscurity by Western scholars in the 1960s, and has been the subject of steadily intensifying reconsideration since then. Regardless of whether the parliament's one-hundredth anniversary really "marks its discovery, not its rediscovery, as an event in American religious history,"[4] the centennial brings to a head the challenge of trying, in Müller's words, "to measure correctly the importance" of the parliament, or, in Goodspeed's, to discern that "meaning" in the parliament which its participants and contemporaries "hardly realized." The present volume is meant to contribute to this ongoing hermeneutic effort.

What were the meaning and significance of the Parliament of Religions, and how are they to be apprehended and assessed? A classic event, the theologian David Tracy reminds us, is no less open to multiple and diverse interpretations than is a classic text, symbol, or person.[5] Such has been and remains the case with the parliament, which is generally viewed as an axial event in the history of religious faiths, American religious history, interfaith dialogue, and even general human history. As this volume demonstrates, the parliament can have numerous meanings, depending upon the particular aspects considered, and the particular perspectives from which those aspects are viewed. The central methodological assumption underlying the present assemblage of lectures, articles and essays corresponds with what Lawrence E. Sullivan has said in a different context with regard to the suspiciousness "histories of religions" often display toward single-stream narrative histories: "History seldom proves to be a simple, singular line of developments. Can single-stream narratives sufficiently penetrate the layered concatenation of events and significations? Any event carries forward many *histories*, contexts that overlap, meanings that contradict and collide with one another."[6]

The Parliament of Religions is a truly remarkable illustration of Sullivan's point. "Every great event is the flower of all the ages which have preceded it," its chairman, John Henry Barrows observed. But

---

[4] Richard Hughes Seager, "General Introduction" to *DRP*, p. 8.

[5] See chap. 1 of David Tracy's *Plurality and Ambiguity: Hermeneutics, Religion, Hope* (San Francisco: Harper and Row, 1987), pp. 1-27, which uses the French Revolution to illustrate a classic event.

[6] Lawrence E. Sullivan, *Histories and Rituals: The Case of a National Rite of Mourning*, Twelfth Annual University Lecture in Religion (Tempe: Arizona State University, 1991), p. 3.

this meeting in Chicago was specially prepared for by at least six factors, or what Sullivan would call histories: the global spread of Christian missions; the growth of the study of comparative religion; the development of English into a lingua franca; facilities for worldwide travel; religious freedom in America; and the attraction of the world's fair.[7] Thus, while the parliament represented a colliding of the numerous religious and denominational traditions (or histories) whose representatives met there, adequate study of the event must ultimately take into account, self-reflectively, the history of the very enterprise of studying religious faiths from "scientific" and "comparative" perspectives—the second of the factors enumerated above. It is often overlooked that the 1893 parliament not only attracted the participation of religious leaders representing their own faiths from within their own traditions, but also drew the involvement of numerous scholars, some of whom, albeit a minority, were devoted to the "scientific," comparative study of religions from without. Having involved the coming into contact of many disparate histories with one another, the parliament in turn spawned what Kitagawa describes as its own "mixed legacies," which include its impact on the study of comparative religion, later to be called also the history of religions.

This book has a circular aim, which is to reassess the meaning and significance and the histories and legacies of the 1893 parliament as a meeting of religious faiths, and to shed light upon the role of the event as a critical moment in the development of the very perspective from which we now reassess it: that of the academic study of religion. Part I reissues from the parliament's original proceedings papers by six scholars of comparative religion articulating their own conceptions of the purpose, method, and scope of their discipline: Merwin-Marie Snell, C.P. Tiele, Albert and Jean Réville, Charles Joseph de Harlez, and Eliza R. Sunderland. Part II contains two articles that appeared during the year after the parliament, one by Barrows, the other by Müller, who appraise the "results" and "significance" of the event and comment on its place in world religious history and its bearing upon the comparative study of religions. Part III, to complete the circle, contains eight contributions from the past ten years by scholars from different areas of religious studies reassessing the 1893 parliament against the background of some of the most significant of the manifold religious, cultural, and scholarly histories, both Eastern and Western,

---

[7] See the article by John Henry Barrows in this volume.

that came into contact there. Perspectives represented include the American, by Marty; South Asian, by Sunrit Mullick and Tessa Bartholomeusz; East Asian, by James Edward Ketelaar; and comparativist, by Kitagawa. In addition, special attention is paid to themes of religious pluralism, by Richard Hughes Seager; religion and literature, by the present author; and women and religion, by Ursula King.

As background to the contents of this volume, several main aspects of the parliament should be considered: its inextricable and ironic historical bond with the Columbian Exposition, which itself represented a point of intersection of a strikingly complex array of cultural, political, philosophical, and theological histories and myths; the parliament as a shared landmark of colliding historical, biblical, and literary associations, and of subsequently mixed legacies in interfaith dialogue, Christian ecumenicism, and the study of comparative religion; the close interrelation of the interfaith, ecumenical, and "scientific" dimensions of the parliament itself, with a special focus on the concept of it as a "hierological museum"; and the recovery of the parliament from near oblivion over the past several decades.

Heavenly Visions, Worldly Intentions

Anyone familiar with the 1893 Parliament of Religions is probably aware of at least the barest facts surrounding it and the world's fair under whose auspices it was held. The Columbian Exposition, the most successful fair ever, is aptly described as "a quintessential event"[8] of late nineteenth-century American history, one that epitomized the hallmarks of the Age of Energy or the Mauve Decade in which it occurred: restless energy, extravagant industry, wealth, grandeur, and optimism. That legendary fair inspired countless catalogues, photograph albums, speeches, essays, novels and poems, and became the subject of half-a-dozen full-length histories consisting of thousands of pages, thus evoking far more written coverage than any other exposition in history.[9]

At the same time, the Parliament of Religions which convened September 11-27 was, as Marty puts it, "the most elaborate display of religious cosmopolitanism yet seen on the continent." From his

---

[8] David F. Burg, *Chicago's White City of 1893* (Lexington: University Press of Kentucky, 1976), p. 1.

[9] Ibid., p. xi.

Americanist vantage, the 1893 parliament was important for having crystallized the ascendant "cosmopolitan habit" among modernists in American theology. As the other contributions to our third part show, the parliament may be seen as well from Asianist, comparativist, literary-historical, and women's-studies perspectives to represent different but equally crucial historical milestones.

There are tremendous ironies about the conjunction of the Parliament of Religions with the Columbian Exposition. While the parliament failed to achieve the primary goal of its mostly Christian American organizers, who had hoped to prove the supremacy of their own faith over others, the exposition marked an important triumph for American industrialism and wealth, and its physical site was viewed by many as a kind of sacred space separate from the profane reality around it. Indeed, the fair was deemed so grand and beautiful that some construed it in decidedly religious, utopian terms as a "Celestial City" or "New Jerusalem" that would live forever in human memory. It appeared as a consecration of American civilization, thus contradicting Mikhail Bakhtin's later notion of carnival as an emphatically subversive tendency in popular culture that expresses the "pathos of change and renewal" and "the sense of the gay relativity of prevailing truths and authorities."[10] The sacred aura that surrounded the Chicago Exposition in the popular imagination serves as an apt reminder that the word "fair" derives from the Latin *feria*, or "holy day," and that the German *Messe* connotes both "mass" and "fair." Henry Adams, who visited the exposition, later equated religion and exposition when he "professed the religion of World's Fairs, without which he held education to be a blind impossibility."[11]

Among the primary motivations of those who planned and oversaw the construction of the Chicago Exposition was their unabashed worldly desire to make it the "greatest fair in history," and thereby to consummate before all the world Chicago's miraculous recovery from the Great Fire of October 1871. Accomplishment of this goal required outdoing the Philadelphia Centennial Exposition and the Paris Exposition mentioned above, and entailed vindicating Chicago against its arch civic rival, New York, which Chicago had to outbid in order to

---

[10] Mikhail Bakhtin, *Rabelais and His World*, trans. Hélène Iswolsky (Bloomington: Indiana University Press, 1984), p. 11.

[11] Henry Adams, *The Education of Henry Adams* (1907; Boston: Houghton, Mifflin, 1961), p. 465, quoted by Robert W. Rydell, *All the World's a Fair: Visions of Empire at American International Expositions, 1876-1916* (Chicago: University of Chicago Press, 1984), p. 3.

host the fair. From April 1890, when President Benjamin Harrison authorized Chicago as the site, through the early stages of the fair's construction, which began in February 1891, reports in New York magazines and newspapers evinced an attitude of jealousy and skepticism. Nonetheless, a Congressional Committee report of May 1892, a year prior to the fair's opening, read: "In its scope and magnificence, the [Chicago] Exposition stands alone. There is nothing like it in all history. It easily surpasses all kindred enterprises."[12]

That prediction was fulfilled from May 1, 1893, when the exposition opened, through its close six months later. The 1,037 acres which the fair encompassed in Jackson Park on the lakefront of Chicago's South Side nearly quadrupled the area of any previous exposition.[13] The area under roof amounted to more than five million square feet, nearly double the amount in the greatest past exposition.[14] In addition to the grand administration building and the individual pavilions representing every state of the nation and numerous foreign governments, there were separate exhibition buildings devoted to such fields and concerns as manufactures (the largest building of the fair), art, women, transportation, forestry, mining, agriculture, to name but a few. Situated around a gigantic human-dug basin and series of lagoons fed by the lake, these buildings were known collectively as the White City, ostensibly for the gleaming stonework of their predominantly neoclassical, domed and colonnaded exteriors. (The unfortunate—even if unintended—double entendre of that name, coming only three decades after the Emancipation Proclamation, and three years after the Massacre of Wounded Knee, speaks for itself.) Finally, extending twelve blocks westward from the White City to Washington Park was the Midway Plaisance, which was lined by concessionary stands, the so-called Bazaar of Nations, and exotic model villages representing the lifestyles and cultures of foreign lands—including the Native American (sic). The exposition's approximate total cost, exclusive of the goods and wares on display, was estimated at thirty-five and a quarter million dollars,[15] which would translate into well over twenty times that amount today.

Masterminded by the Chicago lawyer, civic leader, and Swedenborgian layman, Charles Carroll Bonney (1831-1903), and

---

[12] Quoted by Burg, *White City*, p. 75.
[13] Noted by *A Week at the Fair* (Chicago: Rand, McNally, 1893), p. 35.
[14] Ibid.
[15] Lyman J. Gage, "The Finances of the Exposition," *The Cosmopolitan* 16 (December 1893): 206. See also Burg, *White City*, p. 85.

chaired by Barrows, a prominent Presbyterian minister of Chicago, the Parliament of Religions was officially one of twenty departments of the World's Congress Auxiliary organized under Bonney's leadership in conjunction with the Columbian Exposition.[16] Yet, as the first convention of its kind ever to invite participants from all over the earth and to open its doors to the general public, this parliament turned out to be the most heavily attended of all the exposition's congresses, attracting a total of almost 150,000 spectators[17] over seventeen days. For Barrows, nothing gave a better idea of the public's interest in the parliament than "the fact that the splendors and wonders of the great Fair itself often seemed powerless to divert it."[18] The religions represented and discussed during September 11-27 by the almost two hundred speakers at the parliament—which convened not on the grounds of the fair, but in the newly-built Memorial Art Palace, today's Art Institute, on Michigan Avenue about seven miles north— included Hinduism, Buddhism, Judaism, Roman Catholicism, Eastern Orthodoxy, Protestant Christian denominations, Islam, Shinto, Confucianism, Taoism, Parseeism, Jainism, and various "ethnic" faiths.[19] Well aware that a religion conference and a world's fair

---

[16] For Charles Carroll Bonney's own account see, e.g., his "The Genesis of the World's Religious Congresses of 1893," *The New-Church Review* 1 (January 1894): 73-100.

[17] The figure is given by Barrows, "Review and Summary," in *WPR*, 2:1558.

[18] Barrows, "The History of the Parliament," in *WPR*, 1:111-12.

[19] The parliament met for three sessions (mornings, afternoons, evenings) each day except Sunday in the Art Palace's Hall of Columbus, which could accommodate an audience of 3,000, with standing room for 1,000 more, at times with simultaneous sessions taking place in the neighboring Hall of Washington. Reportedly, the crowds at these sessions were consistently overflowing. Concurrently with the meetings in the Hall of Columbus, a special "Scientific Section" convened September 15, 20-27 in "Hall III." An official day-by-day, session-by-session "Chronicle" of the parliament, including a record of the names of successive speakers, titles or themes of their addresses, with intermittent accounts of memorable incidents that transpired, is found in Barrows, "History," in *WPR*, 1:110-54. (On the "Scientific Section," see pp. 152-54.) A helpful alphabetized listing of the talks by author, with page references to *WPR*, constitutes the "Appendix" to Clay Lancaster, *The Incredible World's Parliament of Religions at the Chicago Columbian Exposition of 1893: A Comparative and Critical Study* (Fontwell, U.K.: Centaur, 1987), pp. 257-64. This list enumerates 196 authors (including the anonymous author of "'Taoism,' a prize essay"), many of whom gave more than one talk. (There are couple of oversights: those whom I noticed missing from this list are Jean Réville, whose parliament address is included in part 1 of the present volume, and a Mr. Nara Sina Satsumchyra, "a Brahman, a member of the School of Philosophy at Madras," who gave a brief untitled address on the eleventh day [see Barrows, "History," in *WPR*, 1:137].) Seager's

seemed strange bedfellows, Barrows tried to justify this convergence of two ostensibly incompatible undertakings by claiming: "The Columbian Exposition which accentuated the material glories of modern civilization needed the Parliament of Religions to bring back to the human mind the greater world of the Spirit."[20] A reporter for *The Cosmopolitan* was alluding to the oddness of Chicago as the location for such a meeting when he wrote, "what a sign of the invincible vitality of Christianity, even in the face of the triumphs of science, is that religions parliament held in the very capital of the positivist, industrial universe."[21]

In speaking of Christianity's "invincible vitality," this reporter was in tune with the attitude shared by Barrows and the parliament's other American Christian organizers, one of whose foremost aims was to prove their own religious faith to be the fulfillment of all others. As Barrows made clear, he and the parliament's other chief promoters

---

"Appendix" to *DRP*, pp. 477-92, contains a list of "those individuals who made *major* addresses at the Parliament," excluding "people who appeared on the floor and made brief statements on the opening and closing days" (p. 477, emphasis mine). This wording is somewhat misleading, because a considerable number of the parliament's papers were actually delivered by persons other than their authors, in most cases because the author had been unable to attend. This list, which is arranged according to the authors' religious traditions (or "delegations"), includes the following: "Buddhism": ten authors, fourteen papers; "Catholicism": eighteen authors, twenty-one papers; "Confucianism": two authors, two papers; "Hinduism": eight authors, ten papers; "Islam": two authors, three papers; "Jainism": one author, one paper; "Judaism": eleven authors, eleven papers; "Orthodox traditions": eight authors, ten papers; "Protestantism": 113 authors, 121 papers; "Shintoism": two authors, two papers; "Taoism": one author (anonymous), one paper; and "Zoroastrianism": two authors, two papers. This list also includes eight authors, nine papers, under "Noted Scholars." Of these, three scholars (J. Estlin Carpenter, C.D. d'Harlez [sic] and Merwin-Marie Snell) and a total of four of their papers are also listed under their respective religious traditions. Thus, according to Seager's list (by my count), a total of 203 "major" papers, poems and sermons by a total of 183 authors were read at the parliament. (The number of presentations actually on Seager's list exceeds by nine the number 194 from which he says the "representative texts" in *DRP* were selected ["Preface," p. 2]; presumably the 194 refers only to those materials that are known to be still extant.) Of these, a total of thirty-nine authors (of a total of forty-six papers) represented non-Christian traditions; a total of 139 authors (of 152 papers) represented some form of Christianity. One author conspicuously missing from Seager's list is Eliza R. Sunderland, whose parliament paper is included in part I of the present volume; as a Unitarian who spoke on comparative religion, she would presumably fall under Seager's "Protestantism" category, and perhaps also that of "Noted Scholars."

[20] Barrows, "Review and Summary," in *WPR*, 2:1569.

[21] Paul Bourget, "A Farewell to the White City," *The Cosmopolitan* 16 (1893): 140.

never conceived of the event as an opportunity to evolve "a cosmic or universal faith"; on the contrary, they believed that the ingredients for such a faith are inherent in Christian faith.

The unabashed missionary aim of the parliament's Christian promoters illustrates an important point about the general theological problem of religious plurality, or the "conflicting truth claims of different religions."[22] This problem, which confronted Western Christendom more and more intensely throughout the nineteenth century as a result of European and American expansionism, is recognized today as one of the most daunting challenges facing Western Christian faith as it approaches its third millennium. According to Alan Race, as discussed in my article, three main attitudes may be adopted by Christians in responding to this challenge. They may reject the other faiths; or acknowledge the spiritual power manifest in other faiths, but reject their salvific sufficiency; or accept all faiths, including Christianity, as possessing partial knowledge of God. While Barrows and most of his Christian colleagues at the parliament steered clear of the first ("exclusivist") position, they also distanced themselves from the third ("pluralist") position, and exemplified the second ("inclusivist") one instead.

Of chief interest here is the close correspondence between this inclusivist, missionary aim behind the Parliament of Religions, and the worldly, political motives behind the exposition. While encompassing what Sydney Ahlstrom calls a period of "crusading Protestantism,"[23] as illustrated by some of the papers presented at the parliament, the final decades of the nineteenth century also saw America's rise to industrial supremacy over other nations, and this development had no little bearing upon the international expositions hosted in this country from 1876 to 1916. Those expositions, including Chicago's, signified victories of cultural hegemony, and were meant to draw popular support for certain domestic and foreign policies, as well as in some cases to legitimate white supremacist theories of evolution and race relations.[24] Conceived and planned in part as a showcase for America's industrial, scientific, and cultural greatness before the

---

[22] The phrase is from the title of chap. 9 of John Hick's *Philosophy of Religion*, 4th ed. (Englewood Cliffs, N.J.: Prentice, 1990).

[23] This phrase furnishes the title for chap. 51 of Sydney E. Ahlstrom, *A Religious History of the American People* (New Haven: Yale University Press, 1972), pp. 857-72.

[24] See Rydell, *All the World's a Fair*, passim. Chap. 2, pp. 38-71, focuses on the Chicago Exposition.

nations of the world, the Columbian Exposition thus found its spiritual counterpart in the Parliament of Religions, which was promoted to demonstrate the presumed supremacy of the Christian religion with which the growth of the American nation had been inseparably bound.

For Kitagawa, the 1893 exposition and parliament find their underlying link in one of the quintessential motifs of their century: "progress." This link helps explain why the lofty terms Barrows used to laud the parliament in his closing address bear such a striking resemblance to those with which the Chicago Exposition's director general, Colonel George R. Davis, had heralded the fair in his address at its dedication ceremony on October 21, 1892. Davis envisioned the fair in terms of America's Manifest Destiny as the culmination of "the ceaseless, resistless march of civilization, Westward, ever Westward," a "natural outgrowth of predestined events."[25] Likewise, Barrows saw the parliament as showing that "mankind is drifting toward religion and not away from it," and as bringing "before millions in Oriental lands the more truthful and beautiful aspects of Christianity."[26] And just as the Colonel saw the White City as a place where all nations could "learn the value of the discovery we commemorate;...the nearness of man to man, the Fatherhood of God and the brotherhood of the human race,"[27] so the Reverend summed up the parliament, adapting an image from Tennyson, as "a shadowy outline of the great last Parliament of Man at which all races, ages and religions are to meet before the Heavenly Judge."[28]

---

[25] Quoted by Burg, *White City*, pp. 102, 104.

[26] Barrows, "Review and Summary," in *WPR*, 2:1569.

[27] Quoted by Burg, *White City*, p. 104.

[28] Barrows, "Review and Summary," in *WPR*, 2:1570. The phrase "parliament of Man" is borrowed from Alfred Lord Tennyson, "Locksley Hall" (1842):
"Till the war-drum throbb'd no longer, and the battle-flags were furl'd
In the Parliament of man, the Federation of the world.
There the common sense of most shall hold a fretful realm in awe,
And the kindly earth shall slumber, lapt in universal law."
From *The Works of Tennyson*, 9 vols., Eversley edition, ed. Hallam Lord Tennyson (London: Macmillan, 1907-08), 2:44-45. Barrows proceeds in his "Review and Summary" to call the parliament "this prophecy of Tennyson's 'Federation of the World'" (*WPR*, 2:1570). As noted by Seager, this verse had become "a kind of unofficial motto of the Parliament" ("General Introduction," *DRP*, p. 5). See, e.g., the article on the parliament by Theodore F. Seward, "The Year 1893 and the Federation of the World," *Christian Thought* (New York: W.B. Ketcham, 1893-94), pp. 376-81, which uses the first two verses quoted above as an opening epigraph.

Unfortunately, such hyperbolic rhetoric of inclusiveness, of which an overabundance was heard at both events, was hardly matched by all the realities of the fair and the parliament with respect to matters of gender, race, and creed, as shall later be discussed. Indeed, in terms of gender, the exclusively masculine stress of such rhetoric—"*man* to *man*," God's "*Father*hood," human "*brother*hood," "Parliament of *Man*"—might seem already to subvert the speakers' intended message.

Perhaps the greatest irony of all emerges when the legacy of the parliament is considered in the light of the popular image of the Columbian Exposition. Just as Barrows's prediction that the parliament would take "rank with the chief events of the century and of all centuries"[29] proved overly bold, so most persons who visited and recorded their impressions of the exposition tended toward hyperbolic laudation. Notwithstanding the bitter dissent of Louis Sullivan, who suggested that the neoclassical style predominant among the fair's buildings would retard the progress of American architecture for at least fifty years,[30] the White City emerges in contemporary accounts and depictions as the epitome of the good, the beautiful, the useful,[31] even the embodiment of the Heavenly City, New Jerusalem, or Utopia.[32] Romantic, dreamlike, nocturnal visions of the White City are expressed in numerous accounts and captured in countless photographs and drawings.[33] In many pictures, the silhouettes of the exotic domed buildings appear aglow beneath a starry or moonlit sky, casting their reflection upon the water of the basin or lagoon. The seeming otherworldliness of this spectacle accounts for the amusing anecdote, recounted by Kitagawa, about two delegates from the Parliament of Religions who perceived the White City as a heaven on earth. Experienced by visitors as a place of such beauty and grandeur that it seemed removed from time (a kind of illusory, locational escape from what Mircea Eliade would call the "terror of history"), the fair was believed by some to be destined to endure "forever" like a dream, long after its physical remains were destroyed, through the indelible

---

[29] Barrows, "Review and Summary," in *WPR*, 2:1570.

[30] Louis Sullivan, *The Autobiography of an Idea* (New York: American Institute of Architects, 1924), p. 325.

[31] E.g., Julian Hawthorne, *Humors of the Fair* (Chicago: Weeks, 1893), p. 205; "Do Not Miss the Fair!," *Century Magazine* 24 (October 1893): 952.

[32] E.g., the stated opinion of W. Hamilton Gibson, as quoted by Frank D. Millet et al., *Some Artists at the Fair* (New York: Scribner, 1893), p. 82; and W. D. Howells, "Letters of an Altrurian Traveller II," *The Cosmopolitan* 16 (December 1893): 218, 220.

[33] E.g., *Century Magazine* 24 (May 1893): 8, 10, 11.

image it had impressed upon human hearts and collective memory.[34] Of thirteen post-exposition novels in which the Chicago World's Fair emerges as a setting or image, one represents the White City in Bunyanesque terms as the City Beautiful and Celestial City, and two others likewise compare it to heaven.[35]

However, such celestial visions of the exposition could not obscure the worldly intentions behind its planning. Much popular rhetoric about the fair tended to synthesize an acknowledgment of the American industrial triumph which the fair signified, with the spiritual vision of a heavenly city which had characterized American utopianism and millenarianism throughout the nineteenth century. Such rhetoric seems almost to have anticipated the thesis Max Weber introduced a decade later, according to which the Protestant ethic and the rise of capitalist economics were related by elective affinities that allowed the Puritan faith to find its legitimation in this-worldly, material success. More to the point is the image of the Chicago Exposition in Robert Herrick's novel *The Memoirs of an American Citizen*, which appeared the same year Weber completed his *Die protestantische Ethik und der Geist des Kapitalismus* (1905):

> The long lines of white buildings were ablaze with countless lights; the music from the bands scattered over the grounds floated softly out upon the water; all else was silent and dark. In that lovely hour, soft and gentle as was ever a summer night, the toil and trouble of

---

[34] E.g., Richard Watson Gilder, "The Vanishing City," *Century Magazine* 24 (October 1893): 868; Gustav Kobbé, "Sights at the Fair," *Century Magazine* 24 (September 1893): 195; Howells, "Letters of an Altrurian Traveller II," p. 231; Arthur Sherburne Hardy, "Last Impressions," *The Cosmopolitan* 16 (December 1893): 195. Perhaps the most imaginative treatment of the problem of the fair's fate is Hjalmar Hjorth Boyesin's "A New World Fable," which creates a "myth" of the sort "we should have found in Homer, Herodotus or Lucretius, if a work even remotely comparable with the World Fair had been achieved and again destroyed, while mankind was young." In this myth, the destruction of the White City is ordered and carried out by "cloud-compelling Zeus," who views the fair as an act of rebellion by mankind against the gods ("A New World's Fable," *The Cosmopolitan* 16 [December 1893]: 176). Contrast the pessimism of Paul Bourget, who reflects: "By a singular contrast, the White City I left, constructed only for a season and finished to the minutest detail, must disappear forever, while the black city [i.e., Chicago], which will endure forever, is only at its commencement" ("A Farewell to the White City" [n. 21 above], p.135).

[35] See Frances Hodgson Burnett, *Two Little Pilgrims' Progress* (New York: Scribner, 1895); Marietta Holley, *Samantha at the World's Fair* (New York: Funk and Wagnalls, 1893), p. 235; and Clara Louise Root Burnham, *Sweet Clover, a Romance of the White City* (Boston: Houghton Mifflin, 1894), pp. 201-02. On these and some of the other thirteen novels concerning the fair see also Burg, *Chicago's White City*, pp. 290-96.

> men, the fear that was gripping men's hearts in the market, fell away
> from me, and in its place came Faith. The people who could dream
> this vision and make it real, those people...—their sturdy wills and
> strong hearts would rise above failure, would press on to greater
> victories than this triumph of beauty—victories greater than the
> world had yet witnessed![36]

The narrator is a capitalist robber baron (Edward Van Harrington) in
the meat-packing industry. What the fair provides him is not the
prospect of a New Jerusalem or heavenly city, but a momentary
respite from the "market." The "Faith" it stirs in him is not spiritual,
but economic. And the "victories" and "triumph" he sees it boding are
not religious, but worldly and imperialist.

Such a spirit of triumphalism, although oriented in Herrick's hero
toward the economic sphere rather than the religious, corresponds
strikingly to the attitude conveyed by the American Christian hosts of
the Parliament of Religions toward their non-Christian guests. But in
this correspondence lies the irony. The parliament did not triumph in
the way its promoters had planned. It hardly substantiated Barrows's
claim that "mankind is drifting toward religion and not away from
it."[37] Nor, of course, did it fulfill its promoters' intention of proving to
everyone's satisfaction the supremacy of Christianity over all other
faiths.

The parliament had a contrary effect on some of its Asian religious
delegates, most notably a Hindu, Swami Vivekananda of India, and
two Buddhists, Anagārika Dharmapāla of Ceylon (today Sri Lanka)
and Shaku Sōen of Japan. As Kitagawa was the first to make clear,
these three young religious reformers picked up on Barrows's notion
of Christianity as the fulfillment of other faiths, appropriated it for
themselves and reversed its Christian claim, developing fulfillment
theories for their own non-Christian faiths. Not only did each of these
Asian speakers return as heroes to their native lands, but some
Americans who had attended the parliament as Christians converted
afterwards to other faiths on the basis of what they heard there. The
lasting American following which Vivekananda attracted at the
parliament is attested by the fact that the Vedanta Society he founded
two years later (1895) continues to maintain centers in a number of
American cities, including Chicago. And the Bahā'ī faith, which was
founded in Iran in 1863 by Mīrza Ḥusayn 'Alī Nūrī (Bahā' Allāh) and

---

[36] Robert Herrick, *The Memoirs of an American Citizen*, ed. Daniel Aaron
(Cambridge, Mass.: Harvard University Press, 1963), p. 147.
[37] Cited above.

first introduced to this country through the parliament, gained enough adherents in the Chicago vicinity to inspire its leader 'Abd al-Bahā to visit there in 1908. He returned several years later to break ground in the northern suburb of Wilmette for the construction of the manificent octagonal temple (dedicated in 1953) which still stands today.[38]

Perhaps the most striking reflection of the immediate effect the parliament had on the way some "average" Americans perceived non-Western religions, especially Hinduism and Buddhism, is a poem that appeared in the Chicago journal *The Open Court*, October 12, 1893, several weeks after the parliament's close: "Aunt Hannah on the Parliament of Religions," by one Minnie Andrews Snell. Together with a much longer poem published the following year by another poet to be discussed later, this poem is one of two literary works from the post-parliament period that take the parliament as their subject or theme.[39] Composed in rustic dialect, the poem's eight four-line stanzas furnish a series of impressions from the perspective of an initially wary Christian woman (Hannah) who, after being discouraged by her minister, attends the parliament, and is won over by the arguments of several of the Asian speakers. Its amusing quaintness aside, this poem exposes an unpleasant dimension of the parliament, the exposition, and their interrelationship that was nevertheless far more real than the utopian images evoked by the rhetoric of Colonel Davis, Chairman Barrows, and many other promoters and witnesses of the events.

In the course of the poem, Hannah's response to the parliament progresses through several stages that approximate what must have

---

[38] The Parliament's bearing on the fortunes of the Vivekananda's Vedanta Society and the Bahā'īs in this country is remarked by Ahlstrom, *Religious History*, pp. 1048, 1050. Ahlstrom does not document his claim regarding the Bahā'īs. But, as noted by Kenten Druyvesteyn, "The World's Parliament of Religions," Ph.D. dissertation, University of Chicago, 1976, pp. 74-75, n. 6 (cited hereafter as Druyvesteyn, diss.), the claim is supported by Marcus Bach, *They Have Found a Faith* (Indianapolis: Bobbs-Merrill, 1946), pp. 189-90. In the parliament's proceedings, the one indirect reference to Bahā'īs is the allusion to "the Babi saint, named Behâ Allah" by Henry Harris Jessup, a Presbyterian missionary from Syria, at the close of his lecture "The Religious Mission of the English Speaking Nations" (in *WPR*, 2:1125). This is believed to be the first mentioning on American soil of the name of the Bahā'ī founder.

[39] The other poem, composed by a Mrs. Eliza Madelina Souvielle, is discussed later in this Introduction. I am not counting the poem by Laura Ormiston Chant, "The World's Parliament," which was composed either before or during the parliament, and was read there by Barrows on its seventeenth and final day. This poem is found in *WPR*, 1:150-51 and *NHP*, pp. 811-12, and reprinted in *DRP*, pp. 455-56.

been the experience of many American fair-goers who attended or looked in upon it out of curiosity. The poem opens (stanzas 1-3):

> Wall—I'm glad enough I'm hum agin—kin rest my weary brain,
> For I've seen an' heered so much *too* much, I guess I've heered in vain.
> I thought th' Fair was mixin' an' th' Midway made me crawl,
> But th' Parl'ment of Religions was th' mixin'est of all!
>
> I seen th' Turks agoing round th' Midway in th' Fair,
> But our minister reproved me when he seen me peep in thair.
> "Defilin' place" he called it, an' th' Turk "a child of sin";
> But th' Parl'ment of Religions took all them heathen in.
>
> It made me squirm a little, to see some heathen's air,
> As he told us Christians 'bout our faults an' laid 'em out so bare,
> But thair flowin' robes was tellin' an' th'air mighty takin' folk,
> So th' Parl'ment of Religions clapped to every word they spoke.

Upon her arrival at the parliament Hannah feels xenophobia and prejudice regarding non-Christian foreigners. Her initial betrayal of these feelings ("It made me squirm a little, to see some heathen's air") is understandable, given that her first exposure to foreign cultures came through her recent visit to the exposition's Midway Plaisance. The Bazaar of Nations featured on the midway consisted of a series of ethnological displays arranged in accordance with the fashionable anthropological theory of evolution to depict "the sliding scale of humanity":[40] the farther one strolled from the White City, the perceived utopia of Western civilization, the farther one descended from more "advanced" races to more "savage" ones, passing from the displays of Teutonic and Celtic culture nearest the White City, through the worlds of Islam and West and East Asia depicted in the Midway's center, to the African and Native American cultures which had their place at the opposite end. That Hannah should be "reproved" by her minister for peeping in the Bazaar should come as no surprise; his condemnation of it ("defilin' place") is consistent with the allusion to "the somewhat shady society of the Midway Plaisance" made by Unitarian Thomas Wentworth Higginson in an extemporaneous, jovial (!) speech at the parliament on its eleventh day—a speech replete with "humor" regarding the racial and ethnic diversity one encountered at the fair, including mocking references to the wives of the Prophet

---

[40] Rydell, *All the World's a Fair*, p. 65. See also in the present volume the essay by Ketelaar.

Muhammad and the ethical code of "Orientals," topped off by an extended Black-Sambo-"servant" joke.[41]

At the parliament, however, Hannah begins to feel approval of the universalist messages of several Eastern spokesmen (those "mighty takin' folk"), and sadness and doubt about the sectarian divisiveness evident among the Protestant Christian representatives (stanzas 4-6):

> I listened to th' Buddhist, in his robes of shinin' white,
> As he told how like to Christ's thair lives, while ours was not—a mite,
> 'Tel I felt, to lead a Christian life, a Buddhist I must be,
> An' th' Parl'ment of Religions brought religious doubt to me.
>
> Then I heered th' han'some Hindu monk, drest up in orange dress,
> Who sed that all humanity was part of God—no less,
> An' he sed we was *not* sinners, so I comfort took, once more,
> While th' Parl'ment of Religions roared with approving roar.
>
> Then a Cath'lic man got up an' spoke, about Christ an' th' cross;
> But th' Christians of th' other creeds, they giv' thair heds a toss.
> When th' Babtist spoke, th' Presbyterians seemed to be fightin' mad,
> 'Tel th' Parl'ment of Religions made my pore old soul feel sad.

As made clear by her descriptions of their appearance and by her summaries of what they said ("how like to Christ's lives thair lives, while ours was not—a mite," and "all humanity was part of God"), the Buddhist and the Hindu by whom Hannah is so deeply impressed are none other than Dharmapāla and Vivekananda. The contrast between the religious universalism preached by these two Eastern reformers, and the credal squabbles between the Baptist and Presbyterian speakers, would surely reinforce Hannah's inchoate suspicion that "to lead a Christian life, a Buddhist I must be." Her parliament experience thus leads her to develop a new openmindedness toward religious diversity (stanzas 7-8):

> I've harkened to th' Buddhist, to th' Hindu an' th' Turk;
> I've tried to find th' truth that in our different sects may lurk,
> 'Tel my pore old brain it buzzes, like its goin' religious mad—
> For th' Parl'ment of religions nigh put out th' light I had.
>
> Must I leave all this sarchin' 'tel I reach th' other side?

---

[41] This speech, printed in small type and tucked into Barrows, "History," in *WPR*, 1:132-36, is recommended reading to any of those who tend to romanticize the parliament. Displaying an editorial precision that seems lacking in other places in his volumes, Barrows inserts in brackets the words "laughter" and "applause" to indicate the half-dozen instances where Higginson's speech was interrupted by the audience's expressions of delight. Barrows's own public commendation of this "beautiful address" (p. 136) is baffling, to say the least.

I'll treat all men as brothers while on this airth I bide,
An' let "Love" be my motto, 'tel I enter in th' door.
Of that great Religious Parl'ment, where creeds don't count no more.

Hannah's resignation "to find th' truth...in our different sects," and to "treat all men as brothers" while awaiting that parliament in heaven "where creeds don't count no more," shows the extent to which she is spiritually transformed by her experience.

Colliding Histories, Mixed Legacies

If the Parliament of Religions was ironically but inextricably linked with the Columbian quatricentennial, as epitomized by Gaston Bonét-Maury's description of the former's chairman as a man "of the spirit of Christopher Columbus,"[42] the parliament also signified the colliding of a remarkably complex array of religious histories, including the traditions of the various faiths and denominations represented there, and the personal religious lives of the individual participants. Those analyzed later by Kitagawa, Mullick, Bartholomeusz, and Ketelaar are among the most remarkable. Here, however, let us consider the multiple histories, myths, and stories that coalesced in the very idea of the Parliament of Religions, as well as the peculiar mixture of legacies that were spawned by the 1893 manifestation of that idea.

Regardless of whether the idea of holding a world's congress of religions in 1893 was originally conceived by Bonney, as is generally accepted, or by two Unitarian ministers of Chicago, Jenkin Lloyd Jones of All Souls Church and David Utter of the First Unitarian Church, as has also been speculated,[43] the Parliament of Religions had significant historical, biblical, and literary prefiguration. According to Barrows, the parliament committee began its work with no prior model in mind, but soon learned of a number of foreshadowings from world history.

---

[42] G. Bonét-Maury, in *Le Revue des Deux Mondes*, Paris (August 1894), cited in *WFP*, p. 35.

[43] See Charles H. Lyttle, *Freedom Moves West: A History of the Western Unitarian Conference, 1852-1952* (Boston: Beacon, 1952), p. 205, cited by Sunrit Mullick, "Protap Chunder Mozoomdar in America: Missionary of a New Dispensation," Doctor of Ministry (D.Min.) dissertation, Meadville/Lombard Theological School, Chicago, Illinois, 1988, pp. 127-28. With regard to the mission of Majumdar (Mozoomdar) to America in 1883, which renewed an already established connection between the Brāhmo Samāj and American Unitarians, Mullick carefully suggests: "While there does not appear to be any direct influence of Mozoomdar on the actual idea of holding a world congress of religions, his message of the meeting of Eastern and Western religions may well have sparked such an idea in the mind of one of the chief architects of the Parliament, the Unitarian minster Jenkin Lloyd Jones" (p. 122).

These included the conference of Buddhists summoned by Aśoka at Pāṭaliputra in 242 B.C.E.; of Christians, by Constantine at Nicaea, 325 C.E.; and of Muslims, Jews, Christians, and Brahmans, by Akbar at Delhi in the sixteenth century. The committee was also told that a similar meeting was conceived by the Moravian bishop, Johannes Comenius (1592-1671). The Free Religious Association of Boston had come up with such a plan in the 1870s. And a sermon on an imaginary convention in Tokyo of religious leaders of the Eastern world had been preached several years prior to the parliament by William Fairfield Warren, then president of Boston University, who, earlier in his career, had occupied the first university chair for comparative religion in America.[44]

Such comparisons, which Müller and others would later reject, were not the last to be made. At the parliament, some of the analogies above were drawn again by speakers. In addition, one speaker told of "a polyglot religious meeting," with "discourses and prayer in five languages—Hawaiian, Portuguese, Japanese, Chinese and English," reportedly held in Hawaii "some months" prior to the Chicago parliament.[45] A dozen years after the parliament, Henry Louis Jordan would refer to an assembly of "Saracen, [Nestorian] Christian, and Buddhist" representatives reportedly convened by Mangu in the mid-thirteenth century, as "the forerunner, though on a much inferior scale," of the 1893 parliament.[46] And Ketelaar, citing Edward Said's discussion of a Christian-Muslim *contraferentia* planned for in the mid-fifteenth century, has recently drawn that unrealized scheme into an implicit comparison with the parliament.

But history in the strict sense of the term was not the only source of perceived foreshadowings for the parliament. Not a few Christian leaders construed the 1893 parliament as antitypic of some of the most profound myths from their tradition, calling the parliament the most important event since the coming of Christ, and portraying it in biblical terms as a defiance of the dispersion of the descendants of

---

[44] Barrows, "History," in *WPR*, 1:8-11. Cf. Mary Eleanor Barrows, *John Henry Barrows: A Memoir* (Chicago: Fleming H. Revell, 1904), pp. 253-54. See also in the present volume the articles by Müller, Seager, and Ziolkowski. On Warren, who had occupied the chair of comparative theology and of history and philosophy of religion at the Boston University from 1873 on, see Louis Henry Jordan, *Comparative Religion: Its Genesis and Growth* (New York: Charles Scribner's Sons, 1905), p. 201 (cited hereafter as Jordan, *Genesis*).

[45] The quote is from Rev. Edward P. Baker, "The Hawaiian Islands," in *WPR*, 2:1070.

[46] Jordan, *Genesis*, p. 134, including n. 2 on that page.

Noah at Babel; a latter-day analogue to the vision of the Transfiguration on Mount Tabor; a larger, "second" Pentecost; an affirmation of Paul's address to the philosophers and Jews upon the Areopagus; and, as mentioned already, a New Jerusalem and Celestial City.[47] That the dream of a religious unity also hearkened back to a venerable theme of religious unity in Western literature was hinted at during the parliament by the allusion by Reform rabbi Kaufman Kohler to the tale of "The Three Rings"; by the occasional appeals made by Barrows and others to pertinent verses of Tennyson and Browning; and by W. A. Martin's observation that "the idea of such a congress had often appeared in fiction and poetry."[48] A century earlier the theme had found popular variations in a pair of American nationalist epics that seem to anticipate the parliament: Elhanan Winchester's *The Process and Empire of Christ* (1793) and Joel Barlow's *Columbiad* (1807), both of which attribute a millennialist significance to the United States and envision a sacred city where the peoples of the world would convene to inaugurate a universal peace.[49]

---

[47] For allusions to Babel see, e.g., John J. Keane, "The Ultimate Religion," in *WPR*, 2:1331; and G. Bonét-Maury in *Le Journal de Genève*, as quoted in *WFP*, p. 35. For comparison to the Transfiguration see, e.g., George Candlin, "Results and Mission of the Parliament of Religions," *The Biblical World* n.s. 5 (1895): 373. For comparisons to the Pentecost see, e.g., George T. Candlin (untitled closing-day address), E.L. Rexford ("The Religious Intent"), George Dana Boardman ("Christ the Unifier of Mankind"), John Henry Barrows ("Review and Summary") in *WPR*, 1:169, 509, 2:1338, 1566 respectively; the remarks from *The Christian World* (London) and Rev. O.P. Gifford quoted in *WFP*, pp. 29, 43; Charles C. Bonney, "The World's Parliament of Religions," *The Monist* 5 (1895): 339; and the poem by Mrs. Eliza M. Souvielle discussed later in this Introduction. For comparisons to Areopagus (Mars Hill) see, e.g., Dionysios Latas ("The Greek Church") and Barrows ("Review and Summary") in *WPR*, 1:358 and 2:1578 respectively. For discussion of such comparisons see in the present volume the articles by Seager and Ziolkowski.

[48] See in this volume the article by Ziolkowski, including n. 19. Although the article focuses upon the theme of religious unity in Western literature, the theme is not exclusive to the West. Dharmapāla probably had Asian literature in mind when he remarked that the parliament had "realized the utopian idea of the poet and the visionary" (quoted beneath his photograph in *WPR*, 2:861).

[49] Elhanan Winchester, *The Process and Empire of Christ, from his birth to the end of the mediatorial kingdom; a poem, in twelve books* (London: T. Gillet, 1793); and Joel Barlow, *The Columbiad, a poem* (Philadelphia: Fry and Kammerer for C. and A. Conrad, 1807), an amplification of his "poem in nine books," *The Vision of Columbus* (Hartford: Hudson and Goodwin, 1787). In Richard Hughes Seager's view, these poems constitute a "script" for the Chicago's Columbian Exposition ("The World's Parliament of Religions, Chicago, Illinois, 1893: America's Religious Coming of Age," Ph.D. dissertation, Harvard University, Cambridge, Mass., 1987, pp. 1-7 [cited hereafter as Seager, diss.]).

That the parliament realized an idea which had hitherto been "uttered now and then by poets only" was suggested the next year (1894) by Max Müller, who was probably unaware that the event had already inspired the composition of a poem of over 3,000 lines, *Sequel to the Parliament of Religions*, by a Mrs. Eliza Madelina (Wilbur) Souvielle, which appeared as a book that same year.[50] In this poem the biblical mythos behind the 1893 parliament achieved its fullest crystallization. Composed in rhymed couplets of iambic pentameter, the poem consists mainly of an imaginary dialogue between "three striking figures, each of Eastern race" on a ship crossing the Atlantic ocean, first on the way to, then on the way back from, the 1893 Parliament of Religions: a Turkish Muslim; a mandarin Confucianist; and a South Asian Buddhist. These three characters discuss and debate the different doctrines and histories of their respective faiths, and on their return trip are joined in this discussion by a (presumably western) Christian "witness" who—undoubtedly reflecting the poet's own beliefs—is allowed the final word. Having described the religion parliament as the "second Pentecost day,"[51] this Christian concludes that the way is now paved for the achievement of what Christ "announced," namely, the "universal brotherhood" of mankind: "The Parliament has this inaugurated, / And prophecy's fulfillment initiated."[52] This conclusion thus accords with the elaborate chart on the book's frontispiece which details the poet's conception of the "Genealogy of Religions." According to this chart, the 1893 parliament "renews and acknowledges the bond of blood and brotherhood" of all humanity, which had been established through the "brotherhood and covenant of safety" with "Noe, tenth from Adam, 3000 B.C.," but which subsequently splintered into the divergent religious traditions of the world. Following its renewal through the parliament, that bond would be "realized" in God's coming "Kingdom."[53]

---

[50] Mrs. Souvielle published her *Sequel to the Parliament of Religions* (Chicago: American Author's Protective Publishing, 1894) under the pseudonym Eben Malcolm Sutcliffe. Her real name does not appear on the cover or title-page, but is disclosed in the entry on that book in *The National Union Catalog Pre-1956 Imprints*, vol. 576. Mrs. Souvielle authored and published under her own name an "American Epic" entitled *The Ulyssiad* (Jacksonville, Fla.: Dacosta, 1896). Whether or not Müller ever came across her work is uncertain.

[51] Souvielle (Sutcliffe), *Sequel*, p. 161.

[52] Ibid., p. 181.

[53] Between Noah and the Parliament of Religions, this frontispiece-chart purports to show how three separate traditions are spawned through Noah's sons: one, through Ham, leads to the "lowest form of idolatry"; another, through

While the interpretation in Mrs. Souvielle's poem might strike readers today as sentimentally overblown and fancifully eccentric, it can hardly be overemphasized how momentous a "landmark" in human history the 1893 parliament seemed to countless contemporaries. In calling the parliament "the first universal council ever held, the first *parliament of man*," Barrows voiced a widely-held opinion, again adopting the emphasized phrase from Tennyson.[54] If not everyone would have shared Barrows's conviction that the event showed mankind to be "drifting toward religion and not away from it," the parliament was perceived by others as "one of the milestones in humanity's *progress*," marking "an era in the religious history and

---

Japheth, leads to "Confucius and ancestral worship"; a third tradition, the central one on the chart, leads through Shem, and later, through the period "when nine generations lived in peace in one house," to the "brotherhood and covenant of promise" with Abraham. Prior to those developments, a crucial year in the development of all three traditions, according to the chart, is "2256 B.C.," when the tradition of Ham "carries to Africa the record of having come from the North"; that of Japeth "carries to China the counsel Yao gave to Shun"; and that of Shem, with Peleg, sees "the earth divided." Later, out of the concubine and two wives of Abraham, five subsequent traditions continue developing: the "idolatry" and Confucian "ancestral worship" spawned by the lineages of Ham and Japeth continue on their own courses; the Ishmaelite tradition spawned by "Hagar of Ham" eventually gives rise to "Mohammedanism"; the Midianite tradition spawned by "Ketura of Japeth" leads through "Jethro or Zoroaster" to Brahmanism and eventually Buddhism; while the tradition of Isaac spawned by "Sarah of Shem" leads through Moses (who is connected with Jethro of the Midianite tradition) to "Jesus the King," whose appearance is followed by "Christianity incorporat[ing] the mythology of all nations," and eventually "Protesting Christianity." As the penultimate development of the central Shemite tradition, "Protesting Christianity" is shown to culminate in the Parliament of Religions, in which it is reunited with the traditions of "Hagar of Ham" ("Mohammedanism") and of "Ketura of Japeth" (Zoroastrianism, Brahmanism, Buddhism), as well as with "idolatry" and "ancestral worship." The author later comments in a brief note on this chart that "the identification of Zoroaster as Jethro is so striking and complete that it seems to solve deep and numerous mysteries; and in these latter days, when so many minds are seeking truth, it will demonstrate the absolute unity of all Truth" (ibid., p. 187).

[54] The quotation of Barrows, with my emphasis, is from his article in this volume. See n. 28 above for the source of the phrase "parliament of man." Compare Barrows's assessment with, e.g., Müller's, in the fifth paragraph of the latter's article in the present volume; and C.H. Toy: "It is perhaps the first universal congress, and it is matter of congratulation that the modern facilities of travel have thus early lent themselves to the successful carrying out of a general convention of men in which religion was the point of attraction" ("The Parliament of Religions," *The New World* 2 [December 1893]: 737). For similar statements by other commentators within the first year after the parliament, see *WFP* intermittently throughout. Ten years later Jordan could still call the event "absolutely *sui generis*" (*Genesis*, p. 198).

progress of the world"; "a new stage in the *evolution* of religion"; a "new, great act in the historic *evolution* of the race."[55]

Of course, "progress" and "evolution," those twin keynotes of late-nineteenth-century thought, have lost their lustre through the theretofore unimaginable horrors of our own century: world wars, genocides, nuclear bombs. But the obsolescence of "progress" and "evolution" as meaningful categories for assessing the significance or worth of a human event does not imply that the parliament made no positive contributions. Kitagawa stresses two: its provision of a "strong stimulus" to the study of comparative religion, evidenced most concretely by the prestigious lectureships resultingly endowed by Mrs. Caroline Haskell, and its initiation of the "dialogue among various religions." To these two contributions a third may be added: the pioneering boost it gave to the then inchoate Christian ecumenical movement.[56]

Consistent with those three contributions, the 1893 parliament can be seen as the starting-point of a trio of separate traditions of international assemblies that persist today. The first tradition concerns the study of comparative religion or the "science of religions." In 1897, in connection with King Oscar II's Silver Jubilee, there was held in Stockholm what was called the Congress of the Science of Religion (*Religionsvetenskapliga Kongressen*), inspired by the Chicago parliament.[57] This Stockholm meeting is considered the second "preliminary"—the Chicago parliament having been the first—to the

---

[55] George S. Goodspeed, "Introduction" to *WFP*, p. 6; Rev. E.M. Wherry, a Presbyterian missionary in India, as quoted in *WFP*, p. 19; Rev. Theodore Munger of New Haven, Connecticut, as quoted in *WFP*, p. 42; excerpt from *The Union Signal* of Chicago, as quoted (with no date given) in *WFP*, p. 44 (all emphases mine). The third of these quotations is reiterated almost verbatim by Paul Carus, "The World's Religious Parliament Extension," *The Monist* 5 (1895): 345, who substitutes the phrase "landmark" for "new stage." Cf. the quotation from Rev. F. Herbert Stead in *WFP*, p. 31

[56] Cf. for example Eck, "Foreword," *DRP*, pp. xv-xvi. Throughout the following discussion I use the term "ecumenical" (from the Greek *oikoumenikós*, "belonging to the whole inhabited world"), in the technical sense in which it has been used since the nineteenth century to refer to an interdenominational movement, especially among Protestants, aimed at achieving universal Christian unity and ecclesiastical union. This use of the term is not to be confused with its increasingly frequent usage elsewhere to refer more generally to a quest for harmony or unity among different religions, of which Christianity is but one.

[57] See Eric J. Sharpe, *Comparative Religion: A History* (1975; 2d edition, La Salle: Open Court, 1987), p. 140 (cited hereafter as Sharpe, *History*).

initial "genuinely scientific congress of comparative religion,"[58] the *Congrés international d'Histoire des Religions* held in Paris, 1900, in connection with that city's international exposition that year. The latter congress led to the ones held for that discipline in St. Louis and Basel (both in 1904), Oxford (1905), Leiden (1912), Lund (1929), Brussels (1935), and Amsterdam (1950), the last of which saw the establishment of the UNESCO-sponsored International Association of the History of Religions (IAHR). Since then, the IAHR has held international congresses in Rome, 1955; Tokyo, 1958; Marburg, 1960; Claremont, 1965; Stockholm, 1970; Lancaster, 1975; Winnipeg, 1980; Sydney, 1985; and Rome, 1990.[59]

A second tradition concerns interreligious or interfaith dialogue. Even before the close of the 1893 parliament a movement called the World's Religious Parliament Extension arose with the expressed intention of becoming a lasting movement "to establish friendly relations among all religions for a better mutual understanding."[60] Despite the historical ineffectuality of this movement, which apparently fizzled out within a decade after its formal inauguration (January 1, 1895),[61] the parliament did spawn a long lineage of

---

[58] The quotation is from Sharpe, *History*, p. 138. But see Sharpe's qualification in the next note below.

[59] The history of all these international congresses from the one in Paris to the one in Claremont (except for the one in St. Louis) is recounted by C.J. Bleeker, "Opening Address," in *Proceedings of the XIth International Congress of the International Association for the History of Religions, held...at Claremont, California, September 6-11, 1965*, 3 vols. (Leiden: Brill, 1968), 1:5. The 1904 St. Louis congress is noted by Jordan, *Genesis*, p. 393. In agreement with Jordan's contention that the 1897 Stockholm congress, not the 1900 Paris one, was "the initial gathering of scholars in this field" (*Genesis*, p. 393 n. 1), Sharpe states in reference to that Stockholm congress: "It is perhaps to be regretted that the subsequent series of international congresses organised by the IAHR should be regarded as having begun with the Paris congress of 1900, rather than with this pioneer assembly" (*History*, p. 140 n. 35). This opinion seems supported by Mircea Eliade's passing reference to those two congresses in his "Chronological Survey: The 'History of Religion' as a Branch of Knowledge," in *The Sacred and the Profane: The Nature of Religion*, trans. Willard R. Trask (New York: Harcourt Brace Jovanovich, 1959), p. 218. Eliade makes no mention of the Chicago parliament.

[60] Carus, "The World's Religious Parliament Extension," p. 345. On the plans behind this movement, see also Bonney, "The World's Parliament of Religions" (n. 47 above), pp. 339-44; and Barrows's passing allusion to it in his article in the present volume.

[61] This short-lived movement was last suggested to be still existing by Paul Carus, as reported in M. Jean Réville, *Congrès international d'histoire des religions* (Paris: Imprimerie Nationale, 1900), p. 6; and by Jordan, *Genesis*, p. 572. For what little else is known about its fate, see Druyvesteyn, diss., pp. 76-79.

international interfaith meetings. This lineage began with the two "Little Parliaments of Religions" held in Japan in 1896 and 1897, and continued with the international interfaith meetings at Boston, 1920; Chicago, 1933, in connection with the city's second World's Fair; London and Cambridge, 1936 and 1938; Bombay, 1936, as part of the Ramakrishna Centenary celebration; Calcutta, 1937; Rishikesh, 1953;[62] and various subsequent smaller meetings between representatives of two or more faiths prior to the two major centenniel congresses planned for this August: the Parliament of the World's Religions in Chicago, and the Sarva-Dharma-Sammelana (Religious People Meeting Together) in Bangalore.

---

[62] See *World Parliament of Religions Commemoration Volume, Issued in Commemoration of the World Parliament of Religions Held at Sivanandanagar, Rishikesh, in April, 1953, as well as, of its Subsequent Anniversary Meetings, and of the Half-Yearly Religions [sic] Federation Incepted in December 1945* [no editor named] (Rishikesh, Himalayas: Sivanandanagar, Yoga-Vedanta Forest University, 1956), which contains a paper by Sri Swami Sadananda, "Religious Parliaments in Retrospect," pp. 25-32, recounting the meetings at Boston (the so-called "International Congress of Religious Liberals"), and Bombay and Calcutta (each called "Parliament of Religions"). On the 1896 and 1897 "parliaments" in Japan, see in the present volume the lecture by Kitagawa. The 1933 Chicago meeting ("World Fellowship of Faith") commemorating the fortieth anniversary of the original parliament is alluded to in the letter of Mr. Ramamurti quoted at the outset of that same lecture by Kitagawa. Between the two meetings in Japan and the one in Boston, there were a number of other interfaith meetings in the United States, and at least one such meeting in China, directly inspired by the 1893 Chicago parliament, but the scope of each was apparently confined to the nation in which it was held. Thus, writing in 1905, Jordan cited "the *New York State Conference of Religion*, organised in 1900,...which meets annually" (*Genesis*, p. 388 n. 2), and "similar Conferences held in other States of the Union," as "the direct fruits of that most stimulating Western impulse" (p. 392) begun by the 1893 parliament. While that New York "Conference" was neither an international congress, nor one that embraced "any great variety of forms of religious belief," Jordan notes, "yet, within its more limited sphere, it seeks to affirm and render visible that religious unity which underlies all religious differences," allowing Jews and Christians of various denominations to "participate freely in its discussions....In like manner, it is no longer an isolated and remarkable occurrence [i.e., after the 1893 parliament] that, in the actual prosecution of Missions, the representatives of Christian and non-Christian Faiths should meet together for free and brotherly conference. Thus, in China in 1904, a group of about one hundred leaders of religious propagandism—Confucianists, Mohammedans, Christians, and others—assembled in Shantung, and frankly discussed the question: How shall we best revive Religion in China?" (p. 392 n. 2).

Having been directly associated with the formation of the
Brotherhood of Christian Unity,[63] the 1893 parliament also pioneered
a third tradition of international assemblies—those convened in the
name of Christian ecumenicism.[64] Anticipated by the parliament, this
tradition "officially" began with the famous 1910 conference of
Edinburgh and continued developing through three distinct
commissions. The International Missionary Council, established in
1921, met in Jerusalem, 1928; Madras, 1938; Whitby, 1947; Willingen,
1952; and Ghana, 1957. The Commission on Life and Work met in
Stockholm, 1925 and Oxford, 1937. And the Faith and Order
Commission met in Lausanne, 1927 and Edinburgh, 1937. The second
and third of those commissions became fused at the founding of the

---

[63] See Seward, "The Year 1893" (n. 28 above), esp. pp. 378-79, 380. A letter read by
Seward to the parliament, stating the character and method of this Brotherhood,
is included in Barrows, "History," in *WPR*, 1:132.

[64] Cf. Robert S. Ellwood: "While the parliament was undeniably liberal
Protestant in tone, it was also a pioneering ecumenical event, international in
scope" ("World's Parliament of Religions," in *The Encyclopedia of Religion*, 16 vols.,
ed. Mircea Eliade [New York: Macmillan, 1987], 15:444); and Eck, for whom the
parliament "might be seen as one of the first events of [Christian] ecumenical
movement, and for many the hopes of Christian unity were the overarching
concern of the Parliament" ("Foreword," *DRP*, p. xv). This connection has been
overlooked in most of the traditional historiography on the ecumenical
movement. For example, the parliament is not mentioned in Robert McAfee
Brown's entry, "Ecumenical Movement," in *The Encyclopedia of Religion*, ed.
Eliade, 5:17-27. Likewise, the parliament goes unmentioned throughout that vast
standard work which Brown calls "the best overall resource" on "the mission and
expansion of Christianity, the movement out of which modern ecumenism
grew" ("Ecumenical Movement," p. 26): Kenneth Scott Latourette's five-vol.
*Christianity in a Revolutionary Age: A History of Christianity in the Nineteenth and
Twentieth Centuries* (New York: Harper, 1958-61), whose third volume focuses on
the Americas, the Pacific, Asia, and Africa in the nineteenth century. In the
comprehensive study, *A History of the Ecumenical Movement, 1517-1948*, ed. Ruth
Rouse and Stephen Charles Neill (1954; 2d ed., Philadelphia: Westminster, 1967),
the parliament is mentioned twice, passingly, both times in connection with the
"great irenic address" (p. 246) of the pioneering Presbyterian ecumenist Philip
Schaff (1819-93) of Union Theological Seminary, an address "now famous" (p.
256), which was presented at the parliament in its ailing author's presence by
Simon McPherson: "The Reunion of Christendom," which seems "prophetic of
the Federal Council [of the Churches of Christ in America] of the 20th century,
and even more so of its successor, the National Council" (p. 256). Schaff's paper
appears in *WPR*, 2:1192-1201, and is, as Seager points out, "representative of a
number of papers [delivered at the parliament] on the prospects of Christian
unity. The quest for Christian unity at the Parliament was one important
dimension...for the larger quest for the religious unity of the world"
("Introduction," *DRP*, p. 36). For Barrows's own remarks on the parliament's
"effect" of "bring[ing] up more prominently than ever the question of the
reunion of Christendom," see his "Review and Summary," in *WPR*, 2:1573.

World Council of Churches (WCC) at Amsterdam in 1948 (two years prior to the founding of the IAHR in that same city, incidentally). After reconvening at Evanston in 1954, the WCC was joined during its third international assembly, in New Delhi, 1961, by the International Missionary Council, and since then has met as a global body in Uppsala, 1968; Nairobi, 1975; Vancouver, 1983;[65] and Canberra, 1991.

The WCC remains at present an organization of Protestant, Anglican, and Orthodox churches which the Roman Catholic Church has consistently refused to join. However, Vatican II (1962-65)—with its decree of *Unitatis Redintegratio* (1964) and attendant declarations on ecumenism[66]—made possible the more open attitude which Rome has displayed toward the WCC since then. This new tone is a far cry from the violent conservative uproar raised within the Catholic hierarchy a hundred years ago against two American liberals from its ranks, Bishop John J. Keane (1839-1918) of Richmond and Cardinal (James) Gibbons (1834-1921), for their participation in the parliament. Keane was removed from his office as the first rector of Catholic University of America three years later (1896), Catholic clergy were forbidden by the Vatican to participate in subsequent religious congresses, and the parliament episode became one in the chain of events that eventually led Pope Leo XIII to issue his encyclical *Testem benevolentiae* (1899) against the perceived dangers posed by "Americanism" to the Catholic church.

The dates and places of the successive post-1893 international assemblies cited above for comparative religion, interfaith dialogue, and Christian ecumenism highlight the lasting, global embrace of three distinct traditions that find a common progenitor in the World's Parliament of Religions. What is particularly fascinating is that this single event could help engender all three traditions. But it must be remembered that the parliament, by its unique conception and circumstances, was not simply an interfaith meeting; also essential to the parliament's nature were the developing intrafaith, ecumenical urge among Christians, and the new vogue for the study of comparative religion in this country. As shall be seen, these three different aspects of the parliament were inextricably interrelated.

---

[65] See Brown, "Ecumenical Movement," pp. 18-21.

[66] Included in Austin P. Flannery, ed., *Documents of Vatican II* (Grand Rapids, Mich.: Eerdmans, 1975), pp. 452-78.

A "Hierological Museum"

The ten officially stated "objects" of the World's Parliament of Religions declared its primary purpose of seeking harmony among different religious traditions: "To bring together in conference, for the first time in history, the leading representatives of the great Historic Religions of the world"; "To show...how many important truths the various Religions hold and teach in common"; "To promote and deepen the brotherhood among religious men of diverse faiths"; and so on.[67] But while this interfaith aspect of the parliament was what most captivated the imagination of its participants and witnesses alike, the event ipso facto became also for Christians an occasion for intrafaith dialogue and pursuit of ecumenical ends. Notwithstanding the sense of interdenominational rivalry that may have occasionally betrayed itself among Christian speakers (as reflected in stanza 6 of the "Aunt Hannah" poem quoted earlier), one witness could observe: "The question of Christian union...from the first was one of the largest issues of the Parliament....For the presence of so many representatives of alien religions facing the Christian speakers forced upon the Christian mind as never before...that all Christians must be 'one' before the unconverted world could know that God had sent [Jesus] to be the Saviour of mankind."[68] Thus "forced," in part, by the parliament's interfaith dimension, the Christian intrafaith, ecumenical dimension was reinforced by the some three dozen denominational and interdenominational congresses held from late August though early October in conjunction with the parliament, almost all of them involving exclusively Christian churches or associations.[69]

---

[67] Quoted by Barrows, "History," in *WPR*, 1:18.

[68] Florence E. Winslow, "A Pen Picture of the Parliament," *Christian Thought*, ed. Charles Deems (New York: W.B. Ketcham, 1893-94), pp. 232-33 (emphasis mine).

[69] See "The Denominational Congresses," in *WPR*, 2:1383-1554, which includes reports on the following denominational congresses, with their names as listed: Advent Church (September 14), African Methodist Episcopal Church (September 22), Seventh-Day Baptist (no date given), Catholic (September 4-9), Christian Science (September 20), Congregational Church (September 10), Women's Congregational (September 11), Disciples of Christ (September 13), Evangelical Association (September 19-21), Society of Friends (with separate sections on Orthodox and Hicksite; no dates given), Jewish (August 27-30), Jewish Women (September 4-7), Lutheran General Synod (September 11-13), Lutheran General Council (September 2), Lutheran Missouri Synod (September 3), Methodist Episcopal (September 25), New Jerusalem Church (no date given), Presbyterian (September 17), Cumberland Presbyterian (no date given), Reformed Episcopal (no date given), Reformed Church in the United States (September 21), Theosophical (September 15-16), Unitarian (September 20-22), United Brethren in Christ (September 14), Universalist Church (September 11), Welsh churches

As a forum for both inter- and intrafaith dialogue, the parliament also furnished an opportunity for each parliamentarian, whether wittingly or not, to engage in comparative religious study, and in turn to see his or her own faith scrutinized as a subject of such study by other parliamentarians and the audience alike.[70] Indeed, the important bearing of the scholarly study of religion on the parliament has not been fully appreciated. It has become a cliché among commentators to say, as Barrows and others claimed at the time, that the parliament gave "a strong impetus to the study of comparative religion."[71] Yet it

---

(September 3), Free Religious Association of America (September 20), King's Daughters and Sons (September 22), Evolutionists (September 27-29), International Board of Women Christian Associations (September 27), Young Women's Christian Associations (October 7), Young Men's Christian Association (no date given). The same part of *WPR* includes reports on inter-denominational congresses on Missions (September 28-October 5), Sunday Rest (September 28-30), and Evangelical Alliance (October 8-15); and reports on the separate presentations by the Anglican Church (September 25), Baptist Churches (September 27), Free Baptist Church (September 25), and German Evangelical Church (September 24); and Swedish Evangelical Mission Covenant in America (September 27).

[70] Cf. Jordan, *Genesis*, pp. 465-66: "But while it was agreed that there should be no publicly instituted comparison of the many Faiths which for seventeen days confronted each other upon the same platform [at the 1893 parliament], there was, in point of fact, a ceaseless and conscious comparison going on in the mind of every interested listener." Barrows, in his article in the present volume, suggests that one of the parliament's aims was "a friendly comparison" of Christianity with other faiths.

[71] Barrows, "Review and Summary," in *WPR*, 2:1569. Barrows reiterated this claim in numerous places, including his article in the present volume; there he comments several times on the parliament's positive impact on the study of comparative religion, asserting at one point that "it has *furnished a stimulus* to further sympathetic inquiry" (emphasis mine) by Christians and non-Christians into each others' faiths. Even earlier, C.H. Toy had predicted in an article three months after the parliament that one of the "direct results" would be "an increase in the interest in the science of the history of religions....A certain number of persons *will be incited* to a sympathetic study of some of these phases of religion." Furthermore, "It may be hoped also that *an impulse has been given* to the study of the nature and function of religion" ("The Parliament" [n. 54 above], pp. 739-40 [emphasis mine]). That same month (December), another journal appeared containing George S. Goodspeed's remark that the parliament "has greatly *stimulated* the interest of thinking people in the study of Comparative Religion" ("Comparative-Religion Notes," *The Biblical World* 2 [1893]: 466 [emphasis mine]; compare the same author's comments in *The Biblical World* 3 [1894]: 128-29). Whether more through the power of suggestion or through the force of facts, other scholars were quick to pick up and reiterate this idea, using the same wording; cf. D.S. Schaff, as quoted from *The Homiletic Review*, New York, in *WFP*, p. 14. By 1905 Jordan could claim that the publication of *WPR* had "done a great deal both to popularise and *to stimulate* advanced research in [comparative religion]" (*Genesis*, p. 198). Almost eighty years later, Joseph M. Kitagawa adapted

is often overlooked that the discipline—or at least the popular conception of it—exerted a crucial influence on the actual formation and carrying out of the parliament. Not only did Bonney and Barrows, as the parliament's two primary promoters, make clear their own long-term personal fascinations with the young growing discipline,[72] but Barrows was quick to cite the growth of comparative religion as one of "the special preparations for this meeting," while F.A. Noble, orthodox Congregationalist, went so far as to say in 1895 that the deepening interest in that field "for the last quarter of a century" had made the parliament "inevitable."[73]

How did the academic study of comparative religion, known today as the history of religions, actually bear upon the parliament? The emergence of a "scientific," historical-critical, and comparative interest in the world's religions as a consequence of the Enlightenment, and the "emancipation" of comparative religion as an "autonomous" scholarly discipline during the second half of the nineteenth century through the work of such "founding fathers" in Europe as Müller, C.P. Tiele, P.D. Chantepie de la Saussaye, and James G. Frazer, have been recounted

---

the same rhetoric in his lecture included in the present volume, where he asserts the parliament "provide[d]...a strong stimulus" to study in the discipline; cf. Kitagawa's similar, earlier remarks about the parliament in his "The History of Religion in America" (1959), in Joseph M. Kitagawa, *The History of Religions: Understanding Human Experience* (Atlanta, Georgia: Scholars Press, 1987), p. 5, where he cites Jordan's discussion; and Joseph M. Kitagawa, "Buddhism in America" (1967), which serves as the "Appendix" to his *On Understanding Japanese Religion* (Princeton, N.J.: Princeton University Press, 1987), p. 318. Kitagawa's statement seems echoed by Eck, "Foreword," *DRP*, p. xiv, who substitutes the phrase "gave an impetus to" for Kitagawa's phrase above, thus returning to the original wording used by Barrows in *WPR* as quoted above. Compare also the remarks of Sydney E. Ahlstrom, *The American Protestant Encounter with World Religions*, Brewer Lectures on Comparative Religion, Beloit College, Beloit, Wisconsin (1962), [n.p., n.d.], as cited by Druyvesteyn, diss., p. 258; and Donald H. Bishop, "America and the 1893 World Parliament of Religions," *Encounter* (Indianapolis) 31 (1970): 358-59. For a critique of this tradition of positive assessments of the parliament's influence on comparative religion, see Druyvesteyn, diss., pp. 251-70, where the author concludes that the parliament "in fact [had]...little demonstrable impact on the growth and development of the serious study of comparative religious studies in America [because] it was not a path-breaking event, but rather a product of its times" (p. 269).

[72] On Bonney's interest from boyhood on in "the science of Comparative Religions," see his "Genesis" (n. 16 above), p. 74; on Barrows's interest, see in the present volume the lecture by Kitagawa.

[73] F.A. Noble, "The Parliament of Religions," *The Advance* 21 (1895): 598; quoted by Bonney, "The World's Parliament of Religions," p. 337. The preceding quotation from Barrows is from his article in the present volume.

well enough elsewhere.[74] The importation of that discipline to American universities and its popularization in this country culminated in the 1893 parliament, which, in Kitagawa's words, "reflected the growing interest of Americans in exotic non-Western religions."[75]

By that time, we should note, the problem of what to call the young discipline—a problem which had plagued its practitioners from the start, and which has never really been settled to everyone's satisfaction—had come to a head,[76] as is reflected in several of the parliamentary papers in this volume. Reacting against the request by the parliament committee that he contribute a paper on "comparative theology," the Dutchman Tiele would contend that English-speaking authors who used that term confused it with "comparative religion." Theology and religion are not the same, he correctly maintained, and therefore comparative theology should signify "comparative study of religious dogmas," while comparative religion should signify "comparative study of the various religions in all their forms." This excursus perhaps was a hidden jab by Tiele at his German-born British rival, Müller, who divided the "science of religion" into two parts, "comparative theology" and "theoretic theology."[77] Whether or not he did have Müller in mind, nonetheless, the problem of nomenclature did not stop for Tiele with the distinction between comparative theology and comparative religion. Comparative theology, he went on to observe, was often taken to mean the "science of religion," with "science" carrying not its limited English denotation, but the more general significance of the Dutch *Wetenschap* or German *Wissenschaft*. Although Tiele would eventually accept "comparative religion" as the

---

[74] In addition to the accounts in Jordan's *Genesis*, Eliade's "Chronological Survey" (n. 59 above), pp. 216-32, and Sharpe's *History*, see those in other standard histories, including vol. 1 of Henri Pinard de la Boullaye, *L'Étude comparée des religions*, 3 vols., 4th ed., revised and augmented (Paris: G. Beauchesne, 1929-31); Gustav Mensching, *Geschichte der Religionswissenschaft* (Bonn: Universitäts-Verlag, 1948), translated by Pierre Jundt as *Histoire de la Science des Religions* (Paris: Lamarre, 1955); and Jacques Waardenburg, *Classical Approaches to the Study of Religion: Aims, Methods and Theories of Research*, 2 vols. (The Hague: Mouton, 1973-74).

[75] Joseph M. Kitagawa, "Humanistic and Theological History of Religions with Special Reference to the North American Scene" (1980), in his *The History of Religions: Understanding Human Experience* (n. 71 above), p. 113.

[76] Thus Jordan would feel the need twelve years later to include in his *Genesis*, a section explicating "Various Names Suggested for this Science" (pp. 24-28).

[77] F. Max Müller, *Introduction to the Science of Religion*, Lectures at the Royal Institution, 1870 (London: Longmans, Green, 1873; reprint New York: Arno Press, 1978), pp. 21-22. For documentation of the use the term "comparative theology" by other authors see Jordan, *Genesis*, p. 27.

most suitable appellation,[78] he would still, in his Gifford Lectures at Edinburgh in 1896 and 1898, employ the term "science of religion"[79]— the Anglicanization, first popularized by Müller, of the German *Religionswissenschaft*, which is traceable to the first decade of the nineteenth century; and of *la science des religions*, the French expression introduced by Prosper Leblanc in the early 1850s and used again in the following decade by the Sanskritist Émile Burnouf, one of Müller's teachers.[80]

Two decades before the parliament, however, Tiele had suggested another term, "hierology," as preferable to "the unhappy name of Science of Religions."[81] Having first cropped up in English during the early nineteenth century to connote "a discourse on sacred things" (as defined by Webster in 1828), the word "hierology" by mid-century denoted, more specifically, hieroglyphic lore and the study of Egyptian records, before evolving also into a colloquial name for the study of the history of religions as a branch of learning.[82] At the parliament, the word would be used by two American advocates of the discipline: by Merwin-Marie Snell, as a synonym for "science of religion," and by Eliza R. Sunderland, as synonynous to "comparative study of religions." Snell, as we shall see, construed the parliament itself through a telling coinage as a "hierological museum."

As the parliament approached, according to Barrows, its organizing committee was delighted and amazed that both "the religious world and the world of scholarship" had become deeply interested in their proposed congress, and there were those, like Max Müller, "who favored it because of the aid it would bring to the study of comparative religion."[83]   Müller, Tiele, and two other well-known European scholars of comparative religion even accepted nominal

---

[78] Cf. Jordan, *Genesis*, p. 27.

[79] E.g., C.P. Tiele, *Elements of the Science of Religion*, 2 vols. (Edinburgh: W. Blackwood and Sons, 1897-99).

[80] For documentation on the histories of the usage of these terms see Pinard de la Boullaye, *L'Étude comparée des religions*, 1:548; cited by Sharpe, *History*, p. 31, n. 7. Cf. Jordan, *Genesis*, p. 25.

[81] C.P. Tiele, "Preface" to his *Outlines of the History of Religion to the Spread of the Universal Religions*, trans. J. Estlin Carpenter (London: Trübner, 1877; 5th ed., 1892), p. vii.

[82] *The Oxford Dictionary of the English Language*, 2d ed., s.v. "hierology." The only example this entry gives of the latter sense of the word is from 1883—i.e., six years after the instance of its usage by Tiele cited in our previous note. *The Oxford Dictionary* also equates this term with "hagiology." See also the discussion of the term in Jordan, *Genesis*, pp. 24-25.

[83] Barrows, "History," in *WPR*, 1:15.

membership on the parliament's advisory council: Eugène Goblet d'Alviella of Belgium, and Otto Pfleiderer of Germany.

However, in spite of the mostly laymen's enthusiasm which Bonney, Barrows, and other American promoters of the parliament exuded for comparative religion, and the support which professional scholars from that discipline showed for the idea of such an event, the actual relationship that emerged between "the religious world and the world of scholarship" in their connection with the parliament proved ambiguous and problematic. To begin with, notwithstanding the parliament's sixth stated "object," which called for the participation of "leading scholars representing" the various non-Christian faiths,[84] it was stressed before the parliament commenced that this was to be, as one organizer put it, "in no sense a scientific congress."[85] Barrows later confirmed this claim:

> It would have been easy to defeat the objects of this meeting by making it chiefly a scientific gathering. But the purpose was not to call together the specialists in comparative religion....Such a proceeding would have killed the parliament. While scholarship was everywhere apparent, technical scholarship was not made supremely prominent, and, according to one participant, "the peculiar charm of this meeting consisted in this, that it did not carry with it the predominant smell of the lamp."[86]

Even leaving aside the question of what Barrows meant by his distinction between "scholarship" (with no adjective) and "technical scholarship," it becomes difficult to assess the actual role played by

---

[84] The full statement of this "goal" reads: "To secure from leading scholars, representing the Brahman, Buddhist, Confucian, Parsee, Mohammedan, Jewish and other Faiths, and from representatives of the various Churches of Christendom, full and accurate statements of the spiritual and other effects of the Religions which they hold upon the Literature, Art, Commerce, Government, Domestic and Social life of the peoples among whom these Faiths have prevailed" (Barrows, "History," in *WPR*, 1:18). It is unclear whether the phrase "scholars" here means (a) scholars who personally adhere to the faiths they are "representing"; or (b) scholars "representing" faiths which they study, but to which they do not necessarily adhere; or both (a) and (b). Interestingly, the statement sets these "representatives of the various Churches of Christendom" apart from the "scholars" of those other "faiths." Compare the statement of the fourth "object": "To set forth, by those most competent to speak, what are deemed the important distinctive truths held and taught by each Religion, and by the various chief branches of Christendom" (ibid.).

[85] Merwin-Marie Snell, "An Exhibit of Religions," *Science* 22 (August 25, 1894): 99.

[86] Quoted from Barrows's article in this volume. The point that the parliament was not meant to be a "scientific" gathering is made also by Toy, "The Parliament," p. 734, as quoted in n. 107 below.

scholars at the parliament because of lack of any consistent boundary drawn in its proceedings between the "religious" and the "scientific." As Kitagawa observes, many professors involved themselves in the parliament as representatives of their denominations: "To be sure, many of them were scholars of Comparative Religion or History of Religions, but they were inclined—theologically and religiously—to share the motto of the Parliament: 'To unite all Religion against all irreligion; to make the Golden Rule the basis of this union; to present to the world...the substantial unity of many religions in the good deeds of the Religious Life...and [to demonstrate] the marvelous Religious progress of the nineteenth century.'"[87] However, not all practitioners of the "scientific" study of religion were prepared to make such concessions to the parliament's "religious" raison d'être. In this regard it is worth quoting Eric J. Sharpe at length:

> The parliament was an encouragement, and a danger, to the emerging science of religion. An encouragement, because it showed the extent to which earlier impatience and intolerance was being overcome. A danger, because it tended to associate at least some comparative religionists (those who dared to associate themselves with it) with an idealistic programme of world peace and understanding....The ideals which were so desirable in the Chicago of the 1890s were not necessarily those of...the European universities, where the science of religion was slowly finding its feet. It was perhaps permissible for Max Müller to associate himself *in absentia* with the parliament; his reputation could bear it. Others held themselves firmly aloof—and have continued to hold themselves aloof from any further such gatherings simply on the grounds that whatever the need for inter-religious understanding, the scientific study of religion, committed to the quest of truth for truth's own sake, ought not to be saddled with such an onerous and subjective incidental.[88]

Let us examine more closely the actual involvement of scholars in the 1893 parliament.

The interests of comparative religion were served to varying degrees of explicitness at the parliament by the following scholars, listed with the titles of the papers which they contributed.[89] The three

---

[87] Kitagawa, "Humanistic and Theological History of Religions," p. 114. Kitagawa's source for the parliament's "motto" is the World's Relgous Congress, *General Programme* (preliminary ed., 1893), p. 19.

[88] Sharpe, *History*, p. 139.

[89] The following list corresponds with the discussion in Druyvesteyn, diss., pp. 243-50, which includes all the authors I mention except Fletcher. Seager's list of "major" parliament addresses in the "Appendix" of *DRP* (see n. 19 above)

most renowned comparativists who contributed papers to the parliament were all Europeans: Müller of Oxford ("Greek Philosophy and the Christian Religion"); Tiele of the University of Leiden ("On the Study of Comparative Theology"); and Albert Réville of the Collège de France ("Conditions and Outlook for a Universal Religion").[90] The other European scholars connected with the discipline, all of them well known, were Jean Réville of the École des Hautes Études ("Principles of the Scientific Classification of Religion"); Léon Marillier of the University of Paris ("The Estimate of Human Dignity in the Lower Religions"); J. Estlin Carpenter, lecturer in comparative religion at Oxford ("The Need for Wider Conception of Revelation, or Lessons from the Sacred Books of the World"); Charles Joseph de Harlez,[91] professor of Oriental languages at the University of Louvain ("The Comparative Study of the World's Religions"); and Conrad von Orelli of Basel University ("The General Belief in the Need of Vicarious Sacrifices").[92] Those American parliamentarians who worked in the field were Crawford H. Toy, professor of Hebrew and Oriental languages at Harvard ("The Relations between Religion and Conduct"); George Park Fisher, an ecclesiastical historian at Yale ("Christianity an Historical Religion"); and George S. Goodspeed, associate professor of comparative religion at the University of Chicago ("What the Dead Religions Have Bequeathed to the Living").[93] Other Americans whose addresses directly concerned comparative religion but who were not professional specialists in the

---

includes those of J. Estlin Carpenter, Alice Fletcher, C.D. d'Harlez (sic), Müller, Albert and Jean Réville, Merwin-Marie Snell, and C.P. Tiele.

[90] All three papers are included in this volume. On their authors, who figure prominently in the historiography of their discipline, see "Notes on the Authors" in the back.

[91] Harlez's name is consistently mis-cited as C.D. d'Harlez in both *WPR* and *NHP*, and seemingly by every subsequent English-speaking scholar and commentator writing on the parliament from the 1890s through the present. My authorities for the correct citation of his name are the title-pages of his many writings published in Belgium and France; the listings under his name in *The National Union Catalog Pre-1956 Imprints*, vol. 231; and the entry on him in *Grand Larousse encyclopedique*, 10 vols. (1960-64), 5:787.

[92] The papers by Jean Réville and Harlez appear in this volume. Those of Marillier, Carpenter, and von Orelli appear in *WPR*, 2:1361, 842-49, and 1041-45 respectively. On Jean Réville and Harlez see "Notes on the Authors" in the back of the present volume. All five of the authors mentioned in the present note, except Harlez, are discussed in Jordan, *Genesis*; see his index for references.

[93] The cited papers of these three authors appear respectively in *WPR*, 2:1009-11, 832-41, and 1:554-64. All three authors are discussed in Jordan, *Genesis*; see his index for references.

area included J.P. Landis, professor of Old Testament and Hebrew at Union Theological Seminary in Dayton, Ohio ("How Can Philosophy Aid the Science of Religion"); Eliza R. Sunderland, Ph.D., of Ann Arbor ("Serious Study of All Religions"); Milton S. Terry, professor at Northwestern University ("The Sacred Books of the World as Literature"); Milton Valentine, president of Gettysburg Theological Seminary in Pennsylvania ("Harmonies and Distinctions in the Theistic Teaching of the Various Historic Faiths"); and Merwin-Marie Snell of Catholic University ("Service of the Science of Religions to the Cause of Religious Unity," "Relations of the Science of Religion to Philosophy," and "Future of Religion").[94]

As impressive as the parliament's representation of comparative religion may seem from this list, certain qualifications must be made. Of the seventeen authors listed, nine, including Fisher and all the Europeans, did not attend the parliament, but sent their papers to be read for them. (Müller, the most celebrated of all the scholars of comparative religion associated with the parliament, would later call his having failed to attend it one of his greatest regrets in life.) So, notwithstanding the considerable number of other speakers at the parliament who were affiliated with academic institutions,[95] the

---

[94] The paper by Sunderland and the first of the three cited papers by Merwin-Marie Snell appear in this volume. The papers of Landis, Terry, and Valentine, and the second and third of Snell's papers appear respectively in *WPR*, 2:960-68, 1:794-704, 280-89, 2:1375, and 1325-27. None of these authors is mentioned in Jordan, *Genesis*. On Sunderland and Snell see "Notes on the Authors" in the back of the present volume.

[95] Not counting the figures listed in the previous paragraph, there were, from America, Charles R. Henderson, E.G. Hirsch, Albion W. Small, and William C. Wilkinson of the University of Chicago; Thomas Dwight, D.G. Lyon, and Francis G. Peabody of Harvard; B.L. Whitman of Colby College in Waterville, Maine; J.A. Howe of Bates College in Lewiston, Maine; A.H. Lewis of Alfred University in New York; Philip Schaff of Union Theological Seminary in New York; Thomas Richey of General Theological Seminary, New York; Waldo S. Pratt of Hartford Theological Seminary; Thomas O'Gorman of Catholic University; John J. Keane, president of Catholic University; J.R. Slattery of St. Joseph Seminary in Baltimore, Maryland; Thomas J. Semmes of the University of Louisiana; Isaac M. Wise, president of Hebrew Union College, Cincinnati, Ohio; Sylvester F. Scovel, president of Wooster University in Ohio; Martin J. Wade of the University of Iowa; Richard T. Ely of the University of Wisconsin; John Gmeiner of St. Thomas Seminary in St. Paul, Minnesota; Charles A. Briggs of Union Theological Seminary in New York. From Canada there was Sir William Dawson of McGill University. And from abroad, there were Minas Tcheraz of the School of Modern Oriental Studies in London; Alfred Williams Momerie of King's College in London; A.B. Bruce of the Free College in Glasgow, Scotland; George Washburn, president of Robert College in Constantinople; Isaac T. Headland of Peking

relatively small group of scholars identifiable with comparative religion who actually spoke there was not nearly as prestigious as might be suggested by the above list of contributing authors.

What was the general reaction to the more "scholarly" papers at the parliament? While it is impossible to know for sure, at least one sobering response can be gleaned from the words with which Laura Ormiston Chant opened her address on "The Real Religion of To-day" immediately after the reading of Tiele's paper: "Dear Friends,—After listening long enough to the science of religion, probably...it may be a little relief to run off, or leave the science of religion to take care of itself for a while and take a few thoughts on religion independent of its science."[96]

As it happened, Chant made this remark before the general assembly during the morning of the parliament's fifth day, at the same time that the so-called "Scientific Section" of the parliament was holding its opening session in a separate hall. Opened in an unsuccessful attempt to divert some of the overflowing crowds from the parliament's main assemblies, this previously unplanned section was "where papers of a more scientific and less popular character were read."[97] Of the comparativists' papers enumerated above, several were delivered in this section: those by the two Révilles, Marillier, and Snell, who chaired the section.[98] The section also featured papers on a wide variety of other topics by a disparate assortment of authors: on Japanese Buddhism, by Peter Goro Kaburaji of Tokyo, Japan and Kinze Riuge M. Hirai of the Myo Shin Ji branch of the Rinzai Zen sect; the influence of Egyptian religion on other religions, by J.A.S. Grant-Bey of Cairo; native religions of the New Hebrides, by Rev. John G. Paton, D.D.; popular superstitions in Morocco and Egypt, by Rev. B.F. Kidder, Ph.D.; the estimate of human

---

University; W.A.P. Martin of Peking Imperial College; Kozaki Horomichi and Matsuyama Takayoshi of Doshisha University in Japan.

[96] In *WPR*, 1:591. Barrows notes that Chant and her address "were welcomed with more than usual demonstrations of interest and applause" ("History," in *WPR*, 1:117).

[97] Barrows, "History," in *WPR*, 1:152. See also ibid., p. 110; and n. 19 above in the present volume.

[98] Although, as cited earlier, Snell's "Future of Religion" is included among papers from the seventeenth day in *WPR*, it is not listed in Barrows's "Chronicle" of the parliament (n. 19 above). It is therefore uncertain whether it was read before the general assembly or in the "Scientific Section," where he had already read his two other two main papers, made several untitled "addresses," and participated on a panel.

dignity in "lower" religions, by L. Mararillier (sic); various schools of Indian religion and philosophy, by Rev. Swami Vivekananda (who made four different addresses in this section), Mr. Narasima Chari, a Brâhman of Madras, Manilal N. D'vivedi, S. Parthacarthy Arjangar of Madras; the Christadelphians, by Mr. Thomas Williams; the Dev Dharm Mission, by Mohun Dev; Shintoism, by Rev. Takayosha Matsugama and Peter Goro Kaburaji; Jainism, by Mr. V.N. (sic) Gandhi of the Bombay Conference of the Jain Faith; North American Indians, by Miss Alice C. Fletcher; future religious unity of humankind, by Rev. Geo. T. Candlin; the Civic Church, by Mr. Wm. T. Stead; Protestant Missions in China, by Rev. Henry Blodget, D.D., of Peking; the Shaker community, by Mr. Daniel Offord; as well as a "Poem of Greeting" by Purnshottam B. Joshi, and symposia and conferences on religion and science, Mormonism, and a number of the topics addressed by the individual papers alluded to above.[99]

Two points are especially worth noting about the "Scientific Section." First, while the vast majority of "major" papers read in all sessions of the parliament were by (mostly Protestant) Christians and largely about explicitly Christian concerns,[100] almost all papers in the "Scientific Section" that were not expressly methodological or comparative in nature focused on ancient, tribal, or non-Western, non-Christian subjects. Of the few exceptions, two papers focused on Christian groups that were decidedly "fringe" or out of the "mainstream" (Mormons and Shakers). Thus the relation in which the "Scientific Section" appears to have stood toward the parliament's implied Christian *centrum* seems analogous to the relation in which the

---

[99] The names and descriptions of the authors in this list are given as they are listed in Barrows, "History," in *WPR*, 1:152-54, although not always in the same order. Fletcher, who read her paper before the general assembly on the twelfth day, is listed as having repeated it in the "Scientific Section" on the sixteenth day; see pp. 138, 154. The symposium on religion and science focused on Sir William Dawson's *Religio Scientiae*, which had been read before the parliament's general assembly and which was read again in the "Scientific Section." That symposium involved Dr. Paul Carus, editor of *The Monist*; Dr. Adolph Brodbeck of Hannover, Germany; Rev. G.T. Candlin of China; Dr. Ernest Faber of China; Rev. Father D'Arby of Paris; Elder B.H. Roberts of Utah; Judge Russell of Chicago (p. 152).

[100] A scan of the titles of "major" parliament addresses by authors listed under "Catholicism," "Orthodox traditions," and "Protestantism" in the "Appendix" to *DRP* reveals some sixty-three to contain such tell-tale terms as "Christ," "Christianity," "Christian," "Bible," "Holy Scripture," "Gospel," "[Christian] Ecumenism," "[Christian] Mission[aries]," or references to a particular Christian "Church" (e.g., "Catholic"), Christian denomination ("Baptist," "Presbyterian," etc.), or Christian figure (e.g., Swedenborg). There is also Müller's paper on "Greek Philosophy and the Christian Religion," listed under "Noted Scholars."

Bazaar of Nations stood toward the exposition's White City.[101] This analogy is supported by the loose, functional affinity between the theory of the "sliding scale of humanity" which underlay the arrangement of the exotic ethnic "displays" along the Midway Plaisance as mentioned earlier, and the three "concentric circles" in whose terms Barrows envisioned the parliament, as explained by Kitagawa: with the Christian assembly in the center, the American religious assembly next to it, and the religions of the world comprising the outer circle. Indeed, in the first of the two volumes of the parliament's papers edited by Barrows, the more vulgar theory of the "sliding scale of humanity" seems to haunt the very layout of the book in one instance. Upon turning the page at the place in Harlez's paper where the author has challenged Darwinian assumptions by denying that there may be "a people without religion, how low soever it may be in the scale of civilization," and that "a few miserable savage tribes [may] be held as specimens of the first human beings," readers will find themselves confronted by a full-page photograph of a dignified, aged, dark-skinned man with a complete facial tatoo, attired in a thickly feathered cloak, beneath which reads the caption: "A NATIVE OF NEW ZEALAND, AN IDOL WORSHIPER."[102]

A second noteworthy point is that, as betrayed by its programme above, the "Scientific Section" had a somewhat misleading title. To be sure, the contents of several of the papers presented there match the connotations of the term "science of religion." Yet, for the most part, for better or worse, the section appears to have offered not so much "science" as the spectacle of Japanese Buddhists representing Japanese Buddhism, Hindus representing Hinduism, a Shaker representing Shakerism, and so forth. Within the context of the parliament, such speakers functioned in effect not as "scientists," but as embodiments of their respective faiths and hence as "specimens," exhibited for scrutiny by an intensely curious audience—including those present who really were, or who imagined themselves to be, "scientists" of religion.

In this respect, the "Scientific Section" conformed to the positivist model on which its chairman, Merwin-Marie Snell, construed the entire parliament. Several weeks before the parliament opened he had touted it as an "exhibit of religions." The parliament was to be

---

[101] Ketelaar makes a similar observation in his essay in this volume.

[102] *WPR*, 1:615, capitalization in the text. Whether this coincidence between text and photo reflects a conscious editorial choice on Barrows's part cannot be known.

"participated in by...the very foremost representatives of hierological science—men like Müller, Tiele, d'Alviella, Harding and the Révilles," wrote Snell, unaware that none of these men would show up. Nonetheless, "the religious bodies participating have at heart...the interests of their own propaganda," hoping to dispel any prejudices of which their systems of belief might be the objects. "But these facts, so far from decreasing the scientific value of the parliament, are really its essential conditions," since "the collection of materials is the most important part of any inductive science," and since the "science of religions" would remain at the level of "empty empiricism...until every class of religious facts shall be recorded with absolute impartiality."[103] As an assemblage of such "facts," the parliament's proceedings would "form an invaluable addition to the materials for the study of religions, but...those who take a scientific interest, in the subject, should attend the parliament in person, so that they may in face-to-face intercourse with the picked representatives of the Christian, Jewish, Moslem and pagan sects and sub-sects,...bring out and note for their own use, and the future uses of science, the many facts....to be collected."[104] True to his word about the value of "face-to-face intercourse," Snell is reported to have "developed a special attachment for the Swamiji [Vivekananda]" at the parliament, and "became through him an ardent devotee of Hinduism."[105]

Snell's ideas about the parliament are developed further in the paper in this volume which he read in opening the first session of the "Scientific Section." There, with his positivist characterization of the parliament again as an "exhibit of religions," and as "a school of comparative religion" and "a vast hierological museum, a collection of religious specimens," the identification of the parliament with the "scientific" aspirations of comparative religion reaches its extreme. But the concept of a "hierological museum" gives pause for reflection. Whether he was aware of it or not, in reconceptualizing the parliament as such, Snell was interpreting its purpose in a way that dramatically rivaled the original implications of its name, derived from the Old French *parlement*, "a speaking." In effect, he shifted the understanding of the parliament from the original emphasis, implicit in its name, on the act of colloquy or speaking that was to take place

---

[103] Snell, "Exhibit of Religions," p. 99.
[104] Ibid., p. 100.
[105] Reported by Sadananda, "Religious Parliaments" (n. 62 above), p. 27.

there among representatives of the world's religions,[106] to an emphasis on the "indispensable value" of that colloquy to its audience (read "hierologists"), whose members were to attend it in the same way as the visitor at a museum views the "specimens" on display, or as the botanist regards the herbarium. Hence Snell's dilettantish conclusion that "everyone who attends [the parliament's] sessions is taking the first step toward becoming a hierologist."

While Snell's "exhibition"-metaphor for the parliament evidently won over Barrows and some other scholars, including Toy and Müller,[107] one basic flaw in the theory behind the metaphor seems to have gone unacknowledged. As any amateur anthropologist knows today, people who are analyzed or observed do not go uninfluenced by the analyst or observer. Likewise, the religious believer who happens to be exposed to some scholarly theory of religions will not be immune to subsequently reconceptualizing his or her own religious beliefs or ideas in the terms of those theories. At the parliament, this truism was manifest as certain speakers from outside academe who gave

---

[106] Recall the use of the term "conference" in the first of the parliament's stated "objects," quoted earlier. The statement of the third of those "objects" likewise refers to the parliament as "a friendly conference" (Barrows, "History," in *WPR,* 1:18).

[107] Barrows affirmed that the parliament's "aim" was "to study all exhibits of the spectrum" ("History," in *WPR,* 1:113). Similarly, C.H. Toy maintains: "It was not intended to be a scientific gathering, but rather a friendly meeting for the *exhibition* of different religious ideas side by side" ("The Parliament," p. 734 [emphasis mine]). For Toy, "The actual appearance of members of various non-Christian faiths in the midst of our modern life is likely to give reality to people's conceptions of these faiths. Those who witnessed or shall read the proceedings of the parliament will probably feel more or less concerned to know something of the history of the systems of belief which were there brought forward" (p. 739). Müller, in his article in the present volume, speaks of the parliament as "exhibiting" the world's religions. However, unlike Toy, he considers the parliament's published proceedings to be ultimately of greater value than the event itself, as shall later be discussed. Also accordant with Snell's museum-goer metaphor for those who attended the parliament is the following opinion expressed by George S. Goodspeed, who participated with Snell in the parliament's "Scientific Section." In his speech before the general assembly, Goodspeed asserted:

> "What is needed in the study of religion to-day, more than anything else, is a study of the manifold facts which religions present, and a rigid abstinence from philosophical theories....
>
> "One great excellence of this Parliament is that *it brings us face to face with these facts.* These brief sessions will do more for the study of religion than the philosophizing of a score of years."
>
> ("What the Dead Religions Have Bequeathed to the Living," in *WPR,* 1:561-62 [emphasis mine].)

addresses representing their own religious traditions, happily invoked definitions and explanations from the writings of famous scholars of religion, most notably Müller, to help frame their own expositions.[108] Religious "specimens" the parliamentarians may have been, but it could by no means be assured in all cases that they had absorbed something from the "science" that studied them. Like the mythologization of the parliament itself, such absorption finds its consummate expression in Mrs. Souvielle's poetic *Sequel to the Parliament of Religions.* There, at one point, the anonymous Christian "witness" invokes the well-known technical distinction between "religion" and "religions" from the opening lecture (1870) of Max Müller's *Introduction to the Science of Religion* (1873) and elsewhere in Müller's writings as being comparable to Tacitus's alleged "prophetic" vision of "the Savior's birth":

> That great and earnest thinker and professor,
> Max Müller, logic's able intercessor,
> Most nobly pleads:
> > "There must be yet conserved
> A 'great and golden dawn of truth' reserved:
> 'There is a true religion still behind
> Those called religions. Happy who can find
> The sacred truth, in days materialistic,
> And tendencies so wholly atheistic.'[109]

Here, the absorption of a tenet from the "science of religion" by the religious subject is so complete that the widely-credited "founder" of that "science" is transformed into the subject's mouthpiece, and the paraphrased words of the "scientist" are rendered to convey the religious vision implicit in the parliament's own motto: "To unite all Religion against irreligion."

The peculiar commingling that occurred at the parliament between "religion" and the "science" devoted to studying it was never to be

---

[108] Consider, e.g., the paraphrasing and appropriation of Müller's definition of religion by the Christian, Lyman Abbott, "Religion Essentially Characteristic of Humanity," in *WPR*, 1:495; the allusion to "Max Müller's gifted lectures" by the Muslim, Mohammed Webb ("The Spirit of Islâm," in *WPR*, 2:990); and the references to Müller, Abraham Kuenen, Ernest Renan, and James Drummond by the Jew, H. Pereira Mendes, "Orthodox or Historical Judaism," in *WPR*, 1:529, 530. For examples of Asian parliamentarians drawing upon the work of Western scholars of comparative religion, see in the article by Seager in the present volume the section entitled "The Men Who Came to Dinner."

[109] Souvielle (Sutcliffe), *Sequel*, pp. 143-44. For the distinction between "religion" and "religions," see Müller, *Introduction to the Science of Religion* (n. 77 above), pp. 16-18.

repeated. Stockholm's 1897 Congress of the Science of Religion, although originally conceived by the Swedenborgian Albert Björck on the Chicago model, did succeed in soliciting the participation of a number of notable scholars, including P.D. Chantepie de la Saussaye, W. Brede Kristensen and Nathan Söderblom. But as Sharpe points out, "many more stayed away, fearing a repetition of Chicago," and the force of Lutheran orthodoxy active there at the time "did more than the Chicago spirit to obscure the spirit of scholarship."[110] The official distancing of all subsequent congresses of history of religions from anything smacking of religious apologetics began three years later at the *Congrès international* for the discipline in Paris. To be sure, direct historical connections between that meeting and its Chicago predecessor are attested by the official tributes paid to Barrows and the memory of the parliament at the *Congrès*, and by the leading roles played there by a number of prominent figures who had been involved in the parliament, including Barrows himself and Albert Réville, the president of *Congrès*.[111] Nonetheless, as one commentator was to point out several years afterwards, the *Congrès* had to be channeled in a purely "scientific" direction, mainly for political and legal reasons obtaining in the French nation:

> The Parliament of Religions which convened at Chicago in 1893 could not be repeated in Paris because in France the principal [sic] of a separation of church and state is interpreted in such a way as to allow the official authorities to do nothing whatever in the line of religion. Accordingly a religious parliament of any character could not have been tolerated on the Exhibition grounds at Paris; but scientific congresses were quite in order, and so there was no opposition to a historical treatment of religion.[112]

Unlike the World's Parliament of Religions, the Paris congress was thus, in Kitagawa's words, "a scholarly, and not a religious,

---

[110] Sharpe, *History*, p. 140.

[111] See Charles Bonney, "Esquisse historique des Congrès des Religions de Chicago en 1893," in *Actes du premier Congrès International d'Histoire des Religions, réuni à Paris, du 3 au 8 septembre 1900 à l'occasion de l'Exposition Universelle*, première partie: *Séances générales* (Paris: Ernest Leroux, 1901), pp. 228-31. Among the names appearing on the lists of the "Commission d'Organisation" (pp. i-ii), "Correspondants du Congrès" (pp. vii-viii), "Bureau du Congrès" (p. ix) and "Membres du Congrès" (pp. x-xxi) are those of the following noteworthy figures, in addition to Barrows and Albert Réville, who had been associated with the 1893 parliament: Jean Réville, Marillier, Bonét-Maury, Goblet d'Alviella, Bonney, Carus, Goodspeed, Toy, Tiele, Carpenter, Müller, and even Vivekananda.

[112] [Anonymous,] "The Basle Congress for the History of Religion," *The Monist* 14 (1904): 770.

conference," and thereby "set the tone...for subsequent Congresses" for the history of religions.[113] But these facts do not render the 1893 parliament irrelevant to the concerns of scholars today. For the problem it highlighted of trying to reconcile the scholar's vocation toward "purely scientific research" with his or her "cultural task," to borrow words from a speech by C.J. Bleeker at the Marburg IAHR congress several decades ago, continued to haunt scholars of religion throughout our century.[114]

Oblivion, Recovery, and Reassessment

The persistence and global embrace of such traditions as the International Association of the History of Religions, the World Council of Churches, and various groups devoted to interfaith dialogue, all of which find a momentous precursor in the World's Parliament of Religions, make all the more curious the fate of its memory. Having provided the end-point for Leonard Woolsey Bacon's highly regarded *History of American Christianity* (1897), and been given a significant account in Jordan's standard history (1905) of comparative religion, the parliament then languished in almost total obscurity in this country for some sixty years,[115] until the appearance of a handful of articles on the parliament during the mid- and late-1960s initiated the restoration of its reputation.[116] Symptoms of the

---

[113] Kitagawa, "Humanistic and Theological History of Religions," p. 116.

[114] Quote from C.J. Bleeker, "The Future Task of the History of Religions," in *X. Internationaler Kongress für Religionsgeschichte, 11.-17. September 1960 in Marburg/Lahn* (Marburg: N.G. Elwert, 1961), pp. 232, 233.

[115] See Leonard Woolsey Bacon, *A History of American Christianity* (New York: Christian Literature Co., 1897), pp. 418-19. Passing references made to the parliament during the period of its near oblivion in the West from 1905 through the early 1960s include those by Stow Persons (1947; reference given in n. 18 of the Seager's article in the present volume), William Warren Sweet, *The Story of Religion in America* (New York: Harper, 1950), p. 378; Kitagawa's article of 1959, "The History of Religions in America" pp. 5-6; Clifton E. Olmstead, *History of Religion in the United States* (Englewood Cliffs, N.J.: Prentice-Hall, 1960), p. 524.

[116] See John R. Betts, "The Laity and the Ecumenical Spirit, 1889-1893," *The Review of Politics* 26 (1964): 3-19; Egal Feldman, "American Ecumenicism: Chicago's World's Parliament of Religions of 1893," *Journal of Church and State* 9 (1967): 180-99; Donald H. Bishop, "Religious Confrontation, a Case Study: The 1893 Parliament of Religions," *Numen* 16 (1969): 63-76; James F. Cleary, "Catholic Participation in the World's Parliament of Religions, Chicago, 1893," *Catholic Historical Review* 55 (1970): 585-609; Bishop, "America and the 1893 World Parliament" (1970; n. 71 above) (all cited by Druyvesteyn, diss., p. 76 n. 1). See also the allusions to the parliament in Winthrop S. Hudson, *Religion in America* (New York: Charles Scribner's Sons, 1965; 2d ed. 1973), pp. 254, 264, 286-87, 425; and in

sudden dissipation of the memory of the parliament early in the century are the pathetically terse and inaccurate entry on the event in a standard reference source, *The Americana* (1903-06),[117] and the absence of any mention of it in the *Encyclopaedia of Religion and Ethics* (1908-26) edited by James Hastings. In contrast, a striking measure of the event's recent retrieval to memory is the inclusion of Robert Ellwood's short but substantial entry on the subject in *The Encyclopedia of Religion* edited by Eliade (1987). That entry, together with eight other references to the parliament elsewhere in the *Encyclopedia,* consecrated the parliament's resurrection from American scholarly oblivion.[118] Seager, focusing on what he sees as a crucial shift in interpretive paradigms within religious studies over the past several decades, provides a compelling explanation for why the parliament could be ignored or forgotten by scholars of American religious history and the history of religions for so long, and then recovered by scholars in those same two fields over the past several decades.[119]

Kitagawa's article of 1967, "Buddhism in America" (n. 71 above), pp. 312, 318, 321, 325.

[117] *The Americana: A Universal Reference Library,* 16 vols., ed. Frederick Converse Beach (New York: Scientific American, 1903-06), s.v. "Congress of Religion." This entry, which never refers to the parliament by its official title, describes this "meeting" as "one of the most interesting events of the great exposition." Yet, despite the fact that all the proceedings of the parliament were in English, this entry reports that "the tenets of the various faiths were expounded in many strange tongues."

[118] *The Encyclopedia of Religion,* s.v. "World's Parliament of Religions," 15:444-45. Other references occur on 2:437, 438; 4:345; 6:358; 12:211; 14:184; 15:292, 567.

[119] See the successive sections on "Slipping through Scholarly Grids" and "Restoration to Memory" in Seager's article in this volume. In documenting that "restoration," Seager does not mention the accounts from the years 1964-70 cited in n. 116 above. He asserts that the parliament "first resurfaced" with the account published in 1971 by Paul A. Carter, and from that point on he traces the restoration of the parliament's reputation "among scholars in the United States" through accounts by Spencer Lavan (1977), Thomas Graham (1979), Rick Fields (1980), Marcus Braybrooke (1980), Carl T. Jackson (1981), Joseph M. Kitagawa (1983; included in this volume), Martin E. Marty (1986; included in this volume), William R. Hutchison (1987), David J. Bosch (1988). For complete references see nn. 18-26 in Seager's article. Other noteworthy accounts from the thirteen years prior to Seager's article (which appeared in 1989) but not mentioned by him are the dissertations of Druyvesteyn (1976), Seager (1987), and Mullick (1988) cited in nn. 38, 43, 49 above; Kitagawa's article of 1980, "Humanistic and Theological History of Religions," pp. 113-115; as well as Lancaster, *The Incredible World's Parliament* (n. 19 above); the *Encyclopedia* entry of 1987 (n. 118 above); and E. Allen Richardson, *Strangers in this Land: Pluralism and the Response to Diversity in the United States* (New York: Pilgrim, 1988), which includes a section, "Tolerance and the Parliament of Religions," pp. 85-94, and other allusions on pp. 45, 84, 159-60,

The parliament's fall into oblivion early in this century was abetted by the lack of any enduring image of it in American literary art, as the two poems by Minnie Andrews Snell and Mrs. Souvielle evidently made no significant impression. To be sure, the doctrine of a "universal religion" expounded so powerfully by Vivekananda at the parliament may seem consonant with the timeworn Western literary theme of religious unity whose prefiguration of the parliament is discussed in my article in this volume. But that doctrine was discouraged by the genteel yet emphatic Christian chauvinism of the parliament's promoters. Having all but entirely disappeared from the Western literature of our century, the theme of religious unity has been replaced by its antithesis, the dispersiveness of Babel—"the fundamental myth in modern literature," according to one scholar. Meanwhile Vivekananda's other main parliament teaching, that of the "God within" each human, ironically became dear to such noted twentieth-century Western novelists as Romain Rolland, Aldous Huxley, and Christopher Isherwood.[120]

Curiously, as Kitagawa observed, over the same period during which the parliament had been forgotten in this country it had remained "vivid in the memories of many religious people in other parts of the world." This is confirmed most explicitly by Tessa Bartholomeusz with regard to contemporary Sri Lanka. However, in the case of a commemorative account prepared by Sri Swami Sadananda on the occasion of the 1953 Parliament of Religions in Rishikesh, such "memories" of the original parliament incorporated a bizarre mythos. Claiming to "enter into the real motives with which [the 1893 parliament] was organized," Sadananda asserts that "the persons who wanted such a Parliament were the leading lights of Roman Catholicism," and that it began "with the support of the

---

201. Since then, in addition to the accounts in this volume by Ketelaar (1990) and Ziolkowski (1993), there have been Eric J. Ziolkowski, "Heavenly Visions and Worldly Intentions: Chicago's Columbian Exposition and World's Parliament of Religions (1893)," *Journal of American Culture* 13 (1990): 9-15; and Eric J. Ziolkowski, "The Literary Bearing of Chicago's 1893 World's Parliament on Religions," forthcoming in the Spring 1993 issue of *The Eastern Buddhist*. See also the works of Kitagawa from the last several years cited in n. 150 below.

[120] See Ziolkowski, "The Literary Bearing of Chicago's 1893 World's Parliament of Religions," passim. The quotation on Babel is from Michael Edwards, "Myth in Twentieth-Century English Literature," *Mythologies, compiled by Yves Bonnefoy: A Restructured translation of "Dictionnaire des mythologies et des religions des sociétés traditionnelles et du monde antique"*, 2 vols., prepared under the direction of Wendy Doniger (Chicago: University of Chicago Press, 1991), 2:785.

Pope".[121] The whole "endeavour" of the parliament was opportunistically initiated by the Catholic Church with the "high hopes" of converting the "many new settlers" of the "new States in the south and the west of the U.S.A.," as well as the "Red Indians," and bringing "the New World...under the influence of Roman Catholicism,...[as] the first step to the restoration of the lost ecclesiastical sway over temporal monarchs":

> If their motives had been purely humanitarian, if they had desired merely to examine impartially the truths embedded in all the religions, no better place could be thought of than England. But no! the Roman Catholics could not—in these days—have any love for Protestant England. There was a danger of the local influence of Protestantism—of Wesleyan Methodism—overpowering Catholicism. So, America was certainly better for their purpose.[122]

From what source Sadananda derived these fantastic ideas of a Catholic conspiracy, if he did not dream them up himself, is a mystery;[123] needless to say, he fails to reconcile them with or even mention the fact that the parliament's acknowledged conceiver, Bonney, was a Swedenborgian layman; that, of the sixteen Chicago clergymen, including Barrows, who were members of the parliament's general organizing committee from start to finish (1889-93), all were Protestant, excepting one Jew and one Catholic; and, indeed, that well over three quarters of the parliament's speakers were Protestants.[124]

Nonetheless, one aspect of Sadananda's account is historically illuminating, although not for a reason he intended. The sanctifying

---

[121] Sadananda, "Religious Parliaments," p. 26.

[122] Ibid., p. 29. This quotation is drawn from a section of Sadananda's paper entitled "Ambitions of the Pope" (pp. 29-30), which immediately follows a section entitled "European Politics and the [Roman Catholic] Church" (pp. 28-29).

[123] One possibility, however, is that they grew out Sadananda's reponse to the fact (as reported by Barrows, "History," in *WPR*, 1:62, 67)—or to some rumor stemming from this fact—that in the parliament's opening session, Cardinal Gibbons had been seated in the center of all the delegates on the stage, and that it was he who then opened the parliament by reading the Lord's Prayer. Sadananda asks his own readers to "visualize" this image of "Cardinal Gibbons, the highest Prelate of the Roman Catholic Church in Western Europe. He was grandly dressed in scarlet robes, and seated upon a chair of state.... The idea was that the grandest of all religions was Christianity in its early form of Roman Catholicism" ("Religious Parliaments," p. 26).

[124] See Barrows, "History," in *WPR*, 1:7-8; and Bonney, "The World's Parliament of Religions," p. 327. Barrows, incidentally, is mentioned twice in Sadananda's "Religious Parliaments" (pp. 26, 30), both times in the same breath as Cardinal Gibbons; it is not clear whether Sadananda is aware that Barrows was Presbyterian, not Catholic.

terms in which he could still stress in 1953 the Chicago triumph of Vivekananda—"whose very admission into the Parliament was a proof of divine grace, (as all who have studied his life know)," and whose speech "came straight from the heart overflowing with love for all God's creation....conquering the hearts of the western people"[125]— serve as a vivid reminder that Vivekananda's enduring, heroic legacy in India was borne out of his success at the parliament. Other 1893 parliamentarians from Asia were likewise lionized in their native lands in the wake of their success at Chicago: most notably the Indian Protap Chandra Majumdar, the Sri Lankan Dharmapāla, and the five Meiji Japanese "champions of Buddhism" (including Shaku), as discussed by Mullick, Bartholomeusz, and Ketelaar. The lasting legacies associating Vivekananda and these other figures with the parliament helps explain why its memory persisted abroad long after it was forgotten in Chicago.

It seems especially appropriate that one of the persons chiefly responsible for restoring the World's Parliament to its rightful place in Western memory as a landmark in religious and cultural history was an Asian-born scholar of the history of religions, a specialist in the religions of the East, and professor at the University of Chicago who delivered his 1983 John Nuveen lecture on the parliament's legacy at the Divinity School, a block away from what was once the Midway Plaisance of the Columbian Exposition. The plan of this volume follows several of Kitagawa's leads, as will be explained.

The Contents of this Volume

Part I

In accordance with Kitagawa's emphasis on the bearing of the parliament upon the study of comparative religion, the first part of this volume reissues from the parliament's proceedings six papers devoted explicitly to expounding the history, scope, aims, and methodologies of that discipline. Of these papers, four are by Europeans, Tiele, Harlez, Albert and Jean Réville, and two by Americans, Snell and Sunderland. The papers by Tiele, Harlez, and Sunderland were read before the parliament's general assembly, the other three, in the "Scientific Section."

Read together, these papers present a provocative cross section of reflection on comparative religion from a moment in its development

---

[125] Sadananda, "Religious Parliaments," pp. 26, 27.

that can seem even further removed from our time than the span of a century might suggest. One telling measure of this distance is the canon of authors in Eliade's well-known retrospective essay (1962) on seminal contributions to "the scientific study of religion" over the period from 1912 to 1962, which includes Émile Durkheim, Max Weber, Wilhelm Schmidt, Joachim Wach, Raffaele Pettazzoni, Sigmund Freud, C.G. Jung, Lucien Lévy-Bruhl, Marcel Mauss, Georges Dumézil, Claude Lévi-Strauss, Rudolf Otto, Gerardus van der Leeuw, to name only some of the most renowned.[126] These primary determiners of the most important twentieth-century trends in the sociological, ethnological, psychological, historical, and phenomenological approaches to religion, all of which have contributed to the discipline of history of religions, stand like a vast wall between us and the 1893 parliamentary "scientists" of religion. Having been altered irreversibly under the theoretical and methodological innovations of the scholars on Eliade's list, some of the lines along which the study of the history of religions is conducted today would not have been recognized by its nineteenth-century "founders." But this is not to deny, as I shall suggest momentarily, that certain ideas and concerns expressed by the parliamentary "scientists" of religion about their discipline find remarkable analogies in much later discussions by historians of religions.

Another tell-tale measure of our distance from the papers by the parliamentary "scientists" of religion is that they were written a decade before the publication of William James's Gifford Lectures (1901-02), *The Varieties of Religious Experience* (1902). James's lectures were important not only substantively as pioneering investigations in the psychology of personal religious life, but historically, because his reading of them at Edinburgh marked the first time that an American scholar was accorded such an honor by a European audience. "It seems the natural thing for us to listen whilst the Europeans talk," James admitted in opening the lectures "with a certain sense of apology": "The contrary habit, of talking whilst the Europeans listen we have not yet acquired."[127] And why not? A decade earlier Max Müller had still been able to call England America's "holy land."

---

[126] See Mircea Eliade, "The History of Religions in Retrospect: 1912 and After," in his *The Quest: History and Meaning in Religion* (Chicago: University of Chicago Press, 1969), pp. 12-36.

[127] William James, *The Varieties of Religious Experience: A Study in Human Nature* (New York: Mentor, 1958), p. 21.

While that "contrary habit" has certainly been acquired since then by American scholars in all areas of learning, James's air of humility would have found special warrant in the utter hegemony of European scholarship in comparative religion at the time, as reflected in the parliament papers by Tiele and Sunderland. In Tiele's overview of seminal contributors to the formation of the discipline from its roots in the eighteenth century to his own time, allusions are made to several dozen European philosophers and scholars, and only one American— William Dwight Whitney. At the same time, aside from Snell's earlier-cited exclamation of almost sycophantic excitement at the prospect of being in the midst of leading European "hierologists" at the parliament, one could not find a better illustration of the deference of American students of the discipline to its European masters than Sunderland's paper. She sets the tone from the start, basing her exposition of "hierology" upon Matthew Arnold's definition of culture. Arnold, as most of her listeners would have known, had helped popularize Ernest Renan's assessment of America as a land of philistines lacking in "general intelligence."[128] That assessment is supported by the cast of scholars on whom Sunderland relies in arguing for the "value and importance of a comparative study of religions"; they are all Europeans: Müller, Tiele, Kuenen, Renan, Albert Réville, William Robertson Smith, Renouf, Chantepie de la Saussaye, and Sayce.

I make this point to stress a difference between the situation of comparative religious studies in Sunderland's time and the one in our own. To be sure, *Religionswissenschaft* was to remain largely a European enterprise well into the twentieth century, as indicated by Eliade's canon. But the study of comparative religion in American universities continued burgeoning after the parliament. The sense of obligation among comparativists of religion in this country to gaze across the Atlantic for guidance at every step was eventually obviated by the emergence here of such an internationally recognized capital of the field as the University of Chicago—whose program in the history of religions had received its initial boost from the parliament, and later blossomed with the arrival of Wach in 1945.[129] The situation of

---

128 See Matthew Arnold's "Preface" to his *Culture and Anarchy: An Essay in Political and Social Criticism* (1869), 3d edition, 1882 (Indianapolis: Bobbs-Merrill, 1971), esp. pp. 13, 15.

129 Kitagawa was insistent on keeping these developments in mind; in addition to his "The History of Religions in America" and "Humanistic Theological History of Religions" (with its "Special Reference to the North American Scene"),

the field today might best be summed up by the title of an address Kitagawa gave in the early 1970s: "The World has Many Centers,"[130] not only those in Europe.

Seager finds the papers by the 1893 parliamentary "scientists" of religion indicative of the "essentially liberal thrust" of the discipline then. In their perspectives and concerns, these papers range from the strictly empiricist (J. Réville), through mixtures of the theological and empiricist (Tiele and A. Réville), two of them with a distinctly Christian twist (Carpenter and Müller), to the combination of the "scientific" with Christian apologetic (Sunderland) or Christian missionary interests (Snell).[131] Indeed, aside from Jean Réville's, the papers contributed by "scientists" hardly amount to a showcase for scholarly objectivity. In any but the Panglossian best of all possible worlds, Snell's repeated emphasis that "hierological" research must be "impartial" would seem irreconcilable with his recommendation that "every missionary school should be a college of comparative religion," and that the knowledge gained through the research of some native religion which a missionary aims at displacing should serve as "a *point d'appui* for the special arguments and claims" of that missionary's own religion. Certainly the interests of pure "science" seem compromised by such utterances of theological identification as Harlez's overture to the audience, "You see that we Christians study your doctrines,...You, on your part, study ours"; or Müller's wish for the parliament to "do excellent work for the resuscitation of pure and primitive ante-Nicene Christianity";[132] or Albert Réville's praising of the event as "the first step...to the truly humanitarian and universal religion"; or Sunderland's overt advocacy of Christianity as an "ideal large enough to include all peoples, tender enough to comfort all, lofty enough to inspire all." Even Tiele, while not identifying himself with any specific

---

both in *The History of Religions: Understanding Human Experience* (n. 71 above), pp. 3-26 and 113-31, see his "The History of Religions at Chicago" and "Joachim Wach," in ibid, pp. 133-44 and 271-74. See also his Introduction, "The Life and Thought of Joachim Wach," in Joachim Wach, *The Comparative Study of Religions*, ed. Joseph M. Kitagawa (New York: Columbia University Press, 1958), pp. xiii-xlviii.

[130] Included in Kitagawa, *The History of Religions: Understanding Human Experience.*, pp. 161-63.

[131] Seager, diss., p. 128-34; quote on p. 128. References to the two parliament papers alluded to here that are not included in the present volume—i.e., those of Carpenter and Müller—were given in earlier in our discussion. In addition to the paper by Snell in this volume, Seager discusses one of Snell's other papers: "The Relations of the Science of Religion to Philosophy," referred to earlier.

[132] Müller, "Greek Philosophy and the Christian Religion," in *WPR*, 2:936.

religious faith or ideal, betrays in his language anything but an "impartial" attitude toward the "conceptions, manners and customs among several backward or degenerate tribes of our own time, giving evidence of the greatest rudeness and barbarousness."

From the entire set of "scientific" papers scattered throughout the parliamentary proceedings, the only one that does not seem to have fallen promptly into oblivion is Tiele's. No fewer than eight of his pronouncements on the history of comparative religion are cited in Jordan's study of that subject. Thus Jordan's readers from 1905 on could learn of (1) the emphasis Tiele placed on the wide divergencies in interpretation of sacred texts separating the greatest masters in the field, alike in Egyptology and Assyriology, Sanskrit and the Zend Avesta; (2) his opinion, shared later by Jordan and Morris Jastrow, that the emergence of comparative religion as a "science" cannot be dated earlier than 1850, and (3) that, contrary to popular opinion, credit for its creation should not go to Müller; (4) his high opinion of Henri Benjamin Constant for having introduced the distinction between the essence and forms of religion, and (5) his proportionately low estimation of Christoph Meiners's *Allgemeine kritische Geschichte der Religionen* (1806-07); (6) his concept of "science" as an "aggregate" of "independent, yet mutually connected" researches; (7) his anxiety that comparative religion would fall prey to dilettantes as a result of becoming a "fashion"; and (8) his conviction that not every student of this "science" should be an "architect," but that most should focus upon a confined section of the field.[133]

Here, despite our temporal removal from Tiele, his opinions and concerns might not seem distant from those of more recent historians of religions. Not only might his judgments on the history of comparative religion almost pass for a very sketchy blueprint for accounts of that history written since Jordan's,[134] but the last three of his opinions and concerns summed up above bear directly upon matters which Eliade and Kitagawa discussed. For example, as if hearkening back to Tiele's remark about dilettantism, Kitagawa

---

[133] See the citations of Tiele in Jordan, *Genesis*, pp. 115, 116-17, 140, 143, 256, 483, 519, 523. With regard to the dating of the emergence of comparative religion to 1850, cf. Morris Jastrow, Jr., *The Study of Religion* (New York, 1901; reprinted, Atlanta, Ga.: Scholars Press, 1981), p. 43.

[134] Many if not most of the authors and texts Tiele refers to in his overview of the history of comparative religion are discussed or mentioned in the standard histories of the discipline by Pinard de la Boullaye, Mensching, Waardenburg, and Sharpe (nn. 57, 59, 74 above).

lamented in the mid-1980s that "many of those who wish to study the history of religions today are rebelling against their own religious traditions..., and not a few are looking for what amounts to a new kind of religion. Some are motivated by misguided enthusiasm for a subject matter that appears to be exotic and alluring....All in all, there seems to be a rather widespread ambiguity about the nature of the discipline in spite of, or because of, its popularity."[135] Eliade, as if elaborating on the sixth and eighth of Tiele's concerns above, insisted that historians of religions should define themselves by their ability "to integrate religious data into a general perspective"; in contrast to Tiele, Eliade challenged the historian of historians precisely to aspire to the broad, integrative role of one who "inform[s] himself of the progress made by the specialists" in related disciplines in order to formulate a more encompassing, "general" understanding of the subject: "One can compare the method of the historian of religions with that of a biologist. When the latter studies, for instance, the behavior of a certain species of insect, he does not take the place of the entomologist. He expands, confronts, and integrates the investigations of the entomologist. To be certain, the biologist, too, is a specialist." But, "he is preoccupied with the general structures of animal life."[136]

Tiele's paper is not alone among the "scientific" papers from the parliament in anticipating later developments in *Religions-wissenschaft*. For example, much is said in those papers that foreshadows specific aspects of the phenomenological branch of the discipline that would later be prepared for by Rudolf Otto, developed by Gerardus van der Leeuw, and continued by Eliade. Just as Jean Réville's impulse toward "classification" of "religious facts and phenomena" looks ahead, perhaps, to the grandiose typologies and "morphologies" of religious data in van der Leeuw's *Phänomenologie der Religion* (1933) and Eliade's *Traité d'histoire des Religions* (1949, *Patterns in Comparative Religion* [1958]), so his rule that such classification must be done to the exclusion of "every abstract principle...imposed from without by a philosophical or theological system" shares an affinity with van der Leeuw's Husserlian emphasis on the need for "intellectual suspense" or "bracketing" of judgments (*epoche*) when engaged in systematic

---

[135] Joseph M. Kitagawa, "The Making of a Historian of Religions," in his *The History of Religions: Understanding the Human Experience* (n. 71 above), p. 101.

[136] Mircea Eliade, "Methodological Remarks on the Study of Religious Symbolism," in *The History of Religions: Essays in Methodology*, ed. Mircea Eliade and Joseph M. Kitagawa (Chicago: University of Chicago Press, 1959), pp. 90-91.

description of the phenomena.[137] What is more, Réville's recommendation that this sort of classification should be done by someone "who knows by experience what religious thought or emotion is," broaches the same issue that Otto would make famous by opening the third chapter of *Das Heilige* (1917) by discouraging any reader who has never had a "deeply-felt religious experience" from reading farther.[138]

Such foreshadowings by the parliamentary comparativists do not stop with Jean Réville. Although his father, Albert, exerted no documentably direct, formative influence upon the concept of Power central to van der Leeuw's *Phänomenologie*, that concept is anticipated by Albert Réville's definition of religion as "that special determination of human nature which causes man to seek...union with a sovereign and mysterious Power." Likewise, Rudolf Otto's explication of the *mysterium* as both *tremendum* and *fascinans* could almost seem drawn from the the senior Réville's description of divine "Power" as "at once attractive and formidable," if we did not know that *Das Heilige* makes no mention of Réville.

The notion the parliamentary comparativists shared of their discipline as a "science" might seem a far cry from Eliade's heralding of the history of religions in 1961 as a "new humanism."[139] Yet Snell and Sunderland seem to have in common with Eliade more than what little is suggested by the etymological kinship between their self-ascribed titles as "hierologists" and that famous neologism so central to Eliade's vocabulary: "hierophany." Snell's comparison of the "hierologist" studying religions at the parliament to the botanist studying "specimens" in the herbarium finds an interesting analogy in Eliade's comparison of the historian of religions to a biologist. Moreover, like Snell's idea of religion as "a universal fact of human experience," Sunderland's understanding of it as "an attribute of humanity, as reason and language are," anticipates one of the stock assumptions dear to countless later historians of religions: the notion of the holy, Power, or the sacred, as construed by Otto, van der Leeuw, and Eliade, as an irreducible element in the lives of the human being, understood as *homo religiosus*. Indeed, Sunderland's observation

---

[137] Gerardus van der Leeuw, *Religion in Essence and Manifestation*, trans. J.E. Turner (1963; Princeton, N.J.: Princeton University Press, 1986), pp. 645-46, 646, n. 1, 683.

[138] Rudolf Otto, *The Idea of the Holy*, trans. John W. Harvey (London: Oxford University Press, 1950), p. 8.

[139] Eliade, "A New Humanism," in *The Quest* (n. 126 above), pp. 1-11.

that, when viewed comparatively, "the petty distinctions of savage, barbarians, civilized and enlightened sink into the background" may stir a sense of déja vu in any reader familiar with Eliade's insistence on "examining the 'lower' and 'higher' religious forms simultaneously, and seeing at once what elements they have in common."[140] And, likewise, if reminded that this insistence stemmed from Eliade's desire not to "make the mistakes that result from an *evolutionist*...perspective,"[141] we might recall that Harlez devoted a substantial portion of his parliament paper a hundred years ago to arguing against precisely those same "mistakes."

Part II

Of the innumerable assessments of the parliament that appeared in the years immediately after it in American and European journals, those by Barrows and Müller in Part II are arguably the two most significant. Barrows's article is one of a number he published on the subject.[142] It is his triumphant eulogy of the event with which his name became almost synonymous. Nowhere is the amalgamation of the "religious" and "scientific" significance he attributed to the parliament more pronounced than in his describing it here, successively, as a place where "multitudes entered anew into the spirit of the Nazarene Prophet," and "a great school of comparative theology," by which he meant comparative religion.[143]

Müller, whom Ketelaar considers the parliament's "guiding light," was also its most famous absentee. His own article opens with a heartfelt statement of regret at having missed this event which he, like Barrows and countless others, now assessed as "unique" and "unprecedented" in world history.[144] Consistent with the concluding remark quoted earlier from his short contribution to the parliament,

---

[140] Eliade, *Patterns in Comparative Religion*, trans. Rosemary Sheed (1958; reprint, New York: Meridian, 1974), p. xvi.

[141] Ibid.

[142] See the listings under Barrows's name in the bibliography of Druyvesteyn's diss., pp. 285-86, which include seven other articles on the parliament.

[143] Cf. John Henry Barrows, "The Religious Possibilites of the World's Fair," *The Chinese Recorder and Missionary Journal* 23 (1892): 550; and his "The World's Parliament," *The Evangelist* 66 (February 7, 1895): 9. Barrows's recommendation in his article in the present volume that comparative religion should "become a study required of all candidates for mission fields" is obviously akin to Snell's earlier-cited conception of the ideal missionary school as "a college of comparative religion."

[144] Compare the views expressed by C.H. Toy and Louis Jordan in n. 54 above.

Müller did not refrain from assessing the meeting theologically, or even theosophically, despite his eminence as a pioneering "scientist" of religion. Indeed, his theosophical assumption, reiterated in this article, that behind all religions lies "one eternal,...universal religion,...to which every man...belongs," emerges as a leitmotiv running through a number of the parliamentary papers, by both Western and Eastern authors. However, that Müller was somewhat out of touch with the true intentions of Barrows, whom he would later meet for the first time in England,[145] is betrayed by his disappointment that the parliament was not used as an occasion "to draw up a small number of articles of faith" for a universal religion. Barrows expressly denies that such a goal was ever pursued by the parliament, which he says proceeded "without concession, without any attempt to treat all religions as equally meritorious,...with no idea of finding or founding any new world-religion."[146] In fact, the official statement of the parliament's third "object" makes the point that the parliament would pursue its aim of promoting "brotherhood among religious men of diverse faiths...*while not seeking to foster the temper of indifferentism, and not striving to achieve any formal and outward unity*"—a point clearly made to defend against attacks by exclusivist Christians who condemned the very idea of setting Christianity in any sort of "comparison" with other faiths, and to assuage the fears of some that the parliament would encourage an attitude of "indifferentism" regarding Christianity's supposed superiority to other faiths.[147]

---

[145] See Mary Barrows, *John Henry Barrows*, pp. 325-26, 357-58.

[146] Cf. Barrows, "Review and Summary," in *WPR*, 2:1572.

[147] The quotation is from Barrows, "History," in *WPR*, 1:18. In his article in the present volume, Barrows makes the point that Christianity "has not been so faultless as to defy competition and comparison." Criticisms of the parliament for its "comparison" of Christianity with other faiths were quite common, and frequently involved attacks on the scholarly enterprise of comparative religion; see, e.g., Arthur T. Pierson, "The Columbian Exposition at Chicago," *The Missionary Review of the World* n.s. 7, no. 1 (1894): 1-10; and the same author's "The Parliament of Religions: A Review," *The Missionary Review of the World* n.s. 7, no. 12 (1894): 881-94. The term "indifferentism," meaning "the principle that differences of religious belief are of no importance; adiaphorism; absence of zeal or interest in religious matters," had been in currency from as early as the 1820s, according to *The Oxford English Dictionary*, 2d ed. Concern over the perceived threat of "indifferentism," which was considered by some a contagion spread by the study of comparative religion, had developed well before the parliament. The term is used in a somewhat different sense by Rev. John G. Fagg, "Recent Criticisms of Missionaries and Missionary Methods," *The Chinese Recorder and Missionary Journal* (December 1890): 553, 556. For an early denial by John Henry Barrows that the parliament would foster "indifferentism," see his article of two

Perhaps the most provocative point of Müller's article is his distinction between the parliament as an act in the "world of deeds," and the recorded proceedings of the event as its surviving "history" in the "world of words." Given his own investment as editor of the monumental *Sacred Books of the East* series, it is not surprising that he should consider the parliament's written proceedings like sacred texts that are "more authoritative" than the historical event that produced them. His further contention that the "usefulness" of the parliament was diminished by the absence of the "sacred books" of the faiths, and by the resulting "impossibility of of checking the enthusiastic descriptions of the supreme excellence of every single religion," reveals how normative an event this "scientist" of religions would have liked the parliament to be. In praising what he saw as the parliament's "idea of exhibiting all the religions of the world," Müller clearly picked up on Snell's idea of it as an "exhibit" or "museum" of faiths. But in Müller's philologically-based approach to comparative religion sacred texts would always take precedence over the sort of living religious "specimens" which Snell was so greatly thrilled to examine on "display."

Part III

Part III juxtaposes the chapter by Marty and the lecture by Kitagawa for several reasons. The two scholars were long-time colleagues at the University of Chicago. Their accounts of the parliament, as shown by Seager, played seminal roles in the critical restoration of the parliament to scholarly memory—hence their recurrent citation in subsequent accounts. And above all, these two accounts complement each other. Both scholars stress the affiliation between the parliament and the exposition. Kitagawa, as we have seen, associates these two events through the idea of "progress," while Marty sums up the parliament as a "world's fair of faiths" rife with "disparities and disputes." Both scholars pay special attention to Barrows, exposing the idiosyncrasies in his parliamentary ideology: Kitagawa, by observing how Barrows mistook the ends of comparative religion for those of theology; Marty, by pointing out that the latter's "blueprint for universalism" was counterbalanced by a belief in the need for "mild [Christian missionary] aggression." Marty focuses on the parliament as the culminating expression of theological

---

years later, "The Religious Possibilities of the World's Fair" (n. 143 above), pp. 551-52.

cosmopolitanism among American modernists, most of whose speeches there smacked instead of parochialism and seemed more "a succession of monologues" than "dialogue." Kitagawa, acknowledging that the parliament was mainly an American Christian assembly, shifts the focus in the middle portion of his lecture to the encounter between Western Christendom and Eastern religions at the parliament.

It is in this regard that Kitagawa makes one of his most important contributions to our understanding of the parliament. His demonstration of how Vivekananda, Dharmapāla, and Shaku Sōen all exemplified a similar kind of religious leadership—he calls them modern religious reformers—follows a typological approach whose methodological roots are traceable back through Kitagawa's mentor, the historian of religions Wach, to the sociologist Weber, as well as to the phenomenologist van der Leeuw.[148] Most significant is his observation of how those Asian reformers reversed the "fulfillment" theory of the parliament's Christian promoters to serve their own religious agendas. An irrepressibly typological thinker, Kitagawa must have also contemplated Vivekananda, Dharmapāla, and Shaku as embodiments of another type of religious leader which he later defined in a different context: the "pious adventurer." To attend the parliament, all three of them, true to this type, had "left their familiar surroundings for uncharted foreign lands for the propagation of the faith or in search of truth."[149] Perhaps Kitagawa's own experience of having left his native Japan for the United States in his mid-twenties to pursue theological studies in this country contributed to his fascination with Vivekananda, Dharmapāla, and Shaku, who were only slightly older when they journeyed from their Asian homelands to Chicago for the parliament.

That Kitagawa never lost his fascination with the parliament is manifest in his recurring references to the event and to those three figures in two of his last published works. For him, the parliament must have furnished a supreme example of what he articulated as the "two-sidedness" of our thinking process and of religion itself—a two-

---

[148] See the typologies of religious leadership and authority in Max Weber, *Economy and Society: An Outline of Interpretive Sociology*, 2 vols., ed. Guenther Roth and Claus Wittich (New York, 1968; Berkeley: University of California Press, 1978), 1:439-68; van der Leeuw, *Religion in Essence and Manifestation*, pp. 650-67; Joachim Wach, *Sociology of Religion* (Chicago: University of Chicago Press, 1944; 1st Phoenix ed., 1962), pp. 331-74.

[149] The reference for this definition by Kitagawa is given in n. 54 of the essay by Ziolkowski in this volume.

sideness summed up by the difference between "autobiographical" and "biographical" perspectives, and between the "inner" and "outer" meanings of religion, common to various religious traditions.[150] If to outsiders Islam is the religion of Muslims, while being to Muslims the religion of truth (to paraphrase the saying Kitagawa attributes to Sir Hamilton Gibb), such a distinction was destined to be blurred at the parliament with regard to any one of the particular faiths represented there. Some faiths were represented by speakers from inner, autobiographical perspectives; others, by speakers from outer, biographical perspectives; and still others, by speakers from both perspectives. Kitagawa explicitly equated the biographical perspective with that of his discipline, the history of religions; but as he well knew, and as we have discussed, those parliamentary papers that were to represent biographical, scholarly views in the name of "science," often conveyed autobiographical, religious views of their authors.[151]

The conflict between autobiographical and biographical perspectives is inherent to the theme of religious pluralism with which Seager is concerned, though he does not discuss it in these terms. His article encapsulates the interpretation developed in his 1987 dissertation on the parliament, establishes the methodology and interpretive "grid" that inform the arrangement of his 1993 edition of selected papers from the event's proceedings, and adumbrates the approach taken in his forthcoming book on the subject. His "grid," through which the various parliamentarians are to be viewed systematically as members of "delegations" from major groups (Protestant, Catholic, Jewish, the various Asian faiths), is designed to attain a more encompassing panorama of the concerns of different traditions. It is on this basis that he can envision the event as a sign that "religious pluralism, like it or not, was in the ascendant." If

---

[150] See Joseph Mitsuo Kitagawa, *The Quest for Human Unity: A Religious History* (Minneapolis: Fortress, 1990), pp. 2-4; and his *The Christian Tradition, beyond Its European Captivity* (Philadelphia: Trinity Press International, 1992) pp. 4-5. The 1893 parliament figures explicitly in both studies; see *The Quest for Human Unity*, pp. 207, 208, 212, 219-20, 232, 246; and *The Christian Tradition*, pp. 62, 63, 199, 207, 229, 251-52.

[151] The fertile conditions for this confusion of the "inner/autobiographical" and "outer/biographical" views at the parliament are already evident in Barrows's statement in his "Preface" regarding the amazing assortment of "types" that participated: "It is my inspiring duty to bring before my readers a most varied and stately procession of living scholars, reformers, missionaries, moral heroes, delvers in the mines of the soul, seekers after Truth, toilers for humanity" (*WPR*, 1:viii).

Seager and I seem to disagree on this point, since I have suggested that the predominant attitude at the parliament was not truly "pluralist," but "inclusivist," it is because we are appealing to different senses of the term "pluralism": while Seager derives from the parliament the lesson that "the existence of radical pluralism is a *fact* of life in American society" (emphasis mine), I use the term explicitly in Alan Race's (and many others') sense of a specific religious *attitude*: the unconditional acceptance of all faiths as possessing partial knowledge of God. These two senses of "pluralism" are equally valid; but their distinction is crucial to note. The undeniable *fact* of religious pluralism, in the sense of a plurality of faiths, does not assure the existence or cultivation of the *attitude* that also goes by that name.[152]

In pursuance of another lead of Kitagawa's, the contributions of Mullick, Bartholomeusz, and Ketelaar are arranged as a set. Each of them, though written independently of the other two, sheds valuable new light upon a different one of the three modern Asian religious reformers linked typologically by Kitagawa. Vivekananda, Dharmapāla, and Shaku Sōen are now examined in greater depth in the separate national as well as religious contexts from which they came to Chicago.

Mullick's comparison of Vivekananda and one of the other major Indian parliamentarians, Protap Chadra Majumdar of the Brāhmo Samāj, is revealing as a reminder that Majumdar, ten years before the parliament, became the first Indian religious leader to visit America, and that this visit "may have created more of a receptivity among Americans toward Indian religions than is acknowledged." Considered in this light, Vivekananda's triumphs at the parliament—triumphs that have eclipsed those of all other Asian speakers in the minds of most historians—would seem to owe a partial debt to his rival, Majumdar.

As posed in the title of her essay, the very question pursued by Tessa Bartholomeusz serves to demythologize a figure whose elevation to a virtually legendary status in his homeland as "*the* Sri Lankan symbol of religious and national pride" began with his mission to the parliament. Offering personally gleaned insights into the popular image of Dharmapāla that still persists in Sri Lanka, Bartholomeusz delves back into his early diaries and writings to show how, after the

---

[152] Compare the "caveats" of Eck, "Foreword," *DRP*, pp. xiii-xiv. David Bishop, in his "Religious Confrontation, a Case Study" (n. 116 above), uses the terms "pluralism," "exclusion," and "inclusion" in much the same sense as I do to analyze the parliament proceedings, although for a different purpose.

parliament, his actual thoughts regarding Buddhism, Sri Lanka, and the Sinhala people do not entirely corroborate that image.

That Dharmapāla, as Bartholomeusz notes, displayed a special fondness for Japanese Buddhism provides an interesting albeit fortuitous link between her essay and Ketelaar's. In the latter, we again meet up with Shaku Sōen, but this time not in a typological association with Vivekananda and Dharmapāla, but in the company of his four fellow-Japanese "champions of Buddhism," with whom he participated in the perceived "duel with Christianity" at Chicago. Ketelaar combines an examination of the motives and beliefs of the five Meiji Buddhist parliamentarians with a thorough investigation of the Darwinian and Müllerian assumptions underlying the whole phenomenon of the parliament. His exposé of the parliament as a Western "staging of the Other" thus prepares for his account of how the parliament in turn was approached by these five "others" there. In this regard a great irony emerges. While "the parliamentarian other was given life [by the Western hosts] so that it could be sacrificed on the altar of evolutionary progress," at least one Japanese Buddhist believed that a future victory of the Buddha dharma was assured by "worldwide evolutionary processes."

My own article shifts the focus back from east to west, and off the realm of history onto that of literature, or more precisely, onto the boundary between those two realms, where literary ideals can often be thwarted upon trying to enter and become manifest within history. Letting my article speak for itself as a demonstration of how this principle of thwarting came into effect at the parliament, I shall end this Introduction with some reflections provoked by Ursula King's essay.

Exclusions and Neglect

While noting that the parliament "was rigidly purged of cranks,"[153] Barrows acknowledged that "the representation of the world's faiths was less complete and imposing" than its promoters had planned, and that the absence of representatives of "Hindu Mohammedanism" and of "Methodist Bishops" was "deplored."[154] Aside from the question of

---

[153] Barrows, "Review and Summary," in *WPR*, 2:1561. See also Mary Barrows, *John Henry Barrows*, pp. 281-83.

[154] These statements are found in Barrows's article in this volume, and in his "Review and Summary," in *WPR*, 2:1561. Apparently Barrows, in acknowledging the absence of "Methodist Bishops," was not counting Bishop Benjamin W.

the representation of women and Native and African Americans, to which we shall turn in a moment, it has also been observed that no Mormons were invited; that, although Catholics and Jews participated, there was no discussion of issues concerning recent immigrant groups such as Germans, Poles and Italians, and central and east European Jews; that Islam was severely underrepresented, perhaps as a result of the rejection by Sultan Abdul Hamid II of his invitation from the parliament committee; and that such relatively modern Asian groups as the Sikhs and the Tibetan Buddhists, like the so-called tribal or ethnic faiths and the whole continents of Africa and South America, had no representation other than what might have been said of them in some "scientific" paper.[155]

In our own time of feminism and "multiculturalism," it may strike some as too easy to highlight the weak spots and gaps in representation at the 1893 parliament. Yet, given the touting of the event by its promoters as the "parliament of Man," the question is begged: of whom did "Man" consist?

Although "Woman" had a whole pavilion devoted to her at the Columbian Exposition, the actual significance of that pavilion was ambiguous.[156] The president of the exposition's Board of Lady Managers, Bertha Honoré Palmer (often referred to as Mrs. Potter Palmer), saw the fair as a turning-point in women's history, as she proclaimed at the exposition's dedication ceremony: "Even more important than the discovery of Columbus, which we are gathered together to celebrate, is the fact that the General Government has just discovered woman."[157] But, as the first part of this claim could have been justly contended by Native Americans, so the second could not have been pleasing to all feminists of the time, with the Nineteenth Amendment (ratified 1920) still almost thirty years away. Elizabeth Cady Stanton, who would contribute a paper to the Parliament of

---

Arnett of the African Methodist Episcopal Church, who did address the parliament.

[155] See Seager, "General Introduction" to *DRP*, pp. 6-7; and, in his essay in the present volume, the section on "A Modern, Democratic, and Somewhat Anarchic Feast."

[156] For extensive analysis of this pavilion, its significance, its displays, the history behind it, and the women involved in it, see Jeanne Madeline Weimann, *The Fair Women* (Chicago: Academy Chicago, 1981).

[157] Rossiter Johnson, *A History of the World's Columbian Exposition*, 4 vols. (New York: D. Appleton, 1897-98), 1:280. Barrows paraphrases this quotation in *WPR*,

Religions to be read there by Susan B. Anthony,[158] remarked that "the Woman's Pavilion on the centennial grounds is an afterthought, as theologians claim woman herself to have been."[159]

Even more disturbing—far more disturbing—is the status, or perhaps lack of status, accorded to Native and African Americans at the fair. As the subject of one of the ethnological "displays" on the Midway Plaisance, Native American culture was relegated to one of the spots farthest from the White City; according to the theory behind the arrangement of those displays, as considered earlier, Native Americans were thus meant to represent for visitors one of the "lowest" peoples on the "scale" of evolution. At the same time, while the "display" of African natives was consigned to an equally "low" position on the Midway, Americans of African descent bizarrely had no official status at all in the fair. This, at least, was the impression made on the great African-American leader and former slave, Frederick Douglass, who served as commissioner from Haiti to the exposition. Amidst the almost overwhelming pomp at the dedication ceremonies, Douglas noticed that not one from the United States' eight million blacks was included among the dignitaries assembled on the main stage. "Glorious" as the ceremonies were, Douglass later reflected, "there was one thing that dimmed their glory. The occasion itself was world embracing in its idea. It spoke of human brotherhood, human welfare and human progress. It naturally implied a welcome to every possible variety of mankind. Yet, I saw, or thought I saw, an intentional slight to that part of the American population with which I am identified."[160]

What sort of representation were women and Native and African Americans accorded at the Parliament of Religions, where, according to Barrows, "equal freedom [was] gladly accorded to all races and both sexes"? Ursula King, in her analysis of the proportion and role of women's voices at the parliament, notes that between nineteen and twenty-one women addressed the parliament (depending on how one's calculation is based), or roughly ten percent of the total number of speakers. Complementing Marty's comment that this percentage of

---

2:1567 in a way that waters down the boldness of Palmer's words. The paraphrase is quoted at length in n. 24 of the essay by King in the present volume.

[158] Stanton's paper, "The Worship of God in Man," is found in *WPR*, 2:1234-36.

[159] Quoted by Weimann, *The Fair Women*, p. 4.

[160] Quoted by Burg, *White City*, p. 109. On racism toward African Americans and the degrading American "Indian exhibits" at the Columbian Exposition, see Rydell, *All the World's a Fair*, pp. 53-55, 63-64.

women at the parliament was larger than such public events would involve for decades to come, King observes that the sort of exclusion of women that might have been expected then at such a gathering proved less in evidence at the parliament than it has in the historiography of the event[161] and in the global interfaith movement it helped initiate.

But, again, what King can say about women at the parliament could not be said at all about Native Americans, and could barely be said about African Americans—namely, that they were there "in their own right and...spoke their own voice." King's prolegomenous effort to recover the "voices" of women from the almost complete silence into which scholars have allowed them to fall might serve also as a reminder of the parliament's bearing on the observation by Charles H. Long that the traditional "approach to American religion has rendered the religious reality of non-Europeans to a state of invisibility."[162] As King and others have observed, no Native Americans appeared at the parliament to represent their own religious faiths. Aside from the paper on Native American religion given there by the anthropologist Fletcher, a pair of papers concerning Native American culture were apparently presented (by non-Native Americans) at the Women's Congregational Congress held in affiliation with the parliament. Perhaps these were all that could be expected three years after Wounded Knee.

In a statement quoted by King, Fletcher herself acknowledged this glaring gap at the parliament. She comes across as exceedingly honest, suggesting—to borrow Kitagawa's terms—that her biographical description of a people's faith from outside, as valuable as that description might be in its own right, cannot substitute for an inner, autobiographical account by that people: "No American Indian has told us," Fletcher reminded her audience, "how his people have sought after God." At least one person missed the point, as betrayed by the following comments made afterwards by an observer: "It was

---

[161] This is true, we might add, even of the one account of the exposition in which some reference to the contributions of women at the parliament might most be expected: Weimann's *The Fair Women*, which makes no mention of the parliament. Although Weimann's focus is on the Woman's Pavilion, some of the more prominent women whom she discusses contributed papers to or appeared at the parliament, including Susan B. Anthony, Bertha Honoré Palmer, and Elizabeth Cady Stanton.

[162] Charles H. Long, "Interpretations of Black Religion in America," in his *Significations: Signs, Symbols, and Images in the Interpretation of Religion* (Philadelphia: Fortress, 1986), p. 149.

not because the American Indian had no faith, nor that his position as the first element, chronologically, of the American Nation was overlooked. All efforts failed to secure his presence; *but in this case an 'absent' Indian proved the best kind of Indian,"*—here, the commentator could not resist an unfortunate pun on the adage that the only good Indian is a dead one—*"for no Indian, living or dead, could have set forth so sympathetically, in gentleness, love and reverence, the features of the primitive religions of the red men of America as did Miss Alice Fletcher,* who has devoted her life to the study of their relics and the service of their peoples."[163]

Unlike Native Americans, African Americans were not an entirely absent race at the parliament. Indeed, despite the Jim-Crow mores of the time, some exuberant utterances were made by white parliamentarians regarding the presence of "Africans." "Dear negro brothers, ye," reads a verse from Laura Ormiston Chant's poem, "The World's Parliament," which Barrows read to the assembly:

> At last at one with you,
> In the most holy name of God,
> The New World welcomes you.
> For all the creeds of men have come to praise,
> And kneel and worship at the great white [!] throne
> Of God...[164]

Although Barrows would accordingly call the parliament "a notable event for the African, whose manhood was fully recognized,"[165] an unabashed condescension was displayed in some of the expressions of that recognition.[166] To be sure, Bishop Benjamin W. Arnett of the African Methodist Episcopal Church could proudly proclaim at the parliament: "I greet the children of Shem, I greet the children of Japheth, and I want you to understand that Ham is here."[167] On the

---

[163] Winslow, "A Pen Picture of the Parliament," p. 233 (emphasis mine).

[164] Quoted by Barrows in "History," in *WPR*, 1:150-51.

[165] Barrows, "Review and Summary," in *WPR*, 2:1569.

[166] Consider the speech given by Rev. J.R. Slattery, of St. Joseph's Seminary, Baltimore, on "The Catholic Church and the Negro." Having opened by declaring, "In the eyes of the Catholic Church the negro is a man" (in *WPR*, 2:1104), Rev. Slattery later recommends with regard to "the formation of [the negro's] character, which is his weak spot": "The building of his character...is best done by the mingled efforts of brotherly white men and worthy black men. His temperament, his passions and other inherent qualities...are beyond his control, and he needs the aid of the best men of his own race, but associated with and not divorced from the coöperation of the best of the white race" (p. 1106).

[167] This quote appears in capital letters beneath the full-page photograph of Arnett in *WPR*, 2:1105.

evening of September 22, marking the thirty-first anniversary of the Emancipation Proclamation, he gave an eloquent address on "what...the negro [has] done with his thirty years of freedom," focusing on achievements of African-American men and women (and he did pay special homage to the latter) in various areas of life, culture, and society. But the fact remains that, aside from this address and the one by Unitarian laywoman Fannie Barrier Williams, no other official speech was given by an African American at the parliament—although Frederick Douglass, upon request, made some short, impromptu remarks at one session, and the African Methodist Episcopal church held a denominational congress of its own in connection with the parliament.[168]

Ten years ago Kitagawa ended his Nuveen Lecture by commending, in his characteristically generous manner, the parliament's "noble legacies that we are proud to inherit." He was referring to the impact of the event on interfaith dialogue and comparative religion, of which we spoke earlier. I am sure he would have agreed that we should also pay critical heed, in the interest of the future of us all, to those other aspects of the parliament whose histories elicit anything but our pride.

---

[168] See B.W. Arnett, untitled address in *WPR*, 2:1101-04, quote on p. 1102; and Fannie Barrier Williams, "What Can Religion Further Do to Advance the Condition of the American Negro?" (pp. 1114-15). A portrait of Williams appears on p. 1147. The remarks by Douglass are recorded in *NHP*, p. 702. For the official report on "The African Methodist Episcopal Church Congress," see "The Denominational Congresses," in *WPR*, 2:1394-96. Pictures of eleven bishops from that church appear on pp. 1393, 1479.

PART I

PROCEEDINGS
1893

SERVICE OF THE SCIENCE OF RELIGIONS
TO THE CAUSE OF RELIGIOUS UNITY

Merwin-Marie Snell

Religion is a universal fact of human experience. There are people without gods, without sacred books, without sacraments, without doctrines, if you will—but none without religion. There is in every human breast an instinct which reaches outward and upward toward the highest truth, the highest goodness, the highest beauty, and which testifies at the same time to the existence of an intimate relation of affection, of honor, and of beauty between each individual person and the surrounding universe.

Everything that exists or can exist may be an object of religious devotion, for everything is in some sense a compendium of the World-All and a symbol of creative power, preserving wisdom and transforming providence. In all the world, from pole to pole, and from ocean to ocean, there lives not one single unperverted human being from whose soul there does not ascend the incense of adoration and in whose hand is not found the pilgrim staff of duty. Mankind is one in the recognition of the relationship between the individual and the cosmos, and one in the effort to manifest and perfect that relationship by sacrifice and service. Superimposed upon this universal foundation

"Service of the Science of Religions to the Cause of Religious Unity" by Merwin-Marie Snell. Reprinted from Walter R. Houghton, ed., *Neely's History of the Parliament of Religions* (Chicago: Neely Publishing Company, 1894), pp. 259-67. A brief abstract of this paper appears in John Henry Barrows, ed., *The World's Parliament of Religions*, 2 vols. (Chicago: Parliament Publishing Company, 1893), 2:1347.

of the spiritual sense, as the late Brother Azarias[1] was wont to describe it, rises a great structure of religious and ethical truths and principles, regarding which there is a substantial agreement among all the branches of the human family. If the precise extent of this agreement can be definitely ascertained, as well as the exact significance and cause of the real or apparent divergences from a common standard, either in the way of omission or addition, the way will be prepared for the complete annihilation of vital religious differences, and the placing of the facts and principles of religions upon an absolutely inexpungable basis.

It cannot be too much insisted upon that for a perfect realization of the highest development and firmest demonstration of religion, the perfection of the science of religion is an indispensable condition. Of this fact the friends of the World's Parliament of Religions cannot permit themselves to doubt; for the parliament itself is a vast hierological museum, a working collection of religious specimens, having the same indispensable value to the hierologist that the herbarium has to the botanist. It is not only an exhibit of religions, but a school of comparative religion, and everyone who attends its sessions is taking the first steps toward becoming a hierologist.

Under these circumstances it is fitting that the science of religions should here receive special attention under its own name. And this all the more as the prejudices and animosities which perpetuate religious disunion are in a large proportion of cases the result of gross misconceptions of the true character of the rival creeds or cults. The anti-Catholic, anti-Mormon, and anti-Semitic agitations in Christendom, and the highly colored pictures of heathen degradation in which a certain class of foreign missionaries indulge, are significant illustrations of the malignant results of religious ignorance.

No one would hate or despise the Catholic Church who knew its teachings and practices as they really are; no one would exclude the Church of the Latter Day Saints from the family of the world's religions who had caught the first glimpse of its profound cosmogony, its spiritual theology and its exalted morality; no one would fail in

---

[1] Patrick Francis Mullany (1847-1893) of the Brothers of the Christian School, known as Brother Azarias, had been an intended parliament speaker. His paper, "The Religious Training of Children," which he completed shortly before his death, was read at the parliament on the seventh day by his brother, Rev. John F. Mullany of Syracuse, New York, and appears in *WPR*, 1:759-66 and *NHP*, pp. 355-63.

respect to Judaism could he once enter into the spirit of its teaching and ritual; and no one would attribute a special ignorance and superstition to the pagan systems as such who had taken the trouble to acquaint himself with their phenomena, and, as it were, enter into union with their inner souls and thus fully perceive the divine truths upon which they rest.

Those who aspire to prepare themselves to give intelligent assistance to the cause of religious unity by a scientific study of religions should bear in mind the following rules:

1. An impartial collection and examination of data regarding all religions without distinction is of primary importance.
2. It is not necessary, however, to doubt or disbelieve one's own creed in order to give a perfectly unbiased examination to all others.
3. In cases where the facts are in dispute the testimony of the adherents of the system under consideration must outweigh those who profess some other religion or none.
4. The facts collected must be studied in due chronological order, and it is not legitimate to construct a history of religions based upon a study of contemporary cults without regard to history.
5. Resemblances in nomenclature, in beliefs, or in customs must not be too hastily accepted as conclusive evidence of the special relationship between systems.
6. Resemblances in ceremonial details must not be considered as necessarily indicating any fundamental similarity or kinship.
7. When any religion or any one of its constituent elements appears to be absurd and false, consider that this appearance may result from an error as to the facts in the case, or misunderstanding of the true significance of those facts.

I believe it to be most certain that every positive element in every religion derives its being from the truth it embodies of the utility of the truth which it subserves; and that every doctrine and practice, especially those which are most widespread, have their roots deep down in the human nature common to us all, and while it may be perfected or superseded it can in no case be permanently eliminated.

It is not necessary to be a scientist by profession in order to give intelligent study to the science of religions. The professional hierologist analyzes and compares religions from a pure love of his science; the man of broadening culture and thought may study them with the practical end of a fuller self-enlightenment regarding his duties to God and the race; and the intelligent religious partisan may seek to master, by means of his science, the secret of religious variations, and to obtain such a knowledge of the relation of other religious systems to his own, their points of agreement and contradiction, and their historic contact as will enable him to carry on a very powerful and fruitful propaganda.

Missionary work, in particular, cannot dispense with this science. I do not refer to Christian missions exclusively, but to missionary work in general, whoever be its objects and whatever its aims, and whether it be Catholic, Protestant, Buddhist, or Muslim. Every missionary school should be a college of comparative religion. It should be realized that ignorance and prejudice in the propagandist are as great obstacles to the spread of any religion as the same qualities in those whom it seeks to win, and that the first requisite to successful missionary work is a knowledge of the truths and beauties of the existing religion, that they may be used as a *point d'appui* for the special arguments and claims of that with which it is desired to replace it.

However, whatever may be the motives of the scientist, the truthseeker, and the propagandist, they must all use the same methods of impartial research; and all work together, even though it be in spite of themselves, for the hastening of the day when mutual understanding and fraternal sympathy, and intelligent appreciation, as wide as the world, shall draw together in golden bonds the whole human family.

All true study of the facts of nature and man is scientific study; all true aspiration toward the ideal of the universe is religious aspiration. Into this union of religious science all men can enter—Catholics, Protestants, Jews, Mormons, Mohammedans, Hindus, Buddhists, Confucianists, Jains, Taoists, Shintoists, Theosophists, Spiritualists, theists, pantheists, and atheists, and none of them need feel out of place; none of them need sacrifice their favorite tenets, and none of them should dare to deny to any of the others a perfect right to stand upon the same platform of intelligent and impartial inquiry and to obtain a free and appreciative audience for all that they can say on their own behalf.

A great deal has been said about the union of science and religion; much more important is the union of all men in science and religion, of which that most remarkable of all human assemblies which this building now shelters is a glorious illustration.

And may this union become ever closer until, under the aegis of the true brotherhood, that demands no surrender of cherished beliefs, but only an opening of the mind and heart upon a broader horizon, the whole race of mankind shall conscientiously and lovingly work together in the quest or illustration of the highest truth and in the teaching and fulfillment of the supremest deity.

On the Study of Comparative Theology

Cornelius Petrus Tiele

I greatly regret that official work of various kinds as well as the peculiar organization of our university system prevents me from attending one of the congresses at Chicago. But for this reason I am the more willing to comply, if possible, with the request which the committee of this congress did me the honor to address to me, viz., to send in a paper on the history and study of comparative theology, to be read at one of the meetings of the congress. When I was ready to enter upon the performing of this task, the first question which presented itself before me was this: What is to be understood by comparative theology? I find that English-speaking authors use the appellation promiscuously with comparative religion, but if we wish the words to convey a sound meaning we should at least beware

"On the Study of Comparative Theology" by C.P. Tiele. Reprinted from both John Henry Barrows, ed., *The World's Parliament of Religions*, 2 vols. (Chicago: Parliament Publishing Company, 1893), 1:583-90, and Walter R. Houghton, ed., *Neely's History of the Parliament of Religions* (Chicago: Neely Publishing Company, 1894), pp. 245-50. Aside from Houghton's omission of the opening three sentences up to the colon, those two texts are identical substantively. However, their paragraphing differs, and Houghton's text is riddled with more spelling errors. Given the occasional awkwardness in prose, both texts seem based on a translation, presumably from the author's native Dutch. The combined version here adapts most of the paragraph breaks of the Houghton text, while, when variances in word choice crop up, usually adapting smoother counterparts from the Barrows text—e.g., "prejudice," as opposed to "side-desires." Misspelled and miscited names and titles have been corrected, and punctuation has sometimes been altered in the interest of coherence. All footnotes are added.

of using these terms as convertible ones. Theology is not the same as religion; and, to me, comparative theology signifies nothing but a comparative study of religious dogmas, comparative religion nothing but a comparative study of the various religions in all their branches. I suppose, however, I am not expected to make this distinction, but comparative theology is to be understood to mean what is now generally called the science of religion, the word "science" not being taken in the limited sense it commonly has in English, but in the general signification of the Dutch *Wetenschap* (High German *Wissenschaft*) which it has assumed more and more even in the Roman languages.

So the history and the study of this science would have to form the subject of my paper, a subject vast enough to devote to it one or more volumes. It is still in its infancy. Although in former centuries its advent was heralded by a few forerunners, as Selden in *De diis Syriis*, de Brosses in *Du Culte des dieux fétiches*, the tasteful Herder[1] and others, as a science it reaches back not much farther than to the middle of the nineteenth century.[2] Dupuis's *Origine de tous les cultes*, which appeared in the opening years of the century, is a gigantic pamphlet, not an impartial historical research.[3] Nor can Creuzer's and Baur's *Symbolik and Mythologie* lay claim to the latter appellation, but are dominated by an a priori and long refuted theory.[4] Meiners's *Allgemeine kritische Geschichte der Religionen* only just came up to the low standard which at that time historical scholars were expected to reach.[5] Much higher stood Benjamin Constant, in whose work, *De la Religion considerée dans sa source, des formes et ses développements*,[6] written with French lucidity, for the first time a distinction was made

---

[1] See the discussion of religion, and of religious stages in history, in J.G. Herder, *Ideen zur Philosophie der Geschichte der Menschheit* (1784-91).

[2] See John Selden, *De diis Syriis* (1617) and Charles de Brosses, *Du Culte de dieux fétiches* (1760).

[3] Charles François Dupuis, *Origine de tous les cultes* (1795). Tiele's claim that this book "appeared in the opening years of the century" is incorrect.

[4] The reference here is to two different works that share the same primary title: Georg Friedrich Creuzer's *Symbolik und Mythologie der alten Völker, besonders der Griechen*, 4 vols. (Leipzig: Leske, 1810-12; 2d, revised ed., Leipzig and Darmstadt: Heyer und Leske, 1819-23; 3d ed., 1836-43); and Ferdinand Christian Baur's *Symbolik und Mythologie, oder die Naturreligion des Altertums*, 2 vols. (Stuttgart: Metzler, 1824).

[5] Christoph Meiners, *Allgemeine kritische Geschichte der Religionen*, 2 vols. (Hannover, 1806-07).

[6] See Benjamin Constant de Rebecque, *De la religion considerée dans sa source, ses formes et ses développements*, 6 vols. (Paris: Bossange Père, Pichon et Didier, 1824-31).

between the essence and the forms of religion, to which the writer also applied the theory of development.

From that time the science of religion began to assume a more sharply defined character, and comparative studies on an ever-growing scale were entered upon, and this was done no longer chiefly with prejudice, either by the enemies of Christianity in order to combat it and to point out that it differed little or nothing [sic] from all the superstitions one was now getting acquainted with, or by the apologists in order to defend it against these attacks, and to prove its higher excellence when compared with all other religions. The impulse came from two sides. On one side it was due to philosophy. Philosophy had for centuries past been speculating upon religion, but only about the beginning of our century had it become aware of the fact that the great religious problems cannot be solved without the aid of history—that in order to define the nature and the origin of religion one must first of all know its development. Already before Benjamin Constant this was felt by others, of whom we will only mention Hegel and Schelling. The *Philosophie der Religion* of one of them, the *Philosophie der Mythologie* of the other, are cast in the mould of a sketch of the history of the development of religious ideas.[7] It may even be said that the right method for the philosophical inquiry into religion was defined by Schelling, at least from a theoretical point of view, more accurately than by anyone else; though we should add that he, more than anyone else, fell short in applying it. Hegel even endeavored to give a classification of religions, which, it is true, hits the right nail on the head here and there, but which as a whole distinctly proves that he lacked a clear conception of the real historical development of religion. Nor could this be otherwise. Even if the one had not been confined within the narrow bounds of an a priori system of the historical data which were at his disposal, even if the other had not been led astray by his unbridled fancy, both wanted the means to trace religion in the course of its developments. Most of the religions of antiquity, especially those of the East, were at that time known but superficially, and the critical research into the newer forms of religion had as yet hardly been entered upon.

One instance out of many: Hegel characterized the so-called Syriac (Aramaic) religions as *die Religion des Schmerzens* (religion of suffering). In doing this he of course thought of the myth and the

---

[7] G.W.F. Hegel, *Vorlesungen über die Philosophie der Religion* (Berlin, 1832); Friedrich W.J. von Schelling, *Philosophie der Mythologie* (Stuttgart, 1857).

worship of Thammuz-Adonis. He did not know that these are by no means of Aramaic origin, but were borrowed by the peoples of western Asia from their eastern neighbors, and are in fact a survival of a much older, highly sensual naturism. Even at the time he might have known that Adonis was far from being an ethical ideal, that his worship was far from being the glorification of a voluntarily suffering deity. In short, it was known that only the comparative method could conduce to the desired end, but the means of comparing, though not wholly wanting, were inadequate.

Meanwhile material was being supplied from another quarter. Philological and historical science, cultivated after strict methods, archaeology, anthropology, ethnology, no longer a prey to superficial theorists and fashionable dilettanti only, but also subjected to the laws of the critical research, began to yield a rich harvest. I need but hint at the many important discoveries of the last hundred years, the number of which is continually increasing. You know them full well, and you also know that they are not confined to a single province nor to a single period. They reach back as far as the remotest antiquity and show us, in those ages long gone by, a civilization postulating a long previous development; they also draw our attention to many conceptions, manners and customs among several backward or degenerate tribes of our own time, giving evidence of the greatest rudeness and barbarousness. They thus enable us to study religion as it appears among all sorts of people and in the most diversified degrees of development. They have at least supplied the sources to draw from, among which are the original records of religion concerning which people formerly had to be content with very scanty, very recent and very untrustworthy information. You will not expect me to give you an enumeration of them. Let me mention only Egypt, Babylonia and Assyria, India and Persia, and, of their sacred books, the *Book of the Dead*; the so-called "Chaldean Genesis"[8] and the Babylonian penitential psalms; and the mythological texts, the Veda and the Avesta. These form but a small part of the acquired treasures, but if we had nothing else it would be much.

I know quite well that at first, even after having deciphered the writing of the first two named and having learned in some degree to understand the languages of all, people seemed not to be fully aware of what was to be done with these treasures, and that the translations, hurriedly put together, failed to lead to an adequate perception of the

---

[8] I.e., the *Enuma elish*.

contents. I know also that even now, after we have learned how to apply to the study of these records the universally admitted, sound philological principles, much of what was believed to be known has been rejected as being valueless. And I know that the questions and problems which have to be solved have not decreased in number, but are daily increasing. I cannot deny that scholars of high repute and indisputable authority are much divided in opinion concerning the explanation of those texts, and that it is not easy to make a choice out of so many conflicting opinions. How much does Brugsch differ in his representation of the Egyptian mythology from Eduard Meyer and Erman![9] How great a division among the Assyriologists between the Accadists or Sumerists, and the anti-Sumerists or anti-Accadists! How much differs the explanation of the Veda by Roth, Müller, and Grassmann, from that by Ludwig, and how different is Barth's explanation from Bergaigne's and Regnaud's![10] How violent was the controversy between Spiegel and Haupt about the explanation of the most ancient pieces in the Avesta![11] And now, in this year of grace, while the younger generation, as Bartholomae and Geldner on the one hand, Geiger, Wilhelm, Hubschmann, Mills on the other hand,[12] are following different roads, there has come a scholar and a man of genius, who is, however, particularly fond of paradoxes—James Darmesteter[13]—to overthrow all that was considered up to his time as

---

[9] Heinrich Karl Brugsch (1827-94); Eduard Meyer (1855-1930); Adolf Erman (1854-1937).

[10] Rudolf von Roth (1821-95); F. Max Müller (1823-1900); Hermann Günther Grassmann (1809-77); Alfred Ludwig (1832-1912); Auguste Barth (1834-1916); Abel Henri Joseph Bergaigne (1838-88); Paul Regnaud (1838-1910).

[11] Tiele's reference here is to Friedrich von Spiegel (1820-1905) and, I suspect, Martin Haug (1827-76) rather than Haupt, which is the name that is given (probably as the result of a stenographic or typographical error) in both the *WPR* and the *NHP* texts of this paper. The methodological controversy to which Tiele is referring here would seem to be the one discussed by James Darmesteter between those, led by Spiegel, who interpreted the Avesta relying chiefly or exclusively on tradition, and those, among whom Haug figured prominently, who interpreted it relying only on comparison with the Vedas. See Darmesteter's "Introduction" to his translation of *The Zend-Avesta*, constituting vols. 4, 23 and 31 of *The Sacred Books of the East*, 50 vols., ed. F. Max Müller (Oxford: Clarendon, 1879-1910), 4:xxvii-xxxi. (The portions in vol. 31 are translated by L.H. Mills.)

[12] Christian Bartholomae (1855-1925); Karl Friedrich Geldner (1853-1929); Wilhelm Geiger (1856-1943); Eugen Wilhelm (1842-1923); Heinrich Hübschmann (1848-1908); Lawrence Heyworth Mills (1837-1918).

[13] James Darmesteter (1849-94), translator of the first two (of three) parts of the Avesta in Müller's *Sacred Books of the East* series. See n. 11 above.

being all but stable, nay, even to undermine the foundations, which were believed safe enough to be built upon.

But all this cannot do away with the fact that we are following the right path, that much has already been obtained and much light has been shed on what was dark. Of not a few of these newfangled theories may be said *nubicula est, transibit*,[14] and at least they are useful in compelling us once more to put to a severe test the results obtained. So we see that the modern science of religion, comparative theology, has sprung from these two sources: the want of a firmer empirical base of operations, felt by the philosophy of religion, and the great discoveries in the domain of history, archaeology, and anthropology.

These discoveries have revealed a great number of forms of religion and religious phenomena which until now were known imperfectly or not at all; and it stands to reason that these have been compared with those already known, and that inferences have been drawn from this comparison. Can anyone be said to be the founder of the young science? Many have conferred this title upon the famous Oxford professor, F. Max Müller; others, among them his great American opponent, the no less famous professor of Yale college, W. Dwight Whitney,[15] have denied it to him. We may leave this decision to posterity. I, for one, may rather be said to side with Whitney than with Müller. Though I have frequently contended the latter's speculations and theories, I would not close my eyes to the great credit he has gained by what he has done for the science of religion, nor would I gainsay the fact that he has given a mighty impulse to the study of it, especially in England and in France.[16]

But a new branch of study can hardly be said to be founded. Like others, this one was called into being by a generally felt want in different countries at the same time and as a matter of course. The

---

[14] "It's just a little cloud; it will pass."

[15] William Dwight Whitney (1827-94) was one of the leading American Indologists of his day.

[16] Cf. C.P. Tiele's remarks several years later on the same question: "As the foundation of this new science had only just been laid, [Müller] could but submit the plan of the building to his readers and hearers. How powerfully he afterwards himself contributed to the building up of our science I need hardly remind you;...His 'Introduction [to] the Science of Religion' [Royal Institution lectures, published in London, 1873]...necessarily dealt with the preliminaries rather than with the results of the science, and was an apology for it more than an initiation into it" (*Elements of the Science of Religion*, 2 vols., Gifford Lectures, 1896, 1898 [Edinburgh: W. Blackwood and Sons, 1897-99], 1:2).

number of those applying themselves to it has been gradually increasing, and for years it has been gaining chairs at universities, first in Holland, afterwards also in France and elsewhere, now also in America. It has already a rich literature, even periodicals of its own. Though at one time the brilliant talents of some writers threatened to bring it into fashion and to cause it to fall a prey to dilettanti—a state of things that is to be considered most fatal to any science, but especially to one that is still in its infancy—this danger has fortunately been warded off, and it is once more pursuing the noiseless tenor of its way, profiting by the fell criticism of those who hate it.

I shall not attempt to write its history. The time for it has not yet come. The rise of this new science, the comparative research of new religions, is as yet too little a feature of the past to be surveyed from an impartial standpoint. Moreover, the writer of this paper himself has been one of the laborers in this field for more than thirty years past, and so he is, to some extent, a party to the conflict of opinions. His views would be apt to be too subjective and could be justified only by an exhaustive criticism of the theories with which he does not agree, a criticism which would be misplaced here, and the writing of which would require a longer time of preparation than has now been allowed to him. A dry enumeration of the names of the principal writers and the titles of their works would be of little use, and would prove very little attractive to you. Therefore let me add some words on the study of comparative theology.

The first, the predominating question, is: Is this study possible? In other words, what man, however talented and learned he may be, is able to command this immense field of inquiry, and what lifetime is long enough for the acquiring of an exhaustive knowledge of all religions? It is not even within the bounds of possibility that a man should master all languages to study in the vernacular the religious records of all nations, not only recognized sacred writings, but also those of dissenting sects and the songs and sagas of uncivilized people. So one will have to put up with translations, and everybody knows that the meaning of the original is but poorly rendered even by the best translation. One will have to take upon trust what may be called second-hand information, without being able to test it, especially where the religions of the so-called primitive peoples are concerned. All these objections have been made by me for having the pleasure of setting them aside; they have frequently been raised against the new study and have already dissuaded many from devoting themselves to it. Nor can it be denied that they contain at least some truth. But if, on account of these objections, the comparative study of religions were to be esteemed impossible, the same judgment would have to be pronounced upon many other sciences.

I am not competent to pass an opinion concerning the physical and biological sciences. I am alluding only to anthropology and ethnology, history, the history of civilization, archaeology, comparative philology, comparative literature, ethics, philosophy. Is the independent study of all these sciences to be relinquished because no one can be required to be versed in each of their details equally well, to have acquired an exhaustive knowledge, got at the mainspring of every people, every language, every literature, every civilization, every group of records, every period, every system? There is nobody who will think of insisting upon this. Every science, even the most comprehensive one, every theory, must rest on an empirical basis, must start from an "unbiased ascertaining of facts." But it does not follow that the tracing, the collecting, the sorting, and the elaborating of these facts and the building up of a whole out of these materials must needs be consigned to the same hands. The flimsily-constructed speculative systems, pasteboard buildings all of them, we have done away with for good and all.

But a science is not a system, not a well-arranged storehouse of things that are known, but an aggregate of researches all tending to the same purpose, though independent yet mutually connected, and each in particular connected with similar researches in other domains, which thus serve as auxiliary sciences. Now the science of religion has no other purpose than to lead to the knowledge of religion in its nature and in its origin. And this knowledge is not to be acquired, at least if it is to be a sound, not a would-be knowledge, but by an unprejudiced historical-psychological research. What should be done first of all is to trace religion in the course of its development, that is to say, in its life, to inquire what every family of religions (as, for instance, the Aryan and the Semitic), what every particular religion, what the great religious persons have contributed to this development; to what laws and conditions this development is subjected; and in what it really consists. Next, the religious phenomena, ideas and dogmas, feelings and inclinations, forms of worship and religious acts are to be examined, to know from what wants of the soul they have sprung and of what aspirations they are the expression. But these researches, without which one cannot penetrate into the nature of religion nor form a conception of its origin, cannot bear lasting fruit unless the comparative study of religions and religious individualities lie at the root of them. Only to a few has it been given to institute this most comprehensive inquiry, to follow to the end this long way. He who ventures upon it cannot think of examining closely all the particulars himself; he has to avail himself of what the students of special branches have brought to light and have corroborated with sound evidence.

It is not required of every student of the science of religion that he should be an architect; yet, though his study may be confined within the narrow bounds of a small section, if he does not lose sight of the chief purpose and if he applies the right method, he too will contribute not unworthily to the great common work.

So a search after the solution of the abstruse fundamental questions would better be left to those few who add a great wealth of knowledge to philosophical talents. What should be considered most needful with a view to the present standpoint of comparative theology is this: Learning how to put the right use the new sources that have been opened up; studying thoroughly and penetrating into the sense of records that on many points still leave us in the dark; subjecting to a close examination particular religions and important periods about which we possess but scanty information; searching for the religious nucleus and meaning of myths; tracing prominent deities in their rise and development, and forms of worship through all the important changes of meaning they have undergone; after this the things thus found have to be compared with those already known.

Two things must be required of the student of the science of religion. He must be thoroughly acquainted with the present state of the research—he must know what has already been got, but also what questions are still unanswered; he must have walked, though it be in quick time, about the whole domain of his science; in short, he must possess a general knowledge of religions and religious phenomena. But he should not be satisfied with this. He should then select a field of his own, larger or smaller according to his capacities and the time at his disposal—a field where he is quite at home, where he himself probes to the bottom of everything, of which he knows all that is to be known about it, and to the science of which he then must try to give a fresh impulse. Both requirements he has to fulfill. Meeting only one of them will lead either to the superficial dilettantism which has already been alluded to, or the trifling of those *doctores umbrarii*, those

Philistines of science, who like nothing better than occupying our attention longest of all with such things as lie beyond the bounds of what is worth knowing. But the last named danger does not need to be especially cautioned against, at least in America. I must not conclude without expressing my joy at the great interest in this new branch of science, which of late years has been revealing itself in the New World.

Conditions and Outlook for a Universal Religion

Albert Réville

We have to do with elements and initial conditions, not with a developed system. They comprise ideas on the universality of religion; on its varieties, on religion in itself, and on its relation to morality. There can be no attempt at a universal confession of faith, for that is far distant.

I. *Universality of Religion.*—To the supreme cause of life must be attributed the radical difference between humanity and animality. It is religion more than all else that differentiates man from the animal. It is a fact whose universality has been vainly contested, which is met as far back as one can go, as far as one can penetrate in the present, which is complex, indefinable, diverse and varied, and yet rests upon something fundamental and substantial, since it bears a common name. Man is by nature a religious being. The absence of religious ideas among peoples on the lowest planes has been asserted, but profounder observation has always proven the allegation erroneous. Religion is a characteristic of human nature. Its continual manifestations, its unceasing action on nations and the mind, and its terrors and joys, passions and activities incontrovertibly prove it an

"Conditions and Outlook for a Universal Religion" by Albert Réville. Reprinted from John Henry Barrows, ed., *The World's Parliament of Religions*, 2 vols. (Chicago: Parliament Publishing Company, 1893), 2:1363-67.

integral part of our constitution. The radically irreligious man is either aborted, infirm or mutilated.

II. *Diversities of Religions.*—Religion has a vast variety of forms and of principles determining them. But fundamental principles dominate these phenomena. A fundamental difference divides them into two groups: monotheistic religions and polytheistic religions. In the monotheistic group man conceives of a single, sovereign Power identical with the first and absolute cause. (The principle implies, as corollary, a central unity of the universe.) Monotheism presents itself under various forms: Judaism, Christianity, Islam, and even Buddhism (Law is Buddhism's supreme god). Polytheism supposes the plurality of the beings who determine the mode of existence and the combination of things. The distinction between monotheism and polytheism is not primitive. Polytheism existed first. The formation of monotheism was due to circumstances of race, place and mental predisposition; but as reason grows stronger and richer, monotheism must finally win the first place. Polytheism contains some sub-groups which in their world-idea approximate to that which is the basis or consequence of monotheism, while others separate from it entirely. In turn many forms of monotheism manifest a continual tendency to moderate the rigor of its principle of divine unity by approximating toward polytheism. In spite of the distinctions which assign religious phenomena to clearly separated categories, the differences do not prevent the opposite principles from becoming weakened at numerous points of contact almost to complete effacement.

Another fact impresses a very marked distinctive character upon monotheistic religions. It manifests itself in the religions which profess to proceed from a supernatural revelation by the One Cause. This fact is intolerance. It says: The special religion revealed by God either through priest or book is alone the absolute truth to which every man is bound to adhere under pain of perdition. Yet intolerance springs from keenest appreciation of religious truth. To escape the indifference which engulfs polytheistic religions in prolonged stagnation it was necessary to pass through intolerance. But it has inflicted terrible evils. At last human feeling, seconded by better understanding of the principles of the highest religion, revolted against theories justifying such horrors.

The great religions remain separated. Shall irreconcilable antagonism be the last word of the history of religion on earth? May there not be, without denying the superiority that each attributes to his own religion, hope for an agreement in the future, founded on rational appreciation of those elements of truth which constitute the substance of a universal religion? For that, it is indispensable to define religion.

III. *Religion in itself.*—There is not yet unanimity in the definition of religion, but the true definition should take account of four facts: (1) Man experiences the need of attaching himself to a Power dominating the phenomena which fill his daily life. (2) His idea of this Power has intimate relations with those of the nature of the world and of himself. (3) His feeling of the existence and action of this Supreme Power is associated with his difficulty, if not inability, in forming an idea of this Sovereign Reality which fully satisfies his reason. (This reality always hides itself behind mystery: the feeling of mystery is always inseparable from the religious sentiment; and sometimes the mystery provokes the sentiment, sometimes the mystery is derived from the sentiment.) (4) The postulate of a supramundane power does not remain an abstraction. It acts powerfully upon life. The religious man seeks to unite personally, in feeling and action, with the Supreme Being. From this practical relation with divinity he derives great joys and tragic terrors. This blending of terror and joy is a characteristic of religion. From such fourfold observation religion may be defined as that special determination of human nature which causes man to seek, above all contingent things, union with a sovereign and mysterious Power, at once attractive and formidable, and impels him to realize this union by acts in keeping with his idea of that Power.

Religion is, therefore, the exercise of the innate natural tendency of the mind. This fact demonstrates the reality of the object. No matter though man form most erroneous notions of that object, or declare it incomprehensible; there could be no tendency without correspondent reality. The primordial doctrine of the religions of the future is the consubstantiality of man with God.

Former definitions have been complicated by the too frequent desire to make morality religion's point of departure or essential element. Religion and morality belong to distinct fields—one can easily imagine a moral atheist—but the two spheres elbow each other and end by uniting. When we would determine the place of religion on the ladder extending from the heavens to the earth, religion's moral worth is a criterion of the highest value.

IV. *Future of Religion.*—Religion will last as long as humanity. Will the diversity and antagonism of the historical religions continue indefinitely? Religion began at a very low level of knowledge, feeling and morality. In its origin it manifested itself under forms everywhere very similar. Thus unity characterized the rise of religion. Is it not probable that at last religion will recover fundamental agreement if not absolute uniformity, reflective and rational unity (scientifically and morally founded) bringing the diversities and hostilities of the past into one harmonious and pacific point of view?

Some forms of religion will disappear of their own accord as civilization extends and in civilized nations penetrates the deep social strata which have long been dominated by the intellectual superiority of the directing classes rather than imbued with their ideas and principles. Naturism, fetishism and polytheism are doomed. Since there are several civilizations, each will penetrate the other, and the religions associated with each will mutually interfere. But what will change the religious complexion of humanity will be the civilization intellectually and morally dominant over the others. It will render universal a mental state to which corresponds the religion sustained and dominated by that condition. Till these predictions be realized can there not be a *modus cogitandi* preparatory to a *modus vivendi* which would replace hostile relations by mutual esteem and good will? We may indicate its elements.

The recognition of religion as inherent and universal requires us to judge even its strangest forms worthy of all respect. In the most uncultured religions are augustness, venerableness and revelation. Man's attempt to commune with ideal Perfection is the fundamental and loftiest truth of human nature. Our duty is to apply this truth to our relations with every religion. For the believer in a collection of truths directly revealed by God it is difficult to recognize valid right in the beliefs of those who reject that revelation, oppose another to it, or reject all miraculous revelation. Paul, however, admitted a degree of inferior revelation worthy of sympathetic veneration. The points upon which religions professing to arise from another revelation accord with the religion of a definite revelation should be to its adherents fragments of divine truth due to natural origin. This is another basis for mutual tolerance and cooperation. The work for theologians and scholars is to seek in each religion its essential foundation. Only when the principles dominating details have been brought out, can rational religious comparison be proceeded with, which shall assign to each religion its right place, its definite rite, in the religion of humanity.

Meanwhile, morals furnish a neutral ground where all religious friends of humanity can meet. Men are everywhere nearer to an understanding of man's duties toward his fellows than of definitions of belief and dogma. Morality is the most active agent in the evolution of religion. The Christian inspired in his relation to non-Christian religions by the truth that purity, integrity, benevolence, active sympathy for every man suffering, the triumphant beauty of gentleness, pardon and generosity, are of universal morality, renders homage to a teaching whose authority he cannot as a Christian contest, whose sublimity he cannot as a thinker deny. Upon morality can be established a sympathetic understanding among the religions.

At present it would be vain to seek doctrinal accord among the great religions. But preparations for that accord can be made by pacifying their relations. This pacification can be obtained by respecting all forms of religious sentiment, by recognizing natural revelation, and by emphasizing the moral content and worth of each religion. This parliament marks the first step in the sacred path that shall one day bring man to the truly humanitarian and universal religion.

Principles of the Scientific Classification of Religions

Jean Réville

The variety of classifications proposed proves that uncertainty still exists as to the principles of classification. This arises from two facts: our knowledge is incomplete; we come to no common understanding as to the characteristics of the several religions.

The chief hindrance to a scientific determination of religions historically known is that each of them includes under a single name the most widely different phenomena.

Rule 1. Recognize that religions are not fixed quantities, nor invariable organic systems, but living organic products of the human mind, in perpetual flux, even when they seem fixed; that under seemingly like external forms they may include very different contents; that in each historic religious unit may be individual manifestations as varied as individual capacities in any modern people. In an inferior religious system may be found ideas, sentiments and practices of a superior order, and inversely. The science of religions is a moral science, and its classifications cannot be rigorous like those of natural science.

"Principles of the Scientific Classification of Religions" by Jean Réville. Reprinted from John Henry Barrows, ed., *The World's Parliament of Religions*, 2 vols. (Chicago: Parliament Publishing Company, 1893), 2:1367-69.

Rule 2. Exclude every abstract principle of classification imposed from without by a philosophical or theological system, and not springing from the facts themselves. Discard as anti-scientific any classification resting upon a distinction between revealed religion and natural religion, primitive monotheism and polytheism, or proposed by the speculative idealism of the Hegelian school, or of the symbolic school, or by the positivism of Comte, or by any systematic or dogmatic notion of history.

Rule 3. Found the classification of religions, to begin with, exclusively on the historic analysis of religious facts and phenomena. Examine inscriptions, documents, national poets, historians, philosophers and dramatists; study cults, rites, practices, popular traditions, usages and morals; examine monuments, plastic representations and religious utensils. Make this analysis in chronological order for each religion historically known, relying on the clearer documents to interpret the more obscure, and applying the general rules of historical criticism. It is better that this should be done by a man who knows by experience what religious thought or emotion is.

Rule 4. In analyzing each religion never forget that it is intimately connected with the civilization of its country, and that if, for convenience of exposition, we study the religion apart from other manifestations of that civilization, we need to keep constantly in view its social environment.

Rule 5. In the most ancient teachings in regard to every religion, as well as in the manifestations of superior religions among their least civilized adherents, we constantly meet beliefs and practices just like those of peoples still uncivilized. In order to understand these primeval or inferior manifestations belonging to a time or a social plane that have no history, we must make a preliminary study of the present religions of uncivilized tribes; not in pursuance of any evolutionist theory, but simply to explain facts otherwise unintelligible by like facts among peoples within reach of our observation.

Rule 6. Complete the analysis of each religion by comparison with the analyses of other religions. Comparison brings out their common characteristics and specific differences, and permits classification in various categories. Such classification may afford instruction, but does not generally offer scientific exactitude without dissecting the history of religions at their various stages of development.

Rule 7. Complete thus the historical criticism by whatever testimonies the analyses have brought to light, clearing up what is obscure in one religion by what is clear in others.

Rule 8. Make this comparison with all the resources at the disposal of science, unaffected by the spirit of system or sect.

Rule 9. The comparison of results obtained by the analytico-historical study of the several religions is the basis of every scientific classification, according either to historic filiation or to form of development. We are not to find historic connection between religious phenomena separated in time or space, except when there is substantial evidence of relation, or when philology shows the common origin of names having a religious use. Otherwise the analogies may simply result from the spontaneous action of the human mind in independent but like conditions.

The study of *religions* must precede the study of *religion*. The only scientific classification is the historic. This springs from the facts instead of being imposed upon them. It is easy to understand these rules—in the present state of science it is hard to apply them.

THE COMPARATIVE STUDY
OF THE WORLD'S RELIGIONS

Charles Joseph de Harlez

It is not without profound emotion that I address myself to an assemblage of men, the most distinguished, come together from all the parts of the world, and who, despite essential divergences of opinion, are nevertheless united in this vast edifice, pursuing one purpose, animated with one thought, the most noble that can occupy the human mind, the seeking out of religious truth. I here have under my eyes this unprecedented spectacle, until now unheard of, of disciples of Kong-fu-tze, of Buddha, of Brahma, of Ahura Mazda, of Allah, of Zoroaster, of Mohammed, of Naka-nusi, or of Laotze [sic], not less than those of Moses and of the Divine Christ, gathered together not to engage in a struggle of hostility or animosity, sources of sorrow and grief, but to hold up before the eyes of the world the beliefs which they profess and which they have received from their fathers—their religion.

"The Comparative Study of the World's Religions" by Charles Joseph de Harlez. Reprinted from John Henry Barrows, ed., *The World's Parliament of Religions*, 2 vols. (Chicago: Parliament Publishing Company, 1893), 1:605-21. Portions from pp. 606, 610-12, and 613 have been omitted. All footnotes are added. A shorter version appears in Walter R. Houghton, ed., *Neely's History of the Parliament of Religions* (Chicago: Neely Publishing Company, 1894), pp. 286-91. Both Barrows and Houghton consistently mis-cite the author's name as C.D. D'Harlez.

Religion! word sublime, full of harmony to the ear of man, penetrating into the depths of his heart and stirring into vibration its profoundest chords.

How goodly the title of our program: "World's Parliament of Religions"! How true the thought put forth by one who took part in its production: "Comparison, not controversy, will best serve the most wholesome and therefore the most divine truth."

Parliament! It is in such an assemblage that the most weighty interests of humanity are discussed, that their most accredited representatives come to set forth what they believe to be most favorable to their development, to their legitimate satisfaction. But in this Parliament of Religions it is not the world that it is question of [sic], but heaven, the final happiness of man.

Truth! The most precious boon of man, which day and night he pursues with all his aspirations, with all his efforts, never fully attaining, but always tearing away more and more the veil that hides it from his view, until he shall contemplate it in its essence amidst celestial splendors.

And do not the different features, the different costumes, the different opinions of the different men and savants here assembled for peaceful deliberation, tell us clearly that all men are brothers, sprung from one Creator, from one common principle, who ought not to tear one another in fratricidal strife, but to cherish one another with mutual love, to aid one another in the pursuit of the great purpose common to all, of that unique end which must assure them happiness eternal, the possession of truth.

No! Catholics faithful to their own teaching will not be wanting in this duty, for their Divine Master has imposed upon them, as his first commandment, resuming all his law, that after the love they owe their Heavenly Father they should love their neighbor as themselves, yea, that they should know how to lay down their lives for his sake. And this neighbor for the Christian is not only the brother bound to him in the unity of faith; no, under the figure of the good Samaritan, the recognized neighbor of the unfortunate Israelite left as dead by robbers, Christ has taught us to recognize the universality of manhood. Yes, whoever you be, children of Brahma, of Shangti, of Allah, of Ahura Mazda, disciples of Kong-fu-tze, of Tao, of Buddha, of Jina, or of whatever other founder of religion amongst men, you are for us Christians that well-beloved neighbor, who may indeed be in error, but who, nonetheless, only all the more, merits all our love, all our devotedness.

[......]

Permit me now to enter upon my subject: "Importance of a Serious Study of All Systems of Religion."

But first let us ask if it is useful, if it is good to give oneself to this study. This is in effect the question which in Europe men of faith put to themselves when this new branch suddenly sprouted forth from the trunk of the tree of science. At first it inspired only repugnance, or at least great distrust. And this was not without reason. The opinions, the designs of those who made themselves its promoters inspired very legitimate suspicions. It was evident that the end pursued was to confound all religions as works of human invention, to put them all upon a common level in order to bring them all into common contempt. The comparative history of religions in the minds of its originators was to be an exposition of all the vicissitudes of human thought, imagination, and, to say the real word, folly. It was to be Darwinism, evolution, applied to religious conditions that were generally held as coming from God. Naturally, then, a large number of the enlightened faithful, some of them eminent minds, seeing only evil and danger in the new science, wished to see its study interdicted and to prevent the creation of chairs in our universities from which it might be taught.

Others, clearer of sight, better informed on prevailing ideas, on the needs of the situation, convinced besides that a divine work cannot perish, and that Providence disposes all things for the greater good of humanity, welcomed without reserve this new child of science, and by their example, as by their words, drew with them into this new field of research even the hesitating and trembling. They thought, besides, that no field of science should or could be interdicted to men of faith without placing them and their belief in a state of inferiority the most fatal, and that to abandon any one of them whatever would be to hand it over to the spirit of system and to all sorts of errors. They judged that any science, seriously controlled in its methods, can only concur in bringing about the triumph of the truth, and that eternal truth must come forth victorious from every scientific discussion, unless its defenders, from a fear and mistrust, injurious alike for it and its divine author, abandon it and desert its cause.

Convinced, therefore, that all mistrust of success is an outrage to truth, they set themselves resolutely to the task, and results have fully justified their confidence and their foresight.

Today the most timid Christian, be he ever so little in touch with the circumstances of the times, no longer dreads in the least the chimerical monsters pictured to his imagination at the dawn of these new studies, and follows with as much interest as he formerly feared the researches, the discoveries, which the savants lay before him.

What study today excites more attention and interest than the comparative study of religions? What object more preoccupies the minds of men than the one resumed in that magic word, Religion! In Christian countries, and this qualification embraces the whole of Europe, with the exception of Turkey, and all of America, three classes of men may be distinguished by their disposition and attitude towards religious questions. Some possessing the truth, descended from on high, study it, search into its depths with love and respect. Others, at the very opposite pole, animated by I-do-not-know-what spirit, wage against it an incessant warfare, and do their utmost to stifle it; others, in fine, ranged between these two extremes, plunged into doubt, ask themselves anxiously what there is in these truths which they see on the one hand exalted with enthusiasm and on the other attacked with fury. In no way formed by education to submit their intelligence to dogmas which they cannot understand, nor to regulate their conduct by inflexible moral precepts, hearing however within them a voice which calls upon them to rise above themselves, they are cast about upon a sea of doubt and anguish, in vain demanding of the earth the balm to cure the evil from which their hearts suffer.

Yes, this voice whispers to their ears the most redoubtable problems that ever man proposed. Whence comes he? Who has placed him upon this earth? Whither does he go? What is his end? What must he do to secure it? Immense horizons of happiness or of misery open out before him, how manage to avoid the one and reach the other?

Long did men seek to stifle the whispered murmurings of conscience; it has triumphed over all resistance. Today, more than ever, as it has been so energetically said, "Man is homesick for the Divine." The Divine! The unbeliever has sought to drive it out through every pass; it has come back more triumphant than ever. So today souls not enlightened by the divine light feel an indefinable uneasiness such as that experienced by the aëronaut[1] in the supra-terrestrial regions of rarefied atmosphere, such as that of the heart when air and blood fail. It is what a French writer belonging to the meditative rationalistic school has so well expressed: "Those who confine themselves to earthly pursuits feel, even in the midst of success, that something is still wanting; that is, whatever they say and whatever they do, man has not only a body to nourish and an intelligence to cultivate and develop, but he has, I emphatically affirm, a soul to satisfy. This soul, too, is in incessant travail, in continual evolution towards the light and the truth. As long as she has not received all light and conquered all truth, so long will she torment man." Yes, man,

Ce dieu tombé qui se souvient des cieux,[2]

as the poet says, finds his soul restless and perplexed when he has not received those glimmers of light which shone upon his cradle.

These aspirations, these indefinable states of the soul in presence of the dreaded unknown, today so common in our midst, are without doubt not unknown in the regions of Asia and Africa. There, too, rationalism, agnosticism, imported from Europe, has made its inroads. But on the other hand, such incertitude is not entirely new. Twenty-five centuries ago the Vedist poets proposed the very problems which today perplex the unbeliever, as we see in the celebrated hymn thought to be addressed to a god, Ka, the fruit of the imagination of interpreters, since this word Ka was merely an interrogative used by the singer of the Ganges in asking what hand had laid the foundation of the world; upon whom depended life and death; who upheld the earth and the stars, etc., questions to which the poet could give only this reply, sad avowal of impotence: "*Kavaiō kō viveda*, Sacred chanters, who knows?"[3]

About the same time, in Asia, another hierophant interrogated his god after the same manner, as we see in the Gatha ix. of the Avesta:

"I beg of thee to tell me in truth, O! Ahura," said he, "what is the origin of Paradise? Who was the procreator, the first father of

---

[1] I.e., the pilot of a hot-air balloon.

[2] From Alphonse de Lamartine, "L'Homme," from his *Premières Méditations poétiques* (1820), in his *Oeuvres poétiques complètes*, ed. Marius-François Guyard (Paris: Gallimard, 1963), p. 6. The quote is taken from the following couplet: "Borné dans sa nature, infini dans ses voeux, / L'homme es un dieu tombé qui se souvient des cieux" ("Finite in his nature, infinite in his desires, / Man is a fallen god who remembers heaven" [Translation mine; Ed.]).

[3] For a standard English rendering of this hymn, see *The Rig Veda: An Anthology*, trans. Wendy Doniger (O'Flaherty) (London: Penguin, 1981), 10.121, pp. 26-28.

sanctity? Who set the sun and the moon in their ways? Who sustains the earth and the clouds? Who gives swiftness to the winds and directs the course of the clouds? What workman with consummate skill has produced the light and the darkness? Who with power has created wisdom sublime? What are thy ordinances and thy teachings? By what sort of sanctification must the world obtain its perfection? How shall I repel the demon? What will be the chastisement of those who repel thy law?"[4]

We see from these short extracts to what a height the reformer of Iran had already raised himself, and how his eye had already caught a glimpse of many of the mysteries of the metaphysical and moral world; how besides his soul was agitated and troubled looking up to that heaven which sent him no light. At the other extremity of the world, the greatest philosopher that China produced, or rather the greatest moralist whose lessons she has preserved, Kong-fu-tze, or, as we call him, Confucius, was bearing witness to the impotence of the mind of man to penetrate the secrets of heaven. To the question which his disciples proposed as to the condition of the soul on leaving this world, he replied by this despairing evasion: "We do not even know life, how can we know death?" *Wei tchi seng, yen tchi sze.*[5]

How many souls at all times and in all parts of the world have been tortured by the same doubts and perplexities? What age has ever counted more than ours?

What then should be the course of men tossed about by incertitude, indefinite aspirations, fear and hope? What, if not to confront the religious problem under all its aspects, to follow all the manifestations of the religious sentiment, to understand their gravity, their bearing, and to seek out under the protection of God, of the God whom their souls know not, the way of truth?

[......]

...The comparative study of religions, better than any other, teaches what ideas constitute the common patrimony of humanity, what consequently belong to human nature and are conformed to reality, for real nature is true. The advocates of unalterable and uncontrolled

---

[4] For an alternate English rendering, see Yasna 44 of the Gāthat Ustavaiti, verses 3-5 in *The Zend-Avesta*, part 3 (of 3 parts), trans. L.H. Mills, in *The Sacred Books of the East*, 50 vols., ed. F. Max Müller (Oxford: Clarendon, 1879-1910), 31:113-14.

[5] A more recent and standard rendering in English reads: "Till you know about the living, how are you to know about the dead?" (*The Analects of Confucius*, trans. Arthur Waley [London: Allen and Unwin, 1938; reprint, New York: Random House, no date], book 11, no. 11, p. 155).

laws in the external world cannot here dissent. Those who believe in a God, the author of this nature, will believe more firmly still, and doubtless not less those who, with the Buddhists, conceive an eternal Dharma, a blind and immutable law, drawing all things into the whirl of irresistible action. The more general, then, both in time and in place, the consent of men upon a dogmatic question, the more will the truth of such a widespread notion impose itself upon minds sincere and not already fixed upon preconceived systems. It is evident on the other hand that in this kind of appreciation it is necessary to take special count of civilized peoples, of those whose intelligence has attained a certain degree of development, and only very little of those unfortunate tribes which have hardly anything more of man than the bodily form.

I come then to consider the important side of the study of religion, that is to say, the results it has to the present day produced and what it is called upon to produce in the future.

How many points cleared up in a few years, thanks to the control exercised upon the first explorers in this field by those who came after them and who had no ready-made system to defend. This is specially true for two concepts upon which we shall principally dwell: the nature of religion and its origin.

[......]

[The study of the religions of the world] has in fact demonstrated in a manner which allows no reasonable doubt that religion is not a creation of the mind of man, still less of a wandering imagination deceived by phantoms, but that it is a principle which imposes itself upon him everywhere and always, and in spite of himself, which comes back again violently into life at the moment it was thought to be stifled, which, try as one may to cast it off from him, enters again, as it were, into man by his every pore.

There is no people without religion, how low soever it may be in the scale of civilization. If there be any in whom the religious idea seems extinct, though this cannot be certainly shown, it is because their intelligence has come to that degree of degradation, in which it has no longer anything human, save the capacity of being lifted to something higher.

Doubtless it is not among idiots that we are to seek out the essential qualities of the human intellect, nor among withered and etiolated plants that we are to study the nature of vegetable life. No more are degenerate beings preserved as the primo-ideal types of their respective species. Still less can a few miserable savage tribes be held as specimens of the first human beings.

The explanations that have been offered of the religious sentiment inborn in man, might be qualified as "truly curious and amusing were it not question of matter so grave."

For some it is *unreflecting instinct*. Be it so; but whence comes this instinct? Doubtless from nature. And nature, what is it? It is reality as we have said. True instinct does not deceive.

For others religion arises from the need man experiences of relationship with superior beings. Correct again. But how has man conceived the notion of beings superior to himself if there are none, and whence arises that natural need which his heart *feels*, if it has its root in nothing, a non-entity? *Ex nihilo nihil*, from nothing nothing comes. Shall I speak of that "celestial harmony which charms the soul and lifts it into an ideal world," of "those visions which float through the imagination of man," and of other like fancies? No, it would be to waste inconsiderately the time of my honored hearers, too precious to be taken up by such trifles. Let us merely note this fact fully attested today. Religious sentiments and concepts are innate in man, they enter into the constitution of his nature, which itself comes from its author and Master; they impose themselves as a duty upon man, as the declaration of universal conscience attests. The idea of a being superior to humanity, its master, comes from the very depths of human nature, and is rendered sensible to the intellect by the spectacle of the universe. No reasonable mind can suppose that this vast world has of itself created or formed itself. This is so true that men of science, the most hostile to religion, the moment they perceive some evidence of design upon a stone, however deeply imbedded in the earth, themselves proclaim *that man has passed here*. And this admirable universe, nay, even that little instrument so wonderful, the human eye, would have been made without anyone putting hand to it! No, a reasonable mind which does not fight against itself for the sake of a system, cannot contradict itself to that degree.

The studies upon which I have the honor of speaking before the World's Parliament have not been less productive as to the explanation of the origin of religions. For upon this ground, as upon the preceding, opinions the most strange, the least rational and the most contradictory, have successively sprung up.

"It is fear that has made the gods," said a Latin poet already two thousand years ago.[6] No, say others, it is a mere tendency to attribute a soul to whatever moves itself. You are mistaken, says a third, it is reverence for deceased ancestors which caused their descendants yet remaining upon earth, to regard them as superior beings. You are astray, exclaims a fourth voice, religion does not arise from any one or other of these or like causes in particular, but from all taken together. Fear, joy, illusions, nocturnal visions, the movements of the stars, etc., etc., have all contributed something, each its own part.

It is not our task to set forth these different opinions, still less to criticize them. We cannot pass in silence the system, till of late universally in vogue in the free-thinking camp, a system whose foundations historical studies have uprooted. I speak of the theory which has borrowed its process from the Darwinian system of evolution, the system of perpetual progress. If you would believe its authors and defenders, primitive humanity had no religious sentiment, not the least notion that raised it above material nature. But feeling in himself a living principle, man attributed the same to whatever moved about him, and thence arose fetishism and animism, which merely endow sensible beings with a living principle, and in some cases with intelligence. This thesis once admitted, there was then a question only of primitive fetishism and animism; it was proposed as an axiom, as a first truth above all demonstration, against which no argument could prevail. They did not perceive, or they did not wish to perceive, that this was a mere begging of the question, an offshoot of the imagination without any root in the ground of facts. They nonetheless continued, however, to build up this castle of cards. After the first stage of fetishism and animism, man would have considered separately the living principles of the beings to which he had attributed it, and this separation would have given rise to the belief in spirits. These spirits growing upon the popular imagination would have become gods, to whom ultimately, after the fashion of earthly empires, they would have given a head. These gods would have at first been exclusively national, then a universal empire would have been

---

[6] Petronius Arbiter (d. 60 C.E.), Fragment 27.1: *Primus in orbe deos fecit timor*. This line is incorporated verbatim by Statius (45-96) in his *Thebaid*, 3.661, and adapted by M. de (Prosper Jolyot) Crébillon in his *Xerxès* (1714), through the voice of Artaban (act 1, sc. 1): "La crainte fit les dieux, l'audace a fait les rois" (*Oeuvres de Crébillon*, 2 vols. [Paris: A.-A. Renouard, 1818], 1:366).

imagined, and national religions would have at length ended, as a last effort of the human mind, in universal religions.

Here, indeed, we have an edifice wonderfully planned and perfectly constructed. This would appear still more plainly were we to describe in detail its parts. Unfortunately one thing is wanting—one thing only, but essential—that is *a little grain of truth*. Not only is the whole of it the fruit of hypothesis without foundation in facts, but religious studies have demonstrated all and each of its details to be false.

First, fetishism is not at all what it was gratuitously pretended to be. The studies of A.B. Ellis, an English Major, whose impartiality is beyond question, have completely put aside the accredited legend.

He had set out for Africa, he himself avows, imbued with the notions which *form the storehouse and equipment* of the greater part of those who occupy themselves with the comparative study of religions. And he expected to find among the negroes of the Gold Coast beliefs and practices in entire conformity with his preconceived ideas. Great, then, was his surprise when he found out that it was nothing of the kind, and that the fetishes were purely and simply *the homes or dwelling places of immaterial divinities*. "This explanation," says he, "differs so much *from all that I had read and heard upon the matter, that I mistrusted it greatly*. It was only after a long examination continued during many months, that I acknowledged myself overcome. No one should be surprised at this; my first convictions were formed by extensive and prolonged studies, and it was necessary for me to have the evidence of facts many times attested in order to put aside my first ideas. Months were necessary to convince me of my error. Several times, also, I thought I had grasped the ideas of the savages, and more attentive examination proved to me that I had been entirely out of the way. Convinced by these repeated experiences, I do not hesitate to say: I no longer believe that fetishism has ever existed, such as it is understood by the partisans of the necessity of a primordial fetishism. Certainly if this theory has no other basis than the supposed religious state of the negroes of Africa, it is utterly without foundation."[7]

---

[7] Although placed between quote marks in the *WPR* text of this paper, this is a paraphrase from A.B. (Alfred Burdon) Ellis (1852-94), *The Tshi-speaking Peoples of the Gold Coast of West Africa: Their Religion, Manners, Customs, Laws, Language, Etc.* (London: Chapman and Hall, 1887), p. 185-86, 189-90. In the *WPR* and *NHP* texts of the present paper, the surname Willis is consistently and erroneously given for Ellis, and the term "Tshi-" from the title is misspelled "Tsi-" in a footnote. The same footnote, the only one accompanying the entire paper, mentions that A.B. Willis (sic) was "Major First West India Regiment." A.B. Ellis did indeed

The learned and truth-loving Major adds this reflection, which would strike everyone if the necessities of a pet system permitted the truth to be recognized. This primitive fetishism is an impossible thing; it could have been produced only when primitive religious ideas had lost their preponderance. To spiritize a stone, a block of wood, one must first have believed in a spirit; to have there imprisoned a god, one must have beforehand believed in a divinity. This is mere elementary logic.

If, moreover, you would know something of the concepts of these so-called fetish peoples, listen to this fragment of cosmogony. See how they here speak to their god:

"For thee, O Whaï, I have great love! From the germ of life arose thought, came the proper instrument of God. Then came the flower and the fruit, and life produced in space the worlds of the night. It was nothing that begot, that nothing foreign to all, that nothing devoid of charm.

"Night conceived its germ and the germ arose existing in itself. It grew in obscurity, and the sap and the juice of life beat with pulsations. I saw dart forth light and the ecstasy of life. Also the productions of the great one (God) spreading out all things filled the heavens and their vast space."

Thus under the hand of god who extends being and creates it, all things spring from nothing, life darts forth and life arises.

These notions, says Max Müller with reason, are superior to many found in the cosmogonies of civilized peoples.

False in its basis, as has been seen, the theory of religious evolution has been battered down in nearly all its positions by the results of the comparative study of religion.

The examples of Egypt, of India, and of China especially, have demonstrated that monotheism real, though imperfect, preceded the luxuriant mythologies whose development astonishes, but is only too easily explained.

In Egypt the divinity was first represented by the sun, then the different phases of the great luminary were personified and deified. In the most ancient portions of Aryan India, the personality of Varuna, with his immutable laws, soars above the figures of Indra and the other devas, who have in great part dethroned him, just as the Jupiter

---

bear that title, as indicated beneath his name on the title-page of *The Tshi-speaking Peoples*, and he also wrote a *History of the First West India Regiment* (London: Chapman, 1885).

of the Greeks supplanted the more ancient Pelasgian Uranos. Among these two last peoples, it is true, monotheism is at its lowest degree; but in China, on the contrary, it shows itself much less imperfect than elsewhere and even with a relative purity. Shang-ti is almost the God of the spritualist philosophy. These facts, we may easily conceive, are exceedingly embarrassing for the adherents of the evolutionary theory; but they worm out of the difficulty in a manner that provokes both sadness and a smile. "It is true," says one, "that monotheism preceded polytheism in Egypt, but *it must* have been itself preceded by primitive animism." This "it must" is worth a measure of gold. Another author whom the sacred books of the Chinese embarrass by sustaining the same theory, simply maintains that these ancient works were composed in the third century before our era. One knows not how to qualify such inexcusable assertions. The thesis of national divinities everywhere preceding the universal divinities is not more solidly grounded. For neither Varuna, nor Brahma, nor Shang-ti, nor Tengri, ever saw their power limited by their devotees to a single country. The theory that fear or ancestral worship gave birth to the gods, receives in China the most formal contradiction. In fact, at the very first appearance of this great empire upon the scene of history, the supreme deity was already considered as the father, the mother, not only of the faithful, but of the entire human race; and the first to receive worship among the dead were not departed relatives, but kings and ministers, benefactors of the people. That it is gratitude which has inspired this worship, is expressly affirmed in the Chinese Ritual.

But I must pause for fear of going beyond proper limits. These considerations will amply suffice to set forth the importance of the comparative history of religions, made under suitable conditions. It remains for us to say a few words about these conditions.

The first is clearly that enunciated in our program. These studies ought to be serious and strictly scientific. They should be based upon strict logic and a thorough knowledge of the original sources. Too long have would-be adepts been given over to fantastic speculations, everywhere seeking an apology for either faith or incredulity. Too long have they limited themselves to superficial views, to summary glimpses, dwelling with complacency upon whatever might favor a pet system. Or else they have been content with documents at second-hand, whose authors themselves had but an imperfect knowledge of what they pretended to treat as masters.

Today the ideas of the learned world and the acknowledged laws of truth no longer tolerate this too easy method of dealing with a science the most important in its results that has ever occupied the human mind. One must now go to the sources themselves and to only the best; must consult native interpreters and above all those who give assurance of fidelity, of complete veracity, by their age not too far removed from the facts which they relate, by their personal character, by the proofs of competence which they give, by their moral integrity, etc.

We may easily understand that in order to be able to choose among them all and to distinguish the sources, it is necessary to know thoroughly the language and the history, both political and literary, of the people whose religious beliefs one would investigate and expose. It is necessary to be a specialist and a specialist competent in this special matter. It is only when the work of such authorized and impartial specialists has been done, that others will be able to draw from the waters which they have collected.

It has been said, it is true, that specialists, too much occupied with details, blinded even by their dust, are incapable of those broad views which are necessary to erect the grand edifices of science. Were this as true as it is false, what would it avail these men of far-reaching vision, or who at least think themselves such, to have constructed an edifice magnificent in appearance, if it is built of worm-eaten wood and sandstone, which breaks or chips off in pieces and can only serve to strew the ground with rubbish?

How many errors fatal to true science have been propagated by men too prone to generalize! Thus some, seeing in a translation of Chinese books that heaven and earth are the father and mother of men, recalled the Uranos and Gea of Hellas, the Dyâvâpethivi of India, and decided that China also had its divine pair, heaven spouse and father, the sea spouse and mother. Now nothing is more false than this explanation. In Chinese, fu-mu, "father-mother," is a compound word whose elements are not taken apart and applied to distinct personages. There is here nothing about a pair of spouses, so much so that in the following phrase, it is said that the sovereign is fu-mu, father-mother of the people. The Chinese author wishes simply to say that heaven and earth sustain and nourish man as parents provide for their children. Nothing more. Adieu then to this celestio-terrestrial pair.

Others have seen in the Tchong or *miem* of the Chinese the *medium* of the Stoics in which virtue consists. Now, this Tchong is a different thing altogether, namely the state of the heart, which like the beam of a balance, keeps always in the middle, inclining neither to the right nor to the left, that is, without any desire of exterior things.

Many also, among those for example who have treated of the religions of China and India, have drawn from the sources without due regard to their different epochs and origins, confounding ages and countries and races, and making of the religious history of these lands the most inextricable hotchpotch ever produced by human pen. We have seen even an acknowledged Chinese scholar present as an antique work, as a source having escaped the influences of Confucianism, the Chinese Ritual (*Li-Ki*) compiled and almost entirely invented in the third century before our era, and the greater part of which is made up of discourses put into the mouth of Confucius.

We have likewise seen a French magistrate flood the world with pamphlets in which he demonstrated by cited texts that the Christian Bible had been copied from the sacred books of India. Now these texts were all false. Nothing is found of them among the monuments of India. And who but a specialist could discover and denounce the fraud?

This leads us to consider the second condition for the serious study of the comparative history of religions; it is the necessity of penetrating oneself with the spirit of the people who form the object of particular research. It is necessary, as it were, to think with their mind and to see with their eyes, making entire abstractions of one's own ideas, under pain of seeing everything in a false light as one sees nature through a colored glass, and of forming religious ideas the most erroneous, and often even the most unjust. What European could, for example, form an exact notion of the *Sadasat*, the being-non-being of the Brahmans (which is not that of Hegel), or the *Khi* of the Chinese, or of the *Dharma* of the Buddhists, if he had not upon these concepts precise and complete ideas? Now to acquire them one must make tabula rasa of his own conceptions, and dream with these peoples; he must also, as is naturally understood, have an exact knowledge of their manner of speaking, of their language and its peculiar terms.

But to arrive at this it is necessary besides to study all religions, even those we may believe to be entirely false, with perfect impartiality, and, I would say even, with a certain sympathy. We are tempted to look upon them as mere products of man's perversity, of his passions, of the ambition of some personage eager for renown, even of the demon. There are certainly some whose origin is far from being pure; besides my honored hearers will all doubtless agree that they cannot be all at the same time true; some among them, and the number must be considerable, are founded in error.

No one will, I think, pretend that God can be at the same time Jupiter, Brahma, Siva, Shamas, Amitabha, etc., etc., or that he authorizes upon the borders of the Ganges or of the Hoang-Ho, what he forbids as a crime against nature at Rome or at Washington, or that he has in the same way sent upon earth his Christ and Mohammed.

In any case, if the first to make innovations without mission, to deny God through fear or cupidity, rendered themselves grievously culpable, we cannot judge the same of men who, raised in a religion in which they sincerely believe, are not ready to abandon it unless an irresistible conviction of their obligation to do so, takes possession of their souls. The ascetic, faithful to his duty, disciple of a religion which we know to be false, but which he thinks true and heaven-inspired, certainly merits our esteem and sympathy so long as we do not know that he resists an interior light which clearly unveils to him the emptiness of his practices.

Are some of our brethren in error? If they are sincere, let us pity them, love them with our whole heart. If they are not, if they resist conscience, let us pity them yet more; let us strive to enlighten them, but by efforts which spring from the heart and go straight to the soul. The heart once gained, the last redoubt of the fortress of the soul is captured.

Besides, how many elevated thoughts, admirable maxims are to be found in certain sacred books of religions very far from our own. The Shis of the Chinese, the sacred chant of Bhagavad Gita or revelations of Krishna to his faithful disciple, the laws of Manu, for instance, would supply us many examples if time permitted me to insert them in this discourse.

Let us begin here, if we would see the truth illumine the eyes of those who look upon these sacred books as inspired. These bright glimpses of truth, these treasures so precious, received from their fathers, will greatly aid them in finding again the true way. No one of my own faith will have, I am confident, the weakness to be troubled at these points of resemblance. They simply show that religious and moral ideas are the common good of humanity, coming to us from nature, and through it from nature's Author.

Permit me to say this word in conclusion: My brothers in our common Creator and Father who now listen to me, we are yet far apart by the diversity of our beliefs, let us at least draw nearer to one another from the present by that brotherly love which is of order divine. That there be no longer among us prepossessions, antipathies of race or doctrine. You see that we Christians study your doctrines, and we wish to do it with justice and good will. You, on your part, study ours, study seriously the Christian faith, the Catholic faith; and these last words I address also to our brothers, Christian like ourselves, but separated from us. Study it not in the works of those who misrepresent it, nor of those who do not recognize its claims; but in the works of its authorized representatives, or its legitimate interpreters. No longer allow yourselves to be told, for example, that Catholics adore the saints, whilst in their eyes the most exalted amongst them, even the Virgin Mother of Christ, are but pure creatures, who owe all their greatness to the divine will. No longer allow that infallibility, so restricted, recognized by our Church, to be confounded in your presence with absolute inerrancy and even impeccability.

Let truth, love, the service of our common Master and Father who is in heaven, be our common good, whilst we hope that one day may be realized the words of the Divine Teacher of men, that the earth will have but one tongue to praise the Creator, and but one sheepfold where its children will find themselves bound together in a union of thought as well as of heart.

SERIOUS STUDY
OF ALL RELIGIONS

Eliza Read Sunderland

My thesis bears the impress of the nineteenth century—the century par excellence in scientific research and classification, which has given us the new lessons of the telescope, the spectroscope and stellar photography; the new earth of geology, chemistry, mineralogy, botany and zoology; and the new humanity of ethnology, philology, psychology, and hierology.

What is the value of this work? I am asked to respond only for one department of it, namely—that of hierology, or the comparative study of religions.

What is the value and importance of a comparative study of religions? What lessons has it to teach? I may answer, first, that the results of hierology form part of the great body of scientific truth, and as such have a recognized scientific value as helping to complete a

"Serious Study of All Religions" by Eliza R. Sunderland. Reprinted from John Henry Barrows, ed., *The World's Parliament of Religions*, 2 vols. (Chicago: Parliament Publishing Company, 1893), 1:622-38. A virtually identical version appears, with several extra introductory paragraphs, in Walter R. Houghton, ed., *Neely's History of the Parliament of Religions* (Chicago: Neely Publishing Company, 1894), pp. 275-86. In the present text, numbered section breaks and all footnotes are added, minor spelling changes are made, though not of names or foreign terms, and a lengthy excursus is omitted (pp. 626-28 of the Barrows text).

knowledge of man and his environment; and I shall attempt to show that a serious study by an intelligent public of the great mass of facts already gathered concerning most of the religions of the world will prove of great value in at least two directions—first, as a means of general; second, as a means of religious culture. Matthew Arnold defines culture as "the acquainting ourselves with the best that has been known and said in the world, and thus with the history of the human spirit."[1] This is a nineteenth-century use of the word.

1.

The Romans would have used instead *humanitas*, or, with an English plural, "the humanities," to express a corresponding thought. The schoolmen, adopting the Latin term, limited its application to the languages, literature, history, art, and archaeology of Greece and Rome, assuming that thither the world must look for the most enlightening and humanizing influences, and, in their use of the word, contrasting these as human products with "divinity," which completed the circle of scholastic knowledge. But the world of the nineteenth century is larger than that of mediaeval Europe, and we may well thank Mr. Arnold for a new word suited to the new times, Culture—acquainting ourselves with the best that has been known and said in the world, and thus with the history of the human spirit. This will require us to know a great body of literature; but when we inquire for the best we shall find ourselves confronted by a vast mass of religious literature. Homer was a great religious poet, Hesiod also. The central idea in all the great dramas of Aeschylus, Sophocles, and Euripides, was religious, and no one need hope to penetrate beneath the surface of any of these who has not a sympathetic acquaintance with the religious ideas, myths, and mythologies of the Greeks. Dante's *Divine Comedy* and Milton's *Paradise Lost* are religious poems, to read which intelligently one must have an acquaintance with medieval mythology and modern Protestant theology. *Faust* is a religious poem.

Then there are the great Bibles of the world, the Christian and Jewish, the Mohammedan and Zoroastrian, the Brahman and Buddhist, and the two Chinese sacred books. It is of these books that Emerson sings:

> Out from the heart of nature rolled

---

[1] This is a close paraphrase of the initial definition Matthew Arnold gives in his *Culture and Anarchy: An Essay in Political and Social Criticism*, 3d edition, 1882, ed. Ian Gregor (Indianapolis: Bobbs-Merrill, 1971), pp. 5-6.

The burdens of the Bible old;
The litanies of nations came,
Like the volcano's tongue of flame,
Up from the burning core below,—
The canticles of love and woe.[2]

He who would be cultured in Matthew Arnold's sense of being acquainted with the history of the human spirit must know these books, and this means a patient, careful study of the growth and development of rites, symbols, myths and mythologies, traditions, creeds and priestly orders, through long centuries of time, from far away primitive nature worship up to the elaborate ritual and developed liturgy which demanded the written book.

But religion is a living power and not, therefore, to be confined to book or creed or ritual. All these religion called into being, and is itself, therefore, greater than any or all of them. So far from being confined to book and creed and ritual, religion has proved, in the words of Dr. C.P. Tiele, one of the most potent factors in human history; it has founded and overthrown nations, united and divided empires; has sanctioned the most atrocious deeds and the most cruel customs; has inspired beautiful acts of heroism, self-renunciation and devotion, and has occasioned the most sanguinary wars, rebellions and persecutions. It has brought freedom, happiness and peace to nations, and, anon, has proved a partisan of tyranny, now calling into existence a brilliant civilization, then the deadly foe to progress, science and art. All this is a part of world history, and the student who ignores it or passes over lightly the religious motive underlying it is thereby obscuring the hidden causes which alone can explain the outer facts of history.

Again, the human spirit has ever delighted to express itself in art. True culture, therefore, requires a knowledge of art. But to know the world's art without first knowing the world's religions would be to read Homer in the original before knowing the Greek alphabet. Why the vastness and gloom of the Egyptian temples? The approaches to them through long rows of sphinxes? What mean these sphinxes and the pyramids, the rock-hewn temple tombs and the obelisks of ancient Egyptian art? Why the low, earth-loving Greek temple, with all its beauty and adornment external? What is the central thought in Greek sculpture? Why does the medieval cathedral climb heavenward itself, with its massive towers and turrets?

---

[2] Lines 13-18 of "The Problem" (1839), in *The Collected Works of Ralph Waldo Emerson*, 12 vols. (Cambridge, Mass.: Riverside Press, 1903-04), 9:6-7.

What is the meaning of the tower temples of ancient Assyria and Babylon, and the mosques and minarets of Western Asia? All are symbols of religious life, and are blind and meaningless without an understanding of that life. Blot out the architecture and sculpture whose motive is strictly religious, and how great a blank remains? Painting and music, too, have been the handmaidens of religion, and cannot be mastered in their full depths of meaning save by one who knows something of the religious ideas and sentiments which gave them birth: eloquence has found its deepest inspiration in sacred themes; and philosophy is only the attempt of the intellect to formulate what the heart of man has felt after and found.

Let a student set himself the task of becoming intelligent concerning the philosophic speculations of the world, and he will soon find that among all peoples the earliest speculations have been of a religious nature, and that out of these philosophy arose. If, then, he would understand the development of philosophy, he must begin with the development of the religious consciousness in its beginnings in the Indo-Germanic race, the Semitic race, and in Christianity. Dr. Pfleiderer shows, in his *Philosophy of Religion on the Basis of Its History*:

> There could have been no distinct philosophy of religion in the ancient world, because nowhere did religion appear as an independent fact, clearly distinguished alike from politics, art and science. This condition was first fulfilled in Christianity. But no philosophy of religion was possible in mediaeval Christianity, because independent scientific investigation was impossible. All thinking was dominated either by dogmatism or by an undefined faith.[3]

If the germs of a philosophy of religion may be found in the theosophic mysticism and the anti-scholastic philosophy of the Renaissance, its real beginnings are to be found not earlier than the eighteenth century. But what a magnificent array of names in the two and a quarter centuries since Spinoza wrote his theologico-political treatise of 1670![4] Spinoza, Leibniz, Lessing, Kant, Herder, Goethe,

---

[3] Although indented in the *WPR* and *NHP* texts of this paper, this passage paraphrases, but does not directly quote, Otto Pfleiderer, *The Philosophy of Religion on the Basis of its History*, 4 vols., trans. Alexander Stewart and Allan Menzies, Theological Translation Fund Library (London: Williams and Norgate, 1886-88), 1:1-2. Cf. 4:275.

[4] The reference is to the *Tractatus theologico-politicus*, whose standard edition in English is *A Theologico-Political Treatise*, included in vol. 1 of *The Chief Works of*

Fichte, Schleiermacher, Schelling, Hegel, and, if we would follow the tendencies of philosophic religious thought in the present day, Feuerbach, Comte, Strauss, Mill, Spencer, Matthew Arnold, Arthur Schopenhauer, Von Hartmann, Lotze, Edward Caird, John Caird, and Martineau.[5] No student who aspires to an acquaintance with philosophy can afford to be ignorant of these thinkers and their thoughts, but to follow most intelligently the thought of any one of them he will need a preliminary acquaintance with hierology through the careful, painstaking, conscientious work in the study of different religions, as has been made by such scholars as Max Müller, C. P. Tiele, Kuenen, Ernest Renan, Albert Réville, Prof. Robertson Smith, Renouf, La Saussaye and Sayce.[6]

If religious thought and feeling is [sic] thus bound up with the literature, art and philosophy of the world, not less close is the relation to the language, social and political institutions, and morals of humanity. It is sacred names quite as often as any other words which furnish the philologist his links in the chain of proofs of relationship between languages. It does not need a Herbert Spencer to point out that political institutions and offices are frequently related to religion as effect to cause; the king's touch and the doctrine of divine right of kings are only survivals from the days of the medicine man and heaven-born chief.

The question concerning the relations of religion to ethics is a living one in modern thought. One class of thinkers insists that ethics is all there is of religion that can be known or can be of value to man; another that ethics if lived will of necessity blossom out into religion,

---

Benedict de Spinoza, unabridged R.H.M. Ewes translation (New York: Dover, 1951, 1955).

[5] The *WPR* and *NHP* texts of this paper erroneously give Schopenhauer the first name Hermann. The full names not supplied for the now less renowned figures of the latter half of this list, with their dates, are Eduard von Hartmann (1842-1906), a synthesizer of Schopenhauer, Hegel, Schelling, and Leibniz; Rudolf Hermann Lotze (1817-81), a German idealist; and James Martineau (1805-1900), an English Unitarian (though he rejected that label from the 1830s on). The dates of the Caird brothers—Edward, the Scottish Hegelian, and John, the philosopher, preacher, and theologian—are respectively 1835-1908 and 1820-98. Regarding Martineau, it is noteworthy that Eliza Sunderland authored *Dr. Martineau's "Study of Religion": A Summary of the Argument* (Toronto, Can., 1889), and co-authored with Jabez Thomas Sunderland a centennial tribute, *James Martineau and his Greatest Book* (Toronto, Can.: W. Tyrrell, 1905).

[6] The full-names not supplied in this list of famous nineteenth-century scholars of religions are Abraham Kuenen, Peter le Page Renouf, Pierre D. Chantepie de la Saussaye, and Archibald Henry Sayce.

since religion is only ethics touched with emotion; another that religion and ethics are two distinct things which have no necessary relation to each other, and still others who maintain that there is no high and persistent moral life possible without the sanctions of religion, and no high and worthy religion possible without an accompanying high morality; that, whatever may be true in low conditions of civilization, any religion adapted to high civilization must be ethical, and any ethical precepts or principles which are helpfully to control men's lives must be rooted in faith.

[......][7]

If the conclusions of all students of hierology shall prove in harmony with the views here expressed as to the close connection in origin and in history, between morality and religion, a connection growing closer as each rises in the scale of worth, until we find in the very highest the two indissolubly united, may we not conclude a wise dictum for our modern life to be "what God in history has joined together let not man in practice put asunder." Rather let him who would lift the world morally avail himself of the motor power of religion; him who would erect a temple of religion see to it that its foundations are laid in the enduring granite of character.

2.

I come now to the second division of my subject, namely, the value of hierology as a means of religious culture. What is religion? Ask the question of an ordinary communicant of any religious order and the answer will in all probability as a rule emphasize some surface characteristic.

The Orthodox Protestant defines it as a creed; the Catholic a creed plus a ritual—believe the doctrines and observe the sacraments; the Mohammedan as a dogma; the Buddhist as an ethical system; the Brahman as caste; Confucianism as a system of statecraft. But let the earnest student ask further for the real meaning in the worshiper of his ritual, creed, dogma, ethics, caste and political ethics, and he will find each system to be a feeling out after a bond of union between the human and the divine; each implies a mode of activity, a process by which the individual spirit strives to bring itself into harmonious

---

[7] In the omitted excursus the author considers the "problem" of the relationship of religion and ethics on the basis of "a wide and careful study of the world's religions" by recapitulating views expressed by C.P. Tiele, *Outlines of the History of Religion, to the Spread of the Universal Religions*, trans. J. Estlin Carpenter (London: Trübner, 1877; 5th ed., 1892); and Albert Réville, *Prolegomena of the History of Religions*, trans. A.S. Squire (London: Williams and Norgate, 1884).

relations with the highest power, will or intelligence. Each is of value in just so far as it is able to inaugurate some felt relation between the worshiper and the superhuman powers in which he believes. In the language of philosophy, each is a seeking for a reconciliation of the ego and the non-ego.

The earnest student will find many resemblances between all these communions, his own included. They all started from the same simple germ; they have all had a life history which can be traced, which is in a true sense a development and whose laws can be formulated; they all have sought outward expression for the religious yearning and have all found it in symbol, rite, myth, tradition, creed. The result of such a study must be to reveal man to himself in his deepest nature; it enables the individual to trace his own lineaments in the mirror, and see himself in the perspective of humanity. Prior to such study, religion is an accident of time and place and nationality; a particular revelation to this particular nation or age, which might have been withheld from him and his, as it was withheld from the rest of the world, but for the distinguishing favor of the divine sovereign of the universe in choosing out one favored people and sending to that one a special revelation of his will.

After such study religion is an attribute of humanity, as reason and language and toolmaking are; needing only a human being placed in a physical universe which dominates his own physical life, which cribs and cabins him by its inexorable laws, and, lo! defying those laws he steps out into the infinite world of faith, of hope, of aspiration, of God. The petty distinctions of savage, barbarian, civilized and enlightened sink into the background. He is a man, and by virtue of his manhood, his human nature, he worships and aspires. A comparative study of religions furnishes the only basis for estimating the relative worth of any religion.

Many of you saw and perhaps shared the smile and exclamation of incredulous amusement over the paragraph which went the rounds of the papers some months ago to the effect that the Mohammedans were preparing to send missionaries and establish a Mohammedan mission in New York City. But why the smile and exclamation? Because of our sense of the superiority of our own form of religious faith. Yet Christianity has utterly failed to control the vice of drunkenness. Chicago today is dominated by the saloons. Nor is it alone in this respect. Christian lands everywhere are dotted with poorhouses, asylums, jails, penitentiaries, reformatories, built to try to remedy evils, nine-tenths of which were caused, directly or indirectly, by the drink habit, which Christendom fails to control and is powerless to uproot. But Mohammedanism does control it in Oriental lands. Says Isaac Taylor: "Mohammedanism stands in fierce opposition to gambling; a gambler's testimony is invalid in law." And further: "Islâm is the most powerful total abstinence association in the world."[8] This testimony is confirmed by other writers and by illustration. If it can do so on the western continent as well, then what better thing could happen to New York, or to Chicago even, than the establishment of some vigorous Mohammedan missions? And for the best good of Chicago it might be well that Mayor Harrison[9] instruct the police that they are not to be arrested for obstructing the highway, if they should venture preach their temperance gospel in the saloon quarters of the city.

But if the study of all religions is the only road to a true definition of religion and classification of religions, it is quite as necessary to the intelligent comprehension of any one religion. Goethe declared long ago that he who knows but one language knows none, and Max Müller applied the adage to religion.[10] A very little thought will show the truth of the application in either case. On the old-time supposition that religion and language alike came down ready formed from Heaven, a divine gift or revelation to man, this would not be true. Complete in itself, with no earthly relationships, why should it need anything but itself for its comprehension? But modern scientific inquiry soon dispels any such theories of the origin of language and religion alike. If the absolute origin of each is lost in prehistoric shadows, the light of history shows each as a gradual evolution or development

---

[8] These statements were presumably made by the prolific English author Isaac Taylor (1785-1865), not to be confused with his son and namesake (1829-1901), the philologist and antiquarian. Cf. the former's claim: "Mohammedans, generally, are more zealous, devout, and fervent than Christians" (*Natural History of Enthusiasm*, from the 9th London edition [New York: Robert Carter, 1855], p. 226).

[9] Carter Henry Harrison (b. 1825) had been elected mayor of Chicago in 1879, 1881, 1883, and 1885, and defeated in 1891, before being elected "World's Fair Mayor" in 1893. Tragically, he was assassinated on the evening of October 28 that year—i.e., barely a month after the present paper was presented at the parliament, and two days before the official close of the Columbian Exposition.

[10] F. Max Müller, *Introduction to the Science of Religion*, Lectures delivered at the Royal Institution, 1870 (London: Longmans, Green, 1873), pp. 15-16. Goethe's saying, "Wer fremde Sprachen nicht kennt, weiss nichts von seiner eigenen," appears as no. 1015 of his *Maximen und Reflexionen* in *Goethes Werke*, 14 vols., Hamburger Ausgabe (Hamburg: Wegner, 1948-60), 12:508.

whose laws of development can to some extent be traced, whose history can be, partially at least, deciphered. But if an evolution, a development, then are both religion and language in the chain of cause and effect, and no single link of that chain can by any possibility be comprehended alone and out of relation to the link preceding and following.

Allow me to illustrate this proposition at some length. I am a Christian. I want to know the nature, meaning and import of the Christian religion. I find myself in the midst of a great army of sects all calling themselves Christians. I must either admit the claim of all or I must prove that only one has right to the name, and to do either rationally I must become acquainted with all. But they absolutely contradict each other, and some of them, at least, the original records of Christianity in both their creed and ritual.

Here is one sect that holds to the unity of God, here another that contends earnestly for a trinity; here one that worships at high altars with burning candles, processions or robed priests, elevation of the host, holy water, adoration of the Virgin Mother, and humble confessional, all in stately cathedrals with stained glass windows, pealing organ and surpliced choir; there another which deems that Christianity is foreign to all such ritual, and whose worship consists in waiting quietly for an hour within the four bare walls of the Quaker meeting house to see if the inner voice hath aught of message from the great enlightening spirit.

How account for such differences when all claim a common source? Only by tracing back the stream of Christian history to its source and following each tributary to its source, thus, if possible, to discover the origin of elements so dissimilar. Seriously entered upon the quest, we discover here a stream of influence from ancient Egypt, "through Greece and Rome bringing to Roman Catholic Christendom," so says Tiele, "the germs of the worship of the Virgin, the doctrine of the Immaculate Conception and the type of its theocracy."[11]

Another tributary brings in a stream of Neo-Platonism with its doctrine of the Word or Logos, there a stream of Greco-Roman mythology with a deifying tendency so strongly developed that it will fall in adoration equally before a Roman emperor or a Paul and Cephas, whose deeds seem marvelous. Another stream from imperial

---

[11] Tiele, *Outlines of the History of Religions*, 5th ed., p. 58. In this edition, the first portion of the passage, while carrying the same meaning, is worded differently from the way Sunderland quotes it.

Rome brings its gift of hierarchical organization, and here a tributary comes in from the German forests bringing the festivals of the sun god and the egg god of the newly developing life of spring. Christianity cannot banish these festivals; too long have they held place in the religious consciousness of the people. She can, however, and does adopt and baptize them, and we have the gorgeous Catholic festivals of Christmas and Easter.

Christianity itself sends its roots back into Judaism, hence, to know it really in its deepest nature we must apply to it the laws of heredity, i.e., we must study Judaism. Judaism has its sacred book, and our task will be easy, so we think. But a very little unbiased study will show us that Judaism is not one, but many. There is the Judaism which talks freely of angels and devils and the future life, happiness or misery; and there is the earlier Mosaism, which knows nothing of angels or devils or of no future life save that of Sheol, in which, as David declares, there is no service of God possible. Would we understand this difference we must note a tributary stream flowing in from Babylonia, and if we will trace this to its source we shall find its fountainhead in the Persian dualism of Ormuzd and Ahriman, the god of light and the god of darkness, with their attendant angels. Only after the Babylonish captivity do we find in Judaism angels and a hierarchy of devils.

Pass back through the Jewish sacred books and strange things will meet us. Here a "Thus saith the Lord" to Joshua, "Slay all the Canaanites, men, women and helpless children, I suffer not one to live."[12] "Sell the animal that has died of itself to the stranger within your gate, but not to those of your own flesh and blood."[13] The Lord comes to dine with Abraham under the oak at Mamre, on his way down to Sodom, to see if the reports of its great wickedness be true, and discusses his plans with his host. Naaman must carry home with

---

[12] Perhaps this passage seems all the more "strange" (to borrow the author's term) because, in fact, nowhere in "the Jewish sacred books" (if by this she means the Hebrew Bible), including the Book of Joshua, does "the Lord" issue this precise order to Joshua with regard to the Canaanites. The wording of this alleged quotation instead calls to mind certain lines from Moses's account in Deuteronomy of his own conquests of Shinon (2:34) and Bashan (3:6). In those passages, although it is God who—to quote from the Revised Standard Version (RSV)—"gave [the enemies] over" to Moses's army (2:33, 3:3), God does not explicitly prescribe the killing of "men, women, and children."

[13] A rather loose rendering of Deut. 14:21, which reads in the RSV: "You shall not eat anything that dies of itself; you may give it to the alien who is within your towns,...or...sell it to a foreigner; for you are a people holy to the Lord your God."

him loads of Palestinian earth if he would build an altar to the God of the Hebrews whose prophet has cured his leprosy.

The Lord guides the Israelites through the wilderness by a pillar of fire by night and of smoke by day, lives in the ark, and in it goes before the Israelites into battle, is captured in the ark and punishes the Philistines till they send him back to his people. The Lord makes a covenant with Abraham, and it is confirmed according to divine command by Abraham slaying and dividing animals and the Lord passing between the parts, thus affirming his share in the covenant.

Is this the same God of whom Jesus taught? This the religion out of which sprang Christianity? How, then, account for the immense distance between the two? To do this we must trace the early Hebrew religion to its source, and then follow the stream to the rise of Christianity, seeking earnestly for the causes of the transformation. What was the early Hebrew religion? A branch of the great Semitic family of religions. What was the religion of the Semites and who were Semites? These questions have been answered in an exhaustive and scholarly manner, so far as he goes, by Professor Robertson Smith, in the volume entitled *The Religion of the Semites*,[14] a volume to which no student of the Old Testament, who wishes to understand that rich treasury of Oriental and ancient sacred literature, can afford not to give a serious study.

The Semites occupied all the lands of Western Asia from the Tigro-Euphrates valley to the Mediterranean sea. They included the Arabs, Hebrews and Phoenicians, the Aramaeans, Babylonians and Assyrians. A comparative study of the religions of all these peoples has convinced scholars that all were developments from a common primitive source, the early religion of the Semites. This religion was first nature worship of the personified heavenly bodies, especially the sun and moon god. Among the Arabs this early religion developed into animistic polydaemonism, and never rises much higher than this; but among the Mesopotamian Semites the nature beings rise above nature and rule it, and one among them rises above all the others as the head of an unlimited theocracy.

If magic and augury remained prominent constituents of their ceremonial religion, they practiced besides a real worship and gave utterance to a vivid sense of sin, a deep feeling of man's dependence,

---

[14] William Robertson Smith, *Lectures on the Religion of the Semites. First Series: The Fundamental Institutions*, Burnett Lectures, 1888-89 (London: A. and C. Black, 1889; new edition, 1894).

even of his nothingness before God, in prayers and hymns hardly less fervent than those of the pious souls of Israel. Among the western Semites the Aramaeans, Canaanites, Phoenicians, seemed to have sojourned in Mesopotamia before moving westward, and they brought with them the names of the early Mesopotamian Semitic gods, with the cruel and unchaste worship of a non-Semitic people, the Akkadians, which henceforth distinguished them from the other Semites. From the Akkadians, too, was probably derived the consecration of the seventh day as a Sabbath or day or rest, afterward shared by the Hebrews.

The last of the Semitic peoples, the Hebrews, seem to be more closely related to the Arabs than to the northern or eastern Semites. They entered and gradually conquered most of Canaan during the thirteenth century, B.C., bringing with them a religion of extreme simplicity, though not monotheistic, and not differing greatly in character from that of the Arabs. Their ancient national god bore the name El-Shaddai, but his worship had given place under their great leader, Moses, to a new cult, the worship of Yahweh, the dreadful and stern god of thunder, who first appeared to Moses at the bush under the name "I am that I am," worshiped according to a new fundamental religious and moral law, the so-called Ten Words. Were this name and this law indigenous to Arabia or a special revelation, *de novo*, to Moses? But whence had Moses the moral culture adequate to the comprehension and appropriation of a moral system so far in advance of anything which we find among other earlier Semites? Nineteenth-century research has discovered an equally high moral code in Egypt, and the very name "Nuk pu Nuk," "I am that I am," is found among old Egyptian inscriptions.[15]

Whatever its origin, this new religion the Hebrews did not abandon to their new home, although they placed their national god, Yahweh, by the side of the deity of the country, whom they called briefly "the Baal," and whom most of them worshiped together with Ashera, the goddess of fertility. After they had left their wandering life and settled

---

[15] The phrase *nuk pu nuk* occurs several times in the *Book of Going Forth by Day*, known also as the *Book of the Dead*. See, e.g., Karl Richard Lepsius, *Das Todtenbuch der Ägypter nach dem hieroglyphischen Papyrus in Turin* (Leipzig: G. Wigand, 1842), 31.4 and 78.21, cited by P. le Page Renouf, *The Origin and Growth of Religion, as Illustrated by the Religion of Ancient Egypt*, Hibbert Lectures, 1879 (New York: Charles Scribner's Sons, 1880), p. 255 ns. 1 and 2. Noteworthily, Renouf cautioned against the already popular assertion that Moses "borrowed" his notion of God— "I am that I am"—from the Egyptian *nuk pu nuk* (pp. 254-55).

down to agriculture, Yahweh, however, as the god of the conquerors, was commonly placed above the others, though his stern character was softened by that of the gentler Baal. Well for Israel and well for the world that these two conceptions of deity came together in Judea twelve centuries before Christ. If the worship of the jealous god, Yahweh, made the Jew stern and uncompromising, it also girded him with a high moral sense whose legitimate outcome was Israel's great prophets; while the fierceness itself, as gradually transformed by the gentler Baal conception of deity, gives us the final outcome, the holy God who cannot look upon sin with the least degree of allowance, and yet pitieth the sinner even as a father pitieth his children. If any have been perplexed over a religion of love, such as Christianity claims to be, proving a religion of bloody wars, persecutions, inquisitions, martyrdoms, mayhap its Hebrew origin may throw light upon the mystery. Jesus' thought of a God, a Father, could not wholly displace at once the old Hebrew Yahweh, the jealous God.

All the Semitic religions, while differing among themselves in the names and certain characteristics of their deities, had much in common. Their gods were all tribal or national gods, limited to particular countries, choosing for themselves special dwelling places, which thus became holy places, usually by celebrated trees or living water, the tree, rock or water often coming to be regarded not simply as the abode, but, as in some sense, the divine embodiment or representative of the god, and hence these places were chosen as sanctuaries and places of worship; though the northern Semites worshiped on hills also, the worship consisting, during the nomadic period, in sacrifices of animals sacred alike to the god and his worshipers, because sharing the common life of both, and to some extent of human sacrifices as well. The skin of the animal sacrificed is the oldest form, says Robertson Smith, of a sacred garment appropriate to the performance of holy function, and was the origin of the expression, "robe of righteousness."[16] Is this the far-away origin of the scarlet robe of office?

All life, whether the life of man or beast, within the limits of the tribe was sacred, being held in common with the tribal god, who was the progenitor of the whole tribal life; hence no life could be taken save in sacrifice to the god without calling down the wrath of the god. Sacrifices thus became tribal feasts, shared between the god and his

---

[16] Smith, *Lectures on the Religion of the Semites*, pp. 438-39.

worshipers, the god receiving the blood poured upon this altar, the worshipers eating the flesh in a joyful tribal feast.

Here, then, was the origin of the Hebrew religion. It was not monotheistic, but what scholars designated as henotheistic, a belief in the existence of many gods, though worshiping only the national god. Thus a man was born into his religion as he was born into his tribe, and he could only change his religion by changing his tribe. This explains Ruth's impassioned words to Naomi: "Thy people shall be my people, and thy God my God."[17] This idea of the tribal god, who is a friend to his own people but an enemy to all others, added to the belief in the inviolability of all life save when offered in sacrifice, explains the decree that an animal dying of itself may not be eaten by a tribesman, but might be sold to a stranger. A tribal god, too, might rightfully enough order the slaughter of the men, women, and children of another tribe whose god had proved too weak to defend them. Life was sacred only because shared with the god, and this sharing was limited to the tribe.

The Hebrew people moved onward and upward from this early Semitic stage, and have left invaluable landmarks of their progress in their sacred books. The story of the sacrifice of Isaac tells of the time when human sacrifices were outgrown. Perhaps circumcision does the same. The story of Cain and Abel dates from the time when agriculture was beginning to take the place of the old nomadic shepherd life. The men of the new calling were still worshipers of the old gods, and would gladly share with them what they had to give— the fruits of the earth. But the clingers to the old life could see nothing sacred in this new thing, and were sure that only the old could be well pleasing to their god.

The god who dined with Abraham under the terebinth tree at Mamre was the early tribal god, El-Shaddai. Naaman was cured of his leprosy because the Jordan was sacred to the deity. It was the thunder god, Yahweh, whom the people worshiped on Sinai and who still bore traces of the earlier sun god as he guided the people in a pillar of fire. The ark is a remnant of fetishism, i.e., a means of putting the deity under control of his worshipers. They can compel his presence on the battlefield by carrying the ark thither, and if the ark is captured the god is captured also.

---

[17] Ruth 1:16.

A powerful element in the development upward of Mosaism was prophecy. The eighth-century prophets had moved far on beyond the whole sacrificial system, when, as spokesman for the Lord, Isaiah exclaims: "I am tired of your burnt sacrifices and your oblations. What doth the Lord require of thee but to do justly, love mercy, and walk humbly with thy God."[18] Jesus condemns the whole theory of holy places when he declares: "Neither on this holy mountain nor yet in Jerusalem shall men think to worship God most acceptably."[19] God is a spirit unlimited by time or place, and they who would worship acceptably must worship in spirit and in truth.

How long the journey from the early tribal, sacrificial, magical, unmoral, fetish, holy place, human sacrifice worship of the early Semites, including the Hebrews, to the universal Fatherhood and brotherhood religion of the sermon on the mount and the golden rule, only those can understand who are willing to give serious study not to the latter alone, but to the former as well. To such earnest student there will probably come another revelation, namely, that there is need of no miracle to account for this religious transformation more than for the physical transformation from the frozen snows of December to the palpitating life of June. They are both all miracle or none. The great infinite life and love was hidden alike in the winter clod and the human sacrifice. Given the necessary conditions, and the frozen clod has "climbed to a soul in grass and flower," the tribal god and the tribal blood bond are seen in their real character as the universal God Fatherhood and man brotherhood. What the necessary conditions were only those shall know who are ready to read God's thoughts after him in the patient researches of scientific investigation.

What is to be the future of this religion which has had so long and varied a history from far away Akkad even to this center of the western hemisphere, and from twenty centuries before Christ to this last decade of the nineteenth century after Christ?

One contribution made by the Hebrew to the Christian Scriptures demands special notice because it occupies so central a place in the development of the Christian system. I refer to the record of a first man, Adam, a Garden of Eden, a fall, an utter depravity resulting, and ending in a universal flood; a re-beginning, and another fall and confounding of speech at Babel. The founder of Christianity never

---

[18] A loose rendering and condensation of Mic. 6:6-8
[19] John 4:21.

refers to these events and the gospels are silent concerning them. Paul first alludes to them, but in his hands and those of his successors they have become central in the theology of Christendom. Whence came this record of these real or supposed events? Genesis is silent concerning its origin. The antiquary delving among the ruins of ancient Chaldea finds almost the identical record of the same series of events upon clay tablets which are referred to an Akkadian people, the founders of the earliest civilization of the Tigro-Euphrates valley, a people not Semitic, but Turanian, related, therefore, to the great Turanian peoples represented by the Chinese, Japanese and Fins.

We started out to make an exhaustive study of Christianity, an Aryan religion, if named from its adherents; Semitic from its origin, we found it receiving tributary streams from three Aryan sources, namely, Alexandrian Neo-Platonism, Pagan Rome and Teutonic Germany; its roots were nurtured in Semitic Hebrew soil which had been enriched from Semitic Assyria, Aryan Persia, Turanian Akkadia and Hamitic Egypt.

Its parent was Judaism, a national religion, limited by the boundaries of one nation. It is itself a universal religion, having transcended all national boundaries. How was this transformation effected? For answer go to Kuenen's masterly handling of the subject, *National Religions and Universal Religions.* If our study has been wide, we have learned that religions, like languages, have a life history of birth, development, transformation, death, following certain definite laws. Moreover, the law of life for all organisms is the same, and may, perhaps, be formulated as the power of adjustment to environment; the greater the adjustability the greater the vitality.

But this means capacity to change. "That which is no longer susceptible of change," says Kuenen, "may continue to exist, but it has ceased to live. And religion must live, must enter into new combinations and bear fresh fruits, if it is to answer to its destiny, if, refusing to crystallize into formulae and usages, it is to work like the leaven, is to console, to inspire and to strengthen."[20] Has Christianity this vital power? "Yes," again answers Kuenen, and quotes approvingly a saying of Richard Rothe: "Christianity is the most mutable of all things. That is its special glory."[21] And why should this

---

[20] Abraham Kuenen, *National Religions and Universal Religions,* Hibbert Lectures, 1882 (New York: Charles Scribner's Sons, 1882), pp. 315-16.

[21] *Stille Stunden. Aphorismen aus Richard Rothes handschriftlichem Nachlass* (Wittenburg: Koelling, 1872), p. 357, quoted by Kuenen, *National Religions,* p. 313.

not be so? Christianity has gathered contributions from many lands and woven them into one ideal large enough to include all peoples, tender enough to comfort all, lofty enough to inspire all—the ideal of a universal human brotherhood bound together under a common Divine Fatherhood.

PART II

APPRAISAL
1894

RESULTS OF THE PARLIAMENT OF RELIGIONS

John Henry Barrows

History has scarcely any contrast to present greater or more instructive than that between "the light of burning heretics," which threw its glare over the enterprise of Columbus, and the purer splendor of a parliament of religions, which cast its radiance, four centuries afterward, over the Columbian anniversary. The human race has been woefully divided by national and other antipathies, especially by those of religion. It is remarkable, therefore, that the first universal council ever held, the first parliament of man, was a religious convention. The world appears to be determined to regard the parliament of religions as vastly significant. To Bishop Coxe, of western New York, an earnest foe of this congress, it is still "one of the most serious events of the kind in the history of humanity, since the wise men from the east came to the cradle of Bethlehem."[1] Castelar writes that, "from the beginning of the world until to-day, history has never recorded an event so momentous as the union, under one roof

---

"Results of the Parliament of Religions" by John Henry Barrows. Reprinted here from *The Forum* 18 (September 1894):54-67, though the same article also appeared in *The Chinese Recorder and Missionary Journal* 26 (March 1895):101-13. Misspellings of names are corrected, and all footnotes are added.

[1] Arthur Cleveland Coxe (1818-96), Bishop in the Protestant Episcopal Church.

and one leadership and for one purpose, of the clergy of the world."[2] A representative voice from Hindustan,—the *Indian Mirror* of Calcutta,—regards the parliament as "the crowning work of the nineteenth century," and "the flower of the tree of religion which mankind has so long watered and pruned." Count D'Alviella, of Brussels, regards it as a fact of great importance "that the programme of the congress was accepted by confessions so diverse and numerous, and that these were drawn to meet on a footing of equality."[3] To Professor Emilio Comba,[4] of Rome, it seemed like reviving the spectacle of the ancient Pantheon, where the priests of many faiths met with a smile, not of cunning, but of courtesy and tolerance. And President Martin writes from the Imperial University of Peking that "it is now evident that the greatest thing at the World's Fair was the parliament of religions, which will be remembered when the marvels of machinery are forgotten."[5]

Though the Congress in Chicago has had many prophecies in literature and many preparations in history, it was, as Rev. M.J. Savage has said, "the first really ecumenical meeting the world has ever seen."[6] Every great event is the flower of all the ages which have preceded it, but the special preparations for this meeting in Chicago were: the almost universal spread of Christian missions; the rise and study of comparative religion; the wide use of the English language, making such a conference possible; international facilities for travel; ample religious freedom in America, where church and state are separated; the attractive opportunity afforded by a world's exposition; and much hard work extending over more than three years. A broad-

---

[2] Emilio Castelar y Ripoll (1832-99), Spanish statesman, orator and author, served as president of the first Spanish Republic from September 1873 to January 1874. The quoted remarks are from his article, "The Parliament of Religions in America," *The Independent* 46 (May 31, 1894): 677. Other remarks of his on the parliament are quoted from the *Globo* of Madrid in *WFP*, p. 34.

[3] Comte Eugène Goblet d'Alviella (1846-1925) was a historian of religions at the University of Brussels. Barrows remarks here in a footnote of his own: "The equality acknowledged was 'parliamentary,' not 'doctrinal.'" Cf. Goblet d'Alviella's remarks in the *Revue de Belgique*, as quoted with no date in *WFP*, p. 36.

[4] Emilio Comba (1839-1904), a noted Italian Protestant historian.

[5] William Alexander Parsons Martin (1827-1916), American Presbyterian clergyman, missionary, and educator, served as president of the Imperial Tungwen College in Peking, China (1869-98), and became head of the New Imperial University of China in 1900. The comment attributed to him here closely resembles a remark of his quoted in *WFP*, p. 26.

[6] Minot Judson Savage (1841-1918), Unitarian author and minister in Chicago (1873-74), Boston (1874-96), and New York (1896-1906).

minded lawyer of Chicago, Mr. Charles C. Bonney, is entitled to the great and lasting honor of having originated and carried to success, in spite of numerous obstacles, the entire scheme of the world's congresses of 1893. The parliament of religions was one of more than two hundred of these conventions, and, according to Mr. Bonney, "the splendid crown" of the series.

With the great peace-bell at the fair, tolling, as many hoped, the death-knell to intolerance; with the rabbis of Israel praying at that hour in all lands that the name of Jehovah might be reverenced over all the earth; with representatives of ten religions gathered beneath one roof; and with a Catholic Cardinal repeating the universal prayer of the world's Saviour, the parliament opened on the 11th of September, 1893. It was indeed a meeting of brotherhood, where "the Brahmin forgot his caste and the Catholic was chiefly conscious of his catholicity"; and where, in the audience, "the variety of interests, faiths, ranks, and races, was as great as that found on the platform." As the representatives of China, Russia, Germany, Hindustan, Sweden and Norway, Greece, France, Africa, the United States, and the all-clasping Empire of Great Britain, from England to New Zealand, uttered their thoughts and feelings, multitudes entered anew into the spirit of the Nazarene Prophet, who seemed always to include the whole world in His purpose and affection.

Professor Toy, of Harvard, has noted the physical difficulties of bringing such a parliament together, and he shows that it might easily have been a ludicrous and melancholy failure.[7] The promoters of the plan were surprised at their own success, though the representation of the world's faiths was less complete and imposing than they had endeavored to achieve. The absence of representatives of Hindu Mohammedanism was deplored. President Miller,[8] of Madras, who was the chairman's chief counselor, despaired for a time of securing any Hindu representation at Chicago. Still the religious life of India spoke through representatives of nearly all its leading systems. Through an address by Vivekananda, and elaborate papers by Professor D'Vivedi and S.P. Aiyangar, different types of Hinduism were presented; Narasima, a graduate of the Christian College at

---

[7] See Crawford Howell Toy (1836-1919), "The Parliament of Religions," *The New World* 2 (1893) : 728-41. Toy, a professor of Hebrew and Oriental languages, had delivered a paper at the parliament, "The Relation between Religion and Conduct" (in *WPR*, 2:1009-11).

[8] President William Miller, of the Christian College of Madras.

Madras, criticised Christian missions; Laksmi Narain, of Lahore, spoke for the Arya Somaj; Gandhi, the acute Bombay lawyer, for Jainism; Mozoomdar and Nagarkar described with great eloquence the principles of the Brahmo Somaj; while Miss Sorabji, Rev. Maurice Phillips, Rev. R.A. Hume, Rev. T.E. Slater, and Rev. T.J. Scott (these last two through papers), spoke for Christianity in India.[9]

Buddhism addressed the parliament through more than a dozen voices, Ceylonese, Japanese, and Siamese, including that of a Siamese prince; the religions of China were treated in seven different papers, the most elaborate of which was by Pung Quang Yu, Secretary of the Chinese Legation; Zoroastrianism was described in two excellent essays; Mohammedanism in four addresses; Shintoism in two, Judaism in twelve; and Christianity—Greek, Latin, Lutheran, Anglican, Reformed, Liberal, New Church—in nearly a hundred. Although much that passed for Oriental religion was a reflection of Christian truth and European philosophy, still the Oriental speakers were, on the whole, fairly representative of the higher ideas of their own faiths, if not of the popular religions. The results accomplished surpassed the popular expectations. Prof. Max Müller, who would have been present had he thought the dream was to be realized, regards the parliament as "one of the most encouraging signs of the times, the first friendly meeting and mutual recognition of all the religions of the world."[10]

---

[9] The speeches alluded to are Vivekananda, "Hinduism," in *WPR*, 2:968-78; Manilal Nabhubhai Dvivedi (D'Vivedi), "Hinduism," in *WPR*, 1:316-32; S. Parthasarathy Aiyangar, "The Tenkalai Sri Vaishnava, or Southern Ramanuja Religion" (not in proceedings); Narasima Charya, untitled address in section on "Criticism and Discussion of Missionary Methods,", in *WPR*, 2:1094-96; Lakshmi Narain, "Orthodox Hinduism and Vedanta Philosophy" (not in proceedings); Virchand A. Gandhi, "The Philosophy and Ethics of the Jains," *WPR*, 2:1222-26; Protap Chandra Majumdar (Protap Chunder Mozoomdar), "The Brāhmo-Somāj," in *WPR*, 1:345-51, and "The World's Debt to Asia," in *WPR*, 2:1083-92; B.B. Nagarkar, untitled "Speech" on the Brāhmo Samāj, in *WPR*, 1:106-107, and "The Work of Social Reform in India," in *WPR*, 1:767-79; Jeanne Sorabji, "Women of India," in *WPR*, 1:1037-38; Maurice Phillips, "The Ancient Religion of India and Primitive Revelation," in *WPR*, 1:296-305; Robert Allen Hume, untitled address in section on "Criticism of Missionary Methods," in *WPR*, 2:1095, and "The Contact of Christian and Hindu Thought: Points of Likeness and of Contrast," in *WPR*, 2:1269-76; T.E. Slater, "Concessions to Native Religious Ideas," *NHP*, pp. 164-67, and "The Present Religious Outlook of India," in *WPR*, 2:1172-78; T.J. Scott, "Divine Providence and the Ethnic Religions," in *WPR*, 2:921-25.

[10] The first part of this statement is quoted, with no source given, in *WFP*, p. 32. Cf. in the present volume the article by F. Max Müller.

It would have been easy to defeat the objects of this meeting by making it chiefly a scientific gathering. But the purpose was not to call together the specialists in comparative religion, to produce learned and critical essays. Such a proceeding would have killed the parliament. While scholarship was everywhere apparent, technical scholarship was not made supremely prominent, and, according to one participant, "the peculiar charm of this meeting consisted in this, that it did not carry with it the predominant smell of the lamp."[11] The parliament was not expected to furnish new facts and ideas to life-long students of comparative religion, but it did something quite as important by drawing popular attention to this vital theme, and by giving the world such a demonstration of its unity and such evidence of brotherhood as had never before been witnessed.

The historian who attempts any adequate review of what the world has said of this meeting is troubled by an embarrassment of riches. The comments which have already reached the chairman would fill more than four thousand pages like those on which this article is printed. According to one religious journal, "when the parliament adjourned, it really began its permanent sessions. Its utterances have continued to echo around the huge whispering-gallery of the world." The study of these criticisms will some day be an important chapter in the progress of comparative religion. By Professor Headland, of the University of Peking, the parliament is regarded as "one of the most stupendous events and undertakings in the religious history of the world"; valuable, among other things, in showing how strong are the great systems with which Christianity is contending, and how stupendous is the task which it has undertaken.[12] According to Dr. Paul Carus it will "exert a lasting influence upon the religious intelligence of mankind."[13] To the Archbishop of Zante it is "a strong foundation-stone for the

---

[11] Evidently quoted from Joseph (Flavius Josephus) Cook (1838-1901), Congregationalist minister, theologian, lecturer, and founder and editor-in-chief of *Our Way*, whose almost identical remark about the parliament in his Boston Monday Lectures series is quoted with no date given in *WFP*, p. 46. Cook gave two presentations at the parliament: "Strategic Certainties of Comparative Religion" (*WPR*, 1:536-42) and "The Worth of the Bible, or Columnar Truths in Scripture" (*WPR*, 2:1072-75).

[12] Isaac Taylor Headland (1859-1942), Methodist Episcopal minister, and missionary to China (1890-1907).

[13] Paul Carus, "The Dawn of a Religious Era," *The Forum* 16 (December 1893): 396.

religious temple of the future."[14] The secretary of the Apostolic Durbar of Calcutta, representing the Brahmo Somaj, looks upon the parliament as the realization of what that Society of the Worshippers of God has been laboring thirty years to achieve, and as an object-lesson of that dispensation which the Brahmo Somaj is now living under, and which St. Paul speaks of as "the dispensation of the fulness of time, in which he might gather together in one all things in Christ."[15] An old Israelite in Germany, who could not read the American papers sent him by his son, an American rabbi, but who looked with wonder at the various pictures of the men and women representing such diverse faiths in the parliament, wrote back: "The times of the Messiah have come."

According to *Le Temps*, of Paris, the parliament was the most novel and amazing spectacle which America has offered. The builder of the exposition, Daniel H. Burnham,[16] said recently that "a thousand years hence about all that the world will remember of the fair will be the parliament"; and to President Higinbotham it is "the proudest work of our exposition."[17] The evident reason for this belief is that, while the fair was no novelty, the parliament was unique and unexampled, and purposed, in a great school of comparative theology,[18] to bring the different faiths into contact and conference; to deepen the spirit of brotherhood; to emphasize the distinctive truths of each religion; to show why men believe in God and the future life; to bridge the chasm of separation between Christians of different names and religious men of all names; to induce good men to work together for common ends; and to promote the cause of international peace.

---

[14] Dionysios Latas, Orthodox Archbishop, presented a paper on "The Greek Church" at the parliament (in *WPR*, 1:352-58).

[15] Paraphrase of Ephesians 1:10.

[16] Daniel Hudson Burnham (1846-1912), chief of construction of the Columbian Exposition, was the most prominent architect of his time in America.

[17] Harlow N. Higinbotham, president of the Columbian Exposition, welcoming address to the parliament, in *WPR*, 1:82. This quote also appears beneath his photo in the frontispiece of vol. 2 of *WPR*. Subsequent statements by others exalting the parliament's historical stature and worth over the exposition's became so common they became cliché; see, e.g., *The New York Herald*, September 17, 1893, as quoted in *WFP*, p. 51; and the article by F. Max Müller in the present volume.

[18] This interesting phrase, which was used by Barrows to describe the parliament in his opening-day "Address" (in *WPR*, 1:75), was adapted by the chairman of the parliament's "Scientific Section," Merwin-Marie Snell, who described the parliament as a "school of comparative religion" (quoted from his paper in the present volume).

From the moment of its inception the proposed congress was attacked on various grounds; and although the great majority of the religious newspapers in America have been friendly to the undertaking, and although the parliament and its literature silenced a vast deal of criticism, still the voice of condemnation and the cries of bigotry and fear have been heard in many lands. It has been stigmatized as "Bedlam," "Babel," and "a booth in Vanity Fair"; and its promoters have been likened to Balaam and Judas Iscariot! All this shows that the parliament has important work yet to do in the world.

The hyper-orthodoxy and exclusiveness which resent the classification of Christianity with other religions should not forget the historic fact that Christianity *is* one of the faiths of the world, competing for the conquest of mankind, and that, historically considered, it has not been so faultless as to defy competition and comparison. "By their fruits ye shall know them."[19] "I shall never forget the lesson which it has been to me," writes Prof. Max Müller, "while walking through the lowest streets of Constantinople, never to see a drunken man or woman." Reasonable men perceive that comparison must be made, and missionaries in the Orient well know that defying competition is a pretty sad business. Why should there be such an apparent lack of faith in Christian truth on the part of some zealous propagandists? Why is it felt that most people cannot be suffered to learn more than one side of this question, and why should noble-hearted disciples of Christ act on the theory that Christianity is darkness rather than light, since it seems to fear such illumination as comes from a friendly comparison with other faiths? And why should those who stab the parliament with Biblical verses omit to quote the comprehensive scriptural declaration that "God is no respecter of persons, but in every nation he that feareth Him and worketh righteousness is acceptable with Him"?[20]

Some have criticised the parliament on the ground that Christian believers must not tolerate error, by which is meant departure from the critic's own interpretations. But what are we going to do with error? Persecute it? If we are not willing to tolerate it, to listen to it, to find out the truth which many be at the heart of it, to supplement it, to enlighten it and remove it, we have no proper place in the

---

[19] Matt. 7:20.

[20] Acts 10:34-35. This passage is also quoted by Max Müller in connection with parliament, in the *Deutsche Rundschau* (Berlin), March 1895, as quoted in *WFP*, p. 36.

humanitarian century. We should go back and take our stand by the side of Torquemada, or the persecuting Protestants of the sixteenth century.

The critics sometimes insist on the unique charms and claims of Christianity, implying that the Christian speakers in the parliament hid the heavenly light under a bushel. Dr. Morgan Dix thinks the Christians who were present "were attacking the Cross of Christ,"[21]— a statement which is fairly questionable after reading the opinion of the missionary, Dr. George William Knox, that "the parliament was distinctively Christian in its conception, spirit, prayers, doxologies, benedictions; in its prevailing language, arguments, and faith."[22] "Amid the bewildering maze of Oriental faiths represented," says one report, "Christianity shone out more luminous than ever as the universal, uplifting force of the world." Strong in its divine certainties and forces, Christianity received meekly the blows dealt at the sins of Christendom. The advances which the Christian faith lovingly made to the non-Christian representatives were no concession of weakness, but an illustration of it consciousness of truth and power. We do well to remember that "the representatives of Christianity" have been so unjust and so cruel in the past to the ancient Oriental religions that "no amount of courtesy or consideration would be excessive compensation."

No other event ever awakened so wide and sympathetic an interest in comparative religion, "the highest study to which the human mind can now devote its energies." The spectacle itself gave vividness and reality to the vague popular notions of the ethnic faiths. Scientific study of this theme has been confined to the few, and scholars are now grateful that the parliament has aroused such general interest in it on the part of educated people. Through the daily press of Chicago, which gave fifty columns each day for seventeen days to the proceedings of the congress, and through the religious press of many lands, the words spoken have already reached millions. The more permanent literary fruitage of this congress, giving its proceedings in books, with more or less fulness, has been large, more than a hundred thousand copies of these various volumes having already been taken. They have gone, not only into the great libraries, into the hands of

---

[21] Morgan Dix (1827-1908).
[22] George William Knox (1853-1912), a missionary of the American Presbyterian Church to Japan.

preachers and scholars, but also into the homes of thoughtful people among the laity of the six continents.[23]

Many hundreds of lectures on the parliament have been delivered in all parts of the world. Prof. G. Bonet-Maury, who ably represented liberal French Protestantism in Chicago, has frequently spoken on the parliament in France.[24] The eloquent voice of Father Hyacinthe has been heard extolling the high purposes of this congress. Count Goblet D'Alviella has lectured on it before the School of Social Sciences annexed to the University of Brussels, and Prof. Max Müller has made it the theme of a discourse in Oxford. In his course of six addresses in Boston, Joseph Cook stoutly championed the parliament from the standpoint of aggressive orthodoxy.[25] The parliament had been a frequent topic of discussion in colleges and Chautauqua assemblies; and at the midwinter fair in San Francisco a congress of religions was addressed by more than twenty speakers. Among the echoes of the parliament, beside the recent Liberal Congress in Chicago, are: the proposition to hold a second parliament in Benares, in regard to which Mr. Dharmapala had already consulted the Maharajah of that ancient and sacred city; and a plan, now well under way, of holding a universal religious parliament in Jerusalem at the opening of the twentieth century.

---

[23] Barrows remarks here in a note of his own: "It is worthwhile to recall that the interest in this literature comes not only from the fact that the parliament dealt with all the highest themes, and was enriched by such minds as those of Cardinal Gibbons, the Archbishop of Zante, Bishop Dudley, [there follows a list of almost seventy other figures associated with the parliament],... and scores beside, but also from the fact that such varied minds were agreed in the sentiments of brotherhood which called the parliament, and which made it, as the Buddhist bishop, Right Rev. Shaku Soyen [Shaku Sōen], believed, 'the greatest spiritual phenomenon ever produced.'"

[24] E.g., his remarks in the two Paris journals, *Revue de l'Histoire des Religions*, and *Revue des Deux Mondes* (August 1894), as quoted in *WFP*, pp. 34, 35. Rev. Gaston Bonét-Maury (1842-1919), professor of church history on the faculty of Protestant theology at the University of Paris, participated at the 1893 parliament, speaking on "The Leading Powers Shaping Religion in France"; see *WPR*, 2:1261-64. He later would also speak at the International Congress of the History of Religions, in Paris in 1900.

[25] On Joseph Cook see n. 11 above. Cf. his assessment of the parliament quoted in *WFP*, pp. 44-45: "[The parliament] received with great favor thoroughly orthodox evangelists; it asserted most devoutly and incisively the Fatherhood of God, the brotherhood of man, and the solidarity of the race; it united Christians and non-Christians every day in the Lord's Prayer; and, to use Dr. Barrows' words, it ended at Calvary."

One of the first fruits of the congress of last September is the gift of $20,000 by Mrs. Caroline E. Haskell to establish a lectureship on comparative religion in the University of Chicago, where that department is already notable. This has been followed by another noble gift by Mrs. Haskell, of $100,000 to build for the university an Oriental museum, to be devoted to lecture-rooms, collections, and studies in the Semitic department.[26] A proposition now comes from a prominent English scholar that a trustworthy and interesting manual of comparative religion should be prepared for the youth in our Sunday-schools. Still further, a religious parliament extension society has been organized, under the presidency of Dr. Paul Carus, to continue the work by promoting a sympathetic and mutual understanding of the world's great faiths.[27]

In these days no study is of the highest value that is not comparative; and some Christians will yet discover that the strongest evidence of Christianity may be furnished by the study which many of them now fear, just as the comparative history of miracles is believed by many to be one of the best defences of Biblical supernaturalism. If Christianity be "the only religion which faces all the facts," it has a magnificent opportunity, both in colleges and mission fields, to vindicate itself. Its apostles need both sympathy and knowledge with regard to the faiths of the world, and the non-Christian peoples need both sympathy and knowledge in regard to Christianity. The parliament, in some measure, answered these requirements; and where it failed,—since doubtless some of the Oriental faiths were not accurately and adequately set forth,—it has furnished a stimulus to further sympathetic inquiry.

The Orientals attending the parliament were deeply impressed by the fraternity and Christian love which invited them, furnished them

---

[26] As indicated by Kenten Druyvesteyn, "The World's Parliament of Religions," Ph.D. dissertation, University of Chicago, 1976, p. 294, the unpublished documentation for the establishment of the famous Haskell lectureship and Haskell Museum is kept in the archives of the president's papers, 1889-1925, at the University of Chicago (box 38, folders 2 and 3 respectively). In October 1894, a month after the present article appeared in *The Forum*, Mrs. Caroline E. Haskell (d. 1900) donated another $20,000 gift to the University of Chicago for the establishment of a second lectureship, the Barrows Lectures on the relationship of Christianity to other religions. The documentation is kept in those same archives (box 8, folder 10). For discussion of the history of both lectureships and the museum, see Druyvesteyn's dissertation, pp. 81-87.

[27] See Paul Carus, "The World's Religious Parliament Extension," *The Monist* 5 (April 1895): 345-53.

hospitality, gave them a free platform, and welcomed their sharpest criticisms of Christendom. The eloquent Buddhist, Mr. Hirai,[28] said to me on leaving for Japan:

> I go back a Christian, by which I mean that Christianity is a religion which I shall be glad to see established in Japan. Only let the Christian missionaries not interfere with our national usages and patriotic holidays. I have been delighted with America and especially with its tolerance. I expected that before I finished my address, criticising false Christianity in Japan, I should be torn from the platform. But I was received with enthusiasm.

Mr. Gandhi, the critic of Christian missions, said: "American Christianity I like, it is something better than what we have usually seen in India." The high priest of Shintoism, Rt. Rev. R. Shibata, and the Buddhist bishop, Zitzusen Ashitsu, write with grateful enthusiasm of their reception in America.[29] The international friendships knit by the Congress of 1893 are a contribution to international peace, while inter-religious good-will is a manifest help to the study of comparative theology.

While modifying some popular views of the Oriental faiths, the parliament is promoting a new and humaner interest in foreign missions, by making the ethnic systems more real, and also more definite, to millions of minds, by showing Christians that these faiths are far from dead, though they many have little life-giving power over their adherents; by setting before the Christian world the magnitude of the task it has undertaken; and by teaching it that it must make its swifter and wider conquests in the future by a better understanding and a larger sympathy, rather than by contemptuous hostility and bigoted exclusiveness. The effect of the parliament was felt immediately, in the magnificent Missionary Congress which followed it,[30] and a new tone of kindliness and tolerance has marked many of the recent gatherings and discussions in foreign missionary societies. What Christendom needs today is to ponder and take to heart the truths proclaimed in the Rev. Mr. Candlin's great address before the parliament, in certain practical regards the chief address made,

---

[28] On Hirai Kinzō (Kinza Riuge M. Hirai) and his participation at the parliament, see in this volume the chapter by James Edward Ketelaar.

[29] At the parliament, Shibata Reiichi (Reuchi Shibata) presented a paper on "Shintoism" (in *WPR*, 1:451-54). On Ashitsu Jitsunen (Zitsuzen Ashitsu) and his participation at the parliament, see in this volume the chapter by Ketelaar.

[30] See the account on "Congress of Missions," in *WPR*, 2:1536-49.

wherein he set forth not only the need of unity, but also the method of sympathetic approach to the foreign faiths.[31] "The glory of Christianity," said Prof. Jowett, "is not to be as unlike other religions as possible, but to be their perfection and fulfilment."[32] As Judaism and Christianity were reconciled in the Epistle to the Hebrews, so Buddhism and Christianity, Hinduism and Christianity, Confucianism and Christianity, Islâm and Christianity, are yet to be reconciled by some supreme minds, who shall show to India, China, Japan, Arabia, that in Christ all that is good and true in these faiths has been embodied and completed by a special revelation.

No intelligent believer in Christian missions has had his faith shaken by the stories,—some of them almost fairy stories,—which two or three delegates to the parliament related. Mr. Vivekananda and Mr. Gandhi have written and spoken against Christian missions in India, and for this we should be thankful, since their criticisms have been buried by Mr. Hume and Mr. Powers under a mountain of facts. Careful inquiry into the effects of Mr. Vivekananda's addresses before our colleges has shown that, instead of discrediting missions, he has led students to investigate with renewed interest the actual religious condition of the people whom he has eulogized. Nothing but advantage will come from hearing all sides of the missionary question. No phenomenon of the century has on the whole been more remarkable than the Christian uprising in Europe and America to give the Gospel to all lands. The splendid record of missions is starred with achievements which no amount of criticism can dim. Let Mr. Mozoomdar and others tell Christianity how its methods can be improved. Let Mr. Candlin and Mr. Hume urge a kindlier spirit in Christian propagandism; let comparative religion become a study required of all candidates for mission fields. The result can be only good. As the *Churchman* says, "it is hard to convert a man unless it is clearly understood what he is to be converted from. Light, knowledge, sympathy are necessary to all missionary work, and surely these may come from so strange a gathering as the parliament of religions." It

---

[31] See George T. Candlin, "The Bearing of Religious Unity on the Work of Christian Missions," in *WPR*, 2:1179-91. Candlin, an English Methodist missionary to China, made several other addresses at the parliament, including some untitled remarks in the section on "Criticism and Discussion of Missionary Methods" (*WPR*, 2:1093-94), and a closing-day address (in *WPR*, 1:168-69).

[32] Presumably from John Henry Jowett (1864-1923), English Congregationalist clergyman.

may be that Christianity needs to be orientalized before the more cultured intellects of the East will generally accept it.

One of the best results of the parliament has been a better understanding, among enlightened minds, between Catholics and Protestants in America. When the American Catholic archbishops, with the knowledge and consent of the Vatican, decided to take part in the parliament, they did much to give the meeting its historic importance. The faithfulness with which they carried out their part of the programme, the ability, courtesy, and kindness of their speakers, made a wholesome impression on many minds; and, although the months which have followed have been filled with acrimonious attacks on the Catholic church, there has yet been a better understanding between many Catholics and Protestants in America than ever heretofore. The fanaticism and wicked folly of the methods of the American Protective Association have not destroyed the recollections of those golden days when, for the first time in history, Protestant and Catholic divines sat together in loving fellowship. The participation of the Catholic bishops made the official refusal of the English Church to participate in the congress appear almost ridiculous. But the generous and liberal sentiments spoken by Cardinal Gibbons, Archbishop Redwood, Bishop Keane, and others, were the features which particularly impressed American Protestants.[33] Count D'Alviella reports that the Catholic journals of Europe have not reproduced these sentiments, and a strong Protestant voice in Italy inquires, If the Protestant in America is justified in his overtures of peace to the Catholic, why should such overtures be refused and condemned in Italy? Is Catholicism liberty in America and intolerance in Europe? How long will this dualism of conscience continue? Words of kindness and conciliation have been spoken by Édouard Naville in the city of Calvin,[34] but they have met no sympathetic response. In America, however, kindly words from Protestant pulpits are met with equal kindness by many Catholic prelates. This is a great surprise to Prof. Auguste Sabbatier, who, in

---

[33] Some nineteen Roman Catholics addressed the parliament. The talks alluded to here by Barrows are James Cardinal Gibbons, Archbishop of Baltimore, "The Needs of Humanity Supplied by the Catholic Religion," in *WPR*, 1:485-93; Archbishop Redwood of New Zealand, untitled opening-day address, in *WPR*, 1:94-95 (a variant version of which appears in *NHP*, pp. 58-60); Rev. John Joseph Keane of New York, "The Incarnation Idea in History and in Jesus Christ," in *WPR*, 2:882-88, and "The Ultimate Religion," in *WPR*, 2:1331-38.

[34] Édouard Naville (1844-1926), Swiss Egyptologist, was a professor at Geneva. The *Forum* text of this paper gives his first name erroneously as Ernst.

the *Journal de Genève,* says of the Catholic dignitaries at the parliament: "Their conduct was so novel, and so in contradiction to the habitual exclusive and uncompromising attitude of the Church of Rome, that in France it seems incredible."[35] Castelar made a great sensation when he informed a company of literary people in his own house that leading Catholic prelates had taken part in the parliament of religions.

It required a parliament of all religions to bring together the first modern parliament of Christendom. An effort less ecumenical would not have brought together the disciples of Christ. It has often been remarked that little sectarianism was preached at the parliament. There Christendom proclaimed its Master. Inevitably this meeting which furnished the prophecy of a reunited church has had large effect on many Christian minds. Discussions of reunion have been increasingly rife. Bishop Keane says that Americans are overeager for speedy results, and he is almost content with saying that "the parliament accomplished itself." It stands as an achieved fact, sublime, impressive, perpetual, a beacon blazing with sacred and unwasting fire. But facts lead to immediate results in the world of the spirit. Feelings are changed, and then convictions. "The solemn charge which the parliament preaches to all true believers is a return to the primitive unity of Christians, as a condition precedent to the conversion of the world." With this faith in their hearts, men are active along various lines. The results may be far off, but they are certain.

It was discovered that Christianity in its main divisions is in harmony on the chief questions of doctrine and duty. The argument of Canon Fremantle, showing that faith in the great central truths of religion has been strengthened by the progress of modern thought, indicated also that these great truths throw into shadow and subordination the elaborate and technical theological creeds, and that the social movement for the common good, in which all Christians may unite, will be recognized more and more as the main part of religion.[36] The group of papers bearing on the social problem, presented by Professors Peabody, Henderson, and Ely, and Drs.

---

[35] Louis Auguste Sabbatier (1839-1901), French Protestant theologian, was one of the founders of the Protestant theological faculty at the University of Paris (1877), where he became dean in 1895.

[36] See W.H. Fremantle, Canon of Canterbury, "The Religious Reunion of Christendom," in *WPR*, 2:1201-09.

Gladden and Small,[37] furnish the divine fire which ought to burn down the barriers of Christian separation. If we can center the interest of Christian minds, both in the greatest themes of practical ethics and in the highest subjects of comparative theology, how divisions over pettier matters will go down! The world needs greater intellects, greater souls, greater men, and, in the divine evolution, the time appears to have come for their appearance. Attention to the supremest concerns of humanity will eliminate unholy fire from the altars at which religious zeal is ministering.

The world will not forget how the venerated Dr. Schaff declared his resolution to speak at the parliament a last word in favor of Christian unity.[38] "He was a prophet," writes Professor Comba, from Rome, "for this word of his was his swan song." One of the chief ideas which the parliament made luminous was a reunited Christendom, the preparation for a Christianized world. Since all the religions found, as Castelar has said, "a common ground in Christianity," and since inevitably the best religion must come to the front, may we not look to see the lines of human progress centering more and more in Christ, the "unifier of humanity"? "Never before in all the earth," writes one student, "has the fact been so vividly set forth that Christianity, and it alone, is large enough to cover the whole round globe, and hold it to the heart of God." In view of the tremendous needs of modern society and the problem of the world's evangelization, Christians will certainly draw closer to each other. Of course every great movement has its reactions, and spiritual contrasts appear in close proximity. The religious world may be all borne along, like the passengers on a ship, in one direction, and yet alienations and quarrels may be intensified among the voyagers. And so in the midst of the progress now apparent we discover American Catholicism eulogizing religious liberty and brotherhood, while in American Presbyterianism appear tendencies which are "Romanizing," exclusive, and reactionary.

---

[37] Francis Greenwood Peabody, of Harvard University, "Christianity and the Social Question," in *WPR*, 2:1024-30; C.R. Henderson, of the University of Chicago, "Individual Effort at Reform not Sufficient," in *WPR*, 2:1061-64; Richard T. Ely, of the University of Wisconsin, "Christianity as a Social Force," in *WPR*, 2:1056-61; Rev. Washington Gladden, "Religion and Wealth," in *WPR*, 2:1068-70; A.W. Small, of the University of Chicago, "The Churches and City Problems," in *WPR*, 2:1079-83.

[38] Philip Schaff, of Union Theological Seminary, "The Reunion of Christendom," in *WPR*, 2:1192-1201.

It was the spirit of fraternity in the heart of America which succeeded in bringing together such widely separated exponents of religion. "Enemies simply met and discovered that they were brothers who had one Father in Heaven." To speak of the deep, tender feelings awakened by the presence at the parliament of the truth-seekers of the Orient, earnest, heart-hungry, believing that they had much to teach as well as something to learn, their "faces set toward God and with some message from God"; to recall the emotions awakened during the great opening and closing hours of the parliament—would be to indulge in what many would deem a sentimental rhapsody; but it is not rhapsody so say that "the age of isolation and hatred has passed, and the age of toleration and scientific comparison has come." Kindlier feelings were certainly engendered at the parliament, and many who looked upon this meeting as a noble humanitarian measure believe that by it prejudices were removed and certain results to civilization made possible. Without concession, without any attempt to treat all religions as equally meritorious, without any compromise of any system of faith and worship, with no idea of finding or founding any new world-religion, with equal freedom gladly accorded to all races and both sexes—the sessions of the parliament continued in practically unbroken harmony. There was a vast significance to human brotherhood in the daily recital of the universal prayer, though the unity of the parliament was that of spirit rather than of creed. If this meeting simply effected a wider diffusion of brotherliness, it deserves, as the London *Daily Telegraph* has said, "a place among the notable events of our age."[39] It was certainly a protest against exclusiveness of feeling, the ignorant pride, the ecclesiastical aloofness, and the dogmatic haughtiness which often prevail. It will be easier henceforth for men to feel "that they do not sully their religious creeds and lives by permitting them to touch any others."

The ethical unity apparent at the parliament was profoundly impressive, and whoever henceforth makes an appeal for international righteousness may quote the universal judgment and sentiment of the congress of religions. Doubtless many will fear that one effect of the parliament will be still further to modify the ancient orthodox teaching in regard to the doom of all those who have not known and accepted the historic Christ. But this result is a benign one. Many of the mistakes the critics of the parliament have made would have been

---

[39] Cf. *The London Daily Telegraph*, as quoted with no date given in *WFP*, p. 29.

avoided had they gained a larger idea of the work of Christ, as the "Original Light enlightening every man that cometh into the world"; and there should be no hesitation to receive as a part of the working creed of Christianity, the verses of Whittier:

Wherever through the ages rise
The altars of self-sacrifice,
Where love its arm has opened wide
Or man for man has calmly died,
I see the same white wings outspread
That hovered o'er the Master's head.[40]

Such are some of the echoes and results of this memorable meeting. The chief promoters of the parliament, grateful for what they have been able to do, would be glad to have done something better and larger. But most of them will be content if the words of Dr. Lyman Abbott shall be prophetic, "that the final issue of the religious parliament will be at once to broaden our conception of Christianity, and to make its acceptance both a logical and a spiritual necessity,"[41] or if the words of Prof. Grose, of the Chicago University, prove historic, that "the parliament was divinely designed to broaden the bounds of human brotherhood and charity; to bring the leaders of the world's religious thought today into bonds of sympathetic acquaintance and fellowship; to reveal spirit unto spirit; and to deepen the universal sense of the fatherhood of God and the brotherhood of man."[42]

---

[40] On the support lent by the American poet John Greenleaf Whittier (1807-92) for the idea behind the parliament, see in this volume the article by Ziolkowski.

[41] Lyman Abbott (1835-1922), pastor of Plymouth Congregational Church and editor-in-chief of *The Outlook*, "Lessons from the Parliament of Religions," *Christian Thought*, ed. Charles Deems (New York: W. Ketcham, 1893-94), p. 223. Abbott had delivered a paper at the parliament entitled "Religion Essentially Characteristic of Humanity," in *WPR*, 1:494-501.

[42] This same statement by Howard Benjamin Grose (1851-1939), clergyman and professor of history, is cited by M.N. Dvivedi in the *Times* of India, Bombay, as quoted with no date given in *WFP*, p. 40. Grose was Editorial Secretary of the American Baptist Home Mission Society.

THE REAL SIGNIFICANCE
OF THE PARLIAMENT OF RELIGIONS

Friedrich Max Müller

There are few things which I so truly regret having missed as the great Parliament of Religions held in Chicago as a part of the Columbian Exhibition. Who would have thought that what was announced as simply an auxiliary branch of that exhibition could have developed into what it was, could have become the most important part of that immense undertaking, could have become the greatest success of the past year, and I do not hesitate to say, could now take its place as one of the most memorable events in the history of the world?

As it seems to me, those to whom the great success of this ecumenical council was chiefly due, I mean President Bonney and Dr. Barrows, hardly made it sufficiently clear at the beginning what was their real purpose and scope. Had they done so, every one who cares for the future of religion might have felt it his bounden duty to take part in the congress. But it seemed at the first glance that it would be a mere show, a part of the great show of industry and art. But instead of a show it developed into a reality, which, if I am not greatly

"The Real Significance of the Parliament of Religions" by F. Max Müller. Reprinted from *The Arena* 11, no. 61 (December 1894):1-14, where the text is accompanied by a note that says it "was read by Professor Müller in Oxford, England, a few months ago." All footnotes are added.

mistaken, will be remembered, aye, will bear fruit, when everything else of the mighty Columbian Exhibition has long been swept away from the memory of man.

Possibly, like many bright ideas, the idea of exhibiting all the religions of the world grew into something far grander than even its authors had at first suspected. Even in America, where people have not yet lost the faculty of admiring, and of giving hearty expression to their admiration, the greatness of that event seems to me not yet fully appreciated, while in other countries vague rumors only have as yet reached the public at large of what took place in the religious parliament at Chicago. Here and there, I am sorry to say, ridicule also, the impotent weapon of ignorance and envy, has been used against what ought to have been sacred to every man of sense and culture; but ridicule is blown away like offensive smoke; the windows are opened and the fresh air of truth streams in.

It is difficult, no doubt, to measure correctly the importance of events of which we ourselves have been the witnesses. We have only to read histories and chronicles written some hundreds of years ago by eye witnesses and by the chief actors in certain events, to see how signally the observers have failed in correctly appreciating the permanent and historical significance of what they saw and heard, or of what they themselves did. Everything is monumental and epoch-making in the eyes of ephemeral critics, but History must wait before she can pronounce a valid judgment, and it is the impatience of the present to await the sober verdict of History which is answerable for so many monuments having been erected in memory of events of men whose very names are now unknown, or known to the stones of their pedestals only.

But there is one fact in connection with the Parliament of Religions which no sceptic can belittle, and on which even contemporary judgment cannot be at fault. Such a gathering of representatives of the principal religions of the world has never before taken place; it is unique, it is unprecedented; nay, we may truly add, it could hardly have been conceived before our own time. Of course even this has been denied, and it has been asserted that the meeting at Chicago was by no means the first realization of a new idea upon this subject, but that similar meetings had taken place before. Is this true or is it not? To me it seems a complete mistake. If the religious parliament was not an entirely new idea, it was certainly the first realization of an idea which has lived silently in the hearts of prophets, or has been uttered now and then by poets only, who are free to dream dreams and to see visions. Let me quote some lines of Browning's, which certainly sound like true prophecy:

Better pursue a pilgrimage
  Through ancient and through modern times,
  To many peoples, various climes,
Where I may see saint, savage, sage
Fuse their respective creeds in one
Before the general Father's throne![1]

Here you have no doubt the idea, the vision of the religious parliament of the world; but Browning was not allowed to see it. *You* have seen it, and America may be proud of having given substance to Browning's dream and to Browning's desire, if only it will see that what has hitherto been achieved must not be allowed to perish again.

To compare that parliament with the council of the Buddhist King Aśoka, in the third century before Christ, is to take great liberties with historical facts. Aśoka was no doubt an enlightened sovereign, who preached and practised religious toleration more truly than has any sovereign before or after him. I am the last person to belittle his fame; but we must remember that all the people who assembled at his council belonged to one and the same religion, the religion of Buddha, and although that religion was even at that early time (242 B.C.) broken up into numerous sects, yet all who were present at the Great Council professed to be followers of Buddha only. We do not hear of Gainas [sic] nor Agîvikas or Brahmans, nor of any other non-Buddhist religion being represented at the Council of Pataliputra.

It is still more incongruous to compare the Council of Chicago with the Council of Nicaea. That Council was no doubt called an ecumenical council, but what was the οἰκουμένη, the inhabited world, of that time, 325 A.D., compared with the world as represented at the Columbian Exhibition of last year? Nor was there any idea under Constantine of extending the hand of fellowship to any non-Christian religion. On the contrary the object was to narrow the limits of Christian love and toleration, by expelling the followers of Arius from the pale of the Christian church. As to the behavior of the bishops assembled at Nicaea, the less that is said about it the better; but I

---

[1] Robert Browning, *Christmas-Eve and Easter-Day* (1850), part 1, section 19, lines 1144-57, in *The Complete Works of Robert Browning, with Variant Readings and Annotations*, general ed. Roma A. King, Jr., 5 vols. (Athens: Ohio University Press, 1961-81), 5:89-90.

doubt whether the members of the Chicago Council, including bishops, archbishops and cardinals, would feel flattered if they were to be likened to the fathers assembled at Nicaea.

One more religious gathering has been quoted as a precedent of the Parliament of Religions at Chicago; it is that of the Emperor Akbar; but although the spirit which moved the Emperor Akbar (1542-1605) to invite representatives of different creeds to meet at Delhi, was certainly the same spirit which stirred the hearts of those who originated the meeting at Chicago, yet not only was the number of religions represented at Delhi much more limited, but the whole purpose was different. Here I say again, I am the last person to try to belittle the fame of the Emperor Akbar. He was dissatisfied with his own religion, the religion founded by Mohammed; and for an emperor to be dissatisfied with his own religion and the religion of his people, augurs, generally, great independence of judgment and true honesty of purpose. We possess full accounts of his work as a religious reformer, from both friendly and unfriendly sources; from Abufazl on one side, and from Badáoní on the other.[2]

Akbar's idea was to found a new religion, and it was for that purpose that he wished to become acquainted with the prominent religions of the world. He first invited the most learned ulemahs to discuss certain moot points of Islam, but we are told by Badáoní that the disputants behaved very badly, and that one night, as he expresses it, the neck of the ulemahs swelled up, and a horrid noise and confusion ensued. The emperor announced to Badáoní that all who could not behave, and who talked nonsense, should leave the hall, upon which Badáoní remarked that in that case they would *all* have to leave.[3] Nothing of this kind happened at Chicago, I believe. The Emperor Akbar no doubt did all he could to become acquainted with other religions, but he certainly was not half so successful as was the president of your religious congress in assembling around him representatives of the principal religions of the world. Jews and Christians were summoned to the imperial court, and requested to translate the Old and the New Testament. We hear of Christian

---

[2] F. Max Müller, *Introduction to the Science of Religion*, Lectures at the Royal Institution, 1870 (London: Longmans, Green, 1873), appendix to lecture 1, pp. 68-100.

[3] Ibid., pp. 83-84. In paraphrasing the translated quote of Badáoní from ibid, Müller exaggerates Badáoní's claim, substituting "they would *all* have to leave" (emphasis in the text) for "*most* of the 'Ulamás would have to leave" (emphasis mine).

missionaries, such as Rodolpho Aquaviva, Antonio de Monserrato, Francisco Enriques and others; nay, for some time a rumor was spread that the emperor himself had actually been converted to Christianity.

Akbar appointed a regular staff of translators, and his library must have been very rich in religious books. Still he tried in vain to persuade the Brahmans to communicate the Vedas to him or to translate them into a language which he could read. He knew nothing of them, except possibly some portions of the Atharva-veda, probably the Upanishads only. Nor was he much more successful with the Zend Avesta, though portions of it were translated for him by one Ardshiv. His minister, Abufazl, tried in vain to assist the emperor in gaining a knowledge of Buddhism; but we have no reason to suppose that the emperor ever cared to become acquainted with the religious systems of China, whether that of Confucius or that of Lao-tze. Besides, there was in all these religious conferences the restraining presence of the emperor and of the powerful heads of the different ecclesiastical parties of Islam. Abufazl, who entered fully into the thoughts of Akbar, expressed his conviction that the religions of the world have all one common ground.[4] "One man," he writes, "thinks that he worships God by keeping his passions in subjection; another finds self-discipline in watching over the destinies of a nation. The religion of thousands consists in clinging to a mere idea; they are happy in their sloth and unfitness of judging for themselves. But when the time of reflection comes, and men shake off the prejudices of their education, the threads of the web of religious blindness break, and the eye sees the glory of harmoniousness." "But," he adds, "the ray of such wisdom does not light up every house, nor could every heart bear such knowledge."[5] "Again," he says, "although some are enlightened, many would observe silence from fear of fanatics, who lust for blood, though they look like men. And should any one muster sufficient courage, and openly proclaim his enlightened thoughts, pious simpletons would call him a madman, and throw him aside as of no account, whilst the ill-starred wretches would at once think of heresy and atheism, and go about with the intention of killing him."[6]

This was written more than three hundred years ago, by a minister of Akbar, a contemporary of Henry VIII; but if it had been written in

---

[4] Ibid., pp. 69-70.
[5] Ibid., p. 70. The wording of this particular translated quote as it appears here differs slightly from its wording in ibid.
[6] Ibid., p. 71.

our own days, in the days of Bishop Colenso and Dean Stanley,[7] it would hardly have been exaggerated, barring the intention of killing such "madmen as openly declare their enlightened thoughts"; for burning heretics is no longer either legal or fashionable. How closely even the emperor and his friends were watched by his enemies we may learn from the fact that in some cases he had to see his informants in the dead of night, sitting on a balcony of his palace, to which his guest had to be pulled up by a rope! There was no necessity for that at Chicago. Your parliament at Chicago had not to consider the frowns or smiles of an emperor like Constantine; it was encouraged, not intimidated, by the presence of bishops and cardinals; it was a free and friendly meeting, nay, I may say a brotherly meeting, and what is still more—for even brothers will sometimes quarrel—it was a harmonious meeting from beginning to end. All the religions of the world were represented at your Congress, far more completely and far more ably than in the palace at Delhi, and I repeat once more, without fear of contradiction, that the Parliament of Religions at Chicago stands unique, stands unprecedented in the whole history of the world.

There are, after all, not so many religions in the world as people imagine. There are only eight great historical religions which can claim that name on the strength of their possessing sacred books. All these religions came from the East; three from an Aryan, three from a Semitic source, and two from China. The three Aryan religions are the *Vedic*, with its modern offshoots in India, the *Avestic* of Zoroaster in Persia, and the religion of *Buddha*, likewise the offspring of Brahmanism in India. The three great religions of Semitic origin are the *Jewish*, the *Christian* and the *Mohammedan*. There are, besides, the two Chinese religions, that of *Confucius* and that of *Lao-tze*, and this is all; unless we assign a separate place to such creeds as Gainism [sic], a near relative of Buddhism, which was ably represented at Chicago, or the religion of the Sikhs, which is after all but a compromise between Brahmanism and Mohammedanism.

All these religions were represented at Chicago; the only one that might complain of being neglected was Mohammedanism.

---

[7] Arthur Penrhyn Stanley (1815-81), English divine, historian and theological writer, was professor of ecclesiastic history at Oxford (1856-63), and appointed dean of Westminster in 1863. John William Colenso (1814-83), was a liberal Anglican bishop of Natal, South Africa (from 1853), and scholar, whose critical writings on the Pentateuch drew tremendous and bitter opposition and led him to be convicted of heresy in 1864 by Cape Town's Bishop Robert Gray. The following year Colenso was acquitted.

Unfortunately the Sultan, in his capacity of Khalif, was persuaded not to send a representative to Chicago.[8] One cannot help thinking that both in his case and in that of the Archbishop of Canterbury, who likewise kept aloof from the congress,[9] there must have been some unfortunate misapprehension as to the real objects of that meeting. The present Sultan is an enlightened and intelligent Mohammedan, and could hardly have wished that his religion should be left without any authoritative representative, in a general gathering of all the religions of the world. It was different with the Episcopalian Church of England, for although the Archbishop withheld his sanction, his church was ably represented both by English and American divines.

But what surprised everybody was the large attendance of representatives of all the other religions of the world. There were Buddhists and Shintoists from Japan, followers of Confucius and Lao-tze from China, there was a Parsee to speak for Zoroaster, there were learned Brahmans from India to explain the Veda and Vedânta. Even the most recent phases of Brahmanism were ably and eloquently represented by Mozoomdar, the friend and successor of Keshub Chunder Sen, and the modern reformers of Buddism in Ceylon had their powerful spokesman in Dharmapâla. A brother of the King of Siam came to speak for the Buddhism of his country. Judaism was defended by learned rabbis, while Christianity spoke through bishops and archbishops, nay, even through a cardinal who is supposed to stand very near the papal chair. How had these men been persuaded to travel thousands of miles, to spend their time and their money in order to attend a congress, the very character and object of which were mere matters of speculation?

Great credit no doubt is due to Dr. Barrows and his fellow-laborers; but it is clear that the world was really ripe for such a congress, nay, was waiting and longing for it. Many people belonging to different religions had been thinking about a universal religion, or at least about a union of the different religions, resting on a recognition of the truths shared in common by all of them, and on a respectful toleration of what is peculiar to each, unless it offended against reason or morality. It was curious to see, after the meeting was over, from how many sides voices were raised, not only expressing approval of what had been done, but regret that it had not

---

[8] See John Henry Barrows, "The History of the Parliament," in *WPR*, 1:20.
[9] See ibid., 1:20-22.

been done long ago. And yet I doubt whether the world would really have been ready for such a truly ecumenical council at a much earlier period. We all remember the time, not so very long ago, when we used to pray for Jews, Turks and infidels, and thought of all of them as true sons of Belial. Mohammed was looked upon as the arch enemy of Christianity, the people of India were idolaters of the darkest die, all Buddhists were atheists, and even the Parsees were supposed to worship the fire as their god.

It is due to a more frequent intercourse between Christians and non-Christians that this feeling of aversion toward and misrepresentation of other religions has of late been considerably softened. Much is due to honest missionaries, who lived in India, China, and even among the savages of Africa, and who could not help seeing the excellent influence which even less perfect religions may exercise on honest believers. Much is also due to travellers who stayed long enough in countries such as Turkey, China or Japan to see in how many respects the people there were as good, nay, even better, than those who call themselves Christians. I read not long ago a book of travels by Mrs. Gordon, called *Clear Round*. The author starts with the strongest prejudices against all heathens, but she comes home with the kindliest feelings towards the religions which she has watched in their practical working in India, in Japan and elsewhere.[10]

Nothing, however, if I am not blinded by my own paternal feelings, has contributed more powerfully to spread a feeling of toleration, nay, in some cases, of respect for other religions, than has the publication of the *Sacred Books of the East*.[11] It reflects the highest credit on Lord Salisbury, at the time secretary of state for India, and on the university of which he is the chancellor, that so large an undertaking could have been carried out, and I am deeply grateful that it should have fallen to my lot to be the editor of this series, and that I should thus have been allowed to help in laying the solid foundation of the large temple of the religion of the future—a foundation which shall be broad enough to comprehend every shade of honest faith in that Power which by nearly all religions is called *Our Father*, a name only, it is true, and it

---

[10] Elizabeth Anna Gordon, *"Clear Round!" Seeds of Story from Other Countries*, new ed., with illustrations, maps and introductory letter from F. Max Müller (London: S. Low, Marston, [1895]). A 3d edition, revised and enlarged, was published by the same press in 1903. The date of the first edition is uncertain.

[11] At the time he wrote this, Müller was still involved in editing this monumental fifty-volume series of translations, published by Oxford's Clarendon Press, 1879-1910.

may be a very imperfect name; yet there is no other name in human language that goes nearer to that forever unknown Majesty in which we ourselves live and move and have our being.

But although this feeling of kindliness for and the desire to be just to non-Christian religions has been growing up for some time, it never before found such an open and solemn recognition as at Chicago. That meeting was not intended, like that under Akbar at Delhi, for elaborating a new religion, but it established a fact of the greatest significance, namely, that there exists an ancient and universal religion, and that the highest dignitaries and representatives of all the religions of the world can meet as members of one common brotherhood, can listen respectfully to what each religion had to say for itself, nay, can join in a common prayer and accept a common blessing, one day from the hands of a Christian archbishop, another day from a Jewish rabbi, and again another day from a Buddhist priest (Dharmapâla). Another fact, also, was established once for all, namely, that the points on which the great religions differ are far less numerous, and certainly far less important, than are the points on which they all agree. The words, "that God has not left Himself without a witness," became for the first time revealed as a fact at your congress.

Whoever knows what human nature is will not feel surprised that every one present at the religious parliament looked on his own religion as the best, nay, loved it all the same, even when on certain points it seemed clearly deficient or antiquated as compared with other religions. Yet that predilection did not interfere with a hearty appreciation of what seemed good and excellent in other religions. When an old Jewish rabbi summoned up the whole of his religion in the words, "Be good, my boy, for God's sake," no member of the Parliament of Religions would have said No; and when another rabbi declared that the whole law and the prophets depend on our loving God and loving our neighbor as ourselves, there are few religions that could not have quoted from their own sacred scriptures more or less perfect expressions of the same sentiment.

I wish indeed it could have been possible at your parliament to put forward the most essential doctrines of Christianity or Islam, for example, and to ask the representatives of the other religions of the world, whether their own sacred books said Yes or No to any of them. For that purpose, however, it would have been necessary, no doubt, to ask each speaker to give chapter and verse for his declaration,—and here is the only weak point that has struck me and is sure to strike others in reading the transactions of the Parliament of Religions. Statements were put forward by those who professed to speak in the name of Buddhism, Brahmanism, Christianity and Zoroastrianism—by followers of these religions who happened to be present—which, if the speakers had been asked for chapter and verse from their own canonical books, would have been difficult to substantiate, or, at all events, would have assumed a very modified aspect. Perhaps this was inevitable, particularly as the rules of the parliament did not encourage anything like discussion, and it might have seemed hardly courteous to call upon a Buddhist archbishop to produce his authority from the Tripitake [sic] or from the nine Dharmas.

We know how much our own Christian sects differ in the interpretation of the Bible, and how they contradict one another on many of their articles of faith. Yet they all accept the Bible as their highest authority. Whatever doctrine is contradicted by the Bible they would at once surrender as false; whatever doctrine is not supported by it they could not claim as revealed. It is the same with all the other so-called book-religions. Whatever differences of opinion may separate different sects, they all submit to the authority of their own sacred books.

I may therefore be pardoned if I think the Parliament of Religions, the record of which has been assembled in forty silent volumes, is in some respects more authoritative than the parliament that was held at Chicago. At Chicago you had, no doubt, the immense advantage of listening to living witnesses; you were *making* the history of the future—my parliament in type records only the history of the past. Besides, the immense numbers of hearers, your crowded hall joining in singing sacred hymns, nay, even the magnificent display of color by the representatives of Oriental and Occidental creeds—the snowy lawn, the orange and crimson satin, the vermilion brocade of the various ecclesiastical vestments so eloquently described by your reporters—all this contributed to stir an enthusiasm in your hearts which I hope will never die. If there are two worlds, the world of deeds and the world of words, you moved at Chicago in the world of deeds. But in the end what remains of the world of deeds is the world of words, or, as we call it, *History,* and in those forty volumes you may see the history, the outcome, or, in some cases, the short inscription on the tombstones of those who in their time have battled for truth, as the speakers assembled at Chicago have battled for truth, for love, and for charity to our neighbors.

I know full well what may be said against all sacred books. Mark, first of all, that not one has been written by the founder of a religion; secondly, that nearly all were written hundreds, in some cases thousands, of years after the rise of the religion which they profess to represent; thirdly, that even after they were written, they were exposed to dangers and interpolations; and fourthly, that it requires a very accurate and scholarlike knowledge of their language and of the thoughts of the time when they were composed, in order to comprehend their true meaning. All this should be honestly confessed; and yet there remains the fact that no religion has ever recognized an authority higher than that of its sacred book, whether for the past or the present or the future. It was the absence of this authority, the impossibility of checking the enthusiastic descriptions of the supreme excellence of every single religion, that seems to me to have somewhat interfered with the usefulness of that great ecumenical meeting at Chicago.

But let us not forget, therefore, what has been achieved by your parliament in the world of deeds. Thousands of people from every part of the world have for the first time been seen praying together, "Our Father, which are in heaven," and have testified to the words of the prophet Malachi, "Have we not all *one* Father, hath not *one* God created us?" They have declared that "in every nation he that feareth God and worketh righteousness is acceptable to Him." They have seen with their own eyes that God is not far from each one of those who seek God, if haply they may feel after Him. Let theologians pile up volume upon volume of what they call theology; religion is a very simple matter, and that which is so simple and yet so all-important to us, the living kernel of religion, can be found, I believe, in almost every creed, however much the husk may vary. And think what that means! It means that above and beneath and behind all religions there is one eternal, one universal religion, a religion to which every man, whether black or white or yellow or red, belongs or may belong.

What can be more disturbing and distressing than to see the divisions in our own religion, and likewise the divisions in the eternal and universal religion of mankind? Not only are the believers in different religions divided from each other, but they think it right to hate and to anathematize each other on account of their belief. As long as religions encourage such feelings none of them can be the true one.

And if it is impossible to prevent theologians from quarreling, or popes, cardinals, archbishops and bishops, priests and ministers, from pronouncing their anathemas, the true people of God, the universal laity, have surely a higher duty to fulfill. Their religion, whether formulated by Buddha, Mohammed or Christ, is before all things practical, a religion of love and trust, not of hatred and excommunication.

Suppose that there are and that there always will remain differences of creed, are such differences fatal to a universal religion? Must we hate one another because we have different creeds, or because we express in different ways what we believe?

Let us look at some the most important articles of faith, such as *miracles, the immortality of the soul,* and *the existence of God.* It is well known that both Buddha and Mohammed declined to perform miracles, nay, despised them if required as evidence, in support of the truth of their doctrines. If, on the contrary, the founder of our own religion appealed, as we are told, to his works in support of the truth of his teaching, does that establish either the falsehood or the truth of the Buddhist, the Mohammedan or the Christian religion? May there not be truth, even without miracles? Nay, as others would put it, may there not be truth, even if resting apparently on the evidence of miracles only? Whenever all three religions proclaim the same truth, may they not all be true, even if they vary slightly in their expression, and may not their fundamental agreement serve as stronger evidence even than all miracles?

Or take a more important point, the belief in the immortality of the soul. Christianity and Mohammedanism teach it, ancient Mosaism seems almost to deny it, while Buddhism refrains from any positive utterance, neither asserting nor denying it. Does even that necessitate rupture and excommunication? Are we less immortal because the Jews doubted and the Buddhists shrank from asserting the indestructible nature of the soul?

Nay, even what is called *atheism* is, often, not the denial of Supreme Being, but simply a refusal to recognize what seem to some minds human attributes, unworthy of the Deity. Whoever thinks that he can really deny Deity, must also deny humanity; that is, he must deny himself, and that, as you know, is a logical impossibility.

But true religion, that is, practical, active, living religion, has little or nothing to do with such logical or metaphysical quibbles. Practical religion is life, is a new life, a life in the sight of God; and it springs from what may truly be called a new birth. And even this belief in a new birth is by no means an exclusively Christian idea. Nicodemus might ask, How can a man be born again? The old Brahmans, however, knew perfectly well the meaning of that second birth. They called themselves Dvi-ga, that is Twice-born, because their religion had led them to discover their divine birthright, long before *we* were taught to call ourselves the children of God.

In this way it would be possible to discover a number of fundamental doctrines, shared in common by the great religions of the world, though clothed in slightly varying phraseology. Nay, I believe it would have been possible, even at Chicago, to draw up a small number of articles of faith, not, of course, thirty-nine, to which all who were present could have honestly subscribed. And think what that would have meant! It rests with us to carry forth the torch that has been lighted in America, and not to allow it to be extinguished again, till a beacon has been raised lighting up the whole world and drawing towards it the eyes and hearts of all the sons of men in brotherly love and in reverence for that God who has been worshipped since the world began, albeit in different languages and under different names, but never before in such unison, in such world-embracing harmony and love, as at your great religious council at Chicago.

In conclusion let me say that I am a very old showman at Oxford University, and I may say truly that there are no strangers that I like so much to conduct personally over Oxford as the Americans. They seem to know what to look for,—they want to see the colleges of Locke, of Adam Smith, of Shelley, of Stanley, and they thoroughly enjoy what they see. They feel at home at Oxford, and they speak of it as their own university, as the glorious nursery of those men whose example has made America as great as she is. They have come on what they call a pilgrimage to England—and it is quite right that the land of their fathers should be to them a holy land. After all, the glories of England are theirs—their fathers fought its battles by land and by sea; their fathers made it a home of freedom; their fathers, when freedom of word and thought and deed seemed threatened for a while, protested, and migrated to found a New England on the other side of the Atlantic.

But blood is thicker than water, thicker even than the Atlantic. With every year the old feeling of brotherhood asserts itself more strongly between Americans and Englishmen, between the Old and the New England. I have many friends in America, not one who is not a friend of England, not one who does not feel that in the struggle for political and religious freedom which looms in the future, Englishmen and Americans should always stand shoulder to shoulder, should form one united people. Whatever may be said against England—and a good deal has been said against her by what I heard an American ambassador call, the other day, "the mischievous boy of the family," always the most popular with mothers, sisters and cousins, if not with fathers and aunts—but whatever has been or may said against England, can you imagine what the world would be without England? And do you believe that New England, Young England, would ever stand by with folded arms to see Old England touched, so long as a drop of Saxon blood was left in the veins of her soldiers and sailors?

Here, too, as in the Parliament of Religions of Chicago, it would be easy to show that the points on which Americans and Englishmen differ are nothing as compared to those on which they agree. Take one instance only. If England and America were to say once for all that there shall be no war without previous arbitration, and that whatever country objects to this article of international faith, shall for the time be excluded from all international amenities, shall be *taboo* politically and financially, the world might breathe again more freely, the poor would be allowed again to eat their bread in peace, we should have what the First Parliament of the World's Religions proclaimed as "the true glory to God." We are all members of the great parliament of the world; let us show that we can be above party, above country, above creed, and that we owe allegiance to truth only, and to that voice of conscience which is the "real presence" in the universal communion of mankind.

PART
III

A Cosmopolitan Habit in Theology

Martin E. Marty

The theological modernists were male members of the privileged subculture, almost all of them Protestant. Far from being reluctant adapters to changes, they wanted to work with the momentum of their faith to advance such change in an effort to be of help to other believers who welcomed the new day but for whom the old statement of faith had become a problem. Their first step in promoting modernism was to seek a universal outlook, to overcome the provincialism that they thought afflicted religion. The Reverend George Gordon of Boston's prestigious Old South Church, saw in modernity the "steady emergence of a cosmopolitan habit."[1] It called forth, he thought, new and pragmatic approaches to religious thought. Weary of pettiness, in the mid-nineties Gordon proclaimed that a vision of a kingdom of the Spirit had risen in his day. This kingdom would appropriate the wealth of all faiths. It would be free because it

---

"A Cosmopolitan Habit in Theology" by Martin E. Marty. This essay originally constituted chap. 2 of Martin E. Marty, *Modern American Religion*, vol. 1: *The Irony of It All: 1893-1919.* ©1986 by the University of Chicago Press. Reprinted here with permission of the author and the University of Chicago Press. The last three paragraphs, which deal with the congress of the Evangelical Alliance, a Protestant ecumenical group, that followed the Parliament of Religions from October 8 to 15, have been omitted.

[1] George A. Gordon, *The Christ of To-Day* (Boston: Houghton Mifflin, 1895), p. 20.

would isolate itself, said the preacher, "from particular times and places."[2]

Such a cosmopolitan habit led the modernists to cherish events that would attract people from their provincial places to confront faiths that reached back to diverse times past. Two years before Gordon wrote, there occurred the most elaborate display of religious cosmopolitanism yet seen on the continent. In Chicago, on a September morning in 1893, in the first year of the fifth American century, four thousand people jammed the Hall of Columbus on the lakefront, there to greet one of the more strange processions in American history. Representatives of dozens of faiths and flags marched past cheering crowds to that hall in what was later to become the city's Art Institute. They moved to a stage for speeches and ceremonies that made up a World's Parliament of Religions. The director of the World's Columbian Exposition, Colonel George R. Davis, had opened that fair itself months earlier. He saw it as a celebration of the ceaseless, irresistible march of civilization. The times were coming to the climax when people would learn, he said, "the nearness of man to man, the Fatherhood of God and the brotherhood of the human race."[3] While his images were all male, his exposition and the parliament also engaged a larger percentage of women than such public events would involve for decades to come.[4] A new era was unfolding.

What united the cosmopolites was a faith that they and the thousands of participants in the two-week parliament were in the vanguard of a religious triumph. Baptist George Dana Boardman of Philadelphia was to look back on the congress as an effort to array if possible all religions against irreligion. Particular religions, he and his colleagues thought, were too divided to accomplish a protest against materialism.[5]

---

[2] Ibid., pp. 28-29.

[3] Quoted by David F. Burg, *Chicago's White City of 1893* (Lexington: University Press of Kentucky, 1976), who accounts for the parliament's opening day (pp. 100-108; quote on p. 104).

[4] For contexts, see Reid Badger, *The Great American Fair: The World's Columbian Exposition and American Culture* (Chicago: Nelson-Hall, 1979), and Jeanne Madeline Weimann, *The Fair Women* (Chicago: Academy Chicago, 1981).

[5] George Dana Boardman, *The Parliament of Religions: An Address before the Philadelphia Conference of Baptist Ministers, October 23, 1893* (Philadelphia: National Baptist Printing Agency, 1893), p. 5.

Reporters were dazzled by the blur of color. The ranking American Catholic prelate, scarlet-robed James Cardinal Gibbons of Baltimore, sat near Oriental delegates "whose many-colored raiment vied with his own in brilliancy," according to one observer.[6] They were followers of Brahma and Buddha and Muhammad. Nearby was yellow-turbaned Vivekananda in red apparel. He shared the stage with B. B. Nagarkar of the Brāhmo-Samāj, a group of Hindu Theists, and Dharmapāla, a Ceylonese Buddhist scholar. There were Parsee and Jain ecclesiastics, Chinese and Japanese delegates, Taoists, Confucians, and Shintoists. Each of them, said the observer, was a picturesque study in color and movement, and all were eager to explain and defend their forms of faith. The more somberly dressed American Protestants who set the stage and called most of the tunes all but blended into the woodwork.[7] These universalizers bowed heads for recitation by Gibbons of "the Universal Prayer," the Lord's Prayer.

The need for a cosmopolitan outlook was obvious to these leaders in 1893. William R. Alger of Boston used timely references to remind conferees of the alternatives. Just before the parliament, Bombay Brahmins and Muhammadans were slaughtering each other, "hating each other more than they loved the generic humanity of God." Christians nearby in Montreal and Toronto were at the point of murdering each other. All over the world, said Alger, and who could gainsay him, hatred was made religion. The hatred of professors of religion for one another "is irreligion injected into the very core of religion." Alger optimistically called his speech "How to Achieve Religious Unity."[8]

Aware that the provincialists and sectarians were sneering at the parliament, speaker after speaker justified it. *Monist* editor Paul Carus, a radical believer in human and religious revolution, gibed back at the throwbacks. Broad Christianity, he announced, must replace their exclusive, bigoted, narrow, and so-called orthodox Christianity. Carus then proclaimed a main modernist tenet. "The nature of religious truth is the same as that of scientific truth. There is but one truth." He could be sympathetic, he said, toward those people who must momentarily pass through all the despair of infidelity and religious emptiness. They were on the way toward modern faith. Any

---

6 Report of Rev. Mr. Wendte of Oakland, California, as cited by Barrows, "The History of the Parliament," in *WPR*, 1:62.

7 See the report of Wendte, as cited by Barrows, "History," in *WPR*, 1:64.

8 William R. Alger, "How to Achieve Religious Unity," in *WPR*, 2:1313.

other kind, since it rejected science, was inevitably doomed. "It cannot survive and is destined to disappear with the progress of civilization."[9]

Only slightly more restrained was Charles Carroll Bonney, who was a partner in promoting the parliament idea. He belonged to the Swedenborgians, or Church of the New Jerusalem, which numbered 7,095 in the 1890 census. Bonney welcomed attendees in the name of the Church of the Holy City, the Church of Reconciliation. Its creed was also modernist: "It comes to reconcile reason and faith, science and religion, miracle and law, revelation and philosophy,...the teachings of sacred scripture and the results of modern research."[10] Like others at the parliament, the Swedenborgians stood by ready to present their church doctrines as the basis of a universal faith. Bonney seemed plausible as he opened the congress by announcing that it would stand in human history like a new Mount Zion, and begin "a new epoch of brotherhood and peace."[11] He was only echoing what Oxford's Max Müller, the most notable scholar of world religion in his day, had said in his letter of regret. Müller could not attend, but he was sure that the congress would be "one of the most memorable events in the history of the world."[12] Bonney, it should be remarked, was sophisticated in his relativism and aware of the tenacity of enduring differences. Meanwhile, he thought, each religion could immediately acquire absolute respect for the religious convictions of others. Each system now stood "in its own perfect integrity, uncompromised, in any degree, by its relation to any other,"[13] but Bonney was an essentialist who believed that there were common essentials by which everyone may be saved, in all the religions.

Bonney's partner was a much more moderate person, no modernist at all. Presbyterian John Henry Barrows, wrote his daughter Mary Eleanor, was a man with a conservative love of tradition and decorum, who contributed Protestant decorousness and manners to the parliament. He was an enigma, she thought, to the less supple orthodox back home who were often "too literally logical to allow for

---

[9] Paul Carus, "Science a Religious Revelation," in *WPR*, 2:980, 981. See also Paul Carus, "The Dawn of a New Religious Era," *The Forum* 16 (November 1893): 388-96.

[10] Charles Carroll Bonney, address to the New Jerusalem Church Congress, in *WPR*, 2:1488

[11] Charles Carroll Bonney, opening-day address, in *WPR*, 1:67

[12] Quoted from Müller's article in this volume.

[13] Bonney, opening-day address, in *WPR*, 1:72.

the spirit blowing where it listeth,"[14] as he himself would allow. When Barrows later went to India to deliver lectures endowed in his honor, fellow Christians there found him orthodox. He was, however, of the new style in temper; his heart was so liberal, so world-embracing, so many-sided, it was said, that it also fit the cosmopolitan mold.

Barrows wanted to be more Christian in particular senses than Carus and Bonney. Those who found limits in his faith and who thus refused to hear its claims of universalism, were unscientific. Christianity was "the only truly redemptive and the only progressive religion."[15] What he called the ethnic faiths were to him often curiosities or moral monstrosities, but he was civil about them and granted them a stage. The Bonney-Barrows tandem displayed some of the inner contradictions of the parliament. Both had a blueprint for universalism, yet one was more repudiative of existing Judaism, Islam, and other non-Christian faiths. Barrows was overt about the need for mild aggression. The parliament, he argued, could accomplish more than any Christian missionary society, because it was under no ecclesiastical dictation, and hence appealed in the spirit of fraternity to high-minded individuals. Barrows had to be emphatic: "The idea of evolving a cosmic or universal faith out of the Parliament was not present in the minds of its chief promoters."[16] The elements of such a faith were already contained, he thought, in the Christian ideal and the Christian scriptures.

What Barrows lived with in ambiguity was simply denounced by Protestants who opposed the parliament. Not all were as strident as prime evangelist Billy Sunday would be years later. Sunday looked back on the parliament as one of the biggest curses that ever came to America.[17] Already in 1892 the Presbyterian General Assembly, speaking for the church to which Barrows belonged, called the anticipated parliament uncalled for, misleading, and hurtful. Arthur Tappan Pierson, a prominent reactionary, knew that the congress gave the impression that Christianity *"may not be the only Divine religion."* Someone, he thought, must expose the puerilities and absurdities, the contradictions and immoralities of heathen faiths. The parliament

---

[14] Mary Eleanor Barrows, *John Henry Barrows: A Memoir* (Chicago: Fleming H. Revell, 1904), p. 162.

[15] John Henry Barrows, "The Greatness of Religion," *Quarterly Calendar,* University of Chicago, 3 (November 1894): 10.

[16] Barrows, "Review and Summary," in *WPR,* 2:1572.

[17] Billy Sunday is quoted in Jacob Henry Dorn, *Washington Gladden* (Columbus: Ohio State University Press, 1966), p. 388.

motto, he thought, should have been "laxity, apathy, and compromise."[18]

The many hundreds of participants dispersed, to enjoy a generally good press. The proceedings of the parliament take up 1,600 pages in two volumes. Scholars were to debate for years to come the complex of parliamentarians' intentions and the frustrations of many of their goals. The swamis and other representatives from Asia packed their robes and sailed for the Orient or stayed as missionaries. Catholics began to argue over what Gibbons had said and whether they should have been there in the first place. Some Christian missionaries grumbled that the parliament had dimmed the luster of their own efforts to convert the heathen. Had unity been achieved at all? No two groups at the event began to merge. Designed to show the unity of faiths, it displayed a split within the company of conveners, a set of disparities and disputes among denominations in this world's fair of faiths. Instead of dialogue a succession of monologues had occurred. Most of the cosmopolitans showed themselves to have been covert or overt parochials. In the Hall of Washington right next door, some forty denominations were to hold their own sideshows in those weeks.[19]

---

[18] Kenten Druyvesteyn, "The World's Parliament of Religions," Ph.D. diss., University of Chicago, 1976, pp. 124-29, 132, cites *Minutes* of the General Assembly of the Presbyterian Church and various writings of Arthur Tappan Pierson against the parliament.

[19] Reports on the denominational congresses make up part 4 of *WPR*, 2:1383-1544.

THE 1893 WORLD'S PARLIAMENT
OF RELIGIONS AND ITS LEGACY

Joseph M. Kitagawa

While visiting India last December, Professor Nathan Glazer found and forwarded to me a letter written by a Mr. Ramamurti of Madras, addressed to the editor of the *Hindu*. The letter reads:

> The first World Parliament of Religions was held in Chicago, U.S., in 1893....The second conference was held in Chicago forty years later and it was called "World Fellowship of Faith"....It was expected at that time that there would be another conference of religions forty years later. That was meant to be in 1973. But there was no conference and forty years went by. Now the fiftieth year [from 1933] is coming,

"The 1893 World's Parliament of Religions and Its Legacy" by Joseph M. Kitagawa. ©1983 by the American Academy of Religion. Originally published as Joseph M. Kitagawa, *The 1893 World's Parliament of Religions and Its Legacy*, eleventh John Nuveen Lecture, 1983 (Chicago: University of Chicago Divinity School; Baptist Theological Union, 1983). Parts of this material were also presented by Dr. Kitagawa as the 75th Anniversary Lecture of the Haskell Lectureship at Oberlin College and as the Stewart Lecture at Princeton University. The entire lecture, with the exception of the opening portion concerning and including the letter from Ramamurti, is reprinted as the "Appendix" to Joseph M. Kitagawa, *The History of Religions: Understanding Human Experience*, AAR Studies in Religion (Atlanta, Ga.: Scholars, 1987), pp. 352-68. Reprinted here, complete with that opening portion, by permission of Scholars Press.

1983, and it is time that Chicago held another conference with another name...fitting the progress of religions during the fifty years....

I do hope this thought will reach Chicago...and competent person or persons will organize the third conference of religions for the unity of all religions. May this message reach Chicago!

I have no illusion that I am that "competent person" who can organize such a congress here this year, or any other year, for that matter; nor do I sense that City Hall has any interest in another parliament or religions in connection with its proposed World Fair in 1992. I have often wondered why the Parliament of Religions, which has been all but forgotten here in Chicago, has remained so vivid in the memories of many religious people in other parts of the world. I have also been intrigued by the fact that such an unprecedented affair as the Parliament of Religions was held as a part of the Columbian Exposition, which marked the four hundredth anniversary of Columbus's discovery of America.

Admittedly, there are many different ways to deal with these questions. I would like to share with you my reflections on the significance of, first, the unlikely convergence of two very different undertakings, that is, the Columbian Exposition and the Parliament of Religions; second, the encounter of Western Christendom and Eastern religions in the nineteenth century as reflected in the parliament; and third, the mixed legacies of the parliament which we have inherited.

Historically, Columbus's discovery of America signified the ascendency of the Western powers, which by the end of the nineteenth century dominated the entire world politically, economically, and culturally. There is much truth in Toynbee's well-known observation that "in the encounter between the [non-Western] world and the West that has been going on...for four or five hundred years...it is the [non-Western] world that has been hit—and hit hard—by the West."[1] The enormous vitality of the West during the past five centuries has been made apparent in the cultural domain through the phenomena of modern nation-states, economic nationalism, a new social structure, and the Renaissance, and in the religious domain through the Reformation and the Counter Reformation.

It was the Renaissance which gave birth to the new conception of "civilization"—that is, Western civilization—as a pseudoreligion of

---

[1] Arnold Toynbee, *The World and the West* (New York: Oxford University Press, 1953), pp. 1-2.

secularized salvation. Rejecting the medieval notion that civilization was subservient to the church, modern Europeans came to regard themselves as the inventors and transmitters of true civilization. The phenomenal expansion of the West, coming as it did after Europe's centuries-old struggle against the world of Islam, convinced many Europeans of the superiority of their culture, their technology, and their socio-economic and political systems. They came to be persuaded that "biology and sociology point to the superiority of...the white races over the coloured races of the earth. Superiority in physical and mental constitution, together with superiority in civilization and organization, entail responsibility as well as privilege."[2] This notion is what Kipling called "the white's man's burden"—the underlying, motivating force implicit in the colonial expansion of the modern West over the non-Western world.

Significantly, Pietist Christians in the eighteenth century rejected the secular view of the human being as the creator of cultural values. Thus the initial ethos of the Christian foreign missions, inaugurated by the continental Pietists and English Evangelicals, ran counter to the spirit of secular Europeans civilization and of colonialism. During the nineteenth century, however, the Christian missionary enterprise in Asia and Africa unwittingly cooperated with European colonialism, and Christianity was propagated for all intents and purposes as one—albeit an important one—of the constituents of Western civilization. The combined forces of Western civilization, Christian missionary activities, and colonial expansion brought about social, political, economic, cultural, and religious changes in much of the non-Western world by the end of the nineteenth century.

The self-confidence of the nineteenth-century West was extravagantly displayed in a series of large-scale exhibits and fairs held in Europe and America, starting with the 1851 Exhibition at the Crystal Palace in Hyde Park, London. The nineteenth century also witnessed the emergence of the United States onto the world stage as a new Western power, whereby eager Americans sponsored their own Crystal Palace exposition in New York in 1853 and a more successful Philadelphia Centennial exposition in 1876. (By the way, the eight million visitors who poured into Philadelphia were fascinated not only by the old Liberty Bell, but also by such new inventions as Alexander

---

[2] Allan John MacDonald, *Trade Politics and Christianity in Africa and the East* (London: Longmans, Green, 1916), p. 270.

Graham Bell's telephone, the Westinghouse air brake, Edison's duplex telegraph, the typewriter, and the sewing machine.) This event was followed by the Paris Exhibition of 1889, which lured the curious multitudes to the newly built Eiffel Tower. Then, in 1893, the Columbian Exposition, the last major exhibition of the nineteenth century, was held in Chicago as the crowning symbol of the achievement of Western civilization during the great century.

The Columbian Exposition was held in Jackson Park and the adjoining Midway. The expansive grounds, far larger than the space occupied by the Philadelphia Exposition, held a series of white buildings with classic facades, one of which was later remodelled as the Museum of Science and Industry. The exposition grounds also had large plazas, lagoons with floating gondolas, and a playground with the first ferris wheel, from which visitors could catch a glimpse of the infant University of Chicago. The designers of the "White City" made full use of electricity, and the great Allis engine in Jackson Park was dramatically started by President Cleveland in the White House at the touch of a magic button.[3]

The more I think about it, the idea of holding such an unprecedented assembly of representatives of the various religions of the world in connection with the Columbian Exposition is not so outrageous after all. As far as we can ascertain, the underlying link between the two events was the motif of "progress"—an idea that was shared by many American civic, government, business, and religious leaders in the nineteenth century. In this regard, we might recall Paul Tillich's distinction between the "concept" of progress, which is just a theoretical abstraction, and the "idea" of progress, which is an interpretation of our historic existence in terms of progress.[4] Religiously, the Jewish and Christian "idea" of progress is traced to the Hebrew scripture, according to which God had chosen a nation and a people and would fulfill his promise to move history toward a specific end. It is significant that the biblically oriented American pioneers interpreted the birth of the new republic in biblical terms. Moreover, many Americans felt that their experience in the nineteenth century of transforming landscape and overcoming frontiers confirmed their faith in progress. In this situation, progress

---

[3] For a description of the physical designs of the Columbian Exposition, see *The White City (As It Was)* (Chicago: White City Art Co., 1894).

[4] Paul Tillich, *The Future of Religions*, ed. Jerald C. Brauer (New York: Harper and Row, 1966), p. 64.

became "not only conscious doctrine but also an unconscious dogma."[5] This dogma was eloquently stated by Charles C. Bonney, an influential lawyer, a civic leader, and a devout Swedenborgian, who first proposed that the Parliament of Religions be held as an integral part of the Columbian Exposition. In his words:

> The coming glory of the World's Fair of 1893 should not be the exhibit...of [only] the material triumphs, industrial achievements, and mechanical victories of man, however magnificent that display may be. Something higher and nobler is demanded by the progressive spirit of the present age...[What is needed is] a congress of statesmen, jurists, financiers, scientists, literati, teachers, and theologians, greater in numbers and more widely representative of all peoples and nations and tongues than any assemblage which has ever yet been convened.[6]

The organizers of the Columbian Exposition accepted Bonney's proposal, and decided to hold the Parliament of Religions with the following charter:

> To unite all Religions against all irreligion; to make the Golden Rule the basis of this union; to present to the world...the substantial unity of many religions in the good deeds of the Religious life; to provide for a World's Parliament of Religions, in which their common aims and common grounds of unity may be set forth, and the marvelous *Religious progress* of the Nineteenth century be reviewed.[7]

The parliament was held from September 11 through 27, primarily at two assembly halls in the present Art Institute on Michigan Avenue. Each hall accommodated 3,000 people, and both were full at every session.

In retrospect, it is evident that the parliament had several layers of meaning. First, in spite of its designation as a "World's Parliament of Religions," it was predominantly an assembly of Christians, and more particularly of American Christians, who constituted the majority of the four hundred delegates. Although the parliament was not an official church assembly, it brought face-to-face representatives of various Christian groups, Roman Catholics, Orthodox, and many Protestant denominations, as well as those of smaller, splinter groups. Moreover, the programs of the parliament, though liberal, had a

---

[5] Ibid., p. 68.

[6] Charles Carroll Bonney, in an article of 1889 in the *Statesman*, cited in "The World's Congresses of 1893," in *NHP*, pp. 15-16.

[7] The World's Religious Congress, *Programme of the World's Religious Congresses of 1893* (preliminary edition, Chicago: Rand, McNally and Co., n.d.), p. 19, italics mine.

definite Christian flavor, with the singing of hymns and the recitation of the Lord's Prayer.

Second, the parliament signified the pluralistic religious reality of North America, epitomized by the presence of many articulate Jewish leaders, who took their rightful place beside Protestant and Roman Catholic leaders. The parliament also demonstrated the growing influence of laymen and laywomen in American religious life.

Third, the parliament presented a Christian theological rationale for inviting representatives of other religions to a common assembly. In the words of Charles Bonney, it was "a friendly conference [based on] the golden rule of Christ: a royal feast to which the representatives of every faith were asked to bring the richest fruits and rarest flowers of their religion."[8] No representative was asked to surrender any conviction he or she believed to be the truth, nor was anyone asked to participate in any part of the program of the parliament which might compromise his relationship to his own religion. Yet even then, some influential leaders, notably the Sultan of Turkey, strongly opposed the idea of the parliament; as a result of such opposition, Islam was represented only by an American convert to Islam and some Western scholars and missionaries who worked among Muslims. Fortunately, though, the parliament was able to attract articulate spokesmen of modern-day Hinduism, Buddhism, and other Eastern religions who came to Chicago in spite of the opposition of their conservative coreligionists at home. In a sense, the parliament dramatically acknowledged the general interest in Eastern religions that was developing among many Americans, an interest that was evidenced by the disproportionate degree of attention given to Eastern representatives by the daily presses; and as might be expected, this aspect of the parliament was condemned by some and praised by others among the Christian leaders and missionaries.

Fourth, while the parliament was an assembly of religious representatives and not a gathering of scholars, it nevertheless called attention to the need for scholarly approaches and resources in dealing with the fact of religious pluralism on the global scene. It is worth mentioning in this regard that Friedrich Max Müller, a leading spokeman of the new discipline of the science of religion (*Religionswissenschaft*), had enthusiastically endorsed the idea of the

---

[8] Charles Carroll Bonney, in *The Monist* 5 (April 1895): 323-24, quoted in *WFP*, p. 56.

parliament but could not attend; nor could another leading scholar, C. P. Tiele, whose paper was presented at the parliament by another representative.[9] But the presence of other important scholars from Europe and North America aroused keen interest among enlightened educators and religious leaders.

As we turn our attention to the encounter between Western Christendom and Eastern religions as reflected in the Parliament of Religions, it is worth recalling that the historic patterns of Christian outreach to the non-Western world, initiated by Iberian maritime kingdoms in the sixteenth century, had already deteriorated by the end of the eighteenth century. This deterioration was due in large part to the decline of Spain and Portugal and to the dissolution of the Society of Jesus. During the nineteenth century, Protestantism, which had been a minority movement in northwest Europe, took the initiative in the overseas missionary enterprise. By the end of the nineteenth century, almost every Christian group "and almost every country, from the Lutheran Church of Finland...to the newest sects in the United States, had its share in the missionary enterprise overseas."[10]

Initially, European colonial authorities were hostile to Christian missionary work. For example, the British East India Company followed the policy that "to hold India in subjugation Christian missionaries must be excluded."[11] Yet, colonial officials soon began to favor Christian missionary work, especially its educational and philanthropic activities. This development resulted in the conscious and unconscious cooperation of Christian missionaries with colonial administrators who reinforced each other in transmitting Western civilization to the non-Western world.

The massive penetration of Western civilization into the East greatly accelerated the disintegration of Asian societies, cultures, and religions during the nineteenth century. Inevitably there developed a deep chasm between the traditional Asian elites, who resented anything new and Western, and the new, Western-educated elites, who scorned old customs and values as a legacy of the backward, feudalistic past. With the passion of new converts, they were determined to interpret their own people's contemporary experiences

---

[9] C. P Tiele's paper is included in this volume. F. Max Müller likewise sent a paper which was read for him at the Parliament: "Greek Philosophy and the Christian Religion," included in *WPR*, 2:935-36 (Ed.).

[10] Stephen Neill, *The Christian Society* (London: Nisbet, 1952), p. 203.

[11] MacDonald, *Trade Politics*, pp. ix-x.

not with the accumulated values and wisdom of Asia, but with the new gospel of Western civilization: liberty, equality, fraternity, democracy, science, and technology. As might be expected, some of the new Asian elites embraced Christianity.

In addition to, or rather, in between the old and the new elites, there emerged a third type of Asian elite, who for lack of a better designation may be called simply "modern religious reformers." Although they were small in number and often criticized, attacked, and ridiculed by both the old and the new elites, these modern religious reformers had the unshakable conviction that their inherited religious and cultural traditions had sufficient resiliency to come to terms with the serious issues raised by modernity. They had been influenced by Western education and Western thought, but they were proud of the languages, cultures, and religions of their homelands. While not engaging in political activities, they were all patriots without being narrow nationalists. None of these figures were scholars by temperament, but they were religious and social reformers, keenly aware of the welfare of their own peoples. They were leaders and practitioners who possessed an astute understanding of their own religious traditions. Moreover, all of them had a global vision. Significantly, it was these modern religious reformers in Asia, and not the old elites or the traditional religious leaders, who responded to the invitation to participate in the Parliament of Religions.

Among those modern Asian religious reformers at the parliament, three are especially important for our consideration: Vivekananda of India (1863-1902), Dharmapāla of Ceylon, now Sri Lanka (1864-1933), and Shaku Sōen of Japan (1859-1919). All of them were relatively young then—Vivekananda was thirty, Dharmapāla was twenty-nine, and Shaku Sōen was thirty-four years of age. They were eager to come to Chicago, not only because they all subscribed to the principle of interreligious understanding and cooperation, but also because they saw in the parliament an opportunity which they had never had: a platform from which to address the whole world. Even though their own homelands were under the strong influence of Western civilization, these three young men had the audacious dream of reversing the tide of history and beginning the Easternization of the West.

Much has been written about Swami Vivekananda, the founder of the Ramakrishna Order. In his time, India was under the rule of the British Crown. English was already the lingua franca of the multilingual Indian subcontinent, and the educated Indians who were exposed to Western social and political philosophies wanted a greater share in the government of their own country. Great famines, such as the ones in Bihar from 1873 to 1883 and in South India from 1876 to 1878, continued to haunt India from inside, while Russian intrigue and Afghan wars threatened her from outside. Articulate, educated youths, dissatisfied with both the general state of unemployment and racial discrimination in government services, were attracted to political activities such as the Indian National Congress, while those more religiously motivated were lured to Hindu reform movements such as Keshab Chandra Sen's Brāhmo Samāj and Dayananda Sarasvati's Ārya Samāj.

Meanwhile, Vivekananda, who had studied law at the University of Calcutta and was about to sail to England for further study, abruptly changed his course and became the disciple of the saintly mystic, Sri Ramakrishna (1836-86). Under Ramakrishna, he endeavored to translate his master's teaching into concrete measures for the reformation of Hinduism and of Hindu society. Vivekananda's neo-Vedantic belief is based on the eternalness of the human soul, which is capable of becoming divine. His message to the world, as presented at the parliament, concerned the supremacy of the eternal principle (*sanātana dharma*) of the Hindu tradition as separated from its metaphysico-social principle and as exemplified by the caste *dharma* (*svadharma*), which is above all creeds and religions, Eastern or Western. He never asked whether such a separation of the eternal *dharma* from the Hindu religious and social tradition was legitimate, he simply preached: "Do not care for doctrines, do not care for dogmas, or sects, or churches, or temples; they count for little compared with the essence of existence in each man which is spirituality."[12] Understandably, his message at the parliament for religious toleration,[13] although reflecting his neo-Hindu perspective, was well received. After the parliament, he spent four years preaching his gospel in America and England, and upon his return to India, founded the Ramakrishna Mission, which now has branches in India as well as in various Western cities.

Dharmapāla—or more precisely, Anagārika Dharmapāla, "the celibate servant of the *Dharma*" (David Hewavitarane)—was a child

---

[12] *Speeches and Writings of Swami Vivekananda* (Madras: n.d.), p. 31.
[13] See "[Opening-day] Speech of Mr. Vivekananda," quoted by John Henry Barrows, "The History of the Parliament," in *WPR*, 1:102.

of Ceylon, the proud homeland of Pali Buddhism, but a homeland that had been occupied successively since the sixteenth century by the Portuguese, the Dutch, and the British. Early in the nineteenth century, the British had guaranteed the protection of Buddhism, but all education was controlled by Christian missionaries. In addition, the introduction of the planting of coffee resulted in the importation of a sizeable number of South Indian Hindu Tamil laborers, who settled in the northern section of Ceylon. With the opening of the Suez Canal in 1869, Colombo became a prosperous center of international trade. Understandably, the growing middle class in Ceylon became heavily westernized in orientation and in daily habits.

Amidst this mixed cultural milieu, through his numerous writings and speeches, the young Dharmapāla advocated the importance of the Buddhist heritage, Buddhist education, and the Singhalese language and culture. In addition, in 1891, two years before the parliament, he founded the Mahā Bodhi Society, originally the Bodhgayā Mahābodhi Society, in Colombo. One of the purposes of this society was to work towards the restoration of the sacred city of Bodhgayā in India as the site for a monastery and college, to be staffed by scholars from various Buddhist nations in Asia. In both of his projects, Dharmapāla was greatly aided by the Buddhist Theosophical Society, founded in Ceylon by Colonel Henry Steel Olcott and Madame Blavatsky; and it was through the activities of the Mahā Bodhi Society in its publications and its educational and evangelistic works that important contributions were made to both the rejuvenation of Buddhism in Ceylon and India and the expansion of Buddhism to the West.

At the parliament, Dharmapāla presented the main tenets of Buddhism with a touch of Theosophy, stressing that "Buddhism is a scientific religion, inasmuch as it earnestly enjoins that nothing whatever be accepted on faith....Buddhism is tantamount to a knowledge of other sciences."[14] Understandably, the scientific nature of Buddhism, an important aspect of modern Buddhism, caught the attention of many people at the parliament. Dharmapāla also offered advice to the Christian missionaries: "If you want to establish Christianity in the East it can only be done on the principles of Christ's love and meekness. Let the missionary study all the religions; let them

---

[14] Dharmapāla, "The World's Debt to Buddha," in *WPR*, 2:878.

[sic] be a type of meekness and lowliness and they will find a welcome in all lands."[15]

Little is known in the West about Shaku Sōen other than that he was instrumental in bringing D.T. Suzuki to the West; but he was a remarkable person in his own right. He was born shortly after Commodore Perry's expeditions, which forcibly opened Japan's doors to the West. During Shaku's childhood, the feudal regime declined and the Meiji imperial regime began its reign. Under the pro-Shinto policy of the imperial regime, Buddhism lost many of its traditional prerogatives. Moreover, Buddhism now faced the massive impact of Western civilization and the newly introduced Christianity. Under these circumstances, the morale of Japanese Buddhists reached its lowest ebb. Fortunately, there were a small number of enlightened Buddhist leaders, including Shaku's own master, Imagita Kōsen (1816-92), who were determined to reform Buddhism for the new age. Thus Shaku, unlike other Buddhist clerics of his time, studied at Keiō Gijuku, the center of the Japanese enlightenment movement, and also spent two years studying in Ceylon and visiting Thailand and China. In 1892, at the age of thirty-three, Shaku became the chief abbot of the prestigious Engaku-ji, Kamakura, and attracted many serious-minded lay disciples, including D.T. Suzuki.

At the parliament, Shaku pleaded for world peace and mutual assistance: "Let us, the true followers of Buddha, the true followers of Jesus Christ, the true followers of Confucius and the followers of truth, unite ourselves for the sake of helping the helpless and living glorious lives of brotherhood under the control of truth."[16] After the parliament, he made two more visits to the West, accompanied by his disciple, D. T. Suzuki, also preparing the ground for Zen Buddhist activities in the West. True to his convictions, when he returned to Japan he was instrumental in organizing the Buddhist-Christian conference of 1896, then known as the "Little Parliament of Religions," against strong opposition from both sides. Parenthetically, at its second meeting in 1897, the main speaker was John Henry Barrows, the permanent chairman of the Chicago Parliament of Religions, about whom I will speak presently.

Even such brief portraits of these three modern religious reformers from the East make it clear, I hope, that what they had expected from

---

[15] Dharmapāla, "Address" in section on "Criticism and Discussion of Missionary Methods," in *WPR*, 2:1093.

[16] Shaku Sōen (Shaku Soyen), "Arbitration Instead of War," in *WPR*, 2:1285.

the parliament was slightly different from the intent of the organizers. To Charles Bonney and his colleagues, the parliament was an "extended Christian feast" to which the representatives of other religions were asked to bring the richest fruits and rarest flowers of their faiths. What the religious reformers from Asia expected to find was a genuine parliament of religions, in which representatives of all religions would share their insights and wisdom as to how each faith could cope with the issues raised by modernity, and how "all religions [could] be united against all irreligion," to use the phrase of the preliminary program of the parliament.

Undoubtedly the most important leader and spokesman of the parliament was the then forty-six-year-old John Henry Barrows, pastor of the First Presbyterian Church in Chicago, who served as the permanent chairman of the parliament. A graduate of Olivet College, Yale University, Union Seminary, and Andover Seminary, Barrows had had pastorates in Kansas, Massachusetts, and Paris. He was a relative newcomer to Chicago, and he liked the city, which was then rebuilding from the devastation of the Great Fire. He quickly made the acquaintance of civic leaders, many of whom supported both the parliament and the new University of Chicago. He was also a great admirer of William Rainey Harper, the energetic first president of the University of Chicago, who held a vision of the "second Reformation" of Christianity through scholarship. It was reported that over 1,000 members were added to Barrows's parish during the first two years of his pastorate. His personality comes through vividly in a letter he wrote a few years after the parliament during his tenure as president of Oberlin College. The letter was addressed to the newborn son of Professor J. Ross Stevenson of McCormick Theological Seminary. It reads:

> My dear William:
> I have just heard of your alighting on this planet and hasten to welcome you to the land of William McKinley and the speech of William Shakespeare. I am sorry that you cannot vote against William Bryan, but your father will do that for you.
>
> As a Republican, a Presbyterian, an American, a Chicagoan, and as the son and heir of such a father and mother your prospects are bright. Be good to your father. Kindly tell them how happy I am for them. Believing that you are "the bright, consummate flower" of the

vanishing century and with all high hopes, I remain, with loving congratulations to your jubilant parents.[17]

The letter was dated November 1, 1900. Incidentally, the baby in question, William Edward Stevenson, later followed Barrows as the eighth president of Oberlin College.

Both as an American and as a Christian, Barrows shared the optimism of his generation. He lived at a time when America was internally recovering from the effects of the Civil War and externally emerging as a new world power. His was also the time when many idealistic young men and women took up evangelistic, educational, and philanthropic activities in far-off lands. Their vision was exemplified by the motto of the Student Volunteer Movement: "The evangelization of the world in this generation."

During the parliament, the tall and genial Barrows, combining learning, rhetorical gifts, and a sense of humor, won the admiration of participants and the press for his intelligence, ability, tact, skill, and courage. He perceived the meaning of the parliament in terms of three concentric circles, with the Christian assembly at its center. Indeed, to him the parliament was the first modern parliament of Christendom and marked an important step toward the prophecy of a united church. In his words: "The solemn charge which the Parliament preaches to all true believers is a return to the primitive unity of the world....The results may be far off, but they are certain."[18]

Next to the Christian center was the circle of the American religious assembly. Following the American principle of religious liberty, this circle demonstrated both a genuine cooperation between Jews, whom he called Old Testament Christians, and Christians, whom he called New Testament Jews, and the growing leadership of women in American religious life.

Third and last came the outer circle comprising all the religions of the world, and on this level, Christianity was one among many faiths "competing for the conquest of mankind."[19] To Barrows, the plurality

---

[17] Printed in Oberlin College *Alumni Magazine* (December 1958). I owe this information to Professor Grover Zinn, Jr.

[18] Quoted directly from the reprint in *WFP*, p. 60, of an excerpt from the article by John Henry Barrows in the present volume. In the original *Forum* text of Barrows's article (i.e., the text reprinted in this volume), the phrase reprinted in *WFP* and quoted by Kitagawa as "the primitive unity of the world," reads "the primitive unity of Christians" (Ed.).

[19] From Barrows's article in this volume.

of religions was a genuine mystery, but he was certain that the deity whom Jews and Christians worship had something to do with all these religions of the world. He asked, "Why should not Christians be glad to learn what God has wrought through Buddha and Zoroaster—through the sages of China, and the prophets of India and the prophet of Islam?"[20]

For Barrows, therefore, what united these three circles of the parliament was the religious quest, the hope, and the longing of the children of the one God, the Christians and the Jews, and adherents of other faiths. As he stated in his opening address:

> We are met as religious men, believing even here [meaning Chicago] in this capital of material wonders, in the presence of an Exposition which displays the unparalleled marvels of steam and electricity, that there is a *spiritual root to all human progress*. We are met in a school of comparative theology...in the temper of love, determined to bury, at least for the time, our sharp hostilities, anxious to find out wherein we agree, eager to learn what constitutes the strength of other faiths and the weakness of our own.[21]

It is interesting to note that Barrows's search for "a spiritual root of all human progress" led him to turn not to theology but to "comparative religion" for illumination. Untrained in any aspect of comparative religion, he had nevertheless an immense admiration for Friedrich Max Müller, that ardent spokesman for the emerging discipline of the science of religion, although Barrows's understanding of comparative religion was much more simplistic and pragmatic than his mentor's explications. For example, Barrows cites the work of Max Müller solely to make his point that the same sun "which shone over Bethlehem and Calvary has cast some celestial illumination and called forth some devout and holy aspirations by the Nile and the Ganges, in the deserts of Arabia and by the waves of the Yellow Sea."[22]

Barrows was entirely clear, however, about the concrete objectives of comparative religion in his time. These objectives were: (1) to present to the West the religious reality of the world, especially undistorted accounts of non-Christian religions, in order to combat general ignorance and prejudice in "Christian lands" concerning other religions; (2) to present to the non-Western world the best available

[20] Barrows, opening-day address, in his "History," in *WPR*, 1:75.
[21] Ibid., italics mine.
[22] Ibid., 1:74-75.

views on the relations of Christianity and other religions; and (3) to probe more deeply into the ancient Near Eastern religious roots which had culminated in the Bible and Christianity. He did not see any fundamental tension between being both a seeker of universal religious truth and a Christian. Accordingly, he was able to welcome openly and warmly the representatives of the many different religions who had gathered together at the parliament; and in his address at the closing session, he stated quite as sincerely: "I desire that the last words which I speak to this Parliament shall be the name of Him to whom I owe life and truth and hope and all things, who reconciles all contradictions, pacifies all antagonisms, and who from the throne of His heavenly kingdom directs the serene and unwearied omnipotence of redeeming love—Jesus Christ, the Saviour of the world."[23]

One can readily understand that the parliament provoked both extremely positive and intensely negative reactions in its contemporaries. Yet as we look back from today's vantage point after ninety years, we can probably assess without undue emotionalism the mixed legacies of the parliament.

First, it is important to point out that, contrary to popular views, the parliament did not initiate comparative religion in America. It did, however, provide such a strong stimulus for the wide acceptance of the study of comparative religion in American colleges, universities, and theological seminaries that in the minds of many Americans comparative religion and the cause of the Parliament of Religions became inseparably related. To be sure, there were some positive results from such an identification. For example, Barrows's contagious enthusiasm for comparative religion, which he called "the highest study to which the human mind can now devote its energies,"[24] caught the imagination of one of his parishioners, Mrs. Caroline Haskell, the widow of the wealthy businessman, Frederick Haskell. In 1894, she established the Haskell Lectureship in Comparative Religion at the infant University of Chicago, expressing herself "in hearty agreement with the conviction that the immense interest awakened by the wonderful Parliament of Religions makes it eminently desirable that the students in the University of Chicago, and the people generally, shall be given wise instruction on this most important of all subjects."[25] Barrows was named the first Haskell Lecturer of this lectureship,

---

[23] John Henry Barrows, closing speech, quoted in his "History," in *WPR*, 1:184.
[24] Quoted from Barrows's article in this volume.
[25] President's Papers, 1889-1925, University of Chicago Archives, box 35, folder 2.

which has since brought many prominent scholars from Asia and Europe, including Professor Mircea Eliade, who subsequently stayed at Chicago.

Later in that same year, Mrs. Haskell offered to the University of Chicago a second endowed lectureship, with the request that this one bear the name of John Henry Barrows. The purpose of this lectureship was the presentation of lectures on "the relations of Christianity and other religions," to be given in India and, if deemed best, in other parts of Asia. Again Barrows became the first lecturer of this series, even though it meant resignation from his pulpit. It is worth noting that this lectureship sent many scholars to India from the University of Chicago, including Dean Charles Gilkey and Professors Bernard E. Meland and James M. Gustafson. Moreover, it was this same Mrs. Haskell who donated to the University Haskell Hall, which for many years housed the Divinity School, the office of the University president, and the Haskell Oriental Museum. At its dedication, Professor George S. Goodspeed spoke on Mrs. Haskell's behalf, expressing the hope that "there will go forth from these halls enlightenment, inspiration, and guidance in that learning which has come from the East and which, culminating in the Book of Books and in the teaching and life of the Son of Man, will ever abide as our most precious possession."[26] The cornerstone of Haskell Hall bears inscriptions in three languages: in Greek, "He was the true light, that, coming into the world, enlighteneth every man"; in Latin, "Light out of the East"; and in Hebrew, "The entrance of thy words giveth light." I am sure that our colleagues in the Anthropology Department, the present inhabitants of Haskell Hall, have some appreciation of these inscriptions.

In 1898, when Barrows became president of Oberlin College, Mrs. Haskell designated funding for another Haskell Lectureship to be based at Oberlin for the promotion of scholarship in oriental literature and its relation to the Bible and Christianity. Like its Chicago forerunner, Oberlin's Haskell Lectureship has brought a number of eminent scholars to this country, including Rudolf Otto, Adolf Deissmann, Günther Bornkamm, and Yihard Yadin.

In addition to the three lectureships established by Mrs. Haskell, around this time a group of scholars on the East Coast were forming

---

[26] Cited in *The Biblical World* n.s. 5 (February 1895): 132-34, reprinted in *WFP*, pp. 12-13 [although not with Goodspeed's remarks (Ed.)].

the American Committee for Lectures on the History of Religions. The chief advocate of this lectureship was Morris Jastrow of the University of Pennsylvania, who is considered to be the "father" of what is today called "religious studies" in America. This lectureship brought T. W. Rhys Davids, Karl Budde, J. J. M. de Groot, Franz Cumont, C. Snouck Hurgronje, and other leading scholars to the United States. In 1937, the lectureship was taken over by the American Council of Learned Societies and has come to be known as the ACLS Lectures on History of Religions.[27] Professor Peter Brown served as the 1982-83 ACLS Lecturer.

Despite—or possibly because of—its lack of clarity as a discipline, the popularity of comparative religion during the first quarter of our century was greatly aided by the spirit of religious liberalism predominant at that time, a spirit which affirmed the oneness of humanity and which had an optimistic vision of social progress. Later, in the 1930s, the sudden decline of comparative religion was accelerated by the impact of neoorthodox theology, the depression, and the impending war.

Ironically, the Parliament of Religions and its advocacy of comparative religion had a very different effect upon Eastern religions than it had upon the American religious scene. Actually, what modern religious reformers from the East, for example, Vivekananda of India, Dharmapāla of Ceylon, and Shaku Sōen of Japan, learned at the parliament was not comparative religion à la Barrows but the Christian formula of "fulfillment" implicit in Barrows's understanding of comparative religion, according to which all the religious quests of the human race, including those of the other great religions, would be "fulfilled" in the Christian gospel. These modern religious reformers in Asia quickly appropriated this "formula" for themselves and reversed the Christian claim, developing "fulfillment" theories from their own faith perspectives.

Following the lead of these early modern religious reformers, many articulate spokesmen of Eastern religions in our time have refined their "apologetics." They do not suggest that Christianity is wrong; rather, they insist that they can embrace Christianity within their particular religious frameworks, much as Barrows and his colleagues

---

[27] See D.H. Daugherty, "Committee on the History of Religions," *ACLS Newsletter* 15 (November 1964): 11-13.

tried to do from a Christian perspective at the parliament. Thus, Sarvepalli Radhakrishnan states:

> The saving knowledge of God is not knowledge and faith in Jesus as a historic person portrayed in the Gospels.... Christ is the spirit of the Supreme, the Eternal Word....
>
> Christian religion is the continuation and restoration of the ancient religions, of something eternal, the Law which Christ came to fulfill but not to destroy....To be a Christian is not the profession of an outward creed but the living of an inward life.[28]

Likewise, Shaku Sōen's disciple, D.T. Suzuki, gives the Zen commentary on the Genesis account of creation:

> When God saw the light which came out of his command, he said, "It is good." This appreciation on the part of God is the first awakening of consciousness in the world; in fact the beginning of the world itself. The mere separation of light and darkness does not demonstrate the beginning. The world starts only when there is mind which appreciates, viz., a mind critically conscious of itself. This is also the eating of "the fruit of the tree which is in the midst of the garden." The eating means "knowing good and evil," appraising the light and darkness, and in this appraisal, in this knowledge, there is the secret of living by Zen.[29]

In retrospect, it becomes clear that what the parliament contributed to Eastern religions was not comparative religion as such. Rather, Barrows and his colleagues should receive credit for initiating what we call today the "dialogue among various religions," in which each religious claim for ultimacy is acknowledged.

Another important fact which those of us interested in religion often forget is that the Parliament of Religions was but one of twenty congresses held as part of the Columbian Exposition, including those on women's progress, the public press, medicine and surgery, temperance, moral and social reform, commerce and finance, music, literature, education, engineering, art, government, science, and philosophy. However successful or unsuccessful they may have been, we cannot help being impressed by the bold vision of the planners of the Columbian Exposition for the "establishment of a universal fraternity of learning and virtue" coupled with the firm affirmation of

---

[28] Sarvepalli Radhakrishnan, *Recovery of Faith* (New York: Harper, 1955), pp. 159-60.

[29] D.T. Suzuki, *Living by Zen* (New York: Rider, 1950), p. 13.

the human capacity to move forward.[30] Yet in their organizational overkill they viewed religion as a single dimension, however important and colorful, of human activities. In so doing, despite the best of intentions they trivialized the very nature of religion itself. This pigeon-holing of religion into one aspect of human life is what Paul Tillich later criticized as the *"Time Magazine* approach to religion," the allocation to it of a small space between sections on theater and sports. Accordingly, many people now take it for granted that if the pope were shot, it would be a religious matter, whereas Hindu-Muslim conflicts in India or Christian-Muslim conflicts in the Philippines are either international or domestic political matters. Be that as it may, we can ill afford to forget the parliament and its mixed legacies which we have inherited, directly or indirectly.

Not so long ago I was showing a Buddhist visitor from Japan around the campus, and as we walked along the Midway, I explained to him that it was the site of the lagoon during the Columbian Exposition. Then I told him that one evening, so the story goes, some leaders of the parliament were aboard a gondola floating over the illuminated waters. Stunned by the beauty of the White City, the Ceylonese Dharmapāla said with a smile, "All the joys of heaven are in Chicago," to which an English delegate replied, "I wish I were sure that all the joys of Chicago are to be in heaven." In reporting this conversation, John Henry Barrows added his comment: "But surely there will be a multitude there, whom no man can number, out of every kindred and people and tongue, and in that perpetual parliament on high the people of God will be satisfied."[31]

Now all of these leaders have joined the heavenly parliament, leaving behind precious memories of a grandiose vision, an undaunted spirit, and a profound dedication to the search for truth in religion—indeed, noble legacies that we are proud to inherit.

---

[30] Charles Carroll Bonney, closing speech, quoted by Barrows, "History," in *WPR*, 1:186.

[31] Reported by Barrows in his closing speech, quoted in his "History," in *WPR*, 1:183.

PLURALISM AND THE AMERICAN MAINSTREAM
The View from the World's Parliament of Religions

Richard Hughes Seager

On September 28, 1893, *The San Francisco Examiner* described the closing day at the World's Parliament in Chicago with the headlines:

A GRAND WORK PERFORMED
GREAT PROGRESS MADE BY THE RELIGIOUS PARLIAMENT
SPREAD OF UNIVERSAL GOSPEL

The *Examiner* reported that throughout the day hundreds of would-be spectators and scalpers charging three and four dollars for tickets gathered on Chicago's downtown streets. The evening plenary session was repeated twice; each time "three thousand men and women were on their feet waving handkerchiefs, clapping hands, and cheering." Julia Ward Howe "kissed her hand in benediction of the Parliament"; the "Jewish rabbi and the Catholic Bishop asked God's blessing upon its work which is now a part of history." Christian and Hebrew, Buddhist and Muslim, the *Examiner* announced, all "spoke for a

"Pluralism and the American Mainstream: The View from the World's Parliament of Religions" by Richard Hughes Seager. ©1989 by the President and Fellows of Harvard College. This article appeared in *Harvard Theological Review* 82 (1989): 301-24. Reprinted by permission of the author and *Harvard Theological Review*.

universal religion, advocated it in fact, and fervently hoped for some such...happy consummation as the outcome of this great and historic gathering."[1]

Astonishment at the success of the parliament was widespread, provoking enthusiastic, caustic, and often excessive commentary. At Oxford, F. Max Müller was moved both to congratulate the assembly's organizers and to clarify a few historical inaccuracies that had crept into the parliament's many praises. No, Müller pointed out, the parliament was not strictly comparable to Aśoka's Pāṭaliputra Council in the third century B.C.E. That had been for Buddhists only. Nor was the parliament like Akbar's Delhi conference in the sixteenth century. Akbar sought a new religion to unite his empire and, unlike the free and friendly atmosphere reported in Chicago, the Delhi proceedings had been fraught with suspicion and political intrigue. It was equally incorrect to compare the parliament to the fourth-century council at Nicaea. Nicaea drew delegates from only a small corner of the inhabited world, and it did not seek to embrace religious diversity, but to expel the Arians from the pale of Christianity. "I repeat once more, without fear of contradiction," Müller concluded, "that the Chicago Parliament stands unique, unprecedented in the whole history of the world."[2]

Müller, the great pioneer of comparative religious history, made a scholarly assessment of the parliament in terms of its antecedents in the entire sweep of world religious history. But many clerical commentators made more strictly religious observations about the assembly, and they tended to inform their varied assessments by drawing analogies between it and events in Christian sacred history. For George Candlin, a liberal and progressive missionary, the encounter among the representatives of the religions of the world was "the Mount Tabor of our experience...[the] holy impulse of those transfigured hours will not be spent while life shall last." For Greek Archbishop Dionysios Latas, it evoked the more traditional image of the missionary as a new Paul, preaching once again to the Athenian pagans on Mars Hill. A more ominous precedent was called to mind by evangelical conservative William Ashmore, a veteran of the China mission. "God's elect flirted with the daughters of Moab," Ashmore lamented, "Israel danced with Baal." The parliament was also hailed

---

[1] *San Francisco Examiner*, September 28, 1893, p. 2.
[2] Quoted from the article by F. Max Müller in this volume.

as a "new and larger Pentecost." Yet, while some read in it signs which pointed to a whole new era in human history, others glimpsed in it a vision of the apocalyptic church.[3]

The parliament was unquestionably a dramatic and extraordinary event, and as the widely varied assessments of its significance suggest, it meant different things for different people. But for all the historical and spiritual insights that could be gleaned from it, it remains a fact that the many lessons of the parliament—whatever they were construed to be—quickly ceased to be of much interest. After a flurry of commentary for several years, the parliament dropped out of the picture, and it is a measure of its plunge into obscurity that Joseph Kitagawa could comment in 1983 that the parliament, while remembered warmly in certain quarters overseas, "has been all but forgotten in Chicago."[4] The weighty volumes of the parliament's published papers have been available in numerous libraries for almost a hundred years,[5] but scholars have yet to make a comprehensive assessment of its significance because the assembly slipped through the grids that have structured the study of religion in the United States for the better part of a century.

Slipping Through Scholarly Grids

Most historians of American religion have long followed in the footsteps of a pantheon of pioneering heroes who have had little in common with the pioneers of world religious history such as F. Max Müller. For Americanists, Protestant church historians such as Philip Schaff, Robert Baird, William Warren Sweet, and a host of others, have been the names to conjure with. Generations of talented and able figures have followed their lead in developing an interpretive grid for American religious history, but one that had little concern for the broader contours of world religious history. This preoccupation with a national field and a simultaneous lack of interest in comparative

---

[3] George Candlin, "Results and Mission of the Parliament of Religions," *The Biblical World* n.s. 5 (1895): 373. See Latas, "The Greek Church," in *WPR*, 1:358. For Ashmore, see A.T. Pierson, "The Parliament of Religions: A Review," *The Missionary Review of the World* n.s. 7 (December 1894): 891-92. For contrasting "New and larger Pentecost" citations, see *WPR*, 1:509; 2:1338, 1346.

[4] Quoted from the lecture by Joseph M. Kitagawa in this volume.

[5] The Barrows volumes are presented as the "official" collection of parliament papers. Other somewhat shorter collections also exist, including *NHP*, and J. W. Hanson, ed., *The World's Congress of Religions: The Addresses and Papers Delivered before the Parliament* (Chicago: W.B. Conkey, 1894).

religion was undoubtedly a factor in the parliament's century of obscurity.

But a more pressing reason runs deeper than that, down into the structure of the traditional discourse on American religious history. R. Laurence Moore has analyzed the ground rules by which scholars studied religion in America well over a century.[6] A central paradigm informing most interpretive scholarship was the contrast between the religious mainstream and fringe. Since the antebellum period, a handful of large and powerful evangelical churches—the mainstream—were presented as the normative description of American religion. Religious groups and trends that diverged from these such unlikely bedfellows as Catholics, Jews, deists, and sectarians—were acknowledged by scholars to exist, but they were seen to be standing on the fringe as a presence deemed both unfortunate and temporary.

Moore argues that the plot of this type of history was informed by an overriding concern for unity among mainstream Protestant churches and by a fundamental assumption that these churches were of determinative importance to both the morality and the religious genius of the nation. Within the perimeter of these ground rules, generations of scholars created what Moore called "the historiography of a desire." Questions asked about American religious history reflected the concerns of historians who, as churchmen hailing from the mainstream, desired that unity, not diversity, would characterize American religion and who presumed that fringe groups would remain more or less irrelevant to the mainstream-dominated center stage.

It was only very recently that this consensus-dominated, mainstream and fringe paradigm was seriously challenged as the norm for American religious history.[7] Sydney Ahlstrom, Edwin

---

[6] R. Laurence Moore, "Protestant Unity and the American Mission—The Historiography of a Desire," in his *Religious Outsiders and the Making of Americans* (New York: Oxford University Press, 1986), pp. 3-21.

[7] An excellent reflection on the historiographic changes at this time can be found in Glenn Bucher, "Options for American Religious History," *Theology Today* 33 (1976): 178-88. Of particular interest is Bucher's observation that from Sydney Ahlstrom's point of view, starting as he did with the Puritan experience in old and New England, the 1960s represented the beginnings of a post-Puritan era in American religious history. For Sidney Mead, however, for whom the fulcrum of American religious history was the eighteenth century, the 1960s represented the natural fulfillment of the ideals of the Enlightenment. In this context, the parliament can be seen either as a harbinger of Ahlstrom's collapse or

Gaustad, Martin Marty, Sidney Mead, and others, most of whom continued to call the mainstream their home, began to lay the groundwork for a new American religious history structured in terms of diversity, not unity. The pluralist religious climate of the late twentieth century increasingly became the starting point from which to survey American religious history. The assumption that there was a single center to the American experience was called into question. A pluralist paradigm moved into prominence in the field and began to force what amounts to a seachange in the way scholars think about American religious history.

Given the older emphasis on unity, consensus, and the importance of the mainstream churches, it is only to be expected that an event noted for its extraordinary diversity would not draw the sustained attention of church historians. Until pluralism became a field preoccupation, the World's Parliament of Religions remained a fringe phenomenon and was more or less forgotten.

But the parliament also slipped through the grid of a second branch of religious studies in the United States, the field of "comparative religions" or "history of religions." The comparativist by nature studies religions in their multiplicity, and his or her task is, as Joseph Kitagawa has suggested, to study "humanity's response to the sacred dimension of life and the world" in the context of the entire sweep of world history.[8] As an unprecedented encounter among the world's great faiths, it might be expected that the parliament would have been

---

of Mead's fulfillment. Given the fact that the parliament was an international rather than a strictly national event, it seems more accurate to see it as a part of the spread of the Enlightenment both in the U.S. and overseas—what William McNeill called the "onset of global cosmopolitanism"—than to confine it within the strictures of American Protestant categories (*A World History* [London: Oxford University Press, 1979], pp. 413-20).

[8] Joseph M. Kitagawa, "Humanistic and Theological History of Religions With Special Reference to the North American Scene," in Peter Slater and Donald Wiebe, eds., *Traditions in Contact and Change: Selected Proceedings of the XIVth Congress of the International Association for the History of Religions* (Waterloo, Ontario: Wilfrid Laurier University Press, 1983), p. 560. I use the term "comparativist" in full knowledge of the fact that many in the field prefer the phrase "historian of religions." In the American field, many historians who no longer think of themselves as "church historians" often call themselves "historians of religion," but do not mean to imply by this that they follow the methods of *Religionswissenschaft*. To avoid undue confusion, I use "Americanist" to refer to those who study religion in the United States and "comparativist" to denote those who study the religions of the world in a more or less comparative framework of understanding.

a prime candidate for analysis and interpretation by scholars in this second branch of religious history. Upon reflection, however, it is not difficult to suggest reasons for their lack of interest.

After the turn of the century, the parliament's limited reputation rested, in great part, on the fact that in Chicago the young discipline of comparative religion had been presented to the public as of a piece with the progressive ideals of Protestant liberalism.[9] It was under the wing of theological liberalism that the discipline began its march into the academy in the post-parliament decades, and the two remained linked for more than a quarter of a century. When Protestant liberals and comparativists began eventually to drift their separate ways, there remained little incentive for the latter to remember, much less to study, the parliament. Comparativists developed their own "mainstream." Paris and the first Congress of the History of Religions of 1900, not Chicago and the parliament of 1893, was recognized as the discipline's inaugural assembly. Historians of religions focused primarily on the "classical" expressions of the world's "great traditions," and they preoccupied themselves with developing text-critical and a variety of historical, anthropological, and phenomenological interpretive skills.[10] Few classically trained comparativists gave attention to the complex and highly variegated contours of modern religious history,[11] and even fewer seem to have

---

[9] Louis Henry Jordan, *Comparative Religion: Its Genesis and Growth* (New York: Charles Scribner's Sons, 1905), pp. 198, 392-93.

[10] Kitagawa, "Humanistic and Theological History," pp. 553-63.

[11] Comparativists whose major concern is with classical expressions of great traditions have often had difficulty in adequately conceptualizing the complex and ambiguous terrain presented by religion in the modern period. Joachim Wach, for instance, went to great lengths to distinguish the criteria of real as opposed to what he called modern "pseudo-religions"; Joachim Wach, *The Comparative Study of Religion*, ed. Joseph M. Kitagawa (New York: Columbia University Press, 1958), pp. 27-58. Kitagawa seems to have maintained this stance in his Nuveen Lecture (in the present volume) when he suggested that in the West the Renaissance gave birth to "a pseudo-religion of secularized salvation" in the form of faith in human progress and civilization. Elsewhere Kitagawa argued that comparativists must develop categories of analysis through the study of "classical forms of religions in which religious manifestations are more clearly discernible than in the ambiguities of modern and less-known pre-civilized situations" ("Humanistic and Theological History," p. 563). For historians whose field of study is the modern period, however, a priori definitions of real and pseudo-religion based on classical examples obfuscate much of what is important in the modern period: the diverse forms of religious experience outside traditional churches; politically tinged religious expressions such as "nationalism" and "civil religion"; and the emergence of syncretistic forms of

wrestled with the complex historiography of the American religious scene.

Other factors undoubtedly contributed to this lack of interest. Modern Asian religions and topics in the East/West encounter tend to be specializations within specializations and are often presented as political and cultural developments in national histories. Despite a great deal of scholarship, a systematic and comprehensive field of study devoted to the modern, global, East/West encounter hardly exists.[12] It is no great wonder that scholars trained to think in terms of Aquinas, Rāmānuja, Śaṅkara, and Chu Hsi would not have been drawn to the relatively meager, modern, and in many respects confusing materials of the parliament.

The self-imposed limits of the two branches of the study of religion in the United States had the effect of doubly marginalizing the parliament, in effect ensuring that the assembly would be more or less banished from history. Only since the 1960s have these two disciplinary traditions begun to undergo internal changes and to enter into a dialogue with one another in a way that would make the parliament ripe for recovery.

A major impetus came from within the field of American religious history. As a result of the gradual shift from a consensus to a pluralist paradigm, new starting points—be they in sectarian, black, women's, Asian, Catholic, or Jewish history—were deemed appropriate in order to draw new, less consensus-dominated, trajectories through national history. It was recognized that a global context was required for a clearer understanding of U.S. religious history, which demanded in turn the abandonment of the older agenda that focused on the

---

religions that are in part by-products of the East/West encounter. It is highly suggestive that Kitagawa understood both the modern and primitive situations to defy the clarity of classical definitions of religion. The "worldview analysis" of Ninian Smart offers a more productive approach to religious history in the modern period. See, e.g., Ninian Smart, *Religion and the Western Mind* (Albany: SUNY Press, 1987).

[12] The numerous studies of selected episodes in the East/West encounter do not constitute a coherent field of study, but considerable and varied attention has been given to the historical construction of the highly ambiguous East/West dichotomy. See, e.g., Stephen N. Hay, *Asian Ideas of East and West: Tagore and His Critics in Japan, China, and India* (Cambridge: Harvard University Press, 1970); Edward W. Said, *Orientalism* (New York: Pantheon, 1978); Bryan S. Turner, *Marx and the End of Orientalism* (London: Allen and Unwin, 1978); and Ashis Nandy, *The Intimate Enemy: Loss and Recovery of Self under Colonialism* (Delhi: Oxford University Press, 1983).

determinative influence of the American frontier.[13] Methods of interpretation once confined to the comparative discipline began to be utilized by those whose field preoccupation was American religious history.[14] Increasing numbers of American specialists had at least an introduction to world religious history, and some scholars with comparative interests turned their attention to the traditions they studied overseas as they appeared with increasing frequency on the American scene.[15]

The momentum of these changes reached two different climaxes with the publication of Sydney Ahlstrom's encyclopedic *A Religious History of the American People* and Catherine Albanese's interpretive

---

[13] Bucher, "Options," pp. 185-88; Sydney Ahlstrom, "The Problem of the History of Religion in America," *Church History* 39 (1970): 230-33.

[14] For an early call for the use of the methodologies of history of religions in the study of American religion, see Jerald C. Brauer, "Changing Perspectives on Religion in America," in Jerald C. Brauer, ed., *Reinterpretation in American Church History* (Chicago: University of Chicago Press, 1968), pp. 1-28. Brauer urged church historians to begin to utilize the insights of the history of religions school, but he considered it prudent for them to limit their attention to Christianity, effectively gutting the comparative dimension to the history of religions project. Cf. his perspective to Kitagawa's, who considered the history of religions school to have as its scope nothing less than "thinking about the religious history of the human race" (Kitagawa, "Humanistic and Theological History," p. 561). For recent studies that have utilized interpretive perspectives from the history of religions school in treatments of standard American church history topics, see Jan Shipps, *Mormonism: The Story of a New Religious Tradition* (Urbana: University of Illinois Press, 1985), and Theodore Dwight Bozeman, *To Live Ancient Lives: The Primitivist Dimension in Puritanism* (Chapel Hill: Published for the Institute of Early American History and Culture, Williamsburg, by the University of North Carolina Press, 1988). In a very different vein, Charles Long has reflected on the broader contours of American civilization, particularly the black experience, with interpretive perspectives derived from phenomenology and linguistic theory; see Charles H. Long, *Significations: Signs, Symbols, and Images in the Interpretation of Religion* (Philadelphia: Fortress, 1986).

[15] One historian working on both Asian and American materials in a history of religions vein is Robert S. Ellwood, Jr.; see his *Religious and Spiritual Groups in Modern America* (Englewood Cliffs, N.J.: Prentice-Hall, 1973); *Alternative Altars: Unconventional and Eastern Spirituality in America* (Chicago: University of Chicago Press, 1979); *The Eagle and the Rising Sun: Americans and the New Religions of Japan* (Philadelphia: Westminster, 1974); and *Japanese Religion: A Cultural Perspective* (Englewood Cliffs, N.J.: Prentice-Hall, 1985). Somewhat different is the work of Charles S. Prebish, ed., *Buddhist Monastic Discipline: The Sanskrit Pratimoksa Sutras of the Mahasamghikas and Mulasarvastivadins* (University Park: Pennsylvania State University Press, 1975), and *American Buddhism* (North Scituate, Mass.: Duxbury, 1979).

survey *America: Religion and Religions.*[16] Ahlstrom pushed the mainstream model of church history to its limit, while at the same time he began to weave hitherto excluded groups such as blacks, spiritualists, and contemporary Asia-inspired movements into the texture of American religious history. Albanese, on the other hand, simply dropped the old paradigm and drew entirely new trajectories inspired by the interpretive methods familiar in comparative religious history.

It is now widely acknowledged that both Ahlstrom's and Albanese's accounts are flawed and in some ways already dated, but both remain at the cutting edge of American religious history. More importantly, with Ahlstrom, Albanese, and the historiographic seachange which they rode to prominence, a cycle of revisionism in the American field seemed, for the moment, to be complete.[17] Once a somewhat cozy subfield in the American Society of Church History, the Americanist guild was transformed in two decades into an immense and highly variegated enterprise. The production of a survey of American religion that combined Ahlstrom's breadth, Albanese's interpretive power, and the new trajectories that have been charted in the last decades is a task that is daunting at best. But more to the point, as scholars explored the substantial gaps created by the field's conversion from a consensus to a pluralist, dissensus paradigm, the parliament slowly began to creep back from obscurity.

---

[16] Sydney Ahlstrom, *A Religious History of the American People* (New Haven: Yale University Press, 1972); and Catherine L. Albanese, *American: Religion and Religions* (Belmont, Cal.: Wadsworth, 1981; 2d, rev. ed., 1992).

[17] Historiographic change has of course continued, particularly as a result of the prominence of a new generation of evangelicals among church historians. For a current historiographic and methodological reflection, see David W. Lotz, "A Changing Historiography: From Church History to Religious History," in David W. Lotz, ed., *Altered Landscapes: Christianity in America 1935-1985* (Grand Rapids: Eerdmans, 1989). Lotz notes the radical religious plurality of contemporary American religion ("a veritable supermarket of faiths" [p. 333]), but his real concern is with a "new style church history" that is both historical-critical and theological, which he describes as "the history of the communal handing on down—the traditioning—of the Christian gospel" as it occurs in preaching, sacraments, worship, missions, catechesis, and biblical exegesis of the "church catholic" (pp. 337-39). Lotz's vision is at once creative and stimulating, but, given the recent emphasis on pluralism, somewhat reactionary. His emphasis on a "church catholic," while recognizing "diversity-in-unity," suggests both an ecumenical spirit and an implicit return to a fundamental emphasis on Christian unity, presumably on evangelical terms.

Restoration to Memory

Until recently, the parliament's slim reputation among scholars in the United States rested on Louis Jordan's early assessment of its pivotal role in the popularization of comparative religion and on Stow Person's suggestion that it was a natural extension of the avant-garde agenda of the largely Unitarian Free Religious Association.[18] But it took the new pluralist paradigm to begin to restore the parliament more fully to memory. In the past fifteen years, the parliament has begun to find its location in the complex terrain of American religious history, but it remains unclear whether its extraordinary nature is to be taken to mean that the assembly should be considered an unusually important or a highly idiosyncratic event in American history.

The parliament first resurfaced when Paul Carter published in 1971 his account of what he called "the spiritual crisis of the Gilded Age." Carter said little of a concrete nature about the event, but he positioned it as the finale to a century in which church schisms, the rise of the social gospel, and the emergence of evolutionary and other naturalistic philosophies had begun to shatter the united front of the antebellum Protestant mainstream. Carter suggested that the consensus rhetoric which was so conspicuous among the parliament's American supporters was superficial and masked serious conflicts, but in his account, the event remained nothing more than a grand and exotic punctuation point to a wonderful if somewhat chaotic century.[19]

Commentary on the parliament then came from a different quarter—from the fringe—with Carl T. Jackson's *The Oriental Religions and American Thought*.[20] Jackson traced the growing interest in the Orient from the early days of the China trade, through the liberal religious interests of Transcendentalists and Theosophists, to the

---

[18] Jordan, *Comparative Religion*, pp. 198, 392-93. Stow Persons, *Free Religion: An American Faith* (New Haven: Yale University Press, 1947), p. 97. Subsequent treatments that link the parliament to Unitarianism include Spencer Lavan, *Unitarians in India: A Study in Encounter and Response* (Boston: Beacon, 1977). Lavan, however, mistook Presbyterian John Henry Barrows, the parliament's chairman, for Samuel J. Barrows, the editor of the Unitarian *Christian Register*. See also Thomas Graham, "Jenkin Lloyd Jones and the World's Columbian Exposition of 1893," *Association for Liberal Religious Studies: Collegium Proceedings* 1 (1979): 62-81.

[19] Paul A. Carter, *The Spiritual Crisis of the Gilded Age* (DeKalb: Northern Illinois University Press, 1971), pp. 199-221.

[20] Carl T. Jackson, *The Oriental Religions and American Thought: Nineteenth-Century Explorations* (Westport, Conn.: Greenwood, 1981), pp. 243-61.

Buddhist craze of Boston's cultural elite and the pioneering studies in comparative religion by American Unitarians. Like Carter, Jackson concluded his account with what amounted to a description of the parliament, but he made the important observation that the Asians in Chicago first had an opportunity to speak to the public about their faiths in their own voices, unencumbered by either the idealism of western liberals or the judgments of Christian missionaries. At about the same time, Rick Fields published his less noticed but valuable work *How the Swans Came to the Lake*, a pioneering historical survey of Buddhism in the United States.[21] Covering much the same ground as Jackson, Fields's phileopietist approach (while until recently a throwback in terms of interpretive developments in mainstream church history), provided a much needed narrative account of an Asian religion's circuitous route into America—from Concord and the Transcendentalist circle to Boulder and Naropa University—by an American who was frankly glad that Buddhism had arrived here.

In the meantime, the parliament was also being discovered from a third direction, by commentators on the histories of the interreligious dialogue movement and the Christian missions. Marcus Braybrooke began his 1980 account of the history of the interfaith movements of the twentieth century with the parliament, noting that "no subsequent interfaith gathering has come near to it in size or complexity." In Braybrooke's account, one dimension of the parliament's importance was made explicit: the wide range of theological positions adopted in the subsequent decades of interfaith dialogue and debate were "nearly all foreshadowed at the Parliament."[22]

More recently, William Hutchison commented on the event in his history of American Protestant missionaries. The issue at stake for mainstream missionaries at the time was to strike a balance between western political and social ideals and traditional Protestant Christianity, between civilizing and evangelizing strategies that were being implemented on the mission fields overseas. For Hutchison, the parliament signaled an attitudinal shift in regard to the evaluation of non-Christian religions that was gradually occurring in the liberal wing of the old Protestant mainstream. Insofar as the parliament was a missionary event, it marked a positive advance over the traditional,

---

[21] Rick Fields, *How the Swans Came to the Lake: A Narrative History of Buddhism in America* (Boulder: Shambala, 1980), pp. 119-29.

[22] Marcus Braybrooke, *Inter-Faith Organizations, 1893-1979: An Historical Directory* (Lewiston, N.Y.: Edwin Mellen, 1980), pp. 8, 7.

militant stance which vilified the heathen, but its liberalism remained highly qualified by a condescending and ethnocentric spirit.[23] In a recent article, David Bosch shared Hutchison's skeptical assessment of the parliament's liberal spirit, but with a different intent. Bosch was concerned with current debates among mainstream missionaries as they articulate new strategies in the light of the world missionary conferences and World Council of Churches meetings from Madras in 1938 to Chiang Mai in 1977. His article represents what will probably be a spate of theological reflections on the relationship between dialogue and mission as we approach the parliament's centennial.[24]

The most substantial accounts of the parliament emerged, perhaps quite predictably, from the faculty of the University of Chicago, an institution likely to be forever associated with the reputation of the parliament, for good or ill. With a coincidental but happy symmetry, one account was written by a prominent historian of American religion, Martin Marty, a chief among the tribe who helped to lay the groundwork for a pluralist-oriented study of American religion. The other was from Joseph Kitagawa, who, possessing a comparativist's magisterial overview of world religions East and West, brilliantly juggled the antipodes to build a firm foundation for understanding the importance of the parliament in a global context.

Marty's account of the parliament opened what he intends to be a four-volume study of religion in the United States in the twentieth century.[25] He located the parliament at the heyday of theological liberalism, when Protestant modernists, with their hopes for global unity and their penchant for optimistic social visions, were ascendant. He correctly pinpointed the idea of "religious cosmopolitanism" as a key idea informing the proceedings, and one can only hope that subsequent historians of liberalism will follow his lead by exploring religious cosmopolitanism, universalism, syncretism, and related ideas. Marty, however, steered his narrative in another direction. In his view, the cosmopolitan spirit of the parliament was transient and fleeting, soon to be challenged by the conservative forces of Protestant fundamentalism, Catholic ultramontanism, and Jewish Zionism, as well as by an increasingly secular spirit in the nation at large. The

---

[23] William R. Hutchison, *Errand to the World: American Protestant Thought and Foreign Missions* (Chicago: University of Chicago Press, 1987), pp. 105-9.

[24] David J. Bosch, "The Church in Dialogue: From Self-Delusion to Vulnerability," *Missiology: An International Review* 16 (1988): 131-47.

[25] See in this volume the chapter by Martin E. Marty.

Asian delegates were of negligible importance in Marty's account, but he portrayed both liberal Catholics and Reform Jews as moving, momentarily at least, in from the fringe towards a soon-to-be troubled mainstream.

Marty's neglect of the Asians is unfortunate, but more or less in keeping with a moderate pluralism that has, since the early 1960s, been regularly inclusive of all parties in "Judeo-Christianity." In this regard the other Chicago scholar, Kitagawa, provided an important corrective.[26] Like Müller, Kitagawa saw the parliament as a unique, epochal encounter between East and West. He set it within the necessary historical framework of the age of discovery, the Catholic and Protestant global missions, and the rise of the modern empires with their triumphalist, often racist celebration of the superiority of western, Christian civilization. He also discussed the important role played by the comparative study of religions in the parliament's interreligious debates. Kitagawa's account lacked a nuanced appreciation of the parliament place in the complex texture of American religious history, but he gave prominent Asians at the assembly such as Vivekananda, Shaku Sōen, and Anagārika Dharmapāla their proper place among the young, modern defenders of Asian traditions who worked to revitalize their traditions at a time when the early nationalist movements were beginning to reshape the contours of world history.

The restoration of the parliament to memory has been undertaken by scholars with a variety of interests over the past two decades. Shifting values among Protestants in the old mainstream, an increasing interest in Asians on the American scene, the rise of ecumenism and interreligious dialogue, and a greater appreciation of the larger frame of modern world religious history have all played a part. But the question remains: Was the parliament, with its qualified but nevertheless real affirmation of religious diversity, an important event or an idiosyncratic event in American religious history?

A Modern, Democratic, and Somewhat Anarchic Feast

Among the theological metaphors used by commentators to reflect upon the parliament was that of a Royal Feast of first fruits and rare flowers offered up to....It is precisely there we hit upon the quandary. Despite much high praise for the parliament as a harbinger of

---

[26] See in this volume the lecture by Kitagawa.

religious unity, a close reading of John Henry Barrows's official edition of the parliament papers impresses one with precisely the news that last century's church historians attempted to suppress: the United States has been for a long time an intractably pluralist nation. To a reader moderately well informed in the arcana of American religious personalities, it seems as though everyone was there. For those converted from the unity-consensus to the pluralist paradigm, the situation in which we find ourselves in late twentieth-century America seems already adumbrated in surprising detail.

Let us limit ourselves for the moment to a look at the trio of Protestant, Catholic, and Jew which Will Herberg christened "equi-legitimate subdivisions" of twentieth-century American religious life, and in so doing first helped to legitimate the pluralist paradigm in the late 1950s.[27] That there were religious differences among these communities a century ago goes without saying. More importantly, the parliament papers also reveal differences within each community, important differences that with our hindsight we can see have not gone away. Whether in Protestantism, Catholicism, or Judaism, strains between traditionalism and modernism were conspicuous, strains which were forcing complex adjustments in all three faiths, reshaping American religion in many different directions in the process.

The question of whether the parliament was cosmopolitan or parochial, liberal or conservative, is not of primary interest to us today. Of greater interest is the fact that the assembly embraced an extraordinary variety of positions simultaneously in a way which defied prophets who sought to find in it a clear indication of a single direction in which we were heading as a nation. If the spirit of the parliament signified anything (that new and larger Pentecost question), it signified that religious pluralism, like it or not, was in the ascendant.

Consider the case of Jews and Roman Catholics, who at the time of the parliament were still seen by an older generation of church historians as outside the mainstream of American religious history. Both groups presented themselves on the parliament floor as comfortable with their own unique locations in, and understandings of, America. But in both cases, tensions were readily apparent within the delegations that would in subsequent decades grow, not only into

---

[27] Will Herberg, *Protestant-Catholic-Jew: An Essay in American Religious Sociology* (Garden City, N.Y.: Doubleday, 1955), p. 227.

major conflicts in their respective denominations, but into conflicts having a significant impact on the entire nation.

The best-known Catholics at the parliament were James Cardinal Gibbons and Fr. John Keane, the rector of Washington's Catholic University. They were among the liberal progressives who soon would become known as the "Americanists," after a chastening by Rome for attempting to make a rapprochement between the traditional dogma of church and the American experience. These liberals, however, were not the entire story, because they were balanced at the parliament by coreligionists such as Monsignor Robert Seton, one-time chamberlain to the fiercely conservative Pius IX and nephew of now-sainted Elizabeth Seton, and Thomas Dwight, Parkman Professor of Anatomy at Harvard University. Seton and Dwight presented papers that attacked the new biblical criticism and the evolutionary hypothesis respectively and more or less restated the case for Catholic traditionalism. Additional papers extolled the papacy, recently disencumbered of its territorial claims, as a potential moral force in world politics and history; reasserted the church's historic role as defender of the poor; and presented the church as standing, beyond mists of ignorance, as Isaiah's mountain top toward which all nations flowed. There were no women, in or out of orders, in the Catholic delegation.[28]

Despite the path taken by Catholicism at Vatican II, the tensions in the delegation are familiar in our current pluralist configuration. The parliament's Americanists were liberal, but distinctly Catholic, having little in common with those prominent Protestants who would become known as new theology men, also present, such as Theodore Munger and Lyman Abbott. Their chastening by Rome meant that a thoroughgoing encounter between traditionalism and modernity would be stalled, reserving Catholicism's tumultuous *aggiornamento* with the modern world for the late twentieth century. Modernist theologies and the higher criticism are now conspicuous in Catholicism, but American Catholics are still (at last check) Roman

---

[28] For issues in Catholicism at this time, see Jay P. Dolan, *The American Catholic Experience* (Garden City, N.Y.: Doubleday, 1985), pp. 303-20. Part of my research design was to assemble papers scattered throughout Barrows's collection into "delegations" from major groups—Protestant, Catholic, Jewish, and the various Asian religions—in order to get a more comprehensive picture of the concerns of different traditions. In addition to papers by individuals cited in text, see papers by Thomas Jenkins Semmes, Charles Francis Donnelly, and Rev. John Gmeiner in *WPR*, 2: 1116-20, 1032-36, 1265-66.

Catholics, and women now play a visible and important, if highly controversial role, in both the parish and the intellectual life of the church. To both the right and left, Catholics have become prominent voices speaking about the moral destiny and economic institutions of the nation, while the papacy has achieved a public prominence unthinkable in the nineteenth century. Little is said in public about Isaiah's mountain top, and since Vatican II Catholics have come to style themselves as a people, presumably among other people, of God. Catholicism did not fade away on the fringe; it emerged as an influential, sometimes liberal, sometimes conservative, force—as an internally pluralist presence—in our late twentieth-century, pluralist nation.

The parliamentary delegates from American Judaism also pointed toward a new pluralist day (and a new pluralist historiography) in American religious history. The distinguished Jewish delegation included framers of the Reform tradition such as Isaac Meyer Wise and more radical reformers such as Kaufman Kohler and Emil Hirsch. But American Judaism was then beginning to undergo major transformations in response to the eastern European migrations. One major force to benefit from this development was conservative Judaism, represented at the parliament by Alexander Kohut. Another was the Zionist homeland movement, which gained support on the parliament floor from Henry Pereira Mendes, leader of the oldline Sephardic community of New York. Women played a conspicuous and varied role in the Jewish delegation, but their subsequent careers displayed the inner tensions in Judaism that were moving the community in very different directions simultaneously. Josephine Lazarus, sister of the more famous Emma, became a vocal advocate of Reform efforts to assimilate eastern European Jews, while Henrietta Szold, in a move somewhat different from Lazarus's, went on to found Hadassah, a major contributor to the success of the Zionist movement in the United States.[29]

Jews at the parliament, like Catholics, displayed internal differentiation that pointed to future complexities, complexities which would not remain quarrels within their own communities, but would come to have a broad and powerful impact on the entire nation. Competing Reform and Orthodox impulses would begin to reshape

---

[29] For issues in Judaism at this time, see Abraham J. Karp, *Haven and Home: A History of the Jews in America* (New York: Schocken, 1985), pp. 84-110.

American Judaism, eventually leading the community a good distance from the liberalism of the classical Reform tradition. The ultimate success of Zionism would come to have an enormous impact on the nation's political life. Protestant church historians of the last century would have found developments that retied modern Catholics to old Rome and modern Jews to old Jerusalem deeply disturbing. But more to the point, the parliament was a harbinger of things to come, not only for Catholics and Jews, but for the nation. With hindsight and the lens of the pluralist, post-consensus paradigm, it is possible to see, not that the parliament anticipated either a conservative or liberal victory, but that it pointed to a more diffuse development of inter- and intra-religious pluralism in an expanding American religious mainstream.

If Judaism and Catholicism displayed the fact that they were becoming worthy if weighty guests at the banquet table of American religious history, the situation was really not so different in Protestantism, where fragmentation, not unity, seemed the order of the day. New theology men such as Abbott and Munger and social gospelers such as Washington Gladden and Richard Ely were highly visible at the parliament, steering one great wing of Protestantism towards naturalism, liberalism, and ethical religion, but so too were Joseph Cook, George Park Fisher, and Luther Townsend, all of whom delivered papers advocating more tightly wrapped and traditional theologies. Protestant women spoke on ethics, the criminal justice system, women in the pulpit, and comparative religion.[30] They naturally tended to hail from the liberal religion end of the spectrum, but Methodist Frances Willard was also there, arguing for temperance and purity, as well as women's rights. Many conservatives avoided the parliament and denounced it after the fact, but a historian well versed in the nuances of current popular Protestant theology might successfully sift through the parliament papers in search of future fundamentalists, holiness advocates, and protopentecostals.

We should also consider that elusive lot, the "secularists," whom John Courtney Murray added to Herberg's Protestant, Catholic, and Jewish troika in another landmark text which helped to legitimate pluralism in the early 1960s.[31] Strict secularists (if such a thing exists in

---

[30] In addition to papers by individuals cited in text, see papers by Anna Spencer, Ida C. Hultin and Antoinette Louisa Brown Blackwell [in *WPR*, 2:1030-31, 1003-05, and 1148-50] and the paper by Eliza R. Sunderland in the present volume.

[31] John Courtney Murray, *We Hold These Truths: Catholic Reflections on the American Proposition* (New York: Sheed and Ward, 1960), pp. 18-22.

the United States) were not present at the parliament. But the American scientific naturalist Paul Carus was there to argue for a new religion based on empirical and evolutionary science, and the German Adolph Brodbeck espoused an altogether noncreedal and non-Christian form of popular idealism. Catholic Merwin-Marie Snell presented comparative religion as a "speculative science" based on both empirical and "metempiric" philosophy, and a number of Protestant liberals, who displayed little interest in Christian dogma, symbol, and creed, discussed the way in which a fundamental spirituality infused all the world's scriptures, literature, music, and culture.[32] One suspects that such eclectic religious sensibilities, although rarely studied sympathetically, are quite prevalent in many quarters today. But they were also there on the parliament floor, a harbinger of a later day when religious humanism would not be synonymous with liberal Christianity.

Other groups which have undergone major twentieth-century developments are, in retrospect, conspicuous by their absence or relative insignificance at the assembly. Mormonism, a religion that has come to play an important role in American historiography despite its original fringe status, had no representation; the parliament was held at a time when the future of Utah/Deseret was under debate. Native Americans, then engaged in a last series of battles over the Great Plains, were represented only by Alice Fletcher, an anthropologist and student of Franz Boas, who delivered a brief paper in the parliament's somewhat unimpressive scientific section. The representation of blacks, Christian or otherwise, was very spotty, a predictable enough development for the Jim Crow decades.[33] But these important exceptions notwithstanding, the parliament was certainly an extraordinary national feast, even if one more modern, democratic, and somewhat anarchic than royal.

---

[32] In addition to papers by individuals cited in text, see papers by Milton Spenser Terry, Theodore Thornton Munger, H.R. Haweis, Waldo Pratt and W.L. Tomlins in *WPR*, 1:694-704, 677-92; 2:947-50, 1005-08, 1302-03; and the paper by Sunderland in the present volume.

[33] B.W. Arnett and D.A. Payne, bishops of the African Methodist Episcopal church, were present. Payne was on the platform at opening day ceremonies; Arnett made a brief address on the twelfth day of the Parliament, the thirty-first anniversary of the Emancipation Proclamation. Fannie Barrier Williams, a black woman and Chicago Unitarian, delivered an address on the role churches could play to advance the American Negro.

Many commentators, however, did not necessarily see it that way. On the parliament floor, Philip Schaff extended a warm hand of fellowship to Greeks, Romans, Lutherans, and the entire spectrum of mainstream churches, and applauded the example of the Waldenses, Anabaptists, Socinians, Unitarians, Universalists, and the Salvation Army, making throughout an appeal to the soul of the one "invisible church" which animated all "the divided visible churches." Historian Leonard Woolsey Bacon looked at the parliament with consensus-oriented eyes as well. The sky of the declining century was "red with promise," he wrote, for a unification of Protestantism's many sects and denominations with the Roman Catholic church; witness "those seventeen wonderful days in September of 1893." Others, however, caught a glimpse of impending chaos and entirely missed the feast. Methodist theologian Charles Little suspected an attempted coup by Catholics and Jews, and, noting the confusing multiplicity of Protestant voices, he warned of the disintegration of the mainstream in the coming century.[34] The parliament was a protean phenomenon which could mean different things for different people, a fact which itself hinted at the passing of a consensus-dominated vision of American religious history.

The Men Who Came to Dinner

Considering only Protestants, Catholics, Jews, and humanists, we are still faced with the most extraordinary ecumenical gathering of the nineteenth or any other century. But that quartet was only a part of the story. I have not discussed the Greeks, Armenians, and Syrians, nor the Swedenborgians, Unitarians, and Universalists, who, although Protestant, deserve special consideration. Of the 216 presentations at the parliament, a total of 109—just over fifty percent—were delivered by those standing on the fringes of the old antebellum, evangelical mainstream. Forty-one were from Asians who, although as far to the fringe as one could possible get, were in fact the real stars of the assembly, who gained much of the public's attention and most of the press.

---

[34] For Schaff, see *WPR*, 2:1192-1201; Leonard Woolsey Bacon, *A History of American Christianity* (New York: Christian Literature Co., 1897), pp. 417-19; Charles Little, "The Chicago Parliament of Religions," *Methodist Review* 76 (March 1894): 213-17.

A historian like Leonard Bacon could dismiss the Asians as "unchristian and antichristian powers,"[35] standing beyond his consensus-vision of a united American church. A theologian like Charles Little could display a different, more metaphysical, side to the unitive wish, by seeing them as incipient Christians, people who were, to use his phrase, "driven to an answer by the imperative energy of the Holy Ghost."[36] But in reality, the Asians arrived in Chicago with their own distinct goals, having little concern for either Christians' hopes for their church or for American religious unity. Unlike the Catholics and Jews, the Asians did not represent communities with deep roots in the colonial experience, and what they hoped to accomplish at the parliament was of a far more radical, epoch-making nature than a move in the direction of the nation's mainstream.

To understand the role of the Asians at the parliament, consider the East and West as two discrete entities, much as Kipling and others were wont to do a century ago, when it was widely considered unlikely that two such different creatures would ever meet. At the time "East" had nothing to do with cold war politics, but referred to a vast stretch of land from the Balkans, through the Levant, Near, Middle, and Far East, including South Asia, to the Pacific. It was the heyday of the European empires, but the international reputation of the United States was relatively untarnished, with five years standing between the parliament and the conquest of the Phillipines.

Within this frame of reference, the encounter on the parliament floor can be considered a call and response, with industrializing America, the young scion of the West, issuing a call for congresses "more widely representative of all peoples and nations and tongues than any assemblage which has ever yet been convened."[37] It was a grand, idealistic, and fundamentally liberal call inviting the Asians to share in an expansive, global vision, but one cast wholly in western, Christian terms and partaking of an often smug largess that depended upon the West's racial, political, economic, and religious hegemony.

The Asian delegation, including as it did Hindus, Buddhists, Confucians, Zoroastrians, Jains, and Shintos—together with Asian Christians—was far from monolithic, but in general their response to America's call entailed both a qualified acceptance and a kind of

---

[35] Bacon, *History*, p. 418.
[36] Little, "The Chicago Parliament," p. 212.
[37] Charles Carroll Bonney, quoted in *Report of the President to the Board of Directors*, Appendix A (Chicago: Rand McNally, 1898), p. 326.

counter-invitation. Many Asians embraced the hopeful prospect of religious harmony and shared with western liberals a global and inclusive vision, but they did so while delivering an outspoken critique of western racism, imperialism, and materialism. They also defended their own ancient faiths, called into question the finality of the Christian religion, and offered to their American audience alternative religious visions with roots struck deep in Asian religious history.

In the remarks of the Asian delegates there emerged common themes. Unfair trade agreements, the loss of national treasure, and the bitter experience of racial exclusion were all of a piece with western imperialism, and were also—as a few Asian delegates were quick to point out—questionable ethics for alleged Christians. Missionaries were also challenged by Hindus, Buddhists, and other non-Christians, as well as by Asian Christians who sought to indigenize the gospel and free themselves from western tutelage. While praising altruistic work, many Asians saw little value in a strictly evangelical mission, which they viewed as both ill-fated and ill-conceived.[38] No Asian delegate, however, criticized Jesus. On the contrary, many expressed for him profound respect as a prophet, guide, and teacher, but this was the Jesus of Palestine, an oriental Jesus, not the unique Savior of the creeds of European and American Christianity.[39]

In a more constructive vein, the Asians offered coherent and informed accounts of their religious traditions. The Tao, Lord Krishna, the Divine Mother, Ahura Mazdā, the Buddhist *dharma*, and the Shinto *kami* were all presented to the American public, often with passion and lucidity. Drawing on the work of scholars in comparative religions, many delegates presented their traditions in a surprisingly modern and sophisticated way. Zoroastrians were not fire worshipers;

---

[38] For examples of Asian criticisms, see *WPR*, 1:432-39, 144-50, 767-812; 2:1012-14, 1283. Asian delegates were more outspoken during the years immediately after the parliament; see, e.g., "Christian Missions: A Triangular Debate Before the Nineteenth Century Club of New York," *The Monist* 5 (January 1895): 264-81, and Purushotam Rao Telang, "Christian Missions as Seen by a Brahman," *The Forum* 18 (September 1894/February 1895): 481-89.

[39] P. C. Mozoomdar's *The Oriental Christ* (Boston: George Ellis, 1883) was popular devotional text with Boston Unitarians in the 1880s. His presentation of the spirit of Christ in "The World's Religious Debt to Asia" is indicative of an understanding of Jesus current in the Brāhmo-Samāj at this time that seems to have informed modernist Buddhists and Hindus alike. See *WPR*, 2:1083-92. See also Churesh Chunder Bose, *The Life of Protap Chunder Mozoomdar*, 2 vols. (Calcutta: Nababidhan Trust, 1940), 2:185-200.

fire was a symbol of the purity and power of divinity. Hindus were not idolaters; images conveyed knowledge of eternal truths to the uneducated, functioning in much the same way as the cross of Christianity and the Ka'bah of Islam. Vedic religion was not polytheistic nature worship; it taught that spiritual unity was at the foundation of the cosmos, a proposition which found its fullest expression in the nondualism of the Advaita Vedanta.[40] What impact these presentations had on the general public is difficult to say, but press response gives one indication. A week into the parliament, the Chicago *Tribune* announced in front-page headlines:

IT POINTS TO UNITY
PARLIAMENT OF RELIGION WILL
BEAR GOOD FRUIT
They Say It Has Opened the Eyes
of the Christian World
WELLS OF TRUTH OUTSIDE[41]

The discovery that there were "wells of truth outside" Christianity was a radical one at the time, and this discovery encouraged the notion, repeated frequently on the parliament floor, that the Asian world faced a new day. In impassioned addresses such as "A Voice from the Young Men of the Orient" by Armenian Herant Kiretchijian, and in the stories of the Hindu reformers as told by B.B. Nagarkar and P.C. Majumdar, the Asians portrayed themselves as wrestling, much like Protestants, Jews, and Catholics in the United States, with the invigorating discovery of the modern age. Vivekananda, still an obscure young ascetic from Bengal, presented Hinduism as the synthesis of all religions and Krishna as an evolving and processing, immutable and eternal, universal deity. Theosophist Anagārika Dharmapāla, a future leader of the Ceylonese Buddhist revival, proclaimed that the Buddhist *dharma*, not Christianity, would reconcile religious aspirations with the scientific spirit of the age. Representatives of modern Asia's most progressive voice, the Brāhmo-Samāj, demanded nothing less than the toppling of all creeds and the

---

[40] *WPR*, 2:906-9, 975-77; 1:318-27.
[41] *Chicago Tribune*, September 17, 1893, p. 1.

harmonizing of all prophets as the religious duty of a new dispensation suitable for a new age.[42]

The great surprise at the parliament was that the American religious cosmopolitans, about whom Martin Marty wrote, discovered they had Asian counterparts overseas. A modern religious spirit seemed to be flourishing worldwide, sending up Hindu and Buddhist, as well as Jewish, Christian, and humanist shoots. The Asians for their part saw Americans as an ally in their struggle for political and religious freedom. "You, citizens of these United States, who, when the right time came, struck for Liberty or Death," proclaimed Hirai Kinzō, a Japanese Buddhist layman, "as you asked for justice from your mother country, we, too, ask justice from these foreign powers."[43] And from the Hindu reformer, B.B. Nagarkar, of the Brāhmo-Samāj: "I entreat you...brothers and sisters of America...give us your earnest advice and cooperation in the realization of the social, political, and religious aspirations of young India."[44] A reader can still sense the energy of the parliament in the cracked and dried pages of Barrows's record of the event. In retrospect, we can see the way in which that new and larger American Pentecost was prescient of a coming century filled with nationalist and religious revivals overseas.

The Asian contribution at the parliament did not end, however, with papers and appeals on behalf of colonized and otherwise beleaguered peoples overseas. It remains a fact that a counter-mission accompanied the Asian's counter-invitation, and in the wake of the parliament, Hindus and Buddhists began their own slouch toward the American mainstream. The Asian mission to America is another story with its own pioneering heroes, its cast of sympathetic seekers, its peaks and valleys of enthusiasm, and, of course, its waves of Asian immigration. That story—the American tours of Vivekananda, Dharmapāla, Majumdar, and others, the founding of the Vedanta Society, the first American Wesak, the arrival of D.T. Suzuki in Illinois, the various Pacific migrations, and all the subsequent events that would lead eventually to the 1960s—cannot detain us here. Suffice it to say, if the parliament was a modern feast for Protestants, Catholics, Jews, humanists, and a good many women, the Asians were the men

---

[42] In addition to papers by individuals cited in text, see papers in *WPR*, 1:345-51 and 2:1226-29 for the reform view of the Brāhmo-Samāj.

[43]"The Real Position of Japan Toward Christianity," in*WPR*, 1:450.

[44]"The Work of Social Reform in India," in *WPR*, 1:779.

who came to dinner, tarried over cognac and cigars, and then never went away.

Looking Down the Road a Piece

The parliament deserves a central place in a pluralistic history of American religion. But it would be wrong to leave the impression that immediately thereafter, in the place of the old-line Protestant mainstream, America witnessed a thousand flowers bloom all in one day. As Marcus Braybrooke noted, the parliament was something of a "seventeen-day wonder,"[45] and as we have seen, it was quickly banished from our collective memory.

In the brief storm raised in the parliament's wake, liberal Protestant opinion about the religions of their new-found Asian colleagues tended to display expansive variations on the consensus-unity theme. Men on the left like Jenkin Lloyd Jones, a Chicago Unitarian, and naturalist Paul Carus looked forward to the dawn of an age of global religious unity on a platform of universal progress.[46] New theology men in the old mainstream were, as Hutchison suggested, more qualified in the liberality, but nonetheless convinced of the universality of their vision. The public might greet with greater enthusiasm the worlds of "apostles of curious face, figure, and attire" than the "more familiar, if soberer, utterances of Anglo-Saxon Christians," wrote Lyman Abbott, but the ultimate effect of the parliament would be "to broaden" Christianity and to make its universal acceptance "both a logical and spiritual necessity." The parliament, liberal missionary George Candlin wrote, marked "a bright new dawn of Gospel morning for the world, for all the world."[47]

But the spectacle in Chicago made many of the more conservative Protestants nervous and a bit vindictive. "A mongrel gathering," sniffed the *Presbyterian Journal*. "Civilization," fumed A. T. Pierson of the *Missionary Review*, "another colossal image of gold all men are now called upon to worship." Charles Little likened the enthusiasm for the parliament—calling it the "melting mood"—to the joy of the

---

[45] Braybrooke, *Inter-Faith Organizations*, p. 8.

[46] Paul Carus, "The World's Parliament Extension," *The Monist* 5 (April 1895): 346-53; Jenkin Lloyd Jones, "The Parliament's Challenge to the Unitarians," *Unity* 32 (January 1894): 306-07.

[47] Lyman Abbott, "Lesson from the Parliament of Religions," in Charles Deems, ed., *Christian Thought* (New York: Wilbur Ketcham, 1893-94), pp. 220-23; letter from George Candlin to Charles Bonney quoted in "The Parliament of Religions," *The Chinese Recorder and Missionary Journal* 25 (January 1894): 36.

French at the Feast of the Federation on the eve of the Terror. But from the far side of the gallery came high and very liberal praise from *The Chicago Tribune*: "There are no longer pagans and heathens."[48]

It is not a part of my argument to say that the parliament caused anything, much less that it caused the collapse of an old consensus-obsessed mainstream. It seems more appropriate to think of it as a kind of grand but temporary interruption in the normal course of events, an interruption indicative of a major modern trend toward the recognition of plurality. Normally segregated forces—Protestants, Catholics, Jews, humanists, Hindus, Buddhists, and so on—were gathered together in one place, allowing everyone to see how truly disparate the nation and the world could be. After a few years of praise and acrimony, things pretty much returned to normal.

But after a century that has witnessed two world wars, the collapse of empires, the rise of Asian nation-states, mass migrations and mass civil rights movements, the burgeoning of science and technology, and the emergence of what we blithely refer to as our global village, there is little sense that we can engineer a return to what a century ago passed for normalcy. A major reorganization of the world has been a central feature of the history of the twentieth century. Radical forms of ethnic and religious pluralism have become the norm in many quarters of the nation. The parliament did not cause any of this, but with the wisdom of hindsight we can see now that it pointed out to us what was on the road ahead.

The last word from the parliament's contemporaries deserves to go to those who most clearly sensed what was down the road a piece, in a new age that would increasingly struggle with religious pluralism, but would grow dubious about universal progress and learn that consensus on religious matters is rarely achieved. For Chicago's Matthew Mark Trumbull, a labor organizer and social radical, the quest for spiritual consensus had been revealed at the parliament to be nothing but an anxious chase after a "phantom of unity." For Unitarian Joseph Henry Allen, the great success of the parliament had been the example of how all the religions of the world might "best flourish, independently, side by side," without having to disguise differences by appeals to the "colorless compromise" of universal faith and the "powerful solvent of metaphysics." A second Unitarian, John

---

[48] For the *Presbyterian Journal*, see press notices reprinted in *Christian Register* 72 (September 1893): 617-18; Pierson, "Columbian Exposition," pp. 9; Little, "Chicago Parliament," pp. 208-9; *Chicago Tribune*, September 24, 1893, p. 12.

White Chadwick, alone among the parliament's commentators, evoked what would become for many the bugbear of the twentieth century: religious relativity. Let the "absolute values [of the various religions] be what they may, relatively, to the peoples who acknowledge them and believe in them," Chadwick wrote; people will one day learn to appreciate the "doctrines and the forms, the mythologies and the idolatries of other faiths" in the same spirit they cherish their own.[49]

As we approach the centennial of the parliament, there is a need for historians of American religions to continue to take a sustained look at religious pluralism in our nation, not simply as a problem that seems to threaten the consensus of a moral and religious mainstream, real or imagined,[50] but as an extraordinary spiritual and social reality. It has become a problematic exercise to think about American religion, particularly in its contemporary manifestations, with shopworn categories such as "mainstream" and "fringe." In the last several decades alone, we experienced first a florescence of Asian religions coinciding with what Ahlstrom called the onset of a "post-Puritan" era in American religious history,[51] then a resurgence of Christian

---

[49] M.M. Trumbull, "The Parliament of Religions," *The Monist* 5 (April 1894): 333-35; Joseph Henry Allen, "The Alleged Sympathy of Religions," *New World* 4 (June 1895): 319-21; John White Chadwick, "Universal Religion," *New World* 3 (September 1894): 411-16.

[50] Almost immediately upon its discovery, religious pluralism was seen by some commentators as a social problem. Among the earliest was Robert Bellah, the first theoretician of civil religion (*The Broken Covenant* [New York: Seabury, 1975]). For a more recent but equally influential discussion, see Richard John Neuhaus, *The Naked Public Square: Religion and Democracy in America*, 2d ed. (Grand Rapids: Eerdmans, 1986). Neuhaus described pluralism as a "legalized secular distortion of Judeo-Christian concern for the marginal," lamented the fact that pluralism tends to undercut dogmatic claims, and correctly pointed to the fact that the meaning of pluralism is in flux in contemporary usage (pp. 144-49). As social commentators and political and moral theologians, Bellah and Neuhaus quite rightly see the challenges presented by pluralism to social and moral consensus. The role of social critic, however, seems somewhat inappropriate to the historian of religions whose major concern is with the analysis and description of the varied forms of human religiosity.

[51] Ahlstrom, *Religious History*, pp. 1037-54. Ahlstrom discussed eastern religion in the United States under the heading "Piety for the Age of Aquarius," lumping together theosophical movements, occultism, and Hinduism, Buddhism, and Bahā'ī. While this is not an inaccurate portrayal of the kaleidoscopic interests of the largely white counter-culture in the 1960s, it does little service to the burgeoning of Asian religions in the United States. Charles Prebish makes a better point when he notes that in the case of Buddhism, "by the close of the decade of the 1960s America had virtually the full range of Buddhist traditions and sects arrive on its soil" (*American Buddhism*, p. 39). Asian religion in immigrant

conservatism as fundamentalists, who had themselves once been pushed to the margin, joined forces with many evangelicals in a new religious right. Fallout at the grassroots from both those movements continues to pit those prophesying a "new age" against those reading signs of the "great apostasy."[52] We can comprehend neither one of these broad developments if they are conceived of as movements on the fringe, yet it seems to accomplish very little to consider them both in an American mainstream.

It seems more to the point for historians to seize the opportunity presented by the extraordinary development the nation has undergone in the past few decades: religious pluralism slowly crept up on us all until suddenly, it seemed, it overtook the mainstream. Plurality replaced consensus as the historians' central paradigm and became as well a prominent national ideal, because plurality became a mainstream experience. From this new perspective, the national religious landscape suddenly appeared as one of extraordinary richness and fascinating complexity.[53] Theologians and consensus

---

communities is a related but different question. For an excellent treatment of the Japanese Buddhist experience on the west coast, see Donald R. Tuck, *Buddhist Churches of America: Jodo Shinshu*, Studies in American Religion 38 (Lewiston, N.Y.: Edwin Mellen, 1987). For religion among recent Indian and Pakistani immigrants, see Raymond Brady Williams, *Religions of Immigrants from India and Pakistan: New Threads in the American Tapestry* (Cambridge: Cambridge University Press, 1988).

52 For a stark contrast between the more popular reaches of these two movements, cf. the interpretations of American religious history implicit in Marilyn Ferguson, *The Aquarian Conspiracy: Personal and Social Transformation in the 1980s* (New York: St. Martin's Press, 1980); and David Hunt, *America: The Sorcerer's New Apprentice: The Rise of New Age Shamanism* (Eugene, Oreg.: Harvest House, 1988). Albanese, reviewing the attempt by sociologists Wade Clark Roof and William McKinney to chart a new emerging center in American religion, noted that fundamentalists and New Agers, for all their differences, share many characteristics of a "species of mysticism" that may be typical of an emerging American "ethnos." Albanese's attempt to characterize American religion in terms of a national style or ethnicity may be more helpful in coming to understand what unites a plural America than attempts to chart a demographic center. See Catherine L. Albanese, "Religion and the American Experience: A Century After," *Church History* 57 (1988): 337-51.

53 David Tracy has recently discussed both the challenge and the opportunity presented by pluralism in all its complexity. Although writing as a theologian, Tracy hits the right beat for a new wave of studies of American pluralism, one more informed by the comparativist's concern for the human experience of the sacred than those older studies which were an outgrowth of the mainstream and fringe model of American religious history; see David Tracy, *Plurality and Ambiguity: Hermeneutics, Religion, and Hope* (San Francisco: Harper and Row, 1987).

theoreticians are not required to cheer, clap hands, and wave handkerchiefs over it all, as many people did at the closing day of the World's Parliament of Religions a century ago. But there is a fundamental lesson from the parliament that historians and theologians alike can learn: the existence of radical pluralism is a fact of life in American society. It is a fact that can be ignored or interpreted out of our field of vision, but it is also a reality—one that cannot be dismissed as a phenomenon on the fringe.

And if the parliament tells us anything at all about the nation's collective religious past, it reminds us that the emergence of a pluralist America was really not so sudden after all. A pluralist current, torrent, or undertow has been flowing right along with the shifting fortunes of a consensus-seeking mainstream for many, many years.

PROTAP CHANDRA MAJUMDAR AND SWAMI VIVEKANANDA AT THE PARLIAMENT OF RELIGIONS
Two Interpretations of Hinduism and Universal Religion

Sunrit Mullick

To many American observers, the Parliament of Religions in Chicago was *the* event of the nineteenth century. While there were protests by some Christian churches on grounds that it was insulting for Christianity to be placed on a par with "heathen" religions, many churches welcomed the step so that Christianity's superiority could be proved once and for all. A middle ground was taken by some who were really motivated by a desire to learn about non-Christian religions.[1] A major accomplishment of Barrows's committee was the presence of a large delegation representing Asian religions. Of this, the delegation from India was impressive. There were Protap Chandra Majumdar and B. B. Nagarkar representing the Brāhmo Samāj, Swami Vivekananda and Narasimha Acarya representing Hinduism, Siddhu Ram and Jinda Ram

---

"Protap Chandra Majumdar and Swami Vivekananda at the Parliament of Religions: Two Interpretations of Hinduism and Universal Religion" by Sunrit Mullick. This essay originally constituted sections of its author's Doctor of Ministry (D. Min.) dissertation, "Protap Chunder Mozoomdar in America: Missionary of a New Dispensation," Meadville/Lombard Theological School, Chicago, Illinois, 1988. Reprinted with permission of the author, and Spencer Lavan of the Meadville/Lombard Theological School. Minor modifications have been made by the author.

[1] For representative positions see *WFP*.

representing Islam, Virchand Gandhi representing Buddhism, C. N. Charkravarti representing Theosophy and Jeanne Sorabji, a convert to Christianity from Zoroastrianism. Protap Majumdar, Vivekananda and Anagārika Dharmapāla, the Buddhist delegate from Ceylon (today Sri Lanka), became acknowledged celebrities of the parliament.[2]

Protap Majumdar was a familiar name to many Americans as author of *The Oriental Christ* and because of his earlier visit to America in 1883.[3] Scholars writing on the East-West encounter of religions have generally neglected to assess the role of Protap Majumdar's first mission to America in 1883. For example, in his book *The Oriental Religions and American Thought* Carl Jackson has made passing reference to Majumdar's 1883 visit as a "lecture visit."[4] Again, in her book *America: Religions and Religion* Catherine L. Albanese has omitted reference to Protap Majumdar's 1883 visit, attributing the growth of Hinduism in America to a "series of missionary movements addressed by Indian spiritual leaders to American converts" beginning with the Vedanta mission of Swami Vivekananda through whom "Hinduism caught the eye of the American public."[5] Both scholars have missed the significance of Protap Majumdar's 1883 visit to America, for this was really the first intentionally missionary effort by a modern Indian religion to America.

Whenever one comes across reference to Protap Chadra Majumdar, it is usually in the context of his leadership in the Brāhmo Samāj and his participation in the Parliament of Religions in Chicago in 1893. But ten years before the Parliament of Religions, Majumdar, as a pioneer of Eastern self-interpretation to America, was really the first Indian intellectual that Americans encountered, and that was the first time an Indian religious leader was on American soil, a precursor of many who came after him—Vivekananda, Rabindranath Tagore, Maharishi Mahesh Yogi and Bhagwan Rajneesh, among others.

Majumdar's 1883 mission, among other factors, may have created more of a receptivity among Americans toward Indian religions than is acknowledged; distinct lines of influence can be traced from that visit to the idea of holding the Parliament of Religions in 1893—particularly

---

[2] Carl T. Jackson, *The Oriental Religions and American Thought: Nineteenth-Century Explorations* (Westport, Conn.: Greenwood, 1981), p. 249.

[3] *WPR*, 1:64, 86.

[4] Jackson, *Oriental Religions*, p. 258. Jackson has erred in dating this visit as "1884."

[5] Catherine L. Albanese, *America: Religions and Religion*, 1st edition (Belmont, Cal.: Wadsworth, 1981), p. 203. These same passages recur in the 2d, rev. edition of Albanese's book of the same title (Belmont, Cal.: Wadsworth, 1992), p. 301, where Majumdar again goes unmentioned.

through Jenkin Lloyd Jones, Unitarian clergyman of All Souls Church, Chicago, with whom Majumdar had developed close connections, and who was one of the chief architects of the parliament.[6]

In his response to the welcome at the inauguration of the parliament on September 11, 1893, Majumdar reiterated what he had said on his first mission to America: that India claimed the attention of the world not merely for her antiquity, but also for her struggle towards modernity. All the great civilizations of the ancient world—Egypt, Greece and Rome—had vanished like a dream, but India, "the ancient among ancients, the elder of the elders, lives to-day with her old civilisation, her old laws, and her profound religion."[7] He went on to trace briefly the evolution of Indian religion from the Vedas to the New Dispensation of the Brāhmo Samāj.

Vivekananda's response was in marked contrast to Majumdar's, and also to that of the other Indian delegates. It was short, terse and pithy. Controverting the opinion that all had voiced, that the Parliament of Religions had ushered in a new era of religious toleration, Vivekananda proclaimed that he was "proud to belong to a religion which had taught the world both tolerance and universal acceptance."[8] He was proud to belong to a nation that had sheltered the persecuted of other lands, such as Jews and Zoroastrians. Without mentioning the West, he laid the charge of sectarianism, bigotry, fanaticism, violence and bloodshed squarely on its shoulders. Proclaiming that all religions led to the same goal, he concluded by hoping that the parliament would sound the death-knell of all fanaticism.

Vivekananda's response contained no apologies for Hindu superstition or backwardness. Trained in the English educational system, in the prime of his youth, dressed in the bright ochre robes of the Hindu monk, Vivekananda's presence was compelling. Dharmapāla was soft-spoken, Majumdar was steady in diction, but Vivekananda took this

---

[6] Jones's role in familiarizing Americans with non-Western religions in general and in the parliament in particular has been undervalued in writings on the subject. For an assessment of Jones's role with special reference to Protap Majumdar, see Sunrit Mullick, "Protap Chunder Mozoomdar in America: Missionary of a New Dispensation," Doctor of Ministry (D. Min.) dissertation, Meadville/Lombard Theological School, Chicago, 1988, pp. 121-35.

[7] Protap Chandra Majumdar, "Response to Welcome," in *Lectures in America and Other Papers* (Calcutta, India: Navavidhan Publication Committee, 1955), p. 2.

[8] Swami Vivekananda, "Response to Welcome," in Eastern and Western Disciples, ed., *The Complete Works of Swami Vivekananda*, 5th ed., 7 vols., Mayavati Memorial Edition (Mayavati, India: Advaita Ashram, 1926-36), 1(1931):1. (Cited hereafter as *Complete Works*.)

opportunity to release the full power of his oratory. Where the other speakers began with "Ladies and Gentlemen" or "Distinguished gentlemen" or "Reverend ministers, most honorable gentlemen, the superiors of this congress," Vivekananda acknowledged no one except "Sisters and brothers of America," giving rise immediately to "a peal of applause that lasted for several minutes."[9] All accounts are unanimous that this address shot him to instant fame.

Swami Vivekananda's meteoric rise to prominence at the Parliament of Religions has caused historians to neglect Majumdar's role. Insofar as Vivekananda helps to throw Majumdar in relief it will be necessary to discuss, without going into detail, Vivekananda's first American visit. In doing so it will become evident that there were, not one, but two interpretations of Hinduism and universal religion presented before the parliament.

A comparative discussion of Majumdar and Vivekananda is an issue delicate in the extreme. Ever since the parliament, there has been bitter acrimony between the followers of the two leaders. The ostensible reason for the rivalry is the claim to fame made for the two men by the rival groups with regard to their impact on the West, represented by the Parliament of Religions. But on a deeper level the rivalry is symptomatic of the psycho-social dynamics set in motion when one civilization responds to another: "The Bengali's psychological uncertainty was heightened by the social consequences of his newly formed relationship with the European."[10]

Swami Vivekananda,[11] whose real name was Narendra Nath Dutta, was born in Calcutta on January 12, 1863 in a wealthy, aristocratic family. His father Visva Nath Dutta was of an agnostic turn of mind. In keeping with his Europeanized tastes, he had the son educated in Western branches of learning. Narenda was a precocious student and though he acquired a fund of knowledge ranging from philosophy to science, he had a hunger for the religious life. When he was in his early teens, Keshab Chandra Sen, the leader of the Brāhmo Samāj, was at the height of his fame and it is said that Bengali youths looked up to him as a model of oratory.

---

[9]Quoted by John Henry Barrows, "The History of the Parliament," in *WPR*, 1:101. In India, this is one phrase for which Vivekananda is universally remembered.

[10] David Kopf, *British Orientalism and the Bengal Renaissance: The Dynamics of Indian Modernization (1773-1835)* (Berkeley: University of California Press, 1969), p. 9.

[11]*Swami* is an honorific title for a celibate monk. *Vivekananda* means "Rejoicer in Conscience."

Narendra joined the Sadharan Brāhmo Samāj and participated in the choral hymn singing, of which he was particularly fond. The legend goes that Narendra, not satisfied with Brāhmo rationalism, desired to see God face to face and so went to Maharshi Debendranath Tagore, the Brāhmo patriarch whom all sections of society revered as a spiritual preceptor. On being told by the Maharshi that even he had not seen God, Narendra went away disappointed. It was then, in his search for the true *guru*, that he met Sri Ramakrishna who unhesitatingly told him that he had indeed seen God and would reveal him to Narendra.[12]

Ramakrishna, born in 1836, was a priest of the temple dedicated to the goddess Kali at Dakshineswar near Calcutta. Ramakrishna was as rustic in his manners and speech as the young Narendra was erudite and sophisticated. The two met in 1881 and, according to legend, Ramakrishna placed his right foot on his body, throwing Narendra into a trance, which the latter interpreted as the spiritual experience of being absorbed in the absolute. Narendra had found his *guru*.

In 1886 Ramakrishna died. The group of young *sannyasis* (celibate monks), of which Narendra, now known as Swami Vivekananda, was one, took formal vows in the presence of one another. This was the founding of the Ramakrishna Order.[13] It appears that the Order was loosely bound, having no formal regulations of conduct or rules of organization. In the next years Vivekananda travelled across the length and breadth of the country, appalled at the sight of the "starving millions" of his people, reeling under several centuries of subjugation by foreign powers. Hereafter, his clarion call was to "give back to the nation its lost individuality and *raise the masses*."[14]

Marie Louise Burke's *Swami Vivekananda: His Prophetic Mission* (1983) provides a picture of the Swami's first American visit in 1893. Unabashedly hagiographic, the book is nevertheless of value because it consists almost entirely of newspaper reports, advertisements, letters

---

[12] Some years ago I learned in private conversation with Professor Surath Chakraborty of the Calcutta Brāhmo Samāj another version of this legend. According to Chakraborty, Narendra went to the Maharshi and asked him if he would teach him the path to *advaita*, i.e., the absolute non-dualism of Śaṅkarācārya in which realization consists of the complete absorption of the human soul (*atman*) in the absolute (*brahman*). The Maharshi had rejected this position and instead told Narendra that God had revealed to him *dvaita-lila* or the divine sport of dualism. Narendra went away disappointed.

[13] Marie Louise Burke, *Swami Vivekananda in the West: New Discoveries*, 3d ed., 6 vols. (Calcutta, India: Advaita Ashrama, 1983-87), 1:12.

[14] Ibid., 14.

and other material that make it possible to judge the American response to the Swami. The accepted notion is that Vivekananda came to Chicago from Calcutta "to speak for Hinduism."[15] This is a popular myth. Vivekananda came to America with a very different mission and his participation at the Parliament of Religions was purely accidental. Both contentions are proved conclusively from Burke.

Vivekananda arrived in Vancouver in July 1893 and reached Chicago some five days later. The parliament was not due to begin till the middle of September, so he left for Boston, for no other reason than that "the cost of living was lower."[16] Here he came in touch with Professor John Henry Wright of Harvard University who persuaded him to attend the Parliament of Religions, introduced him to the parliament authorities as a qualified delegate, gave him financial assistance and arranged for his housing in Chicago.

It was in Massachusetts that the Swami began acquiring celebrity status, not so much as a representative of Hinduism or spiritual preceptor, but as a curio—dressed as he was in his ochre robe and turban. A certain Miss Kate Sanborn of Holliston showed him off as her "Indian Rajah," driving through town in a rented carriage and livery.[17] Burke quotes from the *Boston Evening Transcript* the first direct mention of the Swami which referred to him as a "Brahmin monk."[18] After his meeting with John Wright in August, the Swami got invitations to speak at small gatherings. His addresses before and after the parliament appear to have had a double edge: the patience, non-violence and tolerance of Hinduism were extolled while the English as a race were denounced in venomous terms as irreligious, savage and barbarian.

By this time the press knew that they had a prize in their hands and began pandering to the American penchant for sensationalism. The *Evening News*, for instance, after introducing him as a "learned monk" concluded that the "rajah will wear his native costume";[19] it did not occur to it that for a monk to be a rajah was a contradiction. Its crude journalism is evidence that its readers were probably more interested in a rajah than in a monk.

---

[15] Jackson, *The Oriental Religions*, p. 246. Burke is nowhere referred to by Jackson, neither in footnote nor in bibliography.

[16] Burke, *Swami Vivekananda*, p. 19.

[17] Ibid., pp. 22-23.

[18] Ibid., p. 25.

[19] Ibid., p. 46.

After his success at the Parliament of Religions, Vivekananda's popularity reached phenomenal heights. As one reads through the Burke volume one is struck by the degree to which Americans were captured by his outward appearance. Spirituality became a business venture, using the swami to attract crowds and sell tickets to more than full houses. The chief method of accomplishing this was to advertise him with epithets that grew more and more extravagant as Vivekananda's popularity increased: "High Priest of Brahma,"[20] "Professor Swami Vevekanunda, a Hindu theologian of great learning,"[21] "Viva Kananda, from the oldest monastery in the world,"[22] "Brahmin of the Brahmins."[23] By far the most crass advertisement, more so because of the irony underlying it, was an announcement for "Kananda" at the Detroit Opera House that appeared in the "amusements" column of the *Detroit Tribune* of March 10, 1894.[24]

It is quite evident from the newspaper reports in Burke that Vivekananda became immensely popular with women in particular, over whom he seems to have exerted a powerful magnetism.[25] This phenomenon poses an embarrassment for Burke, so she engages in various kinds of apologetics for the behaviour of the women.[26] This is a curious phenomenon, a discussion of which lies, perhaps, more in the area of psychology than history.

Probably Vivekananda realized that he had become a draw and did not fail to make capital out of it. For his mission in America was not to preach Hindu Vedānta but to raise money for the people of India. Burke quotes, among others, from a letter Vivekananda wrote to the Dewan of Junagad, one of his Indian patrons, "Primarily my coming [to America] has been to raise funds for an enterprise of my own. . . .[The masses] are to be given back their lost individuality. They are to be educated."[27] At the time of the parliament Vivekananda does not seem to have had a well-defined plan for "raising the masses." Unlike the Brāhmo Samāj which already had organized social service departments, Vivekananda

---

[20] Ibid., p. 93.
[21] Ibid., p. 115.
[22] Ibid., p. 139.
[23] Ibid., p. 163.
[24] Ibid., p. 241.
[25] See for example, ibid., pp. 110, 116, 157, 255.
[26] Ibid., pp. 100-01, 116. Protap Majumdar too was besieged by women during his 1883 visit, although far less so than Vivekananda was in 1893.
[27] Ibid., p. 468.

was not part of any institution through which funds could be administered for social action programs.

Vivekananda was greatly moved with compassion by the appalling poverty of the Indian people and also moved with anger against the British whom he accused for the economic exploitation of India. His anger against the British government found vent in his sharp denunciations of the Christian missionaries in India who, unlike the "government," could be easily identified and pointed to, as individuals and groups. Of course the anger of Indians against both British government and Christian missionaries had ample grounds for justification: the former with regard to economic and military imperialism and the latter with regard to religious imperialism. And it is undeniable that each fed into the other.

Vivekananda spoke four times at the Parliament of Religions in addition to speeches at auxiliary conferences. In the opening address he declared that all religions led to the same goal, thus religious intolerance should cease. In the second address "Why We Disagree" he said that every religion imagined that it alone had access to the whole of reality, but no religion, including Hinduism, could ever exhaust reality in its totality. At the closing session he declared, in contrast to the other speakers who waxed eloquent about the era of religious unity that the Parliament of Religions had ushered in, that if anyone thought that this unity would come about by the triumph of any one religion (evidently meaning Christianity) and the destruction of others, "to him I say: 'Brother, yours is an impossible hope'....The Parliament of Religions has...proved...that holiness, purity and charity are not the exclusive possessions of any church in the world....If anybody dreams of the exclusive survival of his own religion and the destruction of the others, I pity him from the bottom of my heart."[28]

Vivekananda set forth his views on Hinduism in a paper he read on September 19, 1893. Hinduism, he said, was a religion that absorbed all religions that clashed with it. Thus it was that though various sects had risen in protest against it, the "immense body of the mother faith" merely sucked them in.[29] Hinduism accommodated the highest philosophy of the Vedānta, the lowest idolatry, the agnosticism of the Buddhists and the atheism of the Jains. The essence of Hinduism which enabled these multifarious contradictions to rest within it was the

---

[28] Vivekananda, "Address At the Final Session," in *Complete Works*, 1:22.
[29] Vivekananda, "Paper on Hinduism," in ibid., p. 4.

common belief in the divinity of the human soul—the Vedāntic doctrine of identity of *atman* and *brahman*. Vivekananda then went on to expound Vedāntic doctrines of immortality, illusion, *karma* and freedom.

Descending from "the aspirations of philosophy to the religion of the ignorant"[30] Vivekananda flatly denied Hindu polytheism, that whipping boy of Christian missionaries. Polytheism, he said, was worship of God through symbols. Christians used many symbols in their worship—the cross, icons and anthropomorphic language. Then he remarked pointedly, "The Hindus have their faults, they sometimes have their exceptions; but mark this, they are always punishing their own bodies, and never for cutting the throats of their neighbours. If the Hindu fanatic burns himself on the pyre, he never lights the fire of Inquisition. And even this cannot be laid at the door of his religion any more than the burning of witches can be laid at the door of Christianity."[31]

Protap Majumdar made two major addresses at the parliament, in addition to brief responses at the opening and closing sessions. Apart from the parliament proper, Majumdar addressed the opening session of the Free Religious Association's Columbian Convention and the International Unitarian Congress. The first address was on "The Brahmo Somaj," delivered on September 13, 1893.[32] The central motif was evolution. Referring to India as the land of evolution, Majumdar traced the rise and development of the Brāhmo Samāj as a new religion that had evolved from "far, far antiquity, from the very roots of our national life, thousands of years ago."[33] He spoke about the social and religious reforms of Ram Mohan Roy and the founding of the Brāhmo community by Debendranath Tagore. He then summarized the three elements of Brāhmo religion that formed the basis of the New Dispensation: acceptance and harmonization of world religions, social action and personal spirituality.

The second address was on "The World's Religious Debt to Asia"[34] delivered on September 22. The motif of this address was spirituality. Asian spirituality embodied in the Hindu Vedas, Zoroastrian Avesta, Jewish psalms and Muslim Qur'an taught the modes of God's self-revelation. The Asiatic saw God in nature; its forces were neither blind nor fantastic, but manifestations of a personal will. Secondly, the Asiatic

---

[30] Ibid.
[31] Ibid., p. 16.
[32] Majumdar, "The Brahmo Somaj," in *Lectures in America*, pp. 4-14.
[33] Ibid., p. 4.
[34] Ibid., pp. 15-32.

beheld God in his own soul through disciplined introspection and prayer, collectively called *yoga*—he realized that his own personality unfolded the Divine Personality. The mystic union was the bedrock of all religious experiences, whether Hindu, Hebrew, Chinese or Christian. Thus it was that "Asia seeking the Universal God in her soul [had] discovered God in all the world."[35] Thirdly, Asia had taught the world to worship—rapturously and joyously. Worship was not a duty with Orientals but a passion, such as Miriam, Muhammad, Hāfiz and the Vaisnavas demonstrated. Finally, Asia had taught the world the practice of renunciation, which denoted curbing of desires and control of the passions. Citing the examples of Jesus, the Buddha, St. Paul and Nānak, Majumdar explained that renunciation meant living in the world but not allowing the world to live in oneself.

In concluding his address Majumdar conceded that perhaps Asians had carried spirituality to extremes, to the neglect of the practical, material demands of life, just as the West had taken the material to extremes. Perhaps one day the resources of East and West would combine

> to support each other's strength, and supply each other's deficiencies. And then that blessed synthesis of human nature shall be established which all prophets have foretold, and all the devout souls have sighed for.[36]

In his closing speech on September 27 Majumdar declared that the Parliament of Religions signified the triumph of the New Dispensation and the fulfillment of Keshab Chandra Sen's prophecy in his 1883 lecture "Asia's Message to Europe": "men and women of varying shades of opinion" had all united "within the magnetic circle of spiritual sympathy," and in the future they would "influence and widen the various denominations to which they belong."[37]

What were the interpretations of Hinduism and universal religion set forth by Vivekananda and Majumdar? Vivekananda became a celebrity as an exponent of that school of Vedāntic Hinduism known as *advaita*, the philosophy of absolute non-dualism or absolute identity of *atman* and *brahman*. In his paper at the parliament, his only discourse on Hinduism, there was one passage where he sketched the *advaita* doctrine: "Perfection is absolute, and the absolute cannot be two or three....When a soul becomes perfect and absolute, it must become one with Brahman,

[35] Ibid., p. 20.
[36] Ibid., p. 28.
[37] Ibid., pp. 30-32.

and it would only realise the Lord as the perfection, the reality, of its own nature and existence, the existence absolute, knowledge absolute, and bliss absolute."[38] In this lecture, he did not spell out *advaita* Vedānta as the universal religion but hinted at it: "If there is ever to be a universal religion, it must be one which will have no location in place or time;...which will recognise divinity in every man and woman, and whose whole scope, whose whole force, will be centered in aiding humanity to realise its own true, divine nature."[39] Marie Louise Burke, one of his earliest disciples, states that the idea of *advaita* Vedānta as the universal religion did not take shape in Vivekananda's mind till much later than the Parliament of Religions: "throughout the large part of 1893 and a large part of 1894 he had not embarked upon the broad and world encompassing mission that he later knew to be his. It appears to have been only towards the end of 1894 and the beginning of 1895 that the fullness of his message to the West began to take shape in his mind and that he settled down to formulate it."[40]

Majumdar's interpretation of Hinduism was in marked contrast to Vivekananda's. He stood clearly in the theistic, dualist, *bhakti* tradition of Indian religiosity. Instead of harking back to the Vedānta as the essence of Hinduism, Majumdar's central motif was evolution. Indian religion had evolved creatively and progressively from the Vedas to its present form in the New Dispensation. Secondly, evolution was not the result of blind forces, but directed by the will be a superintending power—the Spirit of God. The essence of Hinduism, and of all Asian religions, was not realization of the absolute identity of *atman* and *brahman* but the discernment of the Spirit of God in nature, heroes of history and self. The meaning of history was given a new twist in the New Dispensation— following the clash of cultures in the nineteenth century, history could no longer be particularized into Eastern and Western, but must comprise both, giving rise to a new concept of universal human history. The heroes of history belonged to no nation or sect in particular, but must be appropriated by both East and West. So, unlike Vivekananda, Majumdar's interpretation of universal religion was broadly comparative. He admitted strengths and deficiencies in all religions and hence the need for complementarity.

To bring this essay on Vivekananda and Majumdar to a close, a concluding observation is in order. Both men were messengers of Indian

---

[38] Vivekananda, "Paper on Hinduism," in *Complete Works*, 1:11-12.

[39] Ibid., 1:11.

[40] Burke, *Swami Vivekananda*, p. 473.

spirituality to America. Just as their respective interpretations of Hinduism and universal religion stood in marked contrast, so did their personal spirituality, in terms of how they expressed it in their discourses and the impression they left on their audiences as spiritual people. Majumdar was more familiar to Americans than Vivekananda as author of *The Oriental Christ* and because of his earlier missionary visit in 1883. As in that visit, Majumdar described Asian spirituality at the parliament in terms of "devotions, repentance, prayer, praise, faith,"[41] "absolute self-abasement before [God's] majesty,"[42] "meekness, penitence, gentleness, forgiveness, affectionateness...weeping compassion,"[43] "renunciation,"[44] and "poverty, homelessness, simplicity."[45]

Vivekananda, on the other hand, spoke of spirituality in such terms as "lions...souls immortal, spirits free,"[46] "[the spirit] the sword cannot pierce—...fire cannot burn...water cannot melt...air cannot dry,"[47] "the human soul is eternal and immortal, perfect and infinite,"[48] and "ye divinities on earth,—sinners? It is a sin to call a man so; it is a standing libel on human nature."[49]

So we get two versions of spirituality—gentleness and tenderness from the one, strength and power from the other. Majumdar's spirituality was seen for what it was, both in 1883 and in 1893. Burke is crestfallen that her master was not "recognized by all for what he was—the spiritual leader of the age. Some attributed greater spirituality, for instance, to Majumdar, whose talk on the Brāhmo Samāj unaccountably inspired the multitude to rise to its feet and sing the hymn 'Nearer, my God, To Thee.'"[50]

Vivekananda, wherever he appeared and spoke, was the recipient of thunderous applause. He dazzled Americans by his oratory, intellectual power, polemical prowess, biting sarcasm and ready wit. Burke is embarrassed that Vivekananda's spirituality made far less impression on Americans than his intellectual genius, and so she must apologize, as she

---

[41] Majumdar, "The Brahmo Somaj," in *Lectures in America*, p. 11.
[42] Ibid.
[43] Ibid.
[44] Mozoomdar, "The World's Religious Debt to Asia," in ibid., p. 23.
[45] Ibid.
[46] Vivekananda, "Paper on Hinduism," in *Complete Works*, 1:9.
[47] Ibid., 1:7.
[48] Ibid., 1:8.
[49] Ibid., 1:9.
[50] Burke, *Swami Vivekananda*, 1:135.

has done in the case of his appeal to American women: "But somehow this most important aspect of Swamiji's life has been given little importance in his biographies, and his life in America has been so presented as to give the reader the impression that he was primarily a 'man of action,' a lecturer and a writer—spiritually inspired, it is true, but first and foremost an *intellectual* genius. We do not see him as he must have been: continually in a transcendental state of consciousness....The fact is that American devotees view him, not as an intellectual expounder of the Vedānta philosophy, but as the first great prophet sent to this country by God."[51] Burke's apologetic is subjective; her own volume of materials on the Swami's reception in America has no evidence to support her thesis of his "hidden" spirituality.

We are led to conclude then that Vivekananda's message of strength and power prevailed over Majumdar's teaching of gentleness and tenderness. The reason for this victory is explained by placing that message in the psychological climate of late nineteenth-century America. At that time America was spiritually sick:

> [It was] a time when the surface brilliance of America seemed only a gaudy tinsel to hide the spiritual malaise beneath. Recovering from the Civil War and at the same time expanding by leaps and bounds industrially, America was enlarging old cities and creating new ones. People flocked to these cities from the countryside, and people flocked there, too, from abroad, as new waves of immigrants deluged America. This was an age of genuine pluralism but also an age of Protestant predicament, as the old symbols of a supernatural order no longer rang true with everyday American experience.[52]

At the basis of receptivity to *advaita* Vedānta was the predisposition of the late nineteenth-century American psyche toward power. In many ways this was a reaction against the "sin and damnation" theology of traditional Calvinist Protestantism. Philip Rieff has referred to this shift in the American psyche as being one from "religious man" to "psychological man," coterminous with the rise of Freudian psychoanalysis and therapy.[53] Elsewhere Rieff states that with the breakdown of traditional values, norms and ideals which empowered the American individual, now empowerment had to originate within the individual:

---

[51] Ibid., pp. 475, 477.

[52] Albanese, *America: Religions and Religion*, 1st ed., p. 153.

[53] Sigmund Freud, *Therapy and Technique*, ed. Philip Rieff (New York: Collier, 1963), pp. 10-11.

"Freud, knowing there was no cure [for spiritual malaise], in the classical sense of a generalizable conversion experience, sought an increase in human power without reference to any of the established ideals."[54]

Vivekananda's *advaita* Vedānta message of releasing the latent power in human souls was more conducive of acceptance in America than Majumdar's message of tenderness, compassion and self-control. The result of transplanting into the American psyche *advaita* torn out of its Indian religious context is described succinctly by Romain Rolland:

> It is to be feared that this [*yoga*], with its more physiological character, only exercised the great attraction it had in America, because she took it in its most practical sense, as promising material power. A giant with the brain of a child, this people is only interested as a rule in ideas which she can turn to her advantage. Metaphysics and religion are transmuted into false applied sciences, their object being the attainment of power, riches and health—the kingdom of this world....For all Hindu masters of true spirituality, spirituality is an end in itself.[55]

Rolland is not alone in thus describing the American psyche; Catherine L. Albanese corroborates the view of "an America which in the nineteenth century pursued material success and subscribed to the cult of worldly progress."[56] Vivekananda would be frustrated with the rich and wealthy "Vedantists" who would lionize him.[57] Majumdar, Vivekananda, Rolland and Albanese might rail against American "materialist spirituality," but this may be symptomatic of a double-bind in which American religion has been caught—American spirituality may simply be trapped within a materialist model, as may be extrapolated from Max Weber's *The Protestant Ethic and the Spirit of Capitalism*.

In the twentieth century the ramifications of a spirituality of power have had wide-ranging effects on American domestic life as well as on America's role in international politics. Facing the reality of a world teetering on the brink of a nuclear holocaust, there seems to be, in the nineteen-eighties, a sobering of the American psyche away from power to traditional values of love and compassion. A discussion of the shift would be out of place here, but to cite only one example, Majumdar's message of a spirituality of tenderness echoes the cry of environmental ethicists today:

---

[54] Philip Rieff, *The Triumph of the Therapeutic* (New York: Harper and Row, 1966), p. 87.

[55] Romain Rolland, *Prophets of the New India*, trans. E. F. Malcolm-Smith (New York: Albert and Charles Boni, 1930), p. 360.

[56] Albanese, *America: Religions and Religion*, 1st ed., p. 143.

[57] Burke, *Swami Vivekananda*, 1:376-78; Rolland, *New India*, pp. 358-61.

In the West you wrest from Nature her secrets, conquer her, she makes you wealthy and prosperous, you look upon her as your slave and sometimes fail to realise her sacredness. In the East Nature is our Eternal Sanctuary, the throne of our Everlasting Temple; and the sacredness of God's creation is only next to the sacredness of God himself.[58]

To conclude: this essay on Swami Vivekananda and Protap Chandra Majumdar has compared and contrasted, in brief, two major interpretations of Hinduism and universal religion given by them at the Parliament of Religions.

---

[58] Majumdar, "The World's Religious Debt to Asia," in *Lectures in America*, p. 27.

DHARMAPĀLA AT CHICAGO
Mahāyāna Buddhist or Sinhala Chauvinist?

Tessa Bartholomeusz

Introduction

Anagārika Dharmapāla, *the* Sri Lankan symbol of religious and national pride, journeyed to Chicago in 1893 to enlighten the World's Parliament of Religions on the subtleties and complexities of what he called "Arya Dharma," or "Southern Buddhism." Before and after his 1893 mission to America, Dharmapāla published articles on Buddhism in Sri Lanka, then called Ceylon, and gave several lectures on the topic as well. Moreover, he filled his diaries with his own insights into Buddhism on the island and other areas of Asia. In addition to being considered a champion for Buddhism in Sri Lanka then and now, Dharmapāla is considered one of the first Sinhala Buddhist chauvinists.[1] Indeed, there is much in his writings to suggest that he was.[2] Yet, we fail to see him

---

"Dharmapāla at Chicago: Mahāyāna Buddhist or Sinhala Chauvinist?" by Tessa Bartholomeusz. A version of this previously unpublished paper was delivered at a meeting of the Midwest American Academy of Religion at Western Michigan University, Kalamazoo, April 3, 1993. Research for this project was funded by an Indiana University Faculty Development Fellowship. The author would like to thank the Mahābodhi Society in Colombo for allowing her access to Dharmapāla's handwritten diaries, much from which has been published in his *Journal of the Mahā Bodhi Society*. In quotations drawn from Dharmapāla's writings and diaries, diacritics are not used unless they appear in the original.

[1] See, for instance, Stanley Jeyaraja Tambiah, *Buddhism Betrayed: Religion, Politics, and Violence in Sri Lanka* (Chicago: University of Chicago Press, 1992), esp. pp. 5-8.

[2] For instance, in an 1894 piece, he connects the historical Buddha to the Sinhala people by referring to him as "Prince Sakya Sinha" ("India: The Holy Land of the Buddhists," *The Buddhist* 6, no. 8 [March 2, 1894]: 66). In later writings, especially his

accurately if we ignore other strands in his writings, such as the development of his mature thoughts on Buddhism and Sri Lanka. In this study I explore Dharmapāla's attitudes toward Buddhism on the island and, in particular, toward "being Sinhala" at the time that he represented Southern Buddhism at the parliament. I thus go back to his early writings and reevaluate just what it was he actually thought about Buddhism, Sri Lanka, and the Sinhala people in the earliest stages of his missionary career.

Dharmapāla: Forgotten but Recalled

Dharmapāla's name is known throughout contemporary Sri Lanka. Buddhist scholars argue about him; school children study his teachings; patriots and monks alike hold him up as an exemplary Buddhist. A branch of the Mahābodhi Society (MBS) that he established in 1891 for the propagation of Buddhism in Asia continues to thrive in Colombo. Among other things, the MBS organizes lectures in Dharmapāla's honor; coordinates almsgivings for monks; provides relief for Sinhala people who have been displaced by the ethnic strife in Sri Lanka; and provides a venue for various Buddhist groups.

One large, imposing portrait of Dharmapāla hangs in the conference room of the MBS, while one or two smaller photographs of him grace the walls in the main office. Yet we are not asked to remember Dharmapāla by gazing into a likeness of his face, or by visiting his birthplace and remembering his life, as Americans are asked to memorialize their own heroes. Rather, we are asked to think about Dharmapāla's teachings. In my informal interviews with the Society's members and staff over the past several years, I have learned much about contemporary impressions of Dharmapāla's message, yet little about his life. However, most people I interviewed recalled one major event in Dharmapāla's life; as one clerk related to me in 1992—and many others echoed his words—Dharmapāla represented "Sinhala Buddhism in Chicago at the World's Parliament of Religions." My conversations with the clerk reminded me of Joseph Kitagawa's reflections on the parliament. As Kitagawa has remarked, "the Parliament of Religions...has remained so vivid in the memories of

---

1902 "History of an Ancient Civilization," Dharmapāla discusses the "triumphant record of victory [of] the Sinhalese," and glorifies the Buddhist history of the island. For the text, see Anagārika Dharmapāla, *Return to Righteousness*, ed. Ananda Guruge (Colombo: Department of Government Printing, 1991), pp. 479-84. (All references will be to this edition.) Yet he made similar claims for the Burmese and the Japanese. See below.

many religious people in other parts of the world,"[3] including Sri Lanka. Indeed, as my conversations with the clerk of the MBS suggest, the parliament has influenced Dharmapāla's legacy in Sri Lanka.

In the course of my conversations with the clerk, I asked him what Dharmapāla thought about Buddhism in Sri Lanka. Like most who had an opinion about Dharmapāla, the clerk noted that Dharmapāla believed that Sri Lanka has been *the* country where "true" Buddhism—that is, "Sinhala Buddhism"—has always found a home. He was surprised to learn that Dharmapāla in his writings and diaries more often than not as he prepared for the parliament described Buddhism in Sri Lanka as "Arya Dharma" and "Southern Buddhism," rather than "Sinhala Buddhism." He was also shocked to discover that Dharmapāla claimed in his early writings that Buddhism in Sri Lanka was really Mahāyāna.

Dharmapāla's Teachings: The Arya Dharma and Mahāyāna Buddhism

In the early 1890s, the years prior to Dharmapāla's trip to the parliament, Dharmapāla and his colleagues published numerous articles on Buddhism in *The Buddhist: The Organ of the Southern Church of Buddhism*. The journal, inaugurated in 1888, was the main forum for English-speaking Buddhists—the westernized intelligentsia—to discuss Buddhism, as well as other topics, including Christian missionary conversion tactics, education, politics, etc., in Sri Lanka and other Buddhist countries.[4] Like Dharmapāla, most who contributed articles were Buddhist Theosophists, cohorts of the American Colonel Olcott, who along with Madam Blavatsky founded the Theosophical Society in 1875 in New York. Olcott himself wrote frequently for *The Buddhist*,[5] and argued that Buddhism "teaches the highest good without a God; a method of salvation without a vicarious saviour."[6] In other words, he taught that Buddhism is "eminently practical"; Buddhism, unlike

---

[3] Quoted from Joseph M. Kitagawa's lecture in this volume.

[4] The journal is still in publication; it is at present published by the Young Men's Buddhist Association.

[5] In fact, one of the aims of *The Buddhist* was to "take a higher place among the journals devoted to Theosophy and Altruism," and to "place on record the active Theosophic work" ("Ourselves," 4, no. 52 [December 30, 1892]: 412).

[6] *The Buddhist* 4, no. 33 (August 19, 1892): 262. The article is untitled.

Christianity, is a "scientific religion."[7] In *The Buddhist*, Olcott, Dharmapāla, and their colleagues imagined friendships, and then consolidated them; reflected upon an imagined, glorious Buddhist past, and then constructed one; and dreamed of a future in which Buddhism would be restored to its former glory throughout Asia.[8]

In their writings of the early 1890s, contributors to *The Buddhist* very rarely used "Sinhala Buddhism" to describe Buddhism in Sri Lanka. Although some preferred to call Buddhism on the island "Sinhalese Buddhism,"[9] for the most part they referred to it as "Southern Buddhism," or the "ancient Aryan religion."[10] They argued frequently that "the Sinhalese [were] of Aryan origin";[11] they wrote on "The Arya Dharma of Lord Buddha";[12] and they encouraged the study of "Aryan Literature."[13] Some used pseudonyms, such as "an Aryan Buddhist," as they penned their articles.[14] When Indologists—both European and South Asian—argued for the Aryan status of the Sinhalas, the latter could claim to be a superior race as well.[15] The writings of H. Sumangala, Dharmapāla's monk-advisor, best exemplify this ideology, which is especially marked in a letter that he asked Dharmapāla to read at the parliament. Sumangala, perhaps the best-known Buddhist monk in Sri Lanka in the 1890s, began his letter to the parliament by explaining that Buddhists on the island "are followers of Arya Dharma, miscalled Buddhism by Western scholars."[16] Like Dharmapāla and his colleagues

---

[7] Ibid.

[8] For more on the relationship of a print medium to the construction of communities, see Benedict Anderson, *Imagined Communities* (London: Verso, 1983), esp. p. 154. In 1906 Dharmapāla established a Sinhala newspaper, the *Sinhala Bauddhaya*, which likewise linked Sinhala speakers throughout the Sinhala speaking areas of the island. By 1906, Sri Lanka, rather than other Buddhist countries, had become the focus of Dharmapāla's writings. The *Sinhala Bauddhaya* reflects this tendency as well.

[9] For instance, one writer urged that it was the "duty of Sinhalese Buddhists to adopt their own Aryan names and dress" ("Buddhist Boys' Fraternal Association," *The Buddhist* 4, no. 28 [July 15, 1892]: 219). Moreover, in an edition of *The Buddhist* from its earliest year of circulation, "Sinhalese Buddhists" are included in a list of the "so-called communities of the island" ("Correspondence," 1, no. 6 [1889]: 46-47).

[10] "Ourselves," *The Buddhist* 4, no. 52 (December 30, 1892): 412.

[11] "News and Notes," *The Buddhist* 4, no. 47 (November 25, 1892): 376.

[12] "The Arya Dharma of Lord Buddha," *The Buddhist* 4, no. 36 (September 9, 1892): 281.

[13] "The Path," *The Buddhist* 4, no. 26 (July 1, 1892): 200.

[14] E.g., an untitled article in *The Buddhist* 4, no. 6 (February 5, 1892): 48.

[15] See Tambiah, *Buddhism Betrayed*, p. 131.

[16] "Buddhism-Orthodox Southern," in *WPR*, 2:894.

in the early 1890s, Sumangala stressed the Aryan quality of Buddhism in Sri Lanka.[17]

Roughly one year before Dharmapāla set sail for Chicago, *The Buddhist* published an article about the impending parliament. It described the process whereby Rev. John Henry Barrows, the chairman of the parliament, had appointed Dharmapāla as a member of its Advisory Council.[18] According to the article, Barrows asked Dharmapāla "for any suggestions...as to those who might best be invited to take part."[19] The editors of the magazine, Dharmapāla's fellow Theosophists, took it upon themselves to suggest four *laymen* who might be qualified, because "there [were] but a few of the monks who are well acquainted with colloquial English."[20] Among the four laymen were L.C. Wijesinha, a Pāli scholar who had translated the *Mahāvaṃsa*, a fifth century chronicle that glorified the island's Buddhist past. The editors also suggested Dharmapāla. According to *The Buddhist*, of the four only Dharmapāla would be able to make the long journey to America; the others had commitments that prohibited them from representing Southern Buddhism in Chicago.

Dharmapāla began to prepare for the parliament. He and a Burgher,[21] A.E. Buultjens, who in the 1880s had converted to Buddhism though a descendant of the Christian Dutch, set about writing Dharmapāla's speeches. During much of July, 1893, Buultjens concentrated his efforts on helping his fellow Theosophist, Dharmapāla, "write out the Buddhist answers to the questions propounded in the programme of the Chicago Fair."[22] Their answers reflect the nature of Buddhist Theosophy at that time: in their description of Buddhism, they stressed its rational qualities, its affinities with science.[23]

---

[17] This tendency is marked in Dharmapāla's writings. For instance, in his diary entry for September 11, 1894, he scolds Sri Lankan Buddhists and claims that "their Aryan tendencies have deserted them."

[18] "The Parliament of Religions," *The Buddhist* 4, no. 34 (August 26, 1892): 269.

[19] Ibid.

[20] Ibid.

[21] I.e., a descendant of European colonizers.

[22] From Dharmapāla's diary entry for July 15, 1893. On July 17, "Buultjens assited [Dharmapāla] in writing out the questions for the Parliament of Religions. Worked til 5:30"; and on July 18, "From 8 Mr. Buultjens worked til 11 p.m."

[23] See the Guruge edition of Dharmapāla, *Return to Righteousness*, which contains the text of his address to the parliament, "The World's Debt to Buddha." See esp. the sections entitled "Buddhism and Modern Science" (p. 19) and "Can the Knowledge of Religion be Scientific?" (p. 20).

Buultjens was not the only prominent Buddhist of the early 1890s to assist Dharmapāla in educating the Chicago audience on Buddhism. Marie Museus Higgins, a Buddhist Theosophist from America who had helped to establish the first Buddhist girls' school in Colombo, also contributed. While principal of the institution, the Saṅghamittā School for Girls, she posed for a photograph with "the happy smiling children *all Buddhist*),"[24] which was later sent to the parliament. Moreover, she collected "specimens" of her students' "work," and sent them through Lady Havelock, the wife of the British governor of the island.[25] The Buddhist magazine advised its readers that "Visitors to the World's Fair who are the friends of the Saṅghamittā school, should not fail to look in at the Women's Department of the Columbian Exposition and see the work of our Buddhist girls."[26]

Buddhist Theosophists were proud of the progress they had made in educating Buddhist children, especially girls, and Dharmapāla shared their enthusiasm and their success. He agreed with his fellow Theosophists who argued that Buddhist girls are just as deserving of education as boys. Even early Buddhists, they argued, "did not fail to educate women."[27]

Like many Buddhist Theosophists of the 1890s, Dharmapāla argued that the treatment of women under Buddhism demonstrated that Buddhism was superior to the other religions. At the parliament, for instance, Dharmapāla discussed "the benefits conferred on women by Buddhism." He added that "the same rights are given to women as to man. Not the least difference is shown, and perfect equality has been proclaimed. 'Woman,' Buddha says in the *Chulavedala Sutta* and in the *Mahavagga*, 'may attain the highest path of holiness...which is open to man.'"[28] According to Dharmapāla, "The inscriptions of Asoka and the histories of Ceylon, Burmah [sic] and other Buddhist countries prove this,"[29] that is, that women are spiritually equal to men.

Dharmapāla claimed that treatment of women in all Buddhist countries, not just his own, demonstrated the egalitarian nature of Buddhism. In an 1894 article published immediately after his return from Chicago, he praised other Buddhist countries for their enlightened view

---

[24] Editor's "Notes," *The Buddhist* 4, no. 48 (December 2, 1892): 383.
[25] Ibid.
[26] Ibid.
[27] "Responsibility of Buddhists," *The Buddhist*, 4, no. 51 (December 23, 1892): 404.
[28] Dharmapāla, "The World's Debt to Buddha," in *Return to Righteousness*, p. 21 (also in *WPR*, 2:879).
[29] Ibid. (also in *WPR*, 2:879).

of women. For instance, he wrote that "Burma is the land of free women...The Burmese girl is graceful; but the sweetest flower of womanhood is to be found in Japan, the land of chrysanthemums and cherry blossoms; and Japan too is a Buddhist country."[30] Although there is much in Dharmapāla's earlier and later writings to suggest that he mistrusted—even despised—women,[31] he seems to have remained convinced that both women and men can attain enlightenment, and in 1897 even attempted to revive Sri Lanka's defunct order of Buddhist nuns.[32]

There is little hint in his earlier writings—he attended the parliament at twenty-nine—that he held that Sri Lanka, or even the Sinhala people, were *the* only Buddhist beacons for the rest of the world in regard to women or anything else. In fact, shortly after Dharmapāla returned from Chicago, *The Buddhist* published his three-part series of articles, "India: The Holy Land of the Buddhists," in which he argued that *India* was the "Buddhist Jerusalem,"[33] and that "Buddhism [was] the heirloom of the Indian Aryans and India belongs to Buddha."[34] India, rather than Ceylon, captured his attention in the early 1890s.

Dharmapāla's interest in India, specifically the restoration of Bodhgayā as a Buddhist pilgrimage site, nearly prohibited him from representing the Arya Dharma at the parliament. In his 1894 memoirs of the parliament published in *The Buddhist*, Dharmapāla related that his project to liberate the site of the Buddha's enlightenment from Hindus occupied his mind even while he prepared for the parliament. On the thirty-first of March, 1893, he received a cable that he was to start for Chicago by the end of June.[35] That left him with only three months to solicit from fellow Buddhists throughout Asia 100,000 *rupees*—a sizable sum in the 1890s—to bring the Buddhist temple at Bodhgayā into Buddhist possession. He added that if he had had to leave for "Chicago

---

[30] "Diary Leaves of the Buddhist Representative to the World's Parliament of Religions in Chicago," *The Buddhist* 6, no. 6 (February 16, 1894): 42.

[31] For instance, on board ship to Japan in 1902, Dharmapāla wrote in his diary: "Whenever [women] get the opportunity they sin. So far I have kept myself free from their impurities. Now I have passed my youth and I am now a full grown man. I hope in this life that I will not fall into sin. After finishing my active service, may I be allowed to retire into the Himalayan retreats!" (from entry for April 21).

[32] For more on Dharmapāla's attitudes toward women and his project to resuscitate the nuns' lineage, see Tessa Bartholomeusz, *Women Under the Bo Tree: Buddhist Nuns in Sri Lanka* (Cambridge University Press, forthcoming, 1994), chaps. 4 and 5.

[33] "India: Holy Land of the Buddhists" (n. 2 above), p. 66.

[34] Ibid., p. 67.

[35] "Diary Leaves," vol. 6, no. 6 (February 16, 1894); 41.

without having accomplished the object, [that would have been] sufficient to break one's heart."[36] He was finally successful in securing the amount, as well as moving closer to what he perceived to be the "consolidation of the Buddhist nations,"[37] the goal of his Mahābodhi Society. He wrote that the one "motive" that he "had all along to visit America was to disseminate the law of the gentle Lord Buddha abroad, and of bringing into prominence the great idea of the Maha Bodhi Society."[38]

While preparing for the trip to Chicago, Dharmapāla was interviewed by the various presses of the island. He reported that in Chicago, he and the other delegates to the parliament would receive "a right royal welcome."[39] Dharmapāla summarized his expectations thus: "I am looking forward to a delightful time in the west with Mrs. Besant and Countess Wachtmeister who will go along with me from London. I hope to do some useful work. All my expenses to and fro are to be paid by the World's Fair authorities, so that I have not much to complain of, have I?"[40] Having arrived in Chicago, he was quite impressed with its potential as fertile ground for Buddhism. "Materialist Chicago," he wrote just days before the parliament, "will in the 20th century become quite a spiritual centre."[41] With two Buddhist Theosophists at his side, Dharmapāla at the parliament won the sympathy of many, including the American Paul Carus, an influential publisher, who remained his friend and ally. Inspired at the parliament by Dharmapāla and the Zen master, Shaku Sōen,[42] Carus began a prolific career as an author of books and journals on Buddhism, which significantly helped to popularize Buddhism in America.[43]

---

[36] Ibid., p. 43.

[37] "India and Buddhism: A Chat with Mr. Dharmapala, He Represents Southern Buddhism at Chicago," *The Ceylon Independent*, quoted in full in *The Buddhist* 5, no. 26 (July 14, 1893): 207.

[38] "Diary Leaves of the Buddhist Representative to the World's Parliament of Religions in Chicago," *The Buddhist* 6, no. 5 (February 9, 1894): 40.

[39] Ibid.

[40] Ibid.

[41] From Dharmapāla's diary entry for September 6, 1893.

[42] Emma McCloy Layman, *Buddhism in America* (Chicago: Nelson-Hall, 1978), p. 28. Dharmapāla maintained an intellectual relationship with Shaku Sōen for quite some time. He mentioned him from time to time in his writings, especially in his *Journal of the Maha Bodhi Society*. This is especially striking in vol. 6, no. 1 (May 1897), which discusses an ongoing debate between Dharmapāla, Shaku Sōen and Rev. Barrows on the nature of Buddhism. For more on this debate, see below.

[43] For more on Carus, see Thomas A. Tweed, *The American Encounter With Buddhism* (Bloomington: Indiana University Press, 1992).

Dharmapāla arranged to take to the parliament *twenty thousand* copies of the Five Precepts of Buddhism—the fundamentals of Buddhist morality—to distribute in America and at various ports of call along the way.[44] En route to America, his steamer stopped in ports such as Aden, Port Said, and Southampton, to name only a few, where he passed along copies of the Five Precepts to many. He distributed the bulk of them, however, at the parliament, which Dharmapāla considered a success: one American man, C.T. Strauss, even became a Buddhist in a public ceremony in Chicago under Dharmapāla's tutelage.[45] Dharmapāla returned to Sri Lanka via Japan,[46] where he again distributed his leaflets; thus, as he travelled the globe, so did Southern Buddhism, the Arya Dharma.

The Arya Dharma, according to Dharmapāla, found its best expression in Mahāyāna Buddhism. In fact, Dharmapāla's journal entries and articles published immediately before and after he spoke in Chicago suggest he saw himself as a missionary of Mahāyāna Buddhism. From Dharmapāla's 1892 point of view, Buddhism in Sri Lanka was Mahāyāna:

> There have been some who supposed that by the "Mahayana" was meant the Northern Buddhists and by the Hinayana the Southern. Our opinion has always been the reverse of this....that the term Mahayana was applied to the great "Theravadas," *Sthavira Vadas*, and that Hinayana was applied to the seceders who afterwards formed the Northern Buddhist School.[47]

In short, for Dharmapāla, Theravāda Buddhism—the predominant Buddhist school in Sri Lanka—was Mahāyāna and not Hīnayāna as was (and is) commonly claimed.

Along these same lines, Dharmapāla in his *Journal of the Mahā Bodhi Society* immediately prior to the parliament corrected the views of the

---

[44] Bhikshu Sangharakshita, *Anagarika Dharmapala: A Biographical Sketch* (Kandy: Buddhist Publication Society, 1983), p. 60.

[45] Ibid., p. 63. Although Dharmapāla only made one convert to Buddhism during his first trip to the United States, his message and person inspired many. Among those inspired was the elderly Mrs. T.R. Foster, an American philanthropist whom he met in Honolulu on his way home to Sri Lanka. She became Dharmapāla's most generous financial supporter, and with the money she gave him, Dharmapāla built schools, temples, hospitals and other institutions.

[46] This was Dharmapāla's second trip to Japan; according to his diaries, Dharmapāla in 1889 accompanied Olcott to Japan at the invitation of Japanese Buddhists.

[47] "The Maha Bodhi Society," *The Buddhist*, 4, no. 23 (June 10, 1892): 180.

erudite scholar, Sir Monier Williams, on Buddhism in Sri Lanka. In an emphatic tone, Dharmapāla wrote: "The Southern School of Buddhism in the opinion of this great scholar belongs to the Hinayana School. These assertions, founded on no authority, only mislead the world."[48] He added that "We have better authority and reliable sources to show that Buddhism of Ceylon belongs to the oldest school of the Mahayana."[49]

In the years following the parliament, even after meeting Japanese Buddhists and discussing Buddhism with them, Dharmapāla maintained the view that Buddhism in Sri Lanka was Mahāyāna. While aboard ship returning to Sri Lanka from Chicago, Dharmapāla reiterated that Southern Buddhism and Mahāyāna were interchangeable terms; he recorded in his diary that he had discussed with a Japanese delegate to the parliament that "those who think Ceylon Buddhism is Hinayana are wrong."[50] He was outraged to learn after talking to Japanese Buddhist monks shortly after the parliament that they had thought that "Ceylon is Hinayana!"[51] Soon after arriving back in Sri Lanka, he recorded with enthusiasm in his diary that "Bell [an archaeologist] had asked [him] to get a committee formed to restore *dagobas* [Buddhist reliquaries]." He added: "Mahayana Buddhism in Ceylon. Traces discovered by Bell at Wijayarama."[52] Dharmapāla finally had proof of what he had believed all along: Mahāyāna Buddhism had flourished in Ceylon.

What exactly did Dharmapāla mean by "Mahāyāna Buddhism"? It is possible that because "Hīnayāna"—the *small* or *inferior* "vehicle"—was (and is) a pejorative term, Dharmapāla did not want it used of Buddhism in Sri Lanka. He instead preferred to use the term "Mahāyāna"—the *large* or *superior* "vehicle"—to describe Sri Lankan Buddhism. It is possible that the distinction had little to do with doctrinal differences, and more to do with the meaning of the designations. Yet, according to Dharmapāla's later reflections on the differences between Mahāyāna and Hīnayāna Buddhism, he was conversant on the doctrinal distinctions between the two, especially as they relate to liberation:

> The three paths to Nirvana are: *sammasambodhi, pratyeka bodhi, and sravaka bodhi*. The first is the supreme, the second is middling, and the third is low. The Mahayana path is the path of the supreme *bodhisattvas*

---

[48] "The Mayahana School of Buddhism," *The Journal of the Mahā Bodhi Society* 1, no. 1 (May 1892): 5.

[49] Ibid.

[50] From Dharmapāla's diary entry for October 19, 1893.

[51] From Dharmapāla's diary entry for November 30, 1893.

[52] From Dharmapāla's diary entry for September 20, 1894.

who aspire to become Buddhas; the *Majjhima* or *Ekayana* path is for the *pratyeka* Buddhas; and the Hinayana path is for those who wish to enter Nirvana quicker without concerning about the salvation for others.[53]

For Dharmapāla, the Sthavira (Theravāda) School of Sri Lanka, normally associated with the Hīnayāna path, was actually one of the earliest schools of the Mahāyāna.[54] Convinced that the Sthavira School was Mahāyāna—supreme and unselfish—Dharmapāla continued to argue that he was a Mahāyāna Buddhist well after the parliament;[55] he even aspired to become a buddha.[56] Thus, Dharmapāla's defense of Buddhism in Sri Lanka as Mahāyāna had much more to do with what he perceived as its relationship to the altruistic *bodhisattva* path than to the term itself.

In an article he published in 1925 for the journal of the MBS, he wrote about another Mahāyāna Buddhist country, Japan:

> Japan is a kind of beacon light to Asia....Japan is a Buddhist country and the Buddhists call themselves Mahayanists. The Mahayana Buddhists of ancient India were great explorers, they were all over Turkistan, Afghanistan and China preaching the great Doctrine; but the Mahayanist Buddhists of China and Korea are sleeping. It is time for the

---

[53] Dharmapāla, "The Life and Teachings of Buddha," in *Return to Righteousness*, p. 114. The editor, Guruge, does not supply the original date of publication. If the quotation is from Dharmapāla's later years, however, it indeed reflects strands in his earlier thoughts on Buddhism. Several points in this passage are worthy of explication. *Sammāsambhodi* is the perfect enlightenment of someone who then enlightens others; *pratyeka bodhi* is the enlightenment of someone who does not attempt to enlighten others; while *srāvaka bodhi* is the process of enlightenment of a "hearer" or "disciple." *Bodhisattvas* are enlightenment beings who help others attain nirvāna. In connection with their aspiration "to become Buddhas," see below on Dharmapāla's own desire to become a buddha. Finally, "the *Majjhima* or *Ekayana* path...for the *pratyeka* Buddhas" refers to the mediocre path, or path for one, of the solitary Buddha.

[54] Dharmapāla, "The Mahayana School of Buddhism," 5.

[55] In his September 9, 1902 letter to Paul Carus, Dharmapāla explained the differences between Mahāyāna and Hīnayāna: "To be a Buddha and save the world is Mahayana, to be [merely] a disciple *arhat* [one who has atttained *nirvāna*] is Hinayana. The former requires 4 *asankhya kalpas*, the latter one *asankhya kalpa*." In other words, the Hīnayāna path is easier and does not take as long to perfect. He also proved his point by arguing that "the idea of the *Bodhisat* [*bodhisattva*] doctrine is advocated in a Sinhalese work called...*The Ambrosial Drink*." Moreover, "the ancient symbolic architecture found in Anuradhapura...belongs to the Mahayana class." For more of Dharmapāla's correspondence to Carus, see "The Open Court Publishing Company Archives," Special Collections, Morris Library, Southern Illinois University at Carbondale.

[56] In his diary entry for October 5, 1897, Dharmapāla wrote: "I can be an *arahat* but my desire is to be the Supreme Buddha." On December 22 of that same year, he wrote: "May I become Buddha."

Japanese Mahayanist Buddhists to wake up and carry the noble doctrine
to countries that need it.[57]

Like his own Buddhist countrymen and women, Japanese Buddhists
were Mahāyāna Buddhists. In fact, according to Dharmapāla, the
Buddhists of Japan and Sri Lanka had much in common.[58]

In 1902 while in Japan to raise money for the MBS, Dharmapāla made
a speech at the Educational Society in which he argued that the ancestors
of the Japanese were "Vajjian Lichchavis,"[59] a northern Indian tribe
frequently mentioned in the Pali canon. In short, Dharmapāla argued
that Japanese Buddhists, in addition to being Mahāyānists, were Aryans
like their Sri Lankan co-religionists. And like Sri Lankan Buddhists, the
Japanese could also find authority for their practices in the texts.
According to Dharmapāla, "the Shinshu Sect and the Jodo who base
their belief in Amida Buddha [the Buddha of Infinite Light] have the
authority of the Pali texts to accentuate their faith. The Nichiren Sect has
their faith based on the Dhamma; and Pali Buddhism concurs with
them."[60] Thus, for Dharmapāla, Japanese Buddhists were Mahāyāna
Aryans whose beliefs and practices accorded with the Pali canon.

In Dharmapāla's early writings, then, two themes emerge with regard
to Buddhism in Sri Lanka and elsewhere. First, Mahāyāna Buddhists
were not confined to "Northern" Buddhist countries as most people
held; Sri Lanka, though a "Southern" Buddhist country, was also
Mahāyānist.[61] Secondly, Aryan Buddhists were not confined to South
Asia; even the Japanese were descended from an Aryan tribe. Moreover,
both countries proclaimed the Arya Dharma of the Buddha preserved in
the Pali canon.[62] Yet, Dharmapāla in the early years of his missionary
career placed his hopes for a Buddhist revival in Japan rather than in Sri

---

[57] Dharmapāla, "Observations Made During My Tour in Europe," in *Return to
Righteousness*, ed. Guruge, p. 717. The article first appeared in vol. 33 of *The Journal of
the Mahā Bodhi Society* (September 1925).

[58] He wrote much on the affinities between the two countries, and encouraged a
friendship between them. This is especially clear in his "Japan and the Sinhalese
People," *Sarasavisandaresa* (Colombo), March 18, 1902. In the article, he discussed Sri
Lankan monks who had been studying in Japan, and Japanese monks who had been
studying in Sri Lanka.

[59] From Dharmapāla's diary entry for June 21, 1902.

[60] From Dharmapāla's diary entry for May 11, 1902.

[61] There is nonetheless some ambiguity in his writings on Northern and Southern
Buddhism. As we saw above, Dharmapāla had also argued that Northern Buddhists
were Hīnayānists rather than Mahāyānists.

[62] According to his diary entry for July 2, 1902, for instance, Dharmapāla while in
Japan discussed the positive contribution that the "Aryan Doctrine" had made to
Japanese society.

Lanka; according to his diaries, Sri Lanka's "spiritual teachers" were "idle and inactive. Japan's best sons...work[ed] hard day and night."[63] Immediately after the parliament, Dharmapāla wrote, "I have hopes for a better future and that Japan will play an important part in the propagation of Buddhism in India."[64] Moreover, unlike Sri Lanka, "in Japan there had been no contaminating influence of any monotheistic and polytheistic religions. The purifying atmosphere of Buddhism was the only cool zephyr that blew over Japan."[65] In his tacit criticism of the influence of Christianity and what he considered non-Buddhistic practices in Sri Lanka,[66] Dharmapāla argued that Japan was much more prepared than Sri Lanka to take the lead in the revival of Buddhism, but that all Buddhist countries should reclaim their Buddhist heritage. In the years immediately prior to and following the World's Parliament of Religions in Chicago, Dharmapāla in fact urged each Buddhist country that he visited to reaffirm its Buddhist culture; to reestablish life under former Buddhist kings, life before the influence of the West.[67] Among those Buddhist countries, however, Japan stands out as his favorite: he even wrote that it was his "wish to return [to Japan] to settle down and work for Buddhism" there.[68]

Conclusions

As a recent peace walk in Sri Lanka suggests,[69] contemporary Sri Lankan Buddhists invoke Dharmapāla's example to sanction Buddhist behavior. Yet, they do not remember that he called himself a Mahāyāna Buddhist. Nor do they remember that he downplayed the differences among Buddhists in Asia. They do not recall that soon after the mission to Chicago, he argued *against* such illustrious people as Rev. Barrows, the chairman of the parliament, who claimed that "Buddhism is a system which is one thing in Ceylon, quite another in Tibet, and still another in

---

[63] From entry for April 21, 1902.

[64] From entry for November 13, 1893.

[65] From entry for June 5, 1902.

[66] His diaries are replete with criticisms of Buddhism in Sri Lanka at the turn of the century. For instance, according to his February 3, 1898 entry: "Donkeys without brains the present Sinhalese live an assanine [sic] life; but I will bring them back to the lionine [sic] life they lead in the past." Similar attitudes are found in his earlier writings.

[67] "Diary Leaves," pp. 40-43.

[68] From Dharmapāla's diary entry for July 2, 1902.

[69] "Walk Inspires Spiritual Peace, Says Thera," *Daily News* (Colombo), June 25, 1992. In the article, the writer invokes Dharmapāla as someone who "served the people by resorting to non-violent means."

China and Japan."[70] Although, as we have seen, Dharmapāla argued for the supremacy of Mahāyāna Buddhism, he claimed a unity in belief among Buddhists of Asia. For Dharmapāla in the 1890s, "the same fundamental doctrines were preached in all the countries and the same results were brought about everywhere."[71] Dharmapāla thus stressed in his earlier writings that all Buddhist countries and all Buddhist people, not just Sri Lanka and the Sinhala people, were heir to, and responsible for, the "Arya Dharma of Sakya Muni (mis-called) Buddhism."[72] Among them, India was the "holy land," and Japan shone like a bright light.

Since 1893, Sri Lankan Buddhists and others have reflected upon and written about Dharmapāla at the parliament and his impact on Buddhism. Indeed, after the parliament, Dharmapāla became well-known and well-respected at home and abroad;[73] even Barrows, the Christian minister who had helped plan the parliament, became an enthusiastic admirer of Dharmapāla and later visited Dharmapāla's family in Sri Lanka to learn more about Buddhism there.[74] Dharmapāla himself included the parliament as a significant event in his reflections upon his own life.[75]

The parliament was a significant event for other Sri Lankan Buddhists as well. Buultjens, the Theosophist who had helped Dharmapāla write his speeches for his Chicago audience, borrowed a copy of the proceedings soon after Dharmapāla returned in 1894 from his mission of spreading the Arya Dharma in America.[76] Buddhists in Sri Lanka, and especially Buultjens, the editor of *The Buddhist* in its early years, continued to perpetuate Buddhism as rational, scientific, and egalitarian,

[70] "Is There More than One Buddhism?" *Journal of the Mahā Bodhi Society* 6, no. 1 (May 1897): 5.
[71] Ibid. Dharmapāla's attitudes toward Japanese Buddhism are all the more interesting considering the 1990 controversy over an attempt to introduce to the Sri Lankan monastic community a Mahāyāna lineage from Japan. The Sri Lankan monk who tried in vain to establish the lineage was forced to leave the island. Dharmapāla, in his early years, may have encouraged its establishment.
[72] "The Sweet Spirit of Buddhism," *The Journal of the Mahā Bodhi Society* 1, no. 1 (May 1892): 4. The parenthetical remark is in the original.
[73] In a *New York Herald* article, "New Religious Schools" (June 14, 1897), Dharmapāla's main credential as a Buddhist teacher is his association with "the World's Fair's Parliament of Religions."
[74] *The Journal of the Mahā Bodhi Society* 6, no. 6 (October 1897): 41. Dharmapāla was in America on a missionary tour. On some friction that reportedly developed between Barrows and Dharmapāla see n. 67 of the article by Eric J. Ziolkowski in the present volume.
[75] Dharmapāla, *Return to Righteousness*, ed. Guruge, p. 620.
[76] From Dharmapāla's diary entry for March 14, 1894.

much as he had helped Dharmapāla package it for the parliament.[77] When Dharmapāla brought Buddhism back to the island—now legitimated by westerners—he was grandly welcomed with "elephants, drummers, and yellow robed monks,"[78] and the Buddhist revival that was underway picked up speed.[79] He continued to serve as "Manager of Buddhist Schools,"[80] a post he had accepted in 1889. In that post, he helped Olcott, Buultjens, and other Theosophists develop a curriculum for Buddhist children that reflected Buddhism's "rational" and "practical" features. Although he eventually divorced himself from the Buddhist Theosophical Society, he continued "the Buddhist takeover of Western ideas of Buddhism initially started by Olcott."[81] These ideas became the foundation for Buddhist education and, as such, have influenced a significant number of Sri Lankan Buddhists. Dharmapāla's Western "intellectualist representation of Buddhism" still appeals to many Buddhists in Sri Lanka today.[82]

Contemporary Buddhists, too, continue to reflect upon Dharmapāla at the parliament. In an article as recent as 1992, a Buddhist claimed that

> It would be no exaggeration to say, that only Anagarika Dharmapala succeeded in effectively impressing the delegates to the Parliament of Religions about the nobility of Buddhism, while drawing their attention to its great truths. His speech in fact proved an eye-opener to western scholars about the greatness of Buddhism.[83]

Thus, at least one Sri Lankan Buddhist remembers Dharmapāla for being *solely* responsible for popularizing Buddhism in non-Buddhist countries, even though Japanese Buddhists at the parliament contributed much to its popularization.[84] And although Dharmapāla stressed the Aryan

---

[77] As Gananath Obeyesekere has recently argued, Dharmapāla's Theosophical version of Buddhism—"rational religion"—has been appropriated by many Buddhists in Sri Lanka. Although Dharmapāla eventually distanced himself from Olcott and other Theosophists, his version of Buddhism did not change. See Gananath Obeyesekere, "Buddhism and Conscience: An Exploratory Essay," *Daedalus* 12 (1991): 219-39.

[78] Bhikshu Sangharakshita, *Anagarika Dharmapala*, p. 67.

[79] The Buddhist revival in Sri Lanka had been well underway for decades, but was very marked in the 1890s. *The Buddhist* and *The Journal of the Maha Bodhi Society* both helped to perpetuate Dharmapāla's ideas.

[80] Untitled article, *The Buddhist* 1, no. 49 (November 22, 1889): 392.

[81] Obeyesekere, "Buddhism and Conscience," p. 227.

[82] See ibid.

[83] K.D.G. Wimalaratne, "Anagarika Dharmapala and the Parliament of Religions," *Daily News* (Colombo), June 20, 1992, p. 8. The article is complete with photographs of Dharmapāla at the parliament.

[84] See Tweed, *The American Encounter with Buddhism*, passim.

nature of Sri Lankan Buddhism, contemporary Sri Lankan Buddhists stress its "Sinhalaness," so much so that the "Arya Dharma" has now become "Sinhala Buddhism." Sri Lankan Buddhists doubtless will continue to remember Dharmapāla, and continue to invoke him as a shining example of what a Sinhala Buddhist should be. In addition, they doubtless will continue to reflect upon his contribution to the life of Buddhism on the island and in the world. It is very likely that they will also remember him as the *Sinhala* Buddhist,[85] or the *Theravāda* Buddhist,[86] representative to the World's Parliament of Religions, rather than as a Mahāyāna Buddhist, a claim that, for all intents and purposes, has been thoroughly forgotten.

---

[85] See my discussion above of my informal conversations with Buddhists about Dharmapāla.

[86] Wimalaratne, "Anagarika Dharmapala and the Parliament of Religions," p. 8 (emphasis mine).

THE RECONVENING OF BABEL
Eastern Buddhism and the 1893 World's Parliament of Religions

James Edward Ketelaar

The Simidae then branched off into two great stems, the New World and the Old World monkeys; and from the latter, at a remote period, Man, the wonder and glory of the universe, proceeded.
—Charles Darwin,
The Descent of Man, 1883

"Come let us build ourselves a city, and a tower with its top in the heavens, and let us make a name for ourselves, lest we be scattered abroad upon the face of the whole earth." And the Lord came down to see the city and the tower which the sons of men [Adam] had built. And the Lord said, "Behold, they are one people, and they have all one language; and this is only the beginning of what they will do; and nothing that they propose to do will now be impossible for them. Come, let Us go down, and there confuse their language."
—Genesis 11:4-7

"The Reconvening of Babel: Eastern Buddhism and the 1893 World's Parliament of Religions" by James Edward Ketelaar. This essay originally constituted chap. 4 of James Edward Ketelaar, *Of Heretics and Martyrs in Meiji Japan: Buddhism and Its Persecution.* ©1990 by Princeton University Press. Reprinted by permission of the author and Princeton University Press.

The entire world is engaged in a pitched battle of racial competition [jinshu kyōsō]...it is a battle between the yellow and the white races, between Asians and Europeans, and it is truly a battle that will determine the survival or the extinction of each race.
—Editorial in the Shingon Buddhist Journal *Mitsugon Kyōhō*, 1893

Introduction

During the nineteenth century, a dominant characteristic in the relation of the two political entities known as "Japan" and the "West" was that of confrontation: the blatant aggression of Commodore Perry's ironclad fleet; the obstinacy of Townsend Harris and the subsequent establishment of the "unequal treaties" of trade; the tripartite intervention at the conclusion of the Sino-Japanese War; and, in the early twentieth century, the "unsatisfactory" treaties between Russia and Japan at the termination of the Russo-Japanese war.[1] These formal engagements between Japan and the Western powers are characterized by consistent attempts by both parties to dominate and to escape domination. The Iwakura diplomatic mission, as well as the gradually increasing number of technical students that journeyed to Europe and the United States, were deeply concerned not only with the immediate political and economic consequences of their journeys, but also with the national images of Japan in the West and of the West in Japan. One function of the West was to serve as a position external to Japan by which domestic policies could be effectively analyzed. When ideologues such as Shimaji Mokurai or Mori Arinori wrote directly from Paris or Washington, D.C. to both the Ministry of State and the popular press in Japan, they claimed to write from a position of historical, comparative, and scientific, and thus cosmopolitan, truth. The "West," in fact, served as a "created consistency," a "regular constellation of ideas" that was "suitable for study in the academy, for display in the museum,...for theoretical illustration in anthropological, biological, linguistic, racial and

---

[1] This opposition itself—Japan and the West—indicates the somewhat unique status accorded the relation between Japan and the Euro-American powers in the modern period. "Japan" somehow serves as the polar balance of the Western powers and concomitantly signs for all of "Asia" or perhaps "the Orient" itself in this relation. The relation is clearly a problematic one, compounded in part by its near universal acceptance. A locus classicus in this regard is Sir George Sansom's *The Western World and Japan: A Study in the Interaction of European and Asiatic Cultures* (New York: Random House, 1949). An important and intriguing alternative to this method of analysis can be found in Masao Miyoshi's *As We Saw Them: The First Japanese Embassy to the United States* (Berkeley: University of California Press, 1979).

historical theses about mankind and the universe, for instances of economic and sociological theories of development, revolution, cultural personality, national or religious character."[2] Even as the West carefully constructed an image of the "Orient," images of the "West" were used as elements of discursive strategies in Japan that served as a stage for elaborate representations useful to the ideologues' own project. This "imaging" could be carried out, moreover, unencumbered by the need for "accurate" portrayals of the "West itself." The logical extension of this argument is, of course, that neither the "West itself" nor "Asia itself" exists, both serving exclusively as ideological constructs necessary to the continuation of certain definitions of global hegemony. These images partake, in other words, of an "exteriority" to the place of their enunciation. Shimaji, and many others, appropriated certain strategically potent forms found in their journeys and used them to stress or refine items within their political agenda. This, in turn, resulted in a projection of the always already existent character of these newly politicized concerns onto historical narratives. This was a conscious *use*, not a mere *mimicking*, of the West; this is an exercise of what could be called the practice of strategic Occidentalism.

In the mid-fifteenth century, John of Segovia, Nicholas of Cusa, Jean Germain, and Aeneas Silvius (Pius II) attempted to construct a *contraferentia*, or "Conference," between the Christian and the Muslim worlds. This was a fairly sophisticated attempt (that finally was never actualized) to "put a representative Orient in front of Europe, to *stage* the Orient and Europe together in some coherent way."[3] The goal in this conference was that Christianity would finally and completely convince the Muslim world that Islam was in fact "just a misguided version of Christianity." In the late nineteenth century another, more grandiloquent attempt was made to dramatize relations between the "Occident" and the "Orient." This latter event, drawing upon both Darwinistic interpretations of evolution as applied to religious traditions and the newly created "field" of the history of religions as championed by F. Max Müller, was yet another attempt by the "West" to incorporate the "East" into its sphere of operations. Even as the

---

[2] From Edward Said, *Orientalism* (New York: Pantheon, 1978), pp. 7-8. Said's use of these categories is actually applied to the Occident's vision of the Orient. I am suggesting that this is an equally accurate observation when applied to nineteenth-century Japan's conceptions of the West.

[3] Ibid., p. 61.

industrial revolution had lifted the material world to heights heretofore unimagined, nineteenth-century American religionists reasoned, have we not now the capability to unite all of humankind into one global family, joined by a single world religion? Based on this assumption of a link between material and moral sophistication, these self-appointed unifiers sought to convene a "Festival of Peace" among the many nations and religions of the world. They hoped to right the wrong of the first Tower of Babel, "the gate of God," where all "languages were confused" (Hebrew: *balal*), and through this reconvening of Babel construct a new harmony of nations, races, and creeds.

In this essay we will journey to this self-styled tower to God, the World's Parliament of Religions, held for seventeen days in September 1893, in conjunction with the Columbian World's Exposition, in Chicago. Catholic, Protestant, Jewish, Hindu, Buddhist, Shinto, and other representatives gathered before overflowing audiences to deliver the "particular truths" of their respective religions in (more or less) reasoned papers as they sought to construct a program of the universal applicability of certain "transcendent truths." This Icarian task, heralded in newspapers and publications literally around the globe, while claiming to lay the foundation stones of international peace in fact disguised a seething discontent. Christianity, assailed by philosophical materialism and evolutionary theory in Europe and America, meeting with disappointing results in its missionary efforts in the Near and the Far East, desperately needed a reorganization, a rallying point of faith. It needed, some suggested, to reclaim or to rearticulate its God. Members of the "other" religions, generally limited to the so-called Ten Great Religions (more on this below), were painfully aware of the consequences should a Christian-centered world religion be produced. The calling together of representatives of the world's religions was seen by many of those "invited" as a direct challenge. If this challenge could not be met—a duel with Christianity on its own terms in its own land—it would be but a matter of time before Christianity would be deemed the *de facto* victor and claim the spoils: the sole right to define and orchestrate the use of "the absolute." The "victor," in other words, would retain the right to define religion according to standards of its own making, with the assumption that this "definition" would have universal validity. For the Meiji Buddhists this nineteenth-century *contraferentia* was perceived as an international event not to be missed. Buddhism in

Japan, having only recently achieved some domestic institutional security, was continually seeking ways to enhance its position further as a harbinger of civilization and enlightenment. Entrance into the international arena of religious debate was seen as a perfect means by which Buddhism could be proved fit as a vital contributor to the "modern" world. Moreover, the Japanese Buddhists who would journey to Chicago were as certain as their parliamentarian hosts that *their* religion was the one most capable of a dynamic and comprehensive compatibility with the concerns of modern men and women throughout the world. The reconvening of Babel in Chicago was thus not only a threat and a challenge to non-Christian religions; it was also perceived as an opportunity.

Here I will examine the nature of this threat by looking first at the work of Charles Darwin and F. Max Müller in the construction of universalist notions of race and religion central to the operation of the parliament itself. The challenge of the parliament will be discussed vis-à-vis the presence of five Japanese Buddhists (four priests and one layman)[4] who journeyed to Chicago both to engage the "Christian nation of America" in debate over the definition of the true characteristics of a "world religion," and equally to use that engagement as a stage for their activities in the domestic redefinition of Buddhist institutional practices. The discussion of the parliament and the Japanese Buddhists' performances there is thus presented both to accentuate the cosmopolitan nature of nineteenth-century Japanese religionists as they attempted to reconstruct domestic definitions of religion and to highlight the uniquely oppressive character of the discourse upon which they drew for this redefinition.

The Invitation

John Henry Barrows (1847-1902), Chairman of the World's Parliament of Religions, spent the last years of his life on a mission, an "inspiring duty," to bring the unrefracted light of truth, as revealed on

---

[4] The five "champions of Buddhism" (*bukkyō no champion ra*) were Toki Hōryū (Shingon), Ashitsu Jitsunen (Tendai), Shaku Sōen (Rinzai), Yatsubuchi Banryū (Shin), and Hirai Kinzō (layman). In the Buddhists' entourage there were also two interpreters and several newsmen. One Kawai Yoshijirō (Nichiren) arrived too late to present his paper, though it can be found in the World's Parliament chronicle. There was also one representative for Shinto, Shibata Reiichi of the Jikkō sect, and a large number of Japanese Christians led by Kozaki Hiromichi, then President of the Protestant university Dōshisha.

the cross, to those lost in a dimmer illumination, to those who "touched the Great Hand and knew it not."[5]

> We believe that Christianity is to supplant all other religions, because it contains all the truth in them and much besides....As any wise missionary in Bombay or Madras would be glad to gather beneath the shelter of his roof the scholarly and sincere representatives of the Hindu religions, so Christian America invites to the shelter of her hospitable roof, at her Grand Festival of Peace, the spiritual leaders of mankind....Though light has no fellowship with darkness, light does have fellowship with twilight. God has not left himself without witness, and those who have the full light of the cross should bear brotherly hearts towards all who grope in a dimmer illumination.[6]

Barrows, head of the First Presbyterian Church of Chicago; professor of religion at the University of Chicago; Chairman of the Central Committee on Religious Congresses of the World's Congress Auxiliary at the Columbian World's Fair; editor of the official chronicle of the parliament, *The World's Parliament of Religions* (1893); author of the widely read *The Gospels are True Histories* (1891) and of the "literary completion" of the chronicle of the World's Parliament of Religions, *The Christian Conquest of Asia* (1899), and so on, articulates within his life's work the formative impulses of the parliament itself. His faith in his religion, his attitude toward "science," and his desire for the parliament to be an ongoing actualization of "man seeking after God" while simultaneously "[s]triking the noble chord of universal human brotherhood" will provide a narrative to the following discussion.

Ten goals for the World's Parliament of Religions were set forth by the Central Committee, each of which was designed "to win the approval of all broad-minded men." For example: "(1) To bring together in conference, for the first time in history, the leading representatives of the great historic religions of the world. (2) To show men, in the most impressive way, what and how many important truths the various religions hold and teach in common. (3) To promote and deepen the spirit of human brotherhood among religious men of diverse faiths....(10) To bring the nations of the earth into a more friendly fellowship, in the hope of seeking permanent international peace."[7]

---

[5] Part of a rhymed couplet as quoted by John Henry Barrows in his "Preface" to *WPR*, 1:viii.

[6] John Henry Barrows, "The History of the Parliament," in *WPR*, 1:28.

[7] Barrows, "History," in *WPR*, 1:19.

Let me state at the outset that the "spirit of human brotherhood" and the "friendly fellowship" of the "nations of the earth" should be understood as one example of ideas of the transcendent, which, though in a certain fashion conceivable, have no particular existence outside their very conception. Every speech, newspaper article, and social gathering of the time, however, was punctuated with invocations of "fellowship" and "brotherhood," and many people undoubtedly believed in the actualization of these universals and the extinction of difference prerequisite to such a totalization. We must note, in other words, that in response to Barrows's call for brotherhood and the universal truth of Christ (as the two were frequently linked) there was Vivekananda[8] also demanding brotherhood, but he did so by saying: "The Christian is not to become a Hindu or a Buddhist, nor a Hindu or a Buddhist to become a Christian....If anybody dreams of the exclusive survival of his own [religion] and the destruction of others, I pity him from the bottom of my heart."[9] The parliament's attempt at "brotherhood" could exist only given very particular conceptions of race, religion, and nation; it was entirely contingent upon a specific notion of a central defining concept around which all the "others'" concepts were to revolve. But, to the chagrin and fascination of the parliamentarians, these "others" frequently refused the confinement of the preselected roles. They insisted upon other acts, other ideas. We shall see that this was not a denial that resulted in a total dissolution of the projected universal concept, but that the very same code terms were used toward the same ends in a strikingly oppositional manner. Or, in the words of Ashitsu Jitsunen, Tendai representative to the parliament: "While we promulgate our own teachings we must confound those of our enemy. We must use that controlled by the enemy in our attack upon the enemy itself."[10]

"One chief hindrance to missionary progress," Barrows pointed out, "is the misty unreality of the heathen world. We scarcely think of them

---

[8] Born 1863, a student of Ramakrishna, and graduate of the University of Calcutta, Vivekananda took on the role of the "official representative" of the "Hindoo religion." An eloquent and handsome figure, his impression on many at the parliament appears to have been a lasting one. See *WPR*, 1:65, 101-2, 248. For his paper "Hinduism" delivered at the parliament see *WPR*, 2:968-78. [Vivekananda is the subject of much discussion elsewhere in this volume; see esp. the lecture by Joseph M. Kitagawa and the essay by Sunrit Mullick. (Ed.)]

[9] Vivekananda, closing address, quoted by Barrows, "History," in *WPR*, 1:170-71.

[10] Ashitsu Jitsunen, "Bankoku shūkyō daikai sanrei chinjōsho," *Kokkyō* 21 (3/1893): 20.

as our brethren."[11] The nineteenth century's need for the comparative study of religions, publicly expressed in the parliament's seventh goal "to inquire what light each religion has afforded, or may afford to other religions of the world," we should understand as inextricably linked to a Christocentric evangelical mission. Or, to quote Barrows yet again: "Religion, like the white light of Heaven, has been broken into many-colored fragments by the prisms of men. One of the objects of the Parliament of Religions has been to change this many-colored radiance back into the white light of heavenly truth."[12] This Babelian conception of a primordially unified pure religion somehow fractured, frequently cast as differences between light and shadow or between white and the multicolored, is not limited in its use to Barrows's obvious attachment to the metaphor. The Columbian Exposition itself, with its buildings of white granite, was called the White City: "The City so holy and clean / No sorrow can breathe in the air; No gloom of affection or sin / No shadow of evil is there."[13] Moreover, extending from the White City was a central plaisance, a "Midway," established by the Exposition's Department of Ethnology to display by means of archeological collections and several "living exhibitions" the underlying principles of anthropological evolution. Or, in the words of G. Goode Brown, assistant secretary of the Smithsonian Institute and coordinator of ethnological exhibits at the Exposition, the Midway would be "in fact, an illustrated encyclopedia of civilization."[14] The very arrangement of the Midway was based upon a sliding scale of humanity. Nearest to the White City were the Teutonic and Celtic races found in the German and Irish "villages." At the center of the Midway were the Middle Eastern and East Asian exhibitions. And then "we descend to the savage races, the African and the Dahomey, and the North American Indian" at the furthest end of the Plaisance.[15] The White City, resting upon a pyramid formed out of the human races, was presented to the approximately thirty million fair-goers as

---

[11] Quoted in Mary Eleanor Barrows, *John Henry Barrows: A Memoir* (Chicago: Fleming H. Revell, 1904), p. 264.

[12] Barrows, "History," in *WPR*, 1:3.

[13] Robert Rydell, *All the World's a Fair: Visions of Empire at American International Expositions, 1876-1916* (Chicago: University of Chicago Press, 1984), p. 48.

[14] Ibid., p. 45.

[15] Ibid., p. 65. We should recall that the battle of Wounded Knee was but three years past, and that a major attraction, performing daily before packed houses three blocks south of the Exposition's Midway on 63rd Street, was Wild Bill's Congress of Rough Riders.

the natural culmination in the *human race*'s painful climb to the industrial and technical sophistication of the "modern age."

A primary force essential to this formal conceptualizing of different "peoples" in the late-nineteenth-century world expositions (at Chicago and elsewhere) can be located in the work of Charles Darwin (1809-1882).[16] As evidenced at the Columbian Exposition and the World's Parliament of Religions, the overarching principle governing the natural world was determined to be progressive, utilitarian, and (though seldom made explicit, clearly) ruthless. "Civilization" and its material wonders were indeed the result of this inexorable evolutionary advancement of human beings vis-à-vis the material world; moreover, such civilizational advancements necessitated (as determined by "scientific" and "objective" truths) the concomitant destruction of the primitive, the useless, and the unenlightened. The showcase of the Columbian Exposition proved to be a significant institution of higher learning for the average man and woman, a veritable temple of the commonsensical. The display of racial and cultural differences at the Exposition as being not merely "differences" but rather distinct "stages" in a people's "development" formed the basis of a common support for political, economic, and territorial expansionism when carried out in the name of progress and civilization. Much of this argument was taken up with very little modification at the World's Parliament of Religions in order to construct a schematic analysis of the world's religions supportive of the parliament's Eurocentric and Christocentric understanding of the world. Modernization was perceived, in other words, as Westernization. With the above discussion in mind, and in order to set the stage for the World's Parliament and the Japanese Buddhists' presence thereon, here let us turn briefly to the works of Darwin (particularly his later writings) and F. Max Müller. We will be asking about not only the materials of which the parliamentarian stage was constructed, but also the standards the invited representatives would be required to meet and, perhaps more important, the standards they were expected to fail to meet.

Contrary to many naturalists of his age, Darwin chose not to view each human race as constituting a specific species. Gradations of particular characteristics in the so-called races, Darwin reasoned,

---

[16] Ibid, passim.

were too finely differentiated to admit of satisfactory categorization.[17] Darwin, sensitive to the seemingly "insoluble" problem of classification, lamented the misfortune of every naturalist who attempted to determine "how much weight we ought to assign in our classification to strongly marked differences in some few points...and how much to close resemblance in numerous unimportant points."[18] He did not, however, continue to examine by what standards these judgments of "strength" or "importance" could be made. The very "insoluble" nature of the problem was in no small way compounded by the casualness with which the founding judgments were frequently accorded an a priori status. The almost infinite possibility of categorical systems, aided to a large degree by the variously (if at all) defined term "species," certainly led to radically different positions regarding race; but Darwin himself was confident enough to assert that "all the races of men are descended from a single primitive stock" (not, it will be noted, from a "single pair of progenitors").[19]

The crux of Darwin's analysis of difference between peoples and societies is his theory of evolution itself; when crudely expressed for the purposes of our discussions here, this theory can be summarized as follows: "All civilized nations were once barbarous."[20] All forms of life have advanced from the simple to the complex; so too, Darwin asserted, did human society. But it is crucial to recall the consequences of the changes that accompanied this advancement: "Judging from the past, we may safely infer that not one living species will transmit its unaltered likeness into distant futurity."[21] What species then *will* be transmitted and in what form? How do civilizations, that is, survive? There is, for Darwin, a hierarchy of survival; and in spite of his reluctance to treat races as distinct species, Darwin evidently had few

---

[17] There were, however, numerous attempts at definitive categorization of human races into species that ranged in number from two or three to as high as sixty-three distinct races/species. See Charles Darwin's *The Descent of Man and Selection in Relation to Sex* (New York: D. Appleton, 1883), p. 174.

[18] Ibid., p. 153.

[19] Ibid., pp. 176, 180.

[20] Ibid., p. 143. "Proofs" for this assertion offered by Darwin were (1) traces of "primitive" customs in current language, beliefs, and so on; (2) the obvious "advancement" of "savages" when exposed to "civilization," thus showing the dominance of the civilized over the barbarous; and (3) the gradual development of the "highest form of religion" —a righteous God—unknown in ancient times.

[21] Charles Darwin, *The Origin of Species by the Means of Natural Science*, 5th ed. (New York: D. Appleton, 1883), p. 428.

qualms in identifying races as inhabiting particular levels in this hierarchy of civilization.

> At some future period, not very distant as measured by centuries, the civilized races will most certainly exterminate, and replace, the savage races throughout the world. At the same time, the anthropomorphous apes...will no doubt be exterminated. The break between man and his nearest allies will then be wider, for it will intervene between man in a more civilized state, as we may hope, even than the caucasian and some ape as low as a baboon, instead of as now between the negro or Australian and the gorilla.[22]

The means of this destruction, in addition to the common dangers of famine, accident, sickness, low fertility, and infanticide,[23] will be the inevitable "war, slaughter, cannibalism, slavery, and absorption" that follow on the heels of the meeting of advanced and primitive societies. Moreover, this "absorption" will take place relatively quickly, for "when the civilized nations come into contact with barbarians, the struggle is short."[24] Darwin did not seem alarmed by this prophecy; the extinction of races "is the same problem" as the necessary evolutionary extinction evidenced throughout the history of the world.

To acknowledge that some moral sense was "acquired by each individual during his lifetime" Darwin found to be a "serious blemish" in many works of his day and concluded that "based on the general theory of evolution, this is at least extremely improbable."[25] Thus when Darwin invoked the Kantian "ought" and held up "duty" as a cause célèbre,[26] we must recognize both his attempt at a schematic totalization of humanity sharing in a common development of inherent characteristics and his invocation of a developmental ontology—however nonteleological—that brought humans and the lower animals together as (sentient) beings sharing the emotions of "love, memory, attention, curiosity, imitation, reason, etc."[27] To quote Kant: "Duty! Wondrous thought, that workest neither by fond insinuation, flattery, not by any threat, but merely by holding up thy naked law in the soul," and "Two things fill the mind with ever new

---

[22] Darwin, *Descent*, p. 156.

[23] See ibid., p. 182 for an amazing panorama of the "natural" destruction of species.

[24] Ibid.

[25] Ibid., p. 98, n. 5.

[26] See Francis Darwin, *The Life and Letters of Charles Darwin*, 2 vols. (New York: D. Appleton, 1887), 1:227; and Darwin, *Descent*, p. 97.

[27] Darwin, *Descent*, p. 126.

and increasing admiration and awe,....the starry heavens above me and the moral law within me."[28]

This moral law that is found to some degree in all animals, including humans, provides Darwin with a transcendental category for a new organization of the natural world. Further, Darwin goes on to refute the older system by saying "if man had not been his own classifier, he would never have thought of founding a separate order for his own reception."[29] In other words, Darwin made a typically Kantian move in shifting the emphasis from a discussion of eschatology to one of duty ("but man can do his duty"[30]); then, similar to Kant's refusal to acknowledge the hegemony of theology over knowledge and actions, Darwin refused to allow to humankind an irrefutable hegemony in the practice of morality.

The operation of the moral "ought" that Darwin discovered in every animal provided the universal category with which he united humankind, transcendent of race, and animals, transcendent of species. He created a continually evolving ontological hierarchy, the highest point of which in the nineteenth century was the practice of "disinterested love" by the most civilized of races, the Caucasian. ("Disinterested love for all living creatures [is] the most notable attribute of man."[31]) Alongside this universally operative "ought" stood the law of evolution—the continually advancing power of universal growth and increasing complexity. And, in short, sophistication arose concomitantly with the destruction of the simple forms of life. Granted, occasional "lapses" did occur, but when viewed in the passing of centuries these "lapses" appear insignificant. The practice of the highest known morality, "disinterested love," was forced to remain disinterested in the evolutionarily certain "destruction of the races." This is not to suggest that Darwin sought to promote the actual destruction of cultures or races other than his own. His statements are clearly based upon records of his travels and the clear impression left upon him of the trends of "civilization"; as such they provide a glimpse into the difficulties in the material clash of cultures. Much of what Darwin set forth in *The Descent of Man*,

---

[28] The first quote is from Kant's *Metaphysics of Ethics* (1835), p. 136, as cited in Darwin, *Descent*, p. 97; the latter is perhaps the most often quoted phrase of Kant's in this regard, from his *Critique of Practical Reason, and Other Writings in Moral Philosophy*, trans. Lewis Beck (Chicago: University of Chicago Press, 1949), p 258.

[29] Darwin, *Descent*, p. 150.

[30] Francis Darwin, *Life*, p. 277.

[31] Darwin, *Descent*, p. 126.

however, was taken up in theories of evolutionary theology that incorporated a critique of racial difference based upon evolutionary grounds. This uneasy tension between claims to moral superiority, as "proved" by a scientific analysis of the physical world, and the reconciliation to the inevitability of the destruction of beliefs, cultures, and peoples outside the industrialized Caucasian nations, is central to a conception of the World's Parliament of Religions' discourse on humankind and religion and will reappear not infrequently in the pages to follow.

Though clearly disagreeing with certain of Darwin's conclusions (a full discussion of which falls outside our present concerns), the organizers of both of Columbian Exposition and the World's Parliament of Religions were not adverse to using certain of his methodological apparatus to construct their own conception of a universalist discourse upon, in the case of Exposition, human evolution, and at the parliament, the evolution of religions. Further, the World's Parliament of Religions, traversing the same steps of ethnological evolution that led up to the White City, claimed to go yet a step higher. Rather than exhibiting the merely material, the parliament would present the "higher forces which had made civilization itself possible"; it would exhibit "man's intellectual and moral progress"; and it would seek to promote the unity of the world in a way that was not possible by the joint operation of diplomacy and commerce. It was deemed, in fact, a "natural outcome of the spirit of the Prince of Peace" to attempt no less than a universal spiritual unification of the many races found throughout the "civilized" as well as the "uncivilized" worlds. The words of John 10:16 take on new, even ominous, meaning in such a context. "And other sheep I have, which are not of this fold: them also I must bring, and they shall hear my voice: and they shall become one flock, one Shepherd." Evolution was read within its Christian refiguration to extend from the simple to the complex, which is then fully, and finally, united by the pure light of a Christian definition of civilization. The invitations issued by the parliament, and the goals of many of the parliamentarians as well, emerged from an intellectual milieu antithetical to certain conceptions of religion. What, for the parliament, we must now ask, was "religion" and how would the Japanese Buddhists fare within such culture-specific definitional strategies?

Parliamentarian Conceptions of Religion

> Of all antagonisms of belief, the oldest, the widest, the most profound, and the most important, is that between religion and science....It shows itself everywhere throughout the domain of human knowledge affecting man's interpretations alike of the simplest mechanical accidents and of the most complicated events in the history of nations. It has its roots deep down in the diverse habits of thoughts of different orders of minds.[32]

Expanding from this statement, Herbert Spencer (1820-1903) proceeds to constitute religion as the "nescience," always beyond the faculty of knowledge and, as a true absolute, always completely other and thus having logical but no social necessity. This definition of religion was, in fact—even though a somewhat less inflammatory version of religion as found in Darwinist or positivist theories—one of the main targets of nineteenth-century religionists both in Japan and at the parliament. Religion must be equally social, equally personal, and equally absolute; to attempt to relegate it entirely to the "other" was, as far as most parliamentarians were concerned, tantamount to an assertion that there was in fact nothing called religion, or that the only thing that *could* be called religion was no-thing. The occasional reliance upon Spencerian theories (some of which were also taken up by contemporary Theosophists) by nineteenth-century Buddhists and scholars of Buddhism to "explain" certain aspects of the teachings contributed in no small fashion to the ongoing conception of "Asian religion" as a nihilistic quest for annihilation: the search for no-thing. But rather than Spencer's widely read and, in many circles, extremely popular rational proposition called "religion," it was F. Max Müller's (1823-1900) "scientific study of religion" that contributed most directly to both the parliamentarian and Meiji Buddhist attempts to construct a transglobal vision of religious development. Both these visions, though methodologically similar to Müller's work, were produced in a fashion conducive to the even more thoroughgoing opposition of Buddhism and Christianity, East and West.

Even as Goethe sought to avoid philological somnambulism with his edict "he who knows one language, knows none," so too Müller tried to create a language that, ruled by a grammar of Kantian reason,[33] would provide the categories necessary to an examination of

---

[32] Herbert Spencer, *First Principles*, 4th ed. (New York: D. Appleton, 1883), p. 11.

[33] Müller read Kant as the foundation of all modern thought and the culmination of an entire race's development: "The bridge of thoughts and sighs

the eternal and absolute. Müller, distinct from many of his contemporaries, also recognized the basic legitimacy of similar quests when found in radically different cultures, even among the so-called primitives. Müller's use of a Kantian metalanguage, ruled by reason and divorced from the particular passions of dogmatic practices, was directed toward the construction of a discourse concerned exclusively with the articulation and interpretation of the absolute within the historical world. It was used, in Müller's terms, for the examination of the "third faculty" of humankind: the "struggle to conceive the inconceivable," the faculty of a faith in the presence of infinity, or in the operation of the other in thought itself.[34] The three faculties—sense, reason, and faith—poss-essed by all humans in varying degrees, can be equated to three steps necessary to the formulation of Müller's metalanguage of the transcendent. The faculty of sense provides empirical data for historical examination; the faculty of reason allows for the classification of these data for comparative analysis; finally, by means of the third faculty, the operation of the infinite, a truly theoretical or philosophical understanding can be obtained. These three practices when applied to the study religion are called the History of Religion, Comparative Theology, and Theoretical Theology. It perhaps goes without saying that it is only by means of the faculty of reason and the operation of the faculty of the infinite that this very schematic representation can be produced; that is, data are not gathered outside of the operation of reason, nor is the faculty of the infinite divorced from the operation of the senses; these are not mutually exclusive categories.

In order to set this tripartite schema to work, and thereby attempt a theological articulation of the infinite, Müller began by asking "What makes a people?" And, what is perhaps more important, he went on to

---

that spans the whole history of the Aryan world has its first arch in the Veda, and its last in Kant's *Critique [of Pure Reason]*." Müller described his own work as a mere application of Kant's arguments to the fields of religion and mythology and, as evidenced by the dedication of his translation of this *Critique* to the "English speaking race, the race of the future," he also hoped to serve as a link in the "transmission" of this particular form of knowing. For these quotes see Immanuel Kant's *Critique of Pure Reason*, 2 vols., trans. F. Max Müller (London: Macmillan, 1881), 2: xiii, lx.

[34] For a discussion of the "three faculties" see F. Max Müller, *Introduction to the Science of Religion*, Lectures at the Royal Institution, 1870 (London: Longmans, Green, 1873), pp. 18-22; and his *Lectures on the Origin and Growth of Religion, as Illustrated by the Religion of India*, First Hibbert Lectures at Westminster Abbey, 1878 (1879; London: Longmans, Green, 1880), pp. 23-24.

posit exactly what he was attempting to prove: the universality of truth and a common humanity capable of actualizing this truth, or, as he later called it, the divine education of the human race. It was Schelling, says Müller, who impressed upon him the importance of the question of the origin of "a people." Ethnological attempts to classify races (by blood type, skull formation, etc.) failed to account for the "higher and purely moral feeling which binds men together and makes them a people." Schelling suggested that "a people exists only when it has determined itself with regard to its mythology."[35] Müller takes this position a step further and asserts that peoples are constituted by means of the commonality of language and the unifying power of religion, that is, through intimately interconnected operation of expression in language and the codification of the expressible by religion.[36] Müller concluded that it was the unity of the religious life, as proved by a commonality of language, and not notions of nation, state, or shared physical characteristics, that takes precedence in the naming of a people. And it is with the full bravura of nineteenth-century philology that he demonstrates this by means of a comparative analysis of terms that were selected as essential characteristics of religion consistent in use regardless of time, place, and political environment: "prayers, sacrifice, altar, spirit, law, and faith" and of course "God." This list, intriguing in itself, coupled with its analysis, yielded for Müller some not too surprising results.[37]

This attempt to, in effect, determine philologically the "origin of species" presented no difficulties that seriously swayed Müller's confidence. The tenuous link between religion and language he glossed as being a "natural" occurrence; his claim to have identified three world language/religion centers—Aryan, Semitic, and Turanian (the latter was composed of the "Chinese, Mongolians, Finns, Lapps, etc.")—was based upon a Darwinian argument of development from the simple to the complex, which provided no account for the original difference of language, nor did it provide any schema upon which any subsequent comparison could be made.[38] Müller was quite content,

---

[35] Müller's comments can be found in *Science of Religion*, pp. 145, 147, 149; he is quoting from Schelling's *Vorlesungen über Philosophie der Mythologie* (1842).

[36] See also Hegel in his *Philosophy of History*: "The idea of God constitutes the general foundation of a people" (quoted in Müller, *Science of Religion*, p. 149).

[37] For Müller's discussion of these terms and the relation of language to religion see *Science of Religion*, pp. 144-68.

[38] Christianity is identified as the product of the first two "centers" and, Müller claimed, without these antecedents Christianity could not have become "the

here rereading his own typology, to accept on faith the faculty of the infinite as a universal category operative regardless of spatial or chronological particularities. He thus, for example, answered his own rhetorical question "What have we in common with the Turanians?" quite easily: "Very little, it may seem; and yet it is...not the yellow skin and the high cheekbones that make the man. Nay, if we look but steadily into those black Chinese eyes, we shall find that there, too, is a soul that responds to a soul, and that the God whom they *mean* is the same God whom we *mean*, however helpless their utterance, however imperfect their worship."[39]

Müller claimed to refuse the hegemony of Christianity as an absolute determinative of religious practice or conceptualization of the absolute, and he attempted to illustrate the culturally and racially isolated dogma of truth-statements collected throughout Christian history. But he consistently refused to question the status of an infinite godhead at the center of human and cosmic existence. It is this assumption that unites his arguments on the constitution of religion and of a people; it is also an assumption that radically compromises his hope for a metalanguage adequate to the plurality of religious forms. Without assuming a commonality of human experience, Müller thought he would be faced with either an infinity of the utterly contingent or an irrefutable totality of dogmatic theology. He strove to establish a basis of comparison between religious phenomena and in so doing, perhaps inadvertently, actually contributed to the oppressive hierarchy found in evolutionary theology.

Müller's reading of the Biblical conception of universalism reveals to us two goals for comparative religion: (1) to show the operation of the absolute in all times and places ("God shows no partiality") and (2)

---

religion of the world." See, for example, his *Theosophy of Psychological Religion*, Gifford Lectures at the University of Glasgow, 1892 (London: Longmans, Green, 1903), p. 447. Müller's unwillingness to acknowledge a common origin of the world's religions and languages, as well as his lack of discussion accounting for differences evident *prior to a certain selected juncture*, is typical of many uses of evolutionary theory. Under the assumption that evolution described a move from the simple to the complex, it is generally concluded that the origin of any given form must be simple and the origin of all forms must be the simplest. But evolutionary theologians did not, because they could not, claim that the most primitive religion was monotheistic. Rather, we find the nearly oxymoronic conclusion that the truly simple was seen as a collection of the infinite diversity of divinity, while the theologically complex is found in the comprehensive reductionism of monotheism.

[39] Müller, *Science of Religions*, p. 191.

to elucidate the divine education of the human race ("any who fears him does what is right").[40] It is here, while reflecting most clearly the presuppositions of his age and discipline, that Müller makes his most lasting contributions. "Everywhere, whether among the dark Papuan or the yellowish Malay, or the brown Polynesian races,...even among the lowest of the low in the scale of humanity, there are, if we will but listen, whisperings about divine imaginings of a future life; there are prayers and sacrifices which, even in their most degraded and degrading form, still bear witness to that old and ineradicable faith that everywhere there is a God to hear our prayers, if we will but call on Him."[41]

Elsewhere Müller calls these whisperings and imaginings a "hunger," a material quest *for* some*thing*.[42] In spite of exhaustive argumentation to the contrary, Müller asserted that the infinite *could* be a genuine object of our consciousness. As a faithful Kantian, Müller of course disallowed knowing the *Ding an sich*, and yet he did assert that "with every finite perception there is a concomitant perception...of the infinite."[43] For example, the eye can see only to a certain point beyond which the power of sight fails. It is at the precise point of the failure of the senses that we "suffer" from the infinite. Müller's work can be seen as an attempt to provide a chronicle of the attempts by the finite human mind to pierce continually further into the infinite and to "raise the dark perception of [the infinite] into more lucid intuitions and more definite names." Every sense of every human is in every moment "impinged" upon by the "dark pressure of the infinite." It is thus by one's very corporeal existence that there arises the indisputable sentiment of the infinite; this "sentiment" is what Müller identifies as the prehistoric impulse to all religion. It is not surprising then when Müller claims that "theology begins with anthropology."[44] The ontological *unity* of humankind was established

---

[40] Perhaps the most frequently quoted section from the Bible in this regard during the nineteenth century was Acts 10:34-35: "Truly I perceive that God shows no partiality, but in every nation any one who fears him does what is right and acceptable to him."

[41] Müller, *Science of Religions*, pp. 119-20.

[42] See his *Anthropological Religion*, Gifford Lectures at the University of Glasgow, 1891 (London: Longmans, Green, 1892), p. 334.

[43] Ibid., p. 37.

[44] For this discussion see Müller, *Origin and Growth*, pp. 32-50; the quotes are found on pp. 48, 45, and 38. It should be noted, as Müller himself was quite careful to do, that this argument of the infinite as based upon human faculties should be distinguished from the theories found in the work of Müller's

by Müller based upon individual corporeality; he went on to account for *differences* in articulation of the always already impinging infinite by accenting the particularity of any given sense-body that both determines and is determined by the monotony of the finite life of the individual. Müller concludes that the impingement of the infinite, responded to out of a "hunger" for this ever present "beyond," is the "root of the whole historical development of the human faith."[45]

Müller's work was in many ways the guiding light of the World's Parliament of Religions, contributing both a language and a strategy by which the comparative analysis of distinct "religious traditions" could be carried out in an efficient and "scientific" manner. It was used frequently as a means, in fact, to escape the scientificity of Spencer while simultaneously producing a transcendent category of cultural analysis based upon theories of evolutionary development. Müller, a consummate philologist, was the ideal model for a reconvened Babel.[46]

The parliament officially opened on September 11, 1893 with the "Columbian Liberty Bell" tolling ten times, once for each of the "Ten Great Religions." This term appears in a wide variety of literature of the period, and not surprisingly the ten religions that were included varied considerably. Christianity, Judaism, Buddhism, "Mohammedism," Confucianism, and Hinduism were invariably included, strongly reminiscent of Müller's three religious families, the Aryan, Semitic, and Turanian. In addition to these, Jainism,

---

somewhat older contemporary, Ludwig Feuerbach. Feuerbach asserted that human beings make their own gods and thereby become other to themselves: "The conscious subject has for its object the infinity of its own nature." For Müller the infinite other *as infinite other* can never be a manufactured object of a conscious subject. Religion for Müller could never be defined, as it is for Feuerbach, as a "dream of the human mind." For Feuerbach see *The Essence of Christianity*, trans. Marian Evans, 3d ed. (London: Kegan Paul, Trench, Trübner, 1893); for Müller's critique of Feuerbach see his *Origins and Growth*, p. 7.

[45] Müller, *Origin and Growth*, p. 43.

[46] Müller did not attend the Chicago parliament. In a public letter he addressed to Barrows (in *WPR*, 1:935-36 and titled "Greek Philosophy and the Christian Religion") he did, however, make an appeal for the "resuscitation of pure and primitive ante-Nicene Christianity," which he perceived as the last moment in Christian history that the absolute was truly, doctrinally, accessible. The concept of *homoousion* ("of the same substance"), whereby Christ was identified with the absolute *as no other man could be*, Müller asserted, was the mistaken premise upon which 1,500 years of Christian education had been carried out. Not surprisingly, this letter received very little attention at the parliament; Müller's importance there was in the use of his method, not his philosophy.

Zoroastrianism, Taoism, Shinto, Brahmanism, and various geographically defined religious groups such as found in Egypt, Greece, Rome, and Scandinavia were mixed in numerous configurations within this oddly consistent number "ten." Perhaps the most widely read example of the schema contained discussions of each of the Ten Great Religions in turn, "doing full justice to all...acknowledging their partial truth and use," and then proceeded to set forth the truth and value of Christianity as the religion by which all others must by judged. The other religions being both limited in geographical or ethnic scope and fundamentally incapable of evolution can lay claim only to limited notions of "truth"; Christianity, on the other hand, is heralded as the only transethnic, transnational, and thus the only universal religion.[47]

In contrast to the developmental hierarchy of civilization based, as we have seen, on the concerns of the Caucasian and Christian nations stand the concerns of the invited others who attended the parliament. As invited guests they were generally to abide by certain pre-set standards; but they also came with their own agendas and different interpretations of "religion." For example, Pung Kwang Yu, special commissioner to the Columbian Exposition and the World's Parliament of Religion for China, provides us with a list of concerns detailing the definition of religion in use at the parliament. Barrows had suggested to the various delegates to the parliament that they merely "answer certain questions on matters in which the American public is interested." This exposition, it was further requested, should be nontechnical, brief, and in English. The topics to be entertained were (1) God, (2) man, (3) the relation of man to God, (4) the role of woman, (5) education, and (6) social morality.[48] It was hoped that each of these topics would be given a day's or more discussion at the parliament itself; because of the rather haphazard collection of papers, however, this was finally not possible.

Pung's essay on Confucianism, in seven sections and edited to approximately 35,000 words, was not only not brief, but in it he also refused to limit his treatment of Confucian thought to the categories

---

[47] James F. Clarke, *Ten Great Religions: An Essay in Comparative Theology* (Boston: James R. Osgood, 1871), pp. 13-14. Other entertaining examples of this methodology can be found in Marcus Dods, *Mohammed, Buddha, and Christ: Four Lectures on Natural and Revealed Religion* (London: Hodder and Stoughton, 1890).

[48] See Pung Kwang Yu, "Confucianism," in *WPR*, 1:374-75. A similar list can be found in Yatsubuchi Banryū, *Shūkyō daikai hōdō* (Kyoto: Kokyō Shoin, 1894), p. 28, and in Shaku Sōen, *Bankoku shūkyō daikai ichiran* (Tokyo: Omeisha, 1893), p. 9.

suggested by Barrows. As to the discussion of God, problems of creation, and so forth, Pung flatly states "the Confucianists have never indulged in speculations of this nature."[49] Further, since the very term "religion" (Pung quotes Webster here for his definition) is itself contingent upon "feelings toward God," Pung wonders whether he can speak about Confucianism before the parliament at all. For in China, "religion [as defined here] has never been a desirable thing for the people to know and for the government to sanction." Religion served only to promote the "spreading of falsehoods and errors, and finally resulted in resistance to legitimate authority and in bringing calamities upon the country."[50] This is equally true for Christianity, Buddhism, and Taoism; the relative validity of a particular religion is of secondary concern as the "final result is the same": propagating religious doctrines "drives away those who value filial piety, brotherly love, sincerity, truth."[51]

Pung indicates, in other words, the precise point at which the parliamentarian project is at its most oppressive. He refused, first, to confine his remarks to the definition of religion set forth by the parliament, which could *only* result in *all* religions appearing to be concerned with the *same* issues and appearing to be different only as to particular terminology. That is, all religions could appear only as incomplete copies of Christianity. (For example, Buddha was described as Asia's Christ, the Bo Tree was equated with the cross, and the Ganges was called the Indian Jordan.[52]) Second, Pung refused to accept the basic ideological tenet that "religion is the greatest fact of history," and that the culmination of human evolution must needs be articulated in "religious" terms. Yet, in spite of the unqualified directness of these comments, Pung was only *heard* by the "American public" to say that Confucianism was a form of proto-humanism and that humankind is "the heart of heaven and earth. Humanity is his natural faculty and love his controlling emotion."[53] Barrows's desire for the delegates to speak only on nontechnical issues of interest to the general public was thus finally upheld, and Confucianism was "translated" into a promising but lesser developed Chinese-styled

---

[49] Pung, "Confucianism," in *WPR*, 1:376.

[50] Ibid., p. 384.

[51] Ibid., pp. 386-87.

[52] See John H. Barrows, *The Christian Conquest of Asia* (New York: Charles Scribner's Sons, 1899), pp. 165-66, 169.

[53]*Chicago Daily Times*, September 14, 1893, p. 1.

precursor to the Christian message. The success of the parliament's staging of the Other is impressive for both its tenacity of purpose and its ability to refigure even the clearest opposition into harmonious utterance. Participants in the parliament were ready to hear any number of protestations of universal brotherhood; barring few notable exceptions, regardless of what was in fact said, that was exactly what they heard. Parenthetically we should note that part of the responsibility for this problem in Pung's case must be attributed directly to Pung himself. Pung asked Barrows to provide him with suggestions for acceptable comments to be included in his address during the opening ceremonies of the parliament. On the fateful day, Barrows was asked to read Pung's speech (as Pung himself could speak little English) and discovered that he had been handed the exact sheet he had provided Pung weeks before. Barrows, after reading his own remarks as if they were Pung's, was somewhat embarrassed by the "manifestation of welcome and honor as came to no other speaker" and was also oddly but characteristically pleased when the press later remarked that the noble Christian sentiments "spoken by Mr. Pung at the parliament of Religions mark an era in the progress of humanity. Such friendly and magnanimous words indicate that China has been touched by the Christian spirit and is fast coming out into the brotherhood of nations."[54] This is perhaps the clearest example of how the parliament succeeded in providing the "Orient" not only with a voice but also with the language and ideas with which to animate that voice. The parliament, in the guise of Barrows's letter, used "China" to confirm that the parliament's assumptions and strategies vis-à-vis China and Asia were in fact correct. China, in the guise of Pung, unfortunately allowed itself, admittedly after no little resistance, to be constituted as the easily assimilable "other."

The Japanese Buddhists in their speeches were not as critically successful as Pung in their use of the acceptable parliamentarian definition of religion. On the whole their speeches tended to comply with Barrows's initial request to speak only on certain subjects of interest to the American public. When writing in Japanese for the home audience, the Buddhists did so with great strength and conviction; they were also frequently uncompromising in their anti-Christian posturings. But these same "champions of Buddhism" transplanted to Chicago were much more subdued and noticeably less successful in

---

[54] Mary Barrows, *John Henry Barrows*, pp. 284-85.

asserting their own sense of religion and its appropriate manifestations. The Shingon priest Toki Hōryū's (1854-1923) speech, when compared with Barrows's list, proves to be an almost exact copy of Barrows's outline. Except for the vague denial of the "existence of one creator (not by this expression meaning God)," Toki's presentation of "Buddhism in Japan" (the title of his talk), replete with a description of the Buddhist "soul or spirit" as having a "fine phantasmal form," reads very much like a poor copy of Christian doctrine. The inclusion of a photo after his paper in the parliament's chronicle adds a certain insult to the injury Toki had already inflicted on the interpretation of Buddhism offered in his speech. Depicting a mendicant shaman with a portable altar, the "pagan" nature of Buddhism is accented by the title of the photo placed there by the editor (Barrows): "Buddhist priest with portable idol shrine."[55]

Most of the Meiji Buddhists who delivered speeches in Chicago were similarly hampered in their presentations. In attempting to make their messages heard by an audience at the very least unprepared, and frequently hostile as well, they succeeded finally in producing emasculated gestures vaguely directed toward their goals. For example, the Tendai priest Ashitsu Jitsunen's (1841-1921) earlier writings reveal a profound concern about the "savage nature" (*satsubatsu shugi*) of Christianity in the world. He hoped to show at the parliament the "true nature" of religion to be both peaceful and progressive; though Christianity worships a "God of suffering," Ashitsu hoped to explicate the compassionate practice of self-sacrifice and divine labor as found in Buddhism.[56] His lecture before the parliament, however, fraught with translation difficulties, was a detailed and highly technical enumeration of the "Buddha-bodies" (J: *sanshin*; Skt: *trikaya*) as found in Tendai philosophy. Considering the circumstances, this was not a well-chosen topic. Shaku Sōen (1859-1919), a Rinzai priest, chose to lecture on the topic of causality; though his paper in Japanese is a precise and well-handled technical exposition of the Buddhist doctrine of co-dependent origination, the terms used in Chicago, taken directly from language current to contemporary Theosophical discourse, served better in the production

---

[55] *WPR*, 1:553. The photos in *WPR* are themselves an intriguing study of sliding signification. For example, a photo of the Grand Shrine at Ise is labeled simply "Shogunal Tombs."

[56] See Ashitsu Jitsunen, *Nihon shūkyō mirai ki* (Kyoto: Tendai Shūmusho, 1889), pp. 122-27; and Ashitsu, "Sanrei chinjōsho," pp. 19-22.

of an image of Buddhism as quaint and approximate than as the dynamic and socially viable force the Japanese Buddhists hoped to present. As dismal as their English performances may have been (with the exception of the lay Buddhist Hirai Kinzō's [d.1917]), it is important to note that this was but one half of Meiji Buddhism's association with the parliament. The numerous post-parliament press releases *in Japan* were characterized by an unbridled optimism as article after article asserted the joyous and unhindered promulgation of Mahāyanā Buddhism among Westerners saturated with material comforts but sadly lacking in the life of the spirit.

"Religion" at the World's Parliament of Religion was fashioned of elements germane to nineteenth-century America. Articulated with terms drawn from, but not necessarily in agreement with, the work of Darwin and Müller, the global definitional project of the parliament was, as officially chronicled, a great and uncompromised success: the religions of the world were *in fact* reflections of the Christian message; these paler reflections would *someday* each evolve to a position in accordance with those who already lived "within the full light of the cross." As suggested in the discussion of Pung's presentation, the more profound traces of Pung's performance at the parliament were not to be found in his talk (which in fact refuted elements central to the parliament's larger project) but were located in Pung's presence itself. Pung and the invited "others" of the Orient were *by their very participation* already constituted by the parliament as representatives who desired to be *included*. Herein lay the great irony of the parliament. The value of the "others" present at Chicago was their *exteriority* to the Eurocentric and Christocentric world; yet this exteriority could not finally be allowed its full reign. The truly exterior would destroy the universalist assumptions in operation at the base of the parliament's very formation. Pung and the "others" were allowed the status of the familiar other, the weak other, the other to be taught and ushered into the realm of the same—an other willing to sacrifice its exteriority. The parliamentarian other was given life so that it could be sacrificed on the altar of evolutionary progress.

Constructing the Other

In the late nineteenth century's discourse on power, terms such as "race," "nation," and "religion" were used in one of two ways: stressing differentiation, or stressing unification. Particular races were arranged in a hierarchy that described the human race; fragments of the complete religion were straining to cease being religions and to begin participating in religion *itself*. Or so it was argued. Here let us take up some of the specific *images* of race and religion, self and other, as "exhibited" at the parliament.

> Yellow and blue, red and lavender, old gold and green, cardinal, crimson and scarlet...a bewildering kaleidoscope of tints, punctuated and emphasized by the still black and white of American and European....Strange costumes of rich silks, satins, and velvets were next neighbor to common flannel. One son of Asia dressed his limbs in blue and pink percale pantaloons, and another in some soft good of shrimp pink....At the eastern end of the stage sat...[the representatives] from Japan. Their rich silk vestments, delicate in texture, and gorgeous in their richly blended tints and shades, looked in the distance like a flower pot in a garden of black.[57]

The strange, delicate, decidedly feminine garb of those "sons of Asia at the eastern end of the stage" during the parliament's opening ceremony was more than enough to assure the fulfillment of the second goal of the parliament: a display "in the most impressive way." So crucial was this colorful presence to the popular conception of the parliament that after a temporary absence of the Japanese delegation, it was duly noted in the following day's press that the "effect upon the platform picture" was considerably lessened.[58] The very presence of these "delegates from the Orient" was, in many cases, far more crucial a performance than any official presentation they might have made. The Japanese, Chinese, and Indian representatives were consistently front-page news, more frequently for what they wore and did as for what they might have said at the parliament. Clearly, without these representatives there could be no *World's* Parliament; these silk- and velvet-clad souls were the unknown beyond the boundaries of "civilization"; and by their very presence they had given sanction to the unitary power of "Christian America," to the hope of the White City. Or in the words of George Boardman, Baptist from Philadelphia, and the last lecturer at the parliament, "Buddha and his religion are Asiatic; what has Buddha done for the unity of mankind? Why are we not holding our sessions in fragrant Ceylon? Mohammed taught some very noble truths; but Mohammedanism is fragmented and antithetic; why have not his followers invited us to Mecca? But Jesus Christ is the

---

[57] *Chicago Times*, September 12, 1893, p. 1.
[58] *Inter-Ocean*, September 13, 1893, p. 1.

sole bond of the human race; the one nexus of the nations, the great vertebral column of the body of mankind."[59]

The incorporation of non-Christian representatives into the parliament's program was not, however, merely an exercise in a purposeful creative distancing. There was also an equally creative gesture to incorporate their presence into the (almost) familiar. For example, one press release commenting on the opening ceremonies exclaims: "The Orient will be there to recall the Magi."[60] Or again, we find the following comments regarding the Indian representatives during one of the many social events scheduled around the foreign guests: "With their peculiar head gear and flowing robes they recalled pictures of Biblical personages."[61] Barrows himself felt moved to conclude in his last book that Japan was a "wild cherry blossom, gleaming in the morning light of western civilization."[62] India, the ancient cradle of the Aryan religion, had somehow managed to continue in an almost "Biblical" fashion: here ironically synonymous with the uncivilized period of the West's foundation, or in the case of the Magi, in the status of a tributary nation. The Japanese on the other hand, long identified as the "Yankees of the East" and well represented at the Exposition itself,[63] were clearly expected to have an uplifting—that is, Americanizing—influence on all of Asia.

There were times, of course, when neither the image as "other," nor the role as mirror into Christianity's own past, was entirely adequate to the other's presence itself. One such case involved Shibata Reiichi, son of the founder of the Jikko sect of Shinto. The following is excerpted from the day's press following the incident in question. "Women from the audience climbed over chairs and tables to pay their compliments to the distinguished oriental....Then a loud cheer rent the air and there was a mad rush for the platform....The excitement was caused by the High Priest in a spirit of true reciprocity embracing a

[59] George Dana Boardman, "Christ the Unifier of Mankind," in *WPR*, 2:1346.

[60]*Inter-Ocean*, September 11, 1893, p. 1.

[61] Ibid.

[62] Barrows, *The Christian Conquest*, p. 152.

[63] The government of Japan spent over $630,000 in creating its national exhibit at the Exposition, one of the largest expenditures by any foreign nation; an entire construction crew, replete with materials, was sent directly from Japan for building several traditionally styled buildings. The collection of ceramic, textile, and other wares was also of major proportions. See Rydell, *All the World*, pp. 48-51.

couple of ladies. It was over in a moment but in that moment they had felt on their cheeks the kiss of the High Priest of Shintoism."[64]

Though called a "chaste kiss of brotherhood" and an application of an "Eastern custom," that this "little breach of etiquette" should be so quickly forgiven—and the entire event recalled later as "the pleasant little incident"—reflects an elaborate attempt to articulate difference in such a way as to construct a palatable sameness. The shocking scene of an Oriental High Priest kissing several Caucasian gentle ladies in public reinterpreted as "chaste," "customary," and so on, is a creative use of the notions of universal religious equality and transracial universalism to stress, in the words of the parliament's tenth goal, "friendly fellowship, in the hope of securing permanent international peace."

The carnival-like nature of the parliament was not lost on the Japanese Buddhists who journeyed to Chicago. Yatsubuchi Banryū, a Shin priest from Kumamoto, in a speech before the Kyūshū Buddhist Club after returning to Japan from the parliament, noted that upon the arrival in Chicago of the Japanese contingent, "with the speed of a typhoon the news that we had arrived spread throughout the entire city"; wherever they went the priests were mobbed by crowds chanting "The Japanese are here! The Japanese are here!" Yatsubuchi observes that the very presence of the Japanese priests "restored the faith of the local Christian organizers" that there could in fact be a *World's* Parliament of Religions. His understanding of the dramatic nature of the moment was further confirmed by the opening-day ceremonies, which he described as the stage debut (kao mise) of the world's religious actors.[65]

Fashion was ever on the minds of chroniclers of the parliament, and Yatsubuchi's account was no different. He, like many others, used the images found in the dress of the parliamentarians, or rather the reaction to his own, in order to present his own arguments regarding the dire need in the West for true spiritual sustenance. Yatsubuchi spends several pages of his account of the parliament discussing the

---

[64]*Inter-Ocean*, September 14, 1893, p. 1. The *Chicago Daily Tribune* also carried a first-page synopsis of Shibata's "embracing three Caucasian ladies." Shaku notes the incident unabashedly: "Shinshi kifujin shi o yōshite seppun akushu sukoburu tabō o kiwamu." See Shaku, *Bankoku shūkyō daikai ichiran*, p. 25. Not surprisingly Shibata himself makes no note of the incident in his chronicle of the parliament. Barrows, on the other hand, recalls it five years after the fact with great detail and emphasis. See Mary Barrows, *John Henry Barrows*, p. 384.

[65] Yatsubuchi, *Shūkyō daikai hōdō*, pp. 26-29.

Americans' fascination with the Japanese Buddhist priests' silk robes, the very possession of which marked them all as gentlemen of the highest rant and wealth in Westerners' eyes. After a careful listing of costs associated with the Western gentleman's wardrobe, Yatsubuchi suggests that this preoccupation with dress by Westerners is, in fact, a perfect example of the West's preoccupation with wealth and the assumption that there is a direct correlation between the cost of one's possessions and the worth of one's person. Yatsubuchi goes on to note that this is, moreover, but one type of desire (*yokubō*) innate (*sententeki*) to Westerners. In addition to the endless and insatiable quest to possess, finally, the material world, Westerners also seek knowledge of the operation of the natural world and the means to exploit that knowledge to, inevitably, increase their wealth. Western thought is based exclusively on the external world; Yatsubuchi, to prove this assertion, notes that most inventions designed in the West merely extend the knowledge obtainable through the senses to broader (for example, the telescope) or more precise (the microscope) ranges. There are indeed limits to the resources and capabilities used to manipulate or obtain those resources, but, Yatsubuchi observes, there seems to be no limit to the West's collective desires; all aspects of culture—religion, ethics, art, the military, and science (this is Yatsubuchi's list)—are directed exclusively toward the actualization of the West's desire to control the world of form. Further, the true spirit of Westerners can best be seen in their relation to other races of the world, which is inevitably one of subjugation and annihilation. Look, demands Yatsubuchi, at the American Indian and the Africans, but also look at problems much closer to home: India, Annam (Vietnam), Siam, Korea, and China. Japan, he suggests, has been lucky so far. The weak point of the West is, he claims, their unbridled strength; their instinctual need to dominate will be their undoing. "They are slaves to their lifestyles, slaves to their physical desires, and slaves to their wealth." The fascination with the material world in the West, made apparent to Yatsubuchi in part through the banal interest of parliamentarians in the material image of the Orient, was, he concluded, "like a candle in a snowstorm." It gleams brightly and melts all that comes near, but it is also constantly on the verge of extinction with every gust of wind.[66] Yatsubuchi's proposal for the salvation of the West will be taken up in a later discussion.

---

[66] Ibid., pp. 8-12, 33-36.

There were certain disagreeable moments for the Buddhist priests journeying in America as they confronted many of the artifacts of what was being called in late-nineteenth-century Japan, "civilization" for the first time. Confronting Western-style breakfasts (invariably "fried pig fat [bacon] and the eggs of chicken" or "fried chips of ground corn [corn flakes] with the milk of cows"), observing touch dancing (which Yatsubuchi found particularly offensive), or smelling the "excessive use of perfumes on meat-eating Westerners" led Yatsubuchi to exclaim, "this thing they call 'civilization' seems rather like the customs of barbarians."[67] Nevertheless, closer to their areas of expertise, the priests were impressed with both the regularity of Christian religious observations and the unflagging efforts of ministers and missionaries to carry on their work. From the Christian minister who held service on board ship en route to Vancouver, who even administered to those in the lowest classes traveling with the animals and luggage in the ship's hold (the Japanese priests all traveled second class, except for Shaku Sōen, who traveled in first class), to the scriptural exegesis performed in well-received lectures at the parliament, the *social presence* of an interactive faith was made vividly clear to the Meiji Buddhists. Shaku Sōen records in his chronicle of the parliament a lecture on the historical veracity, or lack thereof, of certain passages in the Bible. What intrigued him here was not the speaker's final claim of the Bible's universal validity and superior nature but the disclaimers offered regarding certain factually, scientifically, or historically mistaken passages contained therein. The ancient *recording* of the physical world may in fact contain certain distortions easily discovered by the modern reader ("we know much more than we did"), but the basic transcendent *truths* of the Bible are not thereby rendered inconsequential. Shaku of course linked this apologetic technique directly to current problems in the interpretation of the Buddhist sutras that, ever since Tominaga, had been interpreted in much the same manner as in contemporary Biblical exegesis. The elements of "form" and their underlying "truths" were herein perceived as distinct, in such a manner that the essential teachings of (in Shaku's case) the Buddha need not be seen as defiled by certain technical difficulties.[68]

---

[67] Yatsubuchi Banryū, "Bankoku shūkyō daikai rinseki dōchū ki," *Kokkyō* no. 26 (9/1893): 24-32.

[68] Shaku, *Bankoku shūkyō daikai ichiran*, p. 58. Shibata Reiichi's record of the parliament (*Sekai shūkyōkai enzetsu tekiyō*, 1893) is unfortunately an almost exact duplicate of Shaku's (though shorter). As neither man could speak or read

Due partly to their inability to communicate in English (except for Hirai Kinzō, whose command of the language seems to have been legendary), but more probably due to their concern for constructing their own image of the parliament, all records made by the Japanese priests regularly elide the blatantly confrontational aspects of Christian universalism explicit in numerous speeches at which they were in attendance. Shaku, for example, glosses even the most vitriolic attacks upon non-Christians as attempts at the construction of "universal brotherhood." One Alexander McKenzie, the sole Puritan repre-sentative to the parliament, spoke of the need to fashion "black material into noble men and women" and "red material into respectable men."[69] In Shaku's record, however, McKenzie's call to fashion a "new spiritual republic" (*seishinteki shin kyōwa koku*) was seen not as racist elitism but rather as a sincere attempt to produce a true "global family" (*shikai kyōdai*).[70] The point here is not merely to suggest that the Japanese Buddhists did not understand what "really" happened at the parliament, though language was clearly an important factor in this regard (this was also true in the case of other delegates, for example, Pung). Rather, what this suggests is that the portrayal of the parliament, and the West in general, by these Meiji Buddhists was carried out in a manner conducive to their own goals for the reformulation of domestic institutional Buddhism. The invited Buddhists, like the hosting Christians, saw and heard precisely what they desired. The parliament's emphasis on a transcendent truth over particular issues of historical veracity was, for example, extracted from the uniquely Christian environment of its initial use and was then applied by the Buddhists as their own strategy; the *idea* of a transcendent truth took precedence over the particular version of that truth. Similarly, the Christian emphasis on social work and the

---

English, we can assume that both works are based upon a third text, most likely the notes of their translators Nomura and Noguchi. One major difference between the two is that Shibata's work edits outs the Buddhists' speeches while quoting his own in great detail (in fact much longer than that recorded in *WPR*); similarly, Shaku's version, while more generous to his fellow Buddhists, barely mentions Shibata. Their observations of speakers and the perceived content of all the talks are repeated, however, in much the same language with all the same omissions.

[69] Although there were no "red" delegates among parliamentarians, there were several "black" ministers; I can only assume McKenzie refrained from the use of "yellow material" out of some sense of courtesy to the then-present "delegates from the Orient."

[70] Shaku, *Bankoku shūkyō daikai ichiran*, pp. 8-9.

crossing of class barriers for the sake of religious conversions was seen as yet another important and useful *technique* that could be extracted from its Christian milieu. Tactics such as these, already begun in the "sectarian restoration" of the early Meiji, could be more forcefully articulated in Japan from the privileged "exterior" position of the cosmopolitan interpretation of the "world's religions" as staged in Chicago. The blatant racism and cultural elitism found at the parliament, in its organization and definition and within the presentations, were in fact ironically reconstituted as the *welcoming* of the plurivocal. It was, in other words, a shared assumption by many non-Christian delegates that the very purpose of the parliament was to aid a beleaguered Christianity in meeting the demands of the modern age. The representatives were thus invited to Chicago, this argument went, to teach Christianity both what it lacked and what it had lost.[71]

Though the images of the "other" provided here have been few (entirely out of concern for space), we can conclude that the ethnological hierarchy "displayed" along the Midway was also in operation at the parliament. No representatives of American Indian, African, or other "primitive" religions were invited (presentations were made on these subjects only during some of the "scientific sessions"); the only "other" that could *possibly* be present was one that could be *assimilated*. Assimilation took different guises and was at times severely tried, but the parliamentarian "other," though by definition existing as an exoticism, also needed to meet some fundamental criteria for inclusion among those acceptable as "other." Further, this "other" was by no means merely a passive object of the parliament's construction but was itself engaged in the select imaging of the parliamentarian proceedings and their subsequent interpretation.

On the eleventh day of the parliament, the newly formed Brotherhood of Christian Unity formally presented to the parliament a "formula" designed to "perpetuate the remarkable spirit of unity" at the parliament and to serve "as a suitable bond with which to begin the federation of the world upon a Christian basis." The formula,

---

[71] This was a rather widely accepted interpretation; for the delegates' opinions see Matsuyama Rokuin, *Bankoku shūkyō daikai gi* (Tokyo: Kōbundō, 1893), p. 66, and Yatsubuchi, *Shūkyō daikai hōdō*, p. 50; see also his "Bankoku shūkyō daikai ni tsuite shoshi ni iu," *Dentō*, no. 47 (1893): 5-7.

which gathered numerous signatures, not one of which was from a non-Christian delegate, reads in its entirety as follows: "For the purpose of uniting with all who desire to serve God and their fellow men under the inspiration of the life and teaching of Jesus Christ, I hereby enroll myself as a member of the Brotherhood of Christian Unity."[72]

For Barrows, a man who believed that "the Christian religion is inherently expansive, and the idea of worldwide conquest entered its heart and brain from the very beginning," such a formula was mere common sense.[73] It was his one avowed mission to preach to the world the living "larger Christ," "the Christ who has not forgotten or forsaken any part of the world."[74] The parliament clearly had as an (unexpressed) goal the production of a Christianity that carried with it the gospel that "Paul carried to Rome, and the Puritans to America." It is America, finally, that has the *responsibility* to "set in motion" the "Christian forces" with the "ever-living Son of God marching at the head of Christendom," and to direct these forces as they move upon "vitally intimate" Asia. Only America, claims Barrows, can accomplish what "sixteen centuries of European civilization" have failed to achieve.

But, we might ask, at what cost was such a worldwide unification to be obtained? Barrows answers in language reminiscent of Darwin; religion, like all organisms, evolves, and this evolution itself necessitates the possibility of extinction of certain forms and the survival of others. Judaism, after "acceptance of the truth" of the divinity of Christ, will "be made one" with Christianity. Islam has an even less enviable role in Barrows's schema of religious evolution: "the long blight and agony of Mohammedan rule will be mitigated and the throne of the Arabian prophet will be beaten to fragments by the leaves of the New Testament....And Jesus, in the person of His disciples, shall enter the ancient shrine of Mecca, and there at last the whole truth will be told."[75] Similar futures are foretold for the "acrid expanse, above which hang the mists of restless discontent" called Hinduism and the "wild fantasies" and "partial truths" of Buddhism.[76]

---

[72] Quoted by Barrows, "History," in *WPR*, 1:132.

[73] Barrows, *The Christian Conquest*, p. 222.

[74] Ibid., p. 223.

[75] Ibid., p. 58.

[76] Ibid., pp 90-91, 159, 166, and passim.

In spite of the lofty ideals played large in speeches and in publications, the parliament's certainty that "this world of ours needs Christ," and the willingness and desire to "conquer with love" all peoples of the world, uniting them in that great White City "so holy and clean," describes an irrefutably oppressive ideology thinly disguised with a veneer of evolutionary ethnology, comparative religious studies, and assumptions of a universal brotherhood transcendent of all difference. It is, in other words, a powerful presentation of the *"practical* power" of the idea of the transcendent as set forth by Kant. It is also a clear example of the fiction of certainty perpetuated by dogmatists "unable to establish and defend [their] assertions except by war." The fifth expressed goal of the parliament was "To indicate the impregnable foundations of theism, and the reasons for man's faith in Immortality, and thus to unite and strengthen the forces which are adverse to a materialistic philosophy of the universe." As Kant showed, there *can be no* "reasons" for faith. The "foundations" of theism might be deemed "impregnable" when articulated within a Spencerian system, but this would simultaneously disallow the construction of "forces" operative against a "materialistic philosophy." There is a clear attempt throughout the parliament to disparage mechanical and industrial (i.e., "material") advances and to elevate "religion" as the meaning and the source of all "science." "Science," as one writer expressed it, "is a revelation of God."[77] Darwin's theories of evolution, translated into social (national) and ethnological (racial) terminology, provided the very argument by which nineteenth-century theism attempted to unite its forces against the materialistic advance in which Darwin and Spencer actively participated. Müller did not go to the parliament; his letter calling for a return to the radicality of an ante-Nicene Christianity was read and quietly ignored. Müller was invoked, however, by numerous speakers, almost exclusively to provide expert testimony for claims of the universality of religious experience, of the centrality of the Aryan tradition, or of the final superiority of Christianity. His work in popularizing the comparative study of religion was heralded as having reached full flower in the parliament itself. Müller was, in short, used to provide "reasons for man's faith in Immortality" (a task he himself, clearly, was not totally adverse to take on). But his Kantian

---

77 Paul Carus, ed., *The World's Parliament of Religions and the Religious Parliament Extension* (Chicago: Open Court, 1896); and Paul Carus, "Science a Religious Revelation," in *WPR*, 2:980.

suggestions of the validity of plurivocal enunciations of religious truths and the concomitant assertion that "nineteenth-century Theism" was not the totalizing universal of the world's religious experience (if, indeed, such a thing even existed) could not be heard over the din of the parliamentarians as they tried to baptize the world.

The Champions of Buddhism

The five "champions of Buddhism" (*Bukkyō no championra*)[78] received no official government funding or authorization; they were also not recognized as official representatives of Buddhism by the Buddhist Transsectarian Cooperative Society (*Bukkyō kakushū kyōkai*). This lack of official status had, however, no effect whatsoever on their reception in Chicago, where they were accorded the privilege of speaking for all Buddhists in Japan. The disorganization of the only transsectarian Buddhist organization then in existence was compounded by an open letter sent from an Indian Buddhist reporter resident in the United States.[79] The author asserted that any Buddhist who journeyed to Chicago would serve merely as a source of entertainment for the Christians who would "portray themselves as compassionate and humble lambs and all other religions' representatives as perverse and ravenous jackals." The previous unqualified support for the project quickly disappeared as the various sects envisioned a potentially embarrassing international situation. Perhaps the two most prominent Buddhists of the Meiji era, Nanjō Bun'yū and Shimaji Mokurai, were also prevented from participating by the leaders of their sect.[80] The five Buddhists that did go to Chicago

---

[78] From an editorial, "Bankoku shūkyō daikai o ronzu," in the Shingon journal *Dentō*, no. 37 (1892): 10. See also note 4 above.

[79] This article, first published in the *Buddha's Light* (*Bukkō*) in late 1892, was translated and distributed (it was even rumored solicited) by one Ohara Kakichi, a friend and collaborator of Ashitsu Jitsunen. It subsequently appeared in every major (and most minor) journals within a very short period. The violence of the language shocked many Buddhist supporters of the parliament out of their idealistic conceptions of the parliament's goals; the implications of this commentary should not be underestimated. (See, for example, Suzuki Norihisa, *Meiji shūkyō shichō no kenkyū*, p. 212 for a copy of this letter and a brief commentary.) The quotes here are taken from "Bankoku shūkyō daikai ni taisuru Bukkō kisha no iken," *Mitsugon Kyōhō*, no. 75 (1893): 13.

[80] The *Bukkyō kakushū kyōkai*, the most serious institutional attempt made in the pursuit of a "united Buddhism" and made up of some of the highest ranking clergy of the time, saw its efficacy disappear in an avalanche of intersectarian skirmishes in the debate over the delegate issue.

were thus dependent upon their own temples for support.[81] Only two, Shaku Sōen (Rinzai Zen) and Yatsubuchi Banryū (Pure Land), had any significant clerical rank (abbott); and only Shaku had traveled abroad before (to Siam). Only Ashitsu Jitsunen (Tendai) had published a monograph prior to participation in the parliament,[82] though all were to publish extensively afterwards. None of them, except the lay Buddhist Hirai Kinzō, could speak, read, or write English or any other European language. None of them doubted that they would be participating in a program controlled by Christian luminaries "for the sole purpose of expanding the glory of Christianity." Yet, not surprisingly, none of them doubted their own ultimate victory in this battle of religions, a victory that they assumed was guaranteed by the universal efficacy of the teachings they represented. These difficulties were further compounded by two factors: personal animosity between certain of the delegates themselves, and the role the Nichiren sect was to play in the image of Japanese Buddhism at Chicago. Yatsubuchi, from Kumamoto and lacking extensive scholastic training, looked upon Toki Hōryū (Shingon) and Shaku (both from the capital area), their literary attainments, and their social sophistication as "ostentatious and hypocritical" attempts to impress Westerners with their "civilized nature." Yatsubuchi published several remarks criticizing their, particularly Shaku's, grandstanding. (Toki and Shaku spent their crossing of the Pacific on deck composing classical poetry; Shaku traveled first class and always took his meals in private in his suite.) Shaku responded in his record of the parliament by editing out Yatsubuchi's speech from his work, noting only "it is not really worth recording."[83]

A second complication is found in a letter sent by two high-ranking Nichiren priests, still in Japan, directly to Barrows as chairman of the parliament. Barrows, unable to read Japanese, innocently asked the Shingon priest Toki Hōryū to aid him in translating the letter. This brief epistle stressed in no uncertain terms that the "only true Buddhism" was the teaching of Nichiren; the letter specifically mentions Shingon and the Pure Land teachings as being decadent

---

[81] Shaku was even rumored to have sold some valuable Buddhist paintings to a foreign collector to pay for his trip. See *Hansei Zasshi*, no. 9 (1893).

[82] Ashitsu Jitsunen, *Nihon shūkyō mirai ki*. He was also coeditor with Shimaji and Shaku of the *Bukkyō kakushū kōyō* (1896).

[83] For Yatsubuchi on Shaku and Toki see, for example, "Rinseki dōchū ki," pp. 24-28. For Shaku's remark see his *Bankoku shūkyō daikai ichiran*, p. 67.

bastardizations of Śakyamuni's works and cautions Barrows "not to be fooled by their smooth words" as they have no right to represent Buddhism to the world. Toki and Yatsubuchi both immediately wrote letters to Japan that were published in numerous religious journals. They said, again in no uncertain terms, that the Nichiren priests were "ignorant fools" who seem to take great pleasure in merely attempting to destroy sincere attempts to promulgate Buddhism to the world. The delicacy and value of the first "international" moment of Japanese Buddhism was too great a risk being damaged by some "unskilled and unschooled enemies of the dharma." Their position seems to have been supported; Barrows makes no mention of the incident, nor can it be found in the popular American press of the day. Kawai Yoshijirō, the only follower of Nichiren officially present in Chicago, was not allowed to deliver his paper before the parliament, as the agenda was "full."[84]

In spite of such internal dissension the "champions" did indeed leave their mark on the parliament's proceedings; they also successfully utilized their newly created international positions to direct the ongoing redefinition of Buddhism within Japan. Now let us turn to problems central to the interpretation and presentation of Japanese or Eastern Buddhism at the Chicago parliament.

Nineteenth-century Buddhologists divided the object of their study into the three thematic/geographic divisions of Southern, Northern, and Eastern Buddhism. Southern Buddhism, also known as the Hīnayāna, was generally identified as the "original Buddhism," the purest in form, and (perhaps thus the claim to purity) almost nonextant. The Northern and Eastern forms, both called the Mahāyāna, until around the turn of the century were most frequently described as having "broken away from" the original Southern Buddhism, such that wherever Buddhism appeared, "it has been so modified by the national characteristics and the inherited beliefs of its converts, acting upon the natural tendencies within itself to alteration and decay, that it has developed, under these conditions, into strangely inconsistent and even antagonistic beliefs and practices" from that

---

[84] For the Nichiren letter, and Yatsubuchi's and Toki's responses, see "Bankoku shūkyō daikai kaikaishiki no kōkei," in *Kokkyō*, no. 27 (10/1893): 26-28. This article is a general collection of news and reviews of the first days of the parliament; after appearing here these letters then circulated to journals of Shingon and other sects.

found in the "original" Buddhism.[85] Nineteenth-century Buddhologists would argue that the "benevolent agnosticism" of Southern Buddhism, describing a "passionless yet selfish pursuit for extinction" and tinged with a "bald scepticism and unsettled moral discipline," gave way to belief in a plethora of "hypothetical beings" of fantastic description dwelling in an equally fabulous universe.[86] Buddha, the argument ran, had hoped to rise above the superstitions of the common people, but, even though partially successful, "the clouds returned after the rain." That is to say, the old, dead gods of Brahmanism returned under new names and forms.[87] The most immediate consequence of this line of reasoning was the noticeable lack of concern—disdain might be more accurate—evidenced by scholars and the general public alike for Buddhism as found in China, Korea, and Japan. And it was Eastern Buddhism (i.e., Japanese Buddhism), more than any other, with its particularly "dreadful heresy" of syncretism conjoined with Shinto, that succeeded in "rousing the indignation of students of early Buddhism, like Max Müller."[88] One characteristic student of the science of comparative religions at this time felt compelled to ask, "is Japanese Buddhism really Shintoized Buddhism or Buddhaized Shinto? Which is the parasite and which the parasitized?"[89] This same writer went on to trace the source of the "abomination" of original Buddhism in Japan to the syncretic tendency most clearly seen in the work of Kūkai. This "ecclesiastical dexterity" in coordinating Buddhism with various and sundry folk practices testified to the fact that Japanese Buddhism was merely a "swapping of history for legend and of fact for dogma."[90] The Euro-American parliamentarians at Chicago, as both descendants and participants in this analytical perspective, in fact knew very little of the teachings and practices of their fellow

---

[85] T. W. Rhys Davids, *Buddhism: Its History and Literature* (New York: G.P. Putnam's Sons, 1896), p. 188.

[86] For a typically graphic rendition of Mahāyāna Buddhism by a nineteenth-century commentator see William Elliot Griffis, *The Religions of Japan from the Dawn of History to the Era of Meiji* (New York: Charles Scribner's Sons, 1895), pp. 171-76. See also Barrows, *The Christian Conquest*, p. 154; or, for a more balanced treatment, Rhys Davids, *Buddhism*, passim.

[87] Griffis, *The Religions of Japan*, p. 187.

[88] Only one of the fifty volumes of Müller's major editorial work, the *Sacred Books of the East* series, contains Mahāyāna texts, and they are limited largely to texts used by Shin Buddhism in Japan. We should recall that Nanjō Bunyū, Müller's long-time disciple, was a Shin Buddhist priest and scholar.

[89] Griffis, *The Religions of Japan*, pp. 211-12.

[90] Ibid., p. 221.

parliamentarians from Japan. Moreover, what they did know was decidedly not of a nature conducive to a positive dialogue.

It is interesting, but not surprising, that the Japanese themselves had a very different view of the syncretic nature of the teachings they sought to re-present to the West in Chicago. For example, the Shingon journal *Dentō*, in a review on the World's Parliament of Religions, described *the parliament itself* as a syncretic exercise along the lines of Kūkai's famous *Hasshū-ron* ("Essay on the Eight Teachings"), just on a larger scale. But the parliament, they asserted, being ignorant of the Mahāyāna and dependent upon Christian writers for what they did know about Buddhism, would finally fail to obtain an accurate understanding of the world's true religion. Kūkai, they noted, would not return to this world for another 5,670,000,000 years.[91] Thus what was needed was the (re)birth of an illustrious priest like unto Kūkai himself who, if he were to appear, would doubtlessly go to Chicago and attend the parliament in order to spread the true and comprehensive teaching of the dharma to the benighted West.[92]

Toki Hōryū, the Shingon representative to the parliament, though not possessing the eloquence of a Kūkai, did attempt to show that the Buddhism that was "the spirit of Japan" was indeed the Greater Vehicle, or rather the One Vehicle (Skt.: *Ekayana*).[93] The origin of the Mahāyāna and the Hīnayāna is indeed one, says Toki (along with most other Meiji Buddhists), and he thereby glosses over the difficult chronological problem of Mahāyāna texts (the so-called *Dajo hi bussetsu*, "the Mahayana was not spoken by the Buddha"). Despite this original unity, whereas the Greater Vehicle provides an absolute perspective of this world, the Smaller Vehicle is but a relativistic pursuit of some tranquil other world (*shingai ni jōdo*).[94] The multiplicity of teachings, or Vehicles, Toki attributes to the now very familiar concept of skill-in-means (J:*hōben*), which, as it is presented in Toki's

---

[91] According to Shingon tradition, Kūkai has but retired into meditation (*nyūjō*) and after the completion of this age will return (*shutsujō*) along with the Buddha of the future.

[92] "Bankoku shūkyō daikai o ronzu," *Dentō*, no. 37 (1893): 10.

[93] For Toki's talk, "Buddhism in Japan," see *WPR*, 1:551; and for the Japanese text see "Beikoku Shikago Bankoku Shūkyō Daikai ni okeru Toki sōsho no enzetsu kihitsu," *Mitsugon Kyōhō*, no. 95 (1893): 12-14. The quotes in the text are all from the Japanese version of the speech.

[94] The invocation of the "Pure Land" (*jōdo*) here is an example of the constant subtle infighting that occurred between the priests during their public presentations. Toki, as a Shingon priest, had little that was positive to say about the Shin Pure Land teachings.

paper, is designed to compensate for differences between particular beings' evolutionary development (*nikutai jō no hattatsu*). Toki reads, in other words, the classic Buddhist practice of adapting the message to the listener's ability as an early example of how Buddhism took into account evolutionary differences within specific followers of the Way. The Buddha dharma is here read as an evolutionary practice that is both carried out within history and serves to drive it forth. Further, practices of "idol worship," and the characteristics of "passivity" and "negativity" generally attributed to Buddhism as a whole, Toki suggests should be carefully weighed against the serious differences between the Mahāyāna and Hīnayāna teachings. The simultaneous operation of "form" (*yūkei*) and "formless form" (*mukei*) in the Mahāyāna (saṃsāra is nirvāṇa is saṃsāra) is the "true standard" by which Buddhism needs to be measured, and not by the "law of passive uniformity" or the "delirious condition" of the "calm extinction of mind and body" of the Hīnayāna.

Simultaneously to distancing the conception of the Greater from the Smaller Vehicle, Toki, like many others who attempted to transmit Eastern Buddhism to the West, tried to draw usable parallels between the definitions of Buddhism and Christianity. The Ten Bodhisattva Precepts (J: *bosatsu kai*) would be called the "Ten Buddhist Commandments"; the "formless form" of the "soul or spirit" (*reikon aruiwa seishin*) in Buddhism, or the Shingon teaching of the "True Word" (J: *shingon*, Skt.: *mantra*), would be linked to Christian uses of the "holy ghost" and the "logos," and so forth. But perhaps the most forceful parallel made here was that of the bodhisattva ideal, the "self"-sacrifice of a particular being's salvation (Buddhahood) in the quest for universal salvation. Many European writers, echoing Rhys Davids, would assert that Buddhism was "radically selfish" and that its only form of morality was the determined search for self-extinction and thus a relief from eternal suffering.[95]

The Japanese Buddhists' attempts to present their so-called Eastern version of Buddhism as a legitimate compassionate quest for the complete salvation of *all* beings met with varying degrees of success at the parliament. Christianity, its defenders would stress, from its very inception on the cross has been devoted exclusively to the

---

[95] For example, see Dods, *Mohammed, Buddha, and Christ*, pp. 168-71; Clarke, *Ten Great Religions*, p. 165, where he writes, as for Buddhism "its radical thought is a selfish one"; or Barrows, *The Christian Conquest*, p. 171, where he asserts that Buddhism only teaches you to "be a refuge unto yourself."

compassionate guidance of all humankind. Further, as the Christian claim to universal validity could obviously be made much more effectively if its status as "bearer of the truth of compassion" remained uncontested, the allowance of similar capabilities to Buddhism was not to be given easily. The seeming parallels that could be drawn between Christianity and Japanese Buddhism, though potentially disconcerting, were in fact quickly discarded as superficial mimicry.

> "Almost everything that is distinctive in the Roman form of Christianity is to be found in Buddhism...vestments, masses, beads, wayside shrines, monasteries, nunneries, celibacy, fastings...." Nevertheless, these resemblances are almost wholly superficial and have little or nothing to do with genuine religion. [96]

> There is not a piece of dress, not a sacerdotal, not a ceremony of the court of Rome, which the Devil has not copied in this country [Japan].[97]

Eastern Buddhism, that is, Japanese Buddhism, set out to recast the terms by which it had been defined in the West. Drawing directly from the discursive strategies of nineteenth-century Protestantism Toki, for one, suggested that Buddhism should be described as practicing the "tenderest humanity" and "deepest sympathy" as it followed its "grand aspiration toward universal development and the benefit of mankind." Other writers asserted that Buddhism should be praised for its inherently rational character, its non-prejudicial stance toward women, and its practical and evolutionary, rather than speculative and static, nature.[98] To carry forth this message beyond the confines of the parliament's main stage, the Meiji Buddhists at Chicago held meetings in public halls, coffeehouses, and churches; they distributed literally tens of thousands of pamphlets discussing aspects of Mahāyāna Buddhism. These missionary efforts, the first ever by modern Buddhists, were so positively received that the Meiji Buddhists confidently concluded that the "West's misplaced love for the Hinayana" had been extinguished. By displaying the "brilliant, eternal, universal light of the truth of the Mahayana" while "waving the flag of universal love we have pacified the barbarian heart [*yashin*] of the

---

[96] Griffis, *The Religions of Japan*, pp. 301-02 (commenting on Basil H. Chamberlain's *Things Japanese*).

[97] Clarke, *Ten Great Religions*, p. 139.

[98] For Toki's comments see his "Buddhism in Japan," in *WPR*, 1:551; for the other suggestions see Matsuyama, *Bankoku shūkyō daikai gi*, p. 127.

white race."[99] The "formless form" of Eastern Buddhism, they determined, was precisely the universal principle needed to recast Buddhism as a world religion.

Pre-parliament nineteenth-century Japanese Buddhists were largely unaware of and uninterested in the particular forms of Buddhism found outside their own archipelago. The construction of a New Buddhism, eminently social, practical, and compatible with scientific principles and evolutionary laws, was in its early stages as reactionary as the attempt to distance the Mahāyāna from the Hīnayāna traditions. In the words of Yatsubuchi Banryū, Shin representative to the parliament: "If we desire to extend the influence of Japanese Buddhism to every aspect of our nation then we must, *like the Christianity of America and Europe,* become a Buddhism for the family, a Buddhism of marriage, a Buddhism for the workplace, a Buddhism for the military, a Buddhism for celebration, a Buddhism for all ages."[100]

Ashitsu Jitsunen had previously worked out an eleven-point program for a revitalization of Buddhism.[101] In addition to programs for incorporating Buddhism into each aspect of daily life (in the form of schools, Buddhist doctors, hospitals, and public lecture halls), he proposed the creation of a unified Buddhism: the Śakyamuni sect (J: *Shaka-shū*), transcendent of particular sectarian concerns, philosophically and politically adept, and active in foreign missionary work. Let us note the threefold aim of Ashitsu's proposed "revitalization" of Buddhism: (1) it will prevent further Christian expansion in Japan; (2) it will aid in the management of Japan itself (*kokutai o iji suru*); and (3) it will irrefutably demonstrate that "religion will exist as long as there are people in the world, or, in other words, religion is not bound for extinction as some suggest, but will change in accordance with the needs of the particular time and place....[W]ith

---

[99] A partial list of the texts distributed is *Outlines of the Mahayana as Taught by Buddha: A Brief Account of Shinshū, a Shinshū Catechism, Tendai Religion, Basic Principles of Nichiren,* and *The Essentials of Buddhism.* All were written by the Buddhists who attended the parliament, or by their teachers, and were published by their home churches; most were translated by Noguchi or Hirai. For comments on the publications and the quotes on the victory of the Mahāyāna see *WPR,* 1:442, 549; "Daikai rinsekisha kaeru kongo no undō ikan," *Kokkyō,* no. 28 (1893): 1-3; and "Daikai kichōgo dai'ikkai hōdo," *Kokkyō,* no. 28 (1893): 12-15.

[100] "Daikai no genjō oyobi kansatsu," *Kokkyō,* no. 31 (3/1894): 34-35 (emphasis mine).

[101] Ashitsu, *Nihon shūkyō mirai ki,* pp. 34-38.

these changes religion will be able to evolve (*shinka*) along with the world itself and thereby profit the nation and its people."[102] This amazing mixture of religious exclusivity, nationalism, and a naturalistic vision of a religious ontology was further highlighted by Ashitsu's analysis of Japanese history. By basing his argument upon principles of evolution and the operation of karmic law, Ashitsu interpreted events as individual contributions to the development of the national character of Japan vis-à-vis Buddhism. For example, Tendai Buddhism, after having taken up the sword and straying too far from Saichō's edict to "dwell in temporary huts,...regard living lightly and the law profoundly," had aroused the wrath of Nobunaga. Then, "Hiei merely used Nobunaga to purify itself" by means of its own destruction and thereby contributed significantly to the unification of the nation![103] It was in fact the form of argument used here by Ashitsu—the strength of the nation is derived from the strength of its constituent parts as they themselves evolve—that would be used over and again by "modern" religionists in Japan and elsewhere.

Yatsubuchi Banryū, adopting Comte, took this argument a step further and placed domestic changes within a schema of world evolution and thereby envisioned a universal revolution in the twentieth century: the Fourth Revolution. The sixteenth century saw the destruction of the unity of church and state (*seikyō bunri*) and the concomitant creation of a true religious faith (*shinsei naru shūkyō ryoku*); this was the first revolution in the spiritual development of humankind. The second revolution occurred in the eighteenth-century destruction of aristocratic rule and the establishment of universal rights (*ningen byōdō no dai ken*). The industrial revolution of the nineteenth century, as the third revolution, did indeed provide a freedom based upon the major increase in world wealth, but this new freedom simultaneously resulted in the sacrifice of a large portion of the faith and rights obtained in the first two revolutions. Though the previous revolutions in the spiritual advancement of humankind had been carried out largely in Europe, the culmination of the Three Great Revolutions (*sandai kakumei*) was to be the harmonization of East and West (*tōzai rōyō chōwa*). Moreover, the "general of the revolutionary army of the spiritual world" (*seishinkai kakumeigun no daigenshi*) will

---

[102] Ibid., pp. 55-56.
[103] Ashitsu, *Nihon shūkyō mirai ki*, p. 22.

be the religion of the twentieth century: Buddhism.[104] In other words, Yatsubuchi asserted that Buddhism would bring about the spiritualization of science; the domestic revolution of a newly formed social Buddhism was to coincide with the twentieth century's worldwide revolution of knowledge.

Christianity, unable to turn back the ills of materialistic progress, convened the Parliament of Religions. It sought, the Japanese Buddhists assumed, answers to its own dilemma by turning to the East. One chronicler of the parliament, following Spencer, asserted that the West (Christianity) had failed to actualize the radical distinction between "spiritual" teachings (*seishinteki; kyō*) and "material" study of the world (*bushitsuteki; gaku*).[105] Christianity, overwhelmed in the competition for materialistic survival (*bushitsuteki sezon kyōsō*), had not only lost its raison d'être but had, in fact, directly contributed to the West's "slavery to its own material wealth" (*tomi no dorei*).[106]

Shaku Sōen replied to this plea from Christianity with an explication of the logicality of the operation of Karmic retribution and codependent origination. He spoke of a "logical circle" of causality in operation at each particular configuration of time and space; he went on to link this *law* to the "law of nature," the eternally operating clock describing the "progress of the universe."[107] Since the Karmic Law, like Darwin's own, is applicable to all beings, the moral life of human beings is thereby equally determined by a logical calculus of evolution driven forth by the actions of particular individuals. Yatsubuchi (though disagreeing with Shaku on other issues) elsewhere elaborates that Christianity failed to comprehend modernity because of its failure to understand the evolutionary character of the world. He offered three reasons for this failure: Christianity (1) had elevated human beings almost to a point external to the world by giving them "dominion" over it; (2) had extended the right of dominion to the "chosen" versus the "damned"; and (3) had harbored an exclusive concern with the external world at the expense of the life of the spirit.

---

104 See "Daikai daisankai hōdō: kakumei taikan," *Kokkyō*, no. 30 (1894): 18-20; see also Yatsubuchi, *Shūkyō daikai hōdō*, pp. 50-53.
105 Matsuyama, *Bankoku shūkyō daikai gi*, pp. 71-75.
106 Ibid., p. 95; also Yatsubuchi, *Shūkyō daikai hōdō*, p. 12.
107 Shaku Sōen, "The Law of Cause and Effect, as Taught by Buddha," in *WPR*, 2:829-31.

All three points he traced to the unfortunate insistence upon an external, objective God.[108]

In short, the operation of "science" and the management of society based entirely upon some notion of control over the external world were at once the strength and doom of the West; concomitantly they were perceived as the strength and doom of Christianity in the world. Without the operation of a noncontingent yet immanent spirituality (which, the Meiji Buddhists were certain, had been fully revealed only in the teachings of Eastern Mahāyāna Buddhism), science, society, international politics, and so forth, would be but hollow hulks casting generations into servitude. Conversely, development of the material world based upon such a spirituality would result in a universal attainment to the "realm of the complete, perfect, and true civilization" (*kanzen emman naru shinsei bummei no iki*).[109]

Yatsubuchi, Toki, and Shaku—seemingly oblivious to their own ideologically complex participation in the reinterpretation of Buddhism into a socially efficacious religion—expected such undefined terms as "spirituality," "formless form," and so on, to carry the weight of their arguments. Within their Japanese-language publications the mere invocation of such code terms doubtlessly served more or less adequately to express to their audiences the vast and hopeful future they envisioned for Buddhism and Japan. Their English essays, however, quickly degenerate into bold statements fired without calculus into a poorly understood and largely uncaptivated audience.[110] Parallels between Christianity and Buddhism, produced in part through the incorporation of the prevailing terminology of the nineteenth-century Protestant discourse on religion, were responded to with both disdain and confusion. For example, such statements frequently contributed to the relegation of Buddhist thought to the

---

[108] Yatsubuchi, *Shūkyō daikai hōdō*, pp. 14-17.

[109] Ibid, p. 17.

[110] Regarding the general audience's reception of the Buddhists' *ideas*, there is a revealing comment made by Nomura, the main translator for the Buddhists, and recounted in Shaku's record: Nomura was asked by a gentleman in the audience if he had understood Toki Hōryū's talk on Buddhism. Nomura replied, "Certainly. And yourself?" To which the immediate answer was "Nope!" (*Iya!*) Shaku himself comments on this, saying it was not an unusual occurrence while they were at Chicago, and he lamented the amount of education necessary prior to any possible success in missionary work (Shaku, *Bankoku shūkyō*, p. 39).

"table rapping and spirit talk" of Theosophists along the order of Madame Blavatsky or Colonel Olcott.[111]

Circumambulation of the Globe

> A religious victory is an eternal victory! An indestructible victory! A victory among victories![112]

We should recall that the Buddhist delegates to Chicago were writing of international peace and the unity of humankind on the eve of the Sino-Japanese War. After their return to Japan the link between their missionary work and the national foreign service was strong. Yatsubuchi's discussion of a Fourth Revolution drew ammunition from the Tonghak Rebellion on the Korean peninsula; Ashitsu was attempting to coordinate the Buddhist continental missionary service when war broke out with China in August of 1894; and Shaku eventually spent several months in China organizing priests charged with administering to the troops. With an almost embarrassing rapidity, Buddhists in mid-Meiji Japan, acting under the lingering aftershocks of the early Meiji governmental stance on religion, readily joined Japan's continental expansionist program. Buddhism, they intoned, is both the true source and one of the few (if not the only) remaining bastions of Asian culture. They further asserted that Eastern Buddhism, the most evolutionarily advanced of the various forms of Buddhism (and containing these various forms within it), coupled with the materialistic wealth of (Japanese) technology, will begin the next revolution in Asia. Although there are obvious conceptual similarities between the mid-Meiji Buddhists and late Tokugawa thinkers, notably Sakuma Shōzan (1811-64), in the use of "Asian morality and Western technology," there are also important differences. First, "Asian morality" is specifically and exclusively identified for the Meiji era Buddhists with Japanese Buddhism; second, this New Buddhism is in a *direct relation* to the manipulation of the material world. It is not, as in

---

[111] Griffis, *The Religions of Japan*, pp. 173-74; "Blavatsky Lives: Not in Body but in Spirit," in *Inter-Ocean*, September 16, 1893, p. 1. Colonel Olcott, a sometime Theosophist, was well known in Japan, particularly among Buddhists concerned with the ongoing, and often emotional, debate between Christianity and Buddhism during this period. His popularity in Japan can be attributed largely to his "generous" comments on the Buddhist teachings and a certain derision directed toward the Protestantism of the day.

[112] Kōrai Hōsaku, representative of the Kyūshū Buddhist Youth Group on the occasion of Yatsubuchi's departure for Chicago; in "Yatsubuchi shi no banri ensei wo okuru," *Kokkyō*, no. 23 (6/1893): 24.

the case with Sakuma, a relation of underlying principle and external manifestation. In other words, for the Meiji Buddhists, Buddhism *is* moral and *is* technological; it is also Japan.

Nanjō Bun'yū, in his introduction to the *Short History of the Twelve Japanese Buddhist Sects*, echoing Yatsubuchi (echoing Comte), constructs a tripartite division for describing the development of Japanese Buddhism: ancient Hīnayāna schools, medieval syncretic sects, and the "modern" sects of Pure Land, Nichiren, and Zen.[113] The domestic development of Japanese Buddhism he regards as a microcosmic representation of the evolution of Buddhism itself, as it passed from the Hīnayāna in India, to the major syncretization of the Mahāyāna in China, and then to the "modern" creation of Zen and the faith sects begun in China and "completed" in Japan. Moreover, Nanjō notes that each stage of Buddhism flourished only within the period of its development; a prior age, after providing for advancement to a later one, quietly receded but did not disappear. The Fourth Revolution, borrowing Yatsubuchi's term, must reincorporate the activity of each aspect of Buddhism's history into a unified and universally promulgated teaching. In the introduction to a French translation of Nanjō's work, it is noted that since Indian and Chinese Buddhist practices are all but extinct (due to "connaissance insuffisante des doctrines profondes du Mahayana"), the term "Buddhism" itself can now refer only to Buddhism as found in Japan. "Aussi, ne donnons-nous le nom du Bouddhisme orthodoxe qu'à celui du Japon."[114] Nanjō's conception of the Fourth Revolution, following on the earlier revolutions from India to China to pre-Tokugawa Japan, and Yatsubuchi's, coming in the wake of the religious, political, and industrial revolutions of the West, unite in the form of Japanese Buddhism of the nineteenth century. This "New Buddhism" was conceived of as the moral and humanistic use of material sophistication and, concomitantly, as the rational operation of the Buddha dharma.

---

[113] Nanjio Bunyiu [sic], *A Short History of the Twelve Japanese Buddhist Sects* (Tokyo: Bukkyō Shoeiyaku Shuppan, 1886), pp. xix-xxxi, esp. p. xxix. The French version of this text, based upon Nanjō's English translation and not upon the original essay in Japanese (*Jūni shū kōyō*), provides another useful introduction to early attempts by Japanese Buddhists to "explain" or transmit correctly their doctrines to the West. See Fujishima Ryauon [sic], *Le Bouddhisme Japonais: doctrines et histoire des douze grandes sectes bouddhiques du Japon* (Paris: Maisonneuve et Ch. Leclerc, 1889).

[114] Fujishima, *Le Bouddhisme Japonais*, pp. iv-v.

The World's Parliament of Religions was viewed as an excellent platform from which to launch this quest for the Fourth Revolution. Buddhism could be demonstrated there in all its Mahāyānistic sophistication. (There was, we should note, very little sympathy by the Japanese Buddhists for the Hīnayāna priests from India; Shaku, for example, regularly edited out their speeches from his chronicle of the parliament.) Further, schooling of Buddhist missionaries for the future could be based upon lessons drawn directly from the eclectic atmosphere of heady universalism that permeated the conferences and the long hours spent in the special "Buddhist Room" discussions.[115] The four priests and one layman from Japan, called the "pioneers of Buddhist missionary work" (*bukkyō kaigai sekkyō no kōshisha*), were likened unto the Chinese and Indian priests who carried the dharma from India to China and were assured of the transcendent support of Emperor Kimmei.[116] Moreover, they were advised that as Columbus had merely discovered the "America of form" (in search of wealth in order to finance another crusade against the Muslim world), the Buddhist missionaries would have the opportunity to reveal the "formless America" and thereby create an "unexcelled nation of nirvana" (*mujō no dai nehan koku*).[117] This would serve to further Buddhism's inexorable march to the east, whereby it would both spiritually and, in the bodies of its missionaries and temples, physically circumambulate the globe. Yatsubuchi was perhaps the most active in promoting Buddhist missionary work abroad. He emphasized the need for language and secular education at crucial adjuncts to "rigorous spiritual training" (*seishinteki kunren*) for missionaries. He also suggested two areas that should be of immediate concern for a missionary Buddhism: (1) to work among Japanese immigrants to other nations or, as he called them, "our people, our faithful" (*waga kokumin, waga shinto*); and (2) to provide spiritual "training" (again

---

[115] This was a room within the parliament's building set aside for more "in depth" discussions of Buddhism than were possible otherwise. Hirai, whose superb English made him the most desired speaker there, was said to have been so busy "that he consistently went without meals or rest in order to speak about Buddhism." See Yatsubuchi, *Shūkyō daikai hōdō*, p. 45; Shaku, *Bankoku shūkyō daikai ichiran*, p. 30; and the remarks by Hirai quoted by Barrows, "History," in *WPR*, 1:165-66.

[116] Reigned 539-571; Kimmei is generally recognized as the emperor during whose reign Buddhism first entered Japan.

[117] See "Bankoku Shūkyō Daikai rinsekisha Yatsubuchi o okuru," *Kokkyō*, no. 23 (1893): 1-2, 22-24; "Toki Hōryū shi gai san kōsō ichi koji no raibei no to [michi] ni noboraru ohōji," *Dentō*, no. 51 (1893): 1-3.

kunren, not just "guidance") to the military. "Flashing like a sword and glittering like a flower" (*ken to narite hirameji, hana to narite kagayaku*), the Imperial Army and Navy can, like the faithful Muslims who defeated the Russians in the Crimea, or the soldiers of the Hongan-ji who held back the armies of Nobunaga, face all trials and tribulations with confidence and strength.[118] The Fourth Revolution was to be fought in the name of the Buddha dharma and in the hope of Nirvāṇa by soldier priests (*sōryo hei*) certain of the worldwide evolutionary processes that led up to and assured victory in the upcoming conflict.

Conclusion

The World's Parliament of Religions was constructed out of a patchwork of nineteenth-century evangelical Christianity, particular readings of evolutionary theory as applied to ethnology and cultural anthropology, and the use of positivistic philosophy for the comparative analysis of religion. Eastern Buddhism, in the form of the five Meiji Buddhists at Chicago, was conceived by the West as an object of both fascination and aggression; it was they whose inclusion into the world of the parliament was necessary for the spiritual unification of "all the world." The Japanese Buddhists agreed. But the terms of this unification, though formed out of readings of Darwinian and Spencerian thought, and drawing heavily upon Müller's comparative "Science of Religion," were recast into specifically Buddhist language. Evolution is evident, revolution is imminent; but it is Buddhism, they reasoned, not Christianity, that is most capable of serving as the spiritual guide to technology, as the more universal manifestation of the love of humankind. And not surprisingly, both Christians and Buddhists were convinced they had persuaded the other of the futility of the other's claims and of the final superiority of their own truths.

Hirai Kinzō, lay Buddhist representative to the parliament, was by far the most eloquent of the Buddhist representatives from Japan. As the next day's press releases suggest, his paper, "The Real Position of Japan Toward Christianity," was a genuinely risky presentation of great vehemence. "At the center of the platform stood a slender and delicate looking Japanese priest. His voice trembled in the fervor of his

---

[118] See *Kokkyō*, no. 31 (1894). This, after all that occurred in the early Meiji critique, cannot help but bring pause. The strength of Buddhism, here "as always," is interpreted as being in combat, where life and death are "not-two" at each and every moment.

feeling and the strange robes of his office were forgotten in the eloquence of his utterances....It was like a voice out of darkness, a cry of oppression from a strange land. It came to the thousands of Christians who listened as a thunderblast, and when the priest had finished, the people rose again to their feet and gave him three mighty cheers."[119]

Hirai himself later noted that "I expected that before I had finished my address...I should be torn from the platform." It was indeed so potentially offensive that Barrows had at first refused to allow Hirai to present his paper.[120] Hirai was quite careful to state at the outset of his presentation that the goal of "religious affinity," that is, the goal of the parliament, was being severely impeded by self-motivated diplomats and economically minded persons. Incidents involving this sort of individual can be found literally "everywhere," but one example bearing particular notice is the presence of Christianity in Japan. After recognizing Tokugawa Iemitsu's (1604-51) mid-seventeenth-century suppression of the Shimabara rebellion and his banning of Christianity as a legitimate response to an external government's intended subjugation of Japan, Hirai went on to enumerate the current status of Japan vis-à-vis the so-called Christian Nations. Noting the unequal treaties between Japan and Western powers that guaranteed the latter nations the rights of extraterritoriality and tariff regulation in Japan, and continuing with a heartfelt attack on various injustices against Japanese citizens abroad resulting from exclusionist policies, Hirai goes on to assert that the Japanese people popularly conceived of as "idolaters and heathen" in the West are by virtue of this moral and ontological interpretation of their national essence relegated to a position outside the "principle of civilized law." If Christian ethics is that which, in the guise of international law, maintains that "the rights and profits of the uncivilized, or the weaker, should be sacrificed" for the sake of the

---

[119] *Chicago Daily Times*, September 14, 1893, p. 1.

[120] For Hirai's essay in English see *WPR*, 1:44-50; for the Japanese version see Matsuda Jin'emon, ed., *Hirai Kinzo shi bankoku shūkyō daikai enzetsu* (Kyoto: Yūshichū, 1894). For his comments on the speech's reception see *Kokkyō*, no. 31 (1894): 34; Yatsubuchi, *Shūkyō daikai hōdō*, p. 39; and Shaku, *Bankoku shūkyō daikai ichiran*, p. 130. Regarding the actual presentation of the paper, Barrows himself says only that the paper was "lost" and thus he thought it could not be presented (see Mary Barrows, *John Henry Barrows*, pp. 278, 281), whereas Shaku and Yatsubuchi recount their anger, as well as Hirai's carefully gauged attack, directed toward Barrows for his seeming lack of support.

stronger, then those who "refuse to swallow the sweet and warm liquid of the heaven of Christianity" cannot be seen as unreasonable if they remain "perfectly satisfied to be heathen." Hirai continues by saying that he is confident that there are sincere efforts being made in the West to overcome this "false Christianity" (as an example he notes the Emancipation Proclamation). The emotional conclusion of his presentation was heightened by quoting the preamble to the Declaration of Independence in its entirety and by asserting that the same call of "liberty or death" heard at the founding of America can be heard today in Japan. "If any religion urges the injustice of humanity, I will oppose it, as I have ever opposed it, with my body and soul." Hirai's performance was unsurpassed. He "out-Christianized" the Christians and "out-Americanized" the Americans. His appeal for religious, racial, and national equality for Japan was couched in the same language as the basic sentiments of the founding fathers of the United States. Coupling this appeal for "liberty or death" with the hard facts of an increasingly oppressed Japanese government in the realms of international politics and economics *and* a portrayal of an obviously compromised and divisive history of missionary Christianity in Japan, Hirai succeeded in driving home his point as few foreign delegates were able to do. His use of a realpolitik presentation of current relations stripped away the thin veneer of "brotherhood" that had been evoked by almost every parliamentarian and had been used to cover the severe fissures that riddled the parliament's cosmopolitan project. Hirai laid the groundwork for genuine cultural interaction based upon a healthy respect for real difference.

In the willingness to remain "heathen," which in itself must have been a serious shock to the evangelical sensibilities of the audience, Hirai allowed for the continued possibility of a critique of the universalist conception set forth by Christianity and given form in the Parliament of Religions. His criticisms were not directed solely against the West, for in a later work Hirai makes similar charges against Japan as well; the farce of people's rights in a land governed by wealth and diplomacy, and the resultant servitude of large segments of the populace (women and workers) required for the perpetuation of such a system, is contingent upon some carefully constructed, and co-opted, notion of the "other" *as a means to terminate positions of possibly destructive critique.*[121] Hirai—in notable contradiction to Yatsubuchi,

---

[121] See Hirai's *Shūkyō to seiji* (Kyoto: Kendō Shoin, 1898), passim.

Ashitsu, and Nanjō—asserts that religion, far from being the inviolate locus of any universalist discourse, must remain as a position in flux, a place at risk. Indeed, for Hirai, "religion is the savior of society" (*shūkyō wa shakai no kyūseisha nari*), not because it is social or becomes society itself but *because it remains a position from which forceful critiques of law and of economy within an institutional society can be made.* (This would, of course, include critiques of institutional religion as well.) This very locus of critique, moreover, cannot be thought of as distinct from society (here parting with Kant), for then it purports to be beyond critique itself and is thus rendered ineffective, or rather, contributes to the very discourse it purports to examine (as in Yatsubuchi's Fourth Revolution). The problem here is not so much who has the power but rather power itself. A religious practice that refuses to be either belief in politics or the politics of belief can for the first time allow, perhaps, for the possibility of critical compassion.

The Japanese Buddhists returned to their homeland as true conquering heroes. They were fêted and paraded and traveled the countryside giving speeches on the material marvels of the West and on their own equally marvelous successes in promulgating the teachings of the Buddha. Variously described as "thunder," "brilliant light," or "seeds of the future," the Buddhist presence at the "exposition of humanity" was touted as having refuted conceptions of Buddhism as a historically artificial construct, as nihilism, as idol worship, and as anti- or a-social. The elevation of "Buddhism," conceived of as a cultural product of the particular geopolitical area of the "Orient," to the position of an international and, as the returning parliamentarians would have us believe, sophisticated evangelical tool, was put to immediate use in the domestic reconstruction of images of modern and nationalistic Buddhism. By the close of the nineteenth century the earlier historical, nationalistic, and socio-economic attacks upon Buddhism had indeed largely been put to rest. These themes did, however, remain constant areas of debate. Subsequent domestic versions of the World's Parliament, designed to effect transsectarian and transreligious unity, were held in the last years of the Meiji era. The most widely publicized of these meetings were the two Religionists' Conferences (*Shūkyōka kondankai*). The first, attended by forty-two prominent religious figures representing Shinto, Buddhism, Christianity, and various independent groups, was held for one day 1896; the second was an almost exclusively Christian affair and in fact appears to have been little more than a fête for Barrows, who was on the last leg of his Asian preaching tour. Both of these highly visible meetings claimed to assert the "evolutionary and social" character of religion. However, within late Meiji-era Japan "evolutionary" translated into a willingness to compromise, and "social" was interpreted as the need to cooperate with the state ideological apparatus. Religious unity was obtained, that is, in combined protestations of the reverence for imperial rule.

In 1904, an anti-war essay by Tolstoy was published in both the weekly *Heimin shimbun* and the daily *Tokyo Asahi* newspapers. In this article Tolstoy quotes the contemporarily prominent Zen Buddhist priest Shaku Sōen, also of parliament fame, as he (Sōen) attempted to justify Buddhism's support of recent wars carried out by the Japanese Imperial Army and Navy. Shaku's statement as quoted by Tolstoy, in part, is as follows: "Even though the Buddha teaches not to take another's life, he also teaches that all sentient beings through the exercise of infinite compassion will be united and thereby obtain final and ultimate peace. As means toward the harmonizing of the incompatible, killing and war are necessary."[122]

Shaku, like Yatsubuchi, Shimaji, and to a lesser extent Nanjō, firmly links the world of the spirit and the contemporary world of form. Because of the final, ultimate justification of the perfect unity of the spirit of all humankind, the temporal manipulation of certain "sentient beings" is not only possible, it is in fact necessary. This trend among late Meiji sectarian Buddhists toward what we can call yet another attempt to *unite religion and politics (seikyō itchi)*, this time based upon a new scientism of cooperative global evolution, carried with it consequences, such as evidenced in the quote by Shaku, radically in opposition to some of the fundamental tenets of Buddhism. This new *seikyō itchi* is, distinct from the early Meiji attempt legislated by the government, initiated by the Buddhists themselves and all the more lasting because of it.

Yet, in contrast to such statements by Shaku and like-minded nationalist or imperialist Buddhists, we should also note that Hirai's

---

[122] This quote can be found in Yoshida, *Shakaishi*, p. 433, and in Tamamuro Taijo, *Nihon bukkyōshi*, 3:377-78. Shaku, like many other Meiji era Buddhist priests, actively supported Japan's continental expansion. In 1912 he even made an extensive lecture tour, as a guest of the Southern Manchurian Railways Company, through Korea and Manchuria; the theme of his talks was "the spirit of the Yamato race." See Furuta Shokuin, "Shaku Sōen: The Footsteps of a Modern Zen Master," *Philosophical Studies of Japan* 8 (August 1967): 67-91.

work sought to obtain just the opposite. Though Hirai actually uses the term *seikyō itchi* as both desirable and obtainable, it is meant in a very different way. For Hirai, religion is not used to further the designs of the political world; rather, religion by its very nature necessarily partakes in an undeniable politicality. Religion is an integral element of the social order and as such must serve as both a moral and an ethical guide, as well as a tool for expanded social production and the distribution of wealth, and clearly not as a mere handmaiden to the military. It is not surprising, however, that Hirai's work is all but ignored, whereas the missionary efforts of the sectarian Buddhists are the subject of frequent and extensive praise.

There were other attempts to remove religion from the privileged realm of the religionists. A young reporter at the Religionists' Conferences, Anesaki Masaharu, was convinced that *students* of religion and *religionists* had dramatically different aims in approaching their ostensibly mutual object. (It is interesting and somewhat ironic that Anesaki here has taken up the earlier division—used by, among others, the Ministry of Doctrine—between teaching/*kyō* and study/*gaku*.) The attempt to separate religion from the confines of belief and thus place it within the larger problem of history and society was in fact begun with critiques of Buddhism, such as found in Tominaga's work, several generations prior to this time. Anesaki and others, like his predecessor Kishimoto Nobuta, expanded upon this methodology with the use of contemporary histo-critical and philological techniques. Religion in general, and Buddhism in particular, was being constituted as a discipline, as a field for scientific inquiry. This historicization of Buddhism should not, however, be seen as a withdrawal of Buddhism from society. Rather, following Hirai's claim of the inherent politicality of religion, it is an increased recognition of the volatile nature of conflicting definitions of the absolute. Or, in the words of Murakami Senshō, one of the first generation of Buddhist historians: "It is extremely difficult to criticize war when one's place of enunciation is located within the state. It is only when one takes a position outside the state [for example] in religion...that war can be shown as evil."[123]

---

[123] Yoshida, *Shakaishi*, p. 434.

Waking Up from Akbar's Dream
The Literary Prefiguration of Chicago's 1893 World's Parliament of Religions

※※※

Eric J. Ziolkowski

1.

From Max Müller to Martin Marty, scholarly treatments of Chicago's 1893 World's Parliament of Religions have focused on its momentousness as a watershed event in the history of religions, American religious history, interfaith-dialogue, East-West dialogue, and indeed, human history.[1] Müller, who deeply regretted having failed to attend the parliament, echoed the statements of many when he called it "one of the most memorable events in the history of the world," a convention that "stands unique, stands unprecedented in the whole history of the world."[2] Despite countless similar accolades, however, one of the parliament's most curious aspects has hardly been considered: its prefiguration in Western literature. No one will deny the legacy left in American literature by Chicago's Columbian Exposition, the renowned world's fair of which the religion parliament was one of twenty auxiliary congresses. In its awesome grandeur, that exposition inspired dozens of poems, and figures as an important setting in thirteen novels that appeared in its wake. Consistent with its

"Waking Up from Akbar's Dream: The Literary Prefiguration of Chicago's 1893 World's Parliament of Religions," by Eric J. Ziolkowski. ©1993 by The University of Chicago. Reprinted with permission of The University of Chicago Press from *The Journal of Religion* 73 (1993): 42-60.

[1] For an overview of much of the secondary literature that has built up around this event, see in this volume the article by Richard Hughes Seager.

[2] Quoted from the article by F. Max Müller in this volume.

depiction by contemporary journalists, several of those novels, now obscure, present the fair's "White City" in religious terms as a sacred space removed from the flux of temporality: a "New Jerusalem" or "Celestial City."[3] But the fact that the very conception of a World's Parliament of Religions was anticipated and, as we shall see, to some extent inspired by a certain theme running through prior Western literature, has been overlooked.

This oversight can be explained, in part, by the peculiarly modern Western tendency to construe religion and literature as separate spheres of human activity. This distinction was enforced programmatically by the Columbian Exposition's Congress Auxiliary, whose president was a Chicago lawyer and civic leader, Charles Carroll Bonney. The Congress Auxiliary sponsored a Congress on Literature two months prior to the Parliament of Religions, but apparently made no effort to establish any formal connection between the two meetings. The literary congress, recognized as "the first gathering of its kind ever attempted by an English-speaking people,"[4] and considered widely to be "one of the most significant of all the congresses,"[5] convened July 10-15 and consisted of sections on philology, folkore, history, libraries, and literature proper,[6] as well as branches in copyright law, criticism, and material interests of authors. Aside from the inclusion of religions as a subject for discussion in its folklore section,[7] this congress had no practical bearing on the much more protracted and acclaimed religion parliament that met September 11-27.

Conceived by Bonney, and chaired by a prominent Presbyterian minister of Chicago, John Henry Barrows, the World's Parliament of Religions was heralded as the first convention of its kind ever to invite and attract participants from all over the earth. With a program that included two hundred speakers representing Hinduism, Judaism, Christian denominations, Buddhism, Roman Catholicism, Greek

---

[3] See Eric J. Ziolkowski, "Heavenly Visions and Worldly Intentions: Chicago's Columbian Exposition and World's Parliament of Religions (1893)," *The Journal of American Culture* 13 (1990):9-15, esp. pp. 12-14. See also David F. Burg, "Visions of the Celestial City," chap. 7 of *Chicago's White City of 1893* (Lexington: University of Kentucky Press, 1976), pp. 286-348.

[4] Walter Besant, "Literary Conferences," *The Contemporary Review* 65 (1894): 124. Compare Rossiter Johnson, "The Congress on Literature," chap. 6 of *Congresses*, vol. 4 of *A History of the World's Columbian Exposition Held in Chicago in 1893*, ed. Rossiter Johnson, 4 vols. (New York: D. Appleton, 1897-98), pp. 160-78, see p. 169.

[5] Burg, *Chicago's White City of 1893*, p. 251.

[6] "The Literature Congresses," *The Dial* 15 (July 1, 1893): 5-7.

[7] See Johnson, ed., *History*, 4:176.

Orthodox Christianity, Islam, Shinto, Confucianism, Parseeism, Taoism, Jainism, and certain "ethnic" faiths, the parliament attracted a total of some 150,000 spectators over its seventeen-day period and was esteemed as the Congress Auxiliary's "crowning glory."[8] The event was in Marty's words "the most elaborate display of religious cosmopolitanism yet seen on the continent," epitomizing what he calls the "cosmopolitan habit" among modernists in late nineteenth-century American liberal theology.[9] Although, of the parliament's ten stated objectives, the sixth was "to secure from leading scholars, representing [the world's religions],...full and accurate statements of the spiritual and other effects of the Religions which they hold upon the Literature, Art, Commerce, [etc.]...of the peoples among whom these Faiths have prevailed,"[10] only two of the parliament's papers were devoted to "literary" topics.[11]

While the 1893 parliament has been ignored by literary scholars, and while its debt to Western literature has not been acknowledged by theologians, scholars of religions, or the planners of a 1993 centennial celebration of the original event, the Western literary tradition furnishes an illuminating context in which to consider the event. This tradition, needless to say, yields a plethora of texts reflecting the legacy of religious suspicion, polemics, and intolerance that have plagued the West over the centuries—for example, from the Middle High German poem *Das Jüdel* and Dante's *Inferno* (with its placement of Muhammad ["Mäometto"] and Ali in the eighth of hell's nine circles [canto 28, lines 31-32]), through Tasso's *Gerusalemme Liberata*, Marlowe's *The Jew of Malta*, and Shakespeare's *The Merchant of Venice* of the late sixteenth century, to Byron's *The Giaour* (1813).[12] Nonetheless, as I shall show, the kernel idea of a fraternal meeting of the world's religions is prefigured in a concurrent maverick theme of religious tolerance that had been emergent in Western literature since

---

[8] Charles Carroll Bonney, "The World's Parliament of Religions: Opening Session," in his *World's Congress Addresses* (Chicago: Open Court Publishing, 1900), p. 4. Compare John Henry Barrows, "Review and Summary," in *WPR*, 2:1568-82; the article by Barrows in the present volume; and Rossiter Johnson, "The World's Parliament of Religions," in Johnson, ed., *History*, vol. 4, chap. 8: 221-337.

[9] See Marty's chapter in this volume.

[10] Quoted by John Henry Barrows, "The History of the Parliament," in *WPR*, 1:18.

[11] See Theodore T. Munger, "Christianity as Interpreted by Literature," in *WPR*, 1:677-92; and Milton S. Terry, "The Sacred Books of the World as Literature," in *WPR*, 1:694-704.

[12] I am grateful to Anthony C. Yu for suggesting to me the last four examples listed.

the Middle Ages and that impressed itself upon the parliament's chairman through the poetry of Alfred Tennyson.

The reason that the vision behind this theme did not—and could not—become a reality at the religion parliament might best be explained in terms of the threefold theological distinction between exclusivism (rejection of other faiths), inclusivism (acceptance of the spiritual power manifest in other faiths, but rejection of their sufficiency for salvation apart from Christ), and pluralism (acceptance of all faiths, including Christianity, as possessing partial knowledge of God).[13] The parliament's raison d'être precluded an exclusivist position. This was borne out by the strong dissent expressed by certain religious leaders at the very idea of such a parliament, including the Sultan of Turkey and the Archbishop of Canterbury. The latter's appeal to "the fact that the Christian religion is the one religion" and hence cannot "be regarded as a member of a Parliament of Religions without assuming the equality of the other intended members,"[14] hearkens back uncannily to the classic expression of religious bigotry offered up by the cleric Thwackum in Fielding's *Tom Jones* (1749): "When I mention religion I mean the Christian religion; and not only the Christian religion, but the Protestant religion; and not only the Protestant religion, but the Church of England."[15] As it turned out, however, the parliament stood for an inclusivist rather than a truly pluralist position, as some of the parliament's promoters and participants sought to use the event as a forum in which to demonstrate the supremacy of their own faith over others. Consequently, the parliament failed to enact that imaginative or literary vision that had helped inspire its conception, a vision of genuine religious pluralism that anticipated various pluralist speculations proffered in our own century, including those of Frithjof Schuon (on "the transcendent unity of religions"), William Ernest Hocking (on the possibility of a "world faith"), and John Hick (on the "many names" of God or Ultimate Reality). That failure offers a monumental illustration of what the literary critic Northrop Frye had in mind when he spoke of the capacity of poetry and literature, as opposed to committed religious beliefs, to encourage tolerance:

---

[13] I borrow these well-known categories from Alan Race, *Christians and Religious Pluralism: Patterns in the Christian Theology of Religions* (Maryknoll, N.Y.: Orbis, 1982).

[14] Quoted by Barrows, "History," in *WPR*, 1:20, 22.

[15] Henry Fielding, *The History of Tome Jones, A Foundling*, Modern Library (New York: Random House, 1943), book 3, chap. 3, p. 84.

What produces the tolerance is the power of detachment in the imagination, where things are removed just out of reach of belief and action. Experience is nearly always commonplace; the present is not romantic in the way that the past is, and ideals and great visions have a way of becoming shoddy and squalid in practical life. Literature reverses this process. When experience is removed from us a bit, as the experience of the Napoleonic war is in Tolstoy's *War and Peace*, there's a tremendous increase of dignity and exhilaration....There is an element of illusion even in *War and Peace*, but the illusion gives us a reality that isn't in the actual experience of the war itself: the reality of proportion and perspective, of seeing what it's all about, that only detachment can give. Literature helps to give us that detachment.[16]

I shall return to this point in my conclusion.

2.

While the 1893 Parliament of Religions was truly unprecedented in its global breadth, the idea behind it was not wholly new; indeed, the "quest for human unity" appears to be an irrepressible human impulse whose evolving expressions can be traced through the "inner" as well as the "outer" meanings of the world's religions.[17] As Barrows acknowledged, the parliament committee began its planning under the impression that nothing like the parliament had ever been assembled, let alone dreamed of. Several of the invited speakers soon drew comparisons with the Buddhist council summoned Pāṭaliputra by the Buddhist emperor Aśoka in 242 B.C.E., and the meeting at Delhi of Muslims, Brahmans, Jains, Zoroastrians, Jews, and Christians, sponsored by the sixteenth-century Mogul emperor Akbar, a figure whose life and accomplishments were still not well known in the West at the time of the parliament.[18] However, as Müller and others would

---

[16] Northrop Frye, *The Educated Imagination* (Bloomington: Indiana University Press, 1964), pp. 78-79.

[17] See Joseph Mitsuo Kitagawa, *The Quest for Human Unity: A Religious History* (Minneapolis: Fortress, 1990).

[18] The comparison with Aśoka's Pāṭaliputra congress was first drawn by Anagārika Dharmapāla in his untitled welcoming address during the parliament's opening session (quoted by Barrows, "History" in *WPR*, 1:8, 95). The comparison with Akbar's convention of religious representatives was drawn by Rev. E.L. Rexford and Rev. Joseph Cook, both of Boston, in their respective papers presented during meetings on the fourth day ("The Religious Intent," in *WPR*, 1:509; and "Strategic Certainties of Comparative Religion," in *WPR*, 1:536), and by Prof. J. Estlin Carpenter on the eighth day ("The Need for a Wider Conception of Revelation, or Lessons from the Sacred Books of the World," in *WPR*, 2:842). Compare the remark by Maya Das, a leading Christian of India (quoted by Barrows, "History," in *WPR*, 1:30). Both comparisons were alluded to by Vivekananda on the ninth day ("Hinduism," in *WPR* 2:977). Regarding Akbar's reputation in the West, Vincent Arthur Smith made the following claim

point out, neither of those two meetings, nor the "ecumenical" council of Christians at Nicaea in 325 C.E., was congruous with the 1893 parliament at Chicago; unlike the latter, where all the world religions were represented, the councils of Pāṭaliputra and Nicaea were exclusively Buddhist and Christian affairs, while the Delhi meeting lacked representatives of Buddhism, Confucianism, and Taoism, and was aimed at realizing Akbar's idea of founding a new religion.

More provocative than the comparisons of the 1893 parliament with earlier religious councils is Müller's passing suggestion about its literary pertinence: "If the Religious Parliament was not an entirely new idea, it was certainly the first realization of an idea which has lived silently in the hearts of prophets, or has been uttered now and then by poets only, who are free to dream dreams and to see visions."[19] Rather than pick up on this compelling hint, which anticipates Frye's concept of literature as "man's revelation to man,"[20] scholars who have discussed the parliament after Müller have either overlooked, or been content to ignore, a distinct theme in Western literature that helped inspire its conception. Having emerged in a lineage of medieval European texts, recurred in some works by German and English romantics, and crystallized in English and American literature during the Victorian age, this theme expressed the envisagement of a reconciliation, or an underlying unity, of the world's religions and became both a catalyst to and a symptom of the gradual opening up of Western consciousness toward "Oriental" cultures and religions during the nineteenth century.

Literary reflections on religious pluralism are traceable at least as far back as Judah ha Levi's *Kitab al Khazari* (twelfth century), known also as the *Kuzari*, one of the most important texts of medieval Jewish literature.[21] At the book's opening, the King of the Khazars dreams

---

the exhaustive treatment of the life of Akbar will be in possession of, perhaps, the finest great historical subject as yet unappropriated" (in W.H. Sleeman, *Rambles and Recollections of an Indian Official*, ed. Vincent Arthur Smith, new ed., 2 vols. [Westminster: Archibald Constable, 1893], 1:391 n.2). Smith later quotes that remark in his *Akbar: The Great Mogul 1542-1605* (1917; rev. ed., Oxford: Clarendon Press, 1919), p. v.

[19] Quoted from Müller's article in this volume. Müller was not the first to make this observation; according to Barrows, "Dr. [William Alexander Parsons] Martin, President of the Imperial University of Peking, reported that the idea of such a congress had often appeared in fiction and poetry" ("The History of the Parliament," in *WPR*, 1:8).

[20] Frye, *The Educated Imagination*, p. 105.

[21] Judah Halevi, *The Kuzari (Kitab al Khazari): An Argument for the Faith of Israel*, trans. Hartwig Hirschfeld (1905; reprint, New York: Schocken, 1964).

that his way of thinking is agreeable to God, but not his way of acting, and he is commanded in this dream to seek the work that is pleasing to God. Inspired by the dream, he engages in a series of short dialogues on theological matters with a Hellenistic philosopher, a Christian scholastic, and a doctor of Islam, hearing out each of their arguments for their respective faiths but rejecting them all, before being won over by the contentions for Judaism set forth by a rabbinic sage.

While the bulk of the *Kuzari*—from the rabbi's arrival to the end of the book—constitutes a sustained argument for the religion of Israel alone, the initial theme of the open-minded, truth-seeking king interviewing representatives of several different faiths seems but one step away from conveying a genuinely pluralist message. The same is true of the tale in the *Gesta Romanorum* of a dying man who has two duplicates made of his precious ring and then bequeaths one each to his three sons; the tale concludes with a demonstration of the authenticity of the real ring (symbolizing Christian faith, as opposed to Jewish or Islamic) through its power to effect a miracle.[22] A Christian transformation of a Jewish anecdote found in the *Scebet Jehuda*, this frequently rehearsed story[23] drops its exclusivist (some would say bigoted) message when it is retold in the *Novellino* or *Cento novelle antiche* (late-thirteenth or early fourteenth century; tale 73), in Boccaccio's *Decamerone* (mid-fourteenth century; day 1, tale 3), and in G.E. Lessing's verse drama *Nathan der Weise* (1779). In these later versions, a cautious Jew tells the story to avoid an awkward situation before the Sultan of the Saracens, and asserts that the real ring's authenticity must remain undetermined in this world. Told this way, the parable implies that competing religious systems, or at least the three "revealed" monotheisms, have equal claims to truth. In the *Novellino* and the *Decamerone*, whose authors lived in the wake of the crusades, the parable conveys a daring lesson of religious tolerance, if not agnosticism as well.[24] In *Nathan der Weise*, which was written in a

---

[22] "Of the Triple State of the World," tale 89 of *Gesta Romanorum: Entertaining Stories Invented by the Monks as a Fire-Side Recreation and Commonly Applied in Their Discourses from the Pulpit Whence the Most Celebrated of Our Own Poets and Others Have Extracted Their Plots*, trans. Charles Swan, Broadway Translations, 1st ed. (London: George Routledge, [1924]), p. 215.

[23] Documentation of the various texts in which this story recurs from the thirteenth century on is provided by Peter Demetz in his section on "Traditionen der Märe von den drei Ringen," in his *Gotthold Ephraim Lessing: Nathan der Weise* (Berlin: Ullstein, 1966), pp. 200-16.

[24] For example, Robert Burton, *Anatomy of Melancholy*, ed. A. R. Shilleto, 3 vols. (London: George Bell and Sons, 1893), 3:445, cited by Thomas G. Bergin, *Boccaccio* (New York: Viking, 1981), p. 359, n. 30, who observes that "Filomena's listeners,

much more tolerant time (despite the official silencing of Lessing shortly before for his having edited a historical-critical work on Jesus by the free-thinker H. S. Reimarus), the same parable illustrates the play's claim to a unified humanity transcending racial and credal differences.

The theme of Lessing's play, summed up by Paul Tillich as "the relativism of religions,"[25] finds a striking variation in the earliest of William Blake's illuminated prints, *All Religions are One*. Engraved in England in 1789, a decade after *Nathan der Weise* appeared in Germany, this terse text comprises an "argument" and seven aphoristic "principles," of which the last three read as follows:

> PRINCIPLE 5. The Religions of all Nations are derived from each Nations different reception of the Poetic Genius which is every where call'd the Spirit of Prophecy.
>
> PRINCIPLE 6. The Jewish & Christian Testaments are An original derivation from the Poetic Genius. This is necessary from the confined nature of bodily sensation.
>
> PRINCIPLE 7th. As all men are alike (tho' infinitely various) So all Religions & as all similars have one source.
>
> The true Man is the source he being the Poetic Genius.[26]

Consistent with the tendency to naturalize the supernatural that M. H. Abrams has shown to typify romantic literature,[27] Blake's idea that all religions are one is inextricably related to his own theory of art. That idea, as Frye, interprets it, "means that the material world provides a universal language of images and that each man's imagination speaks that language with his own accent. Religions are grammars of this language."[28]

The groundwork that was being laid for a scientific study of comparative religion during the time of Lessing and Blake was directly

---

perhaps a little uneasy, make no comment on her story" (p. 229). J.H. Whitfield points out that the *Decameron*'s version of this tale "has been taken sometimes...as the coming of the Renascence, setting men free from the restraints of religion and morality" (*A Short History of Italian Literature* [Harmondsworth, Middlesex: Penguin, 1960], p. 58).

[25] Paul Tillich, *A History of Christian Thought, from Its Judaic and Hellenistic Origins to Existentialism*, ed. Carl E. Braaten (New York: Simon and Schuster, 1967), p. 369.

[26] William Blake, *The Complete Poetry and Prose of William Blake*, ed. David V. Erdman, rev. ed. (Garden City, N.Y.: Anchor, 1982), pp. 1-2.

[27] See M.H. Abrams, *Natural Supernaturalism: Tradition and Revolution in Romantic Literature* (New York: Norton, 1973).

[28] Northrop Frye, *Fearful Symmetry: A Study of William Blake* (1947; reprint, Princeton, N.J.: Princeton University Press, 1969), p. 28.

pertinent to their respective notions of the relativism and the oneness of religions. Both authors were participants in the eighteenth-century debate over the concept of natural religion and in the growing discussion on the relationships between different types of religion. On the one hand, Lessing's little treatise *Die Erziehung des Menschengeschlechts* (1780; *The Education of the Human Race*), which traces a development from polytheism, through the monotheism of Judaism and the ethic of Christianity, to an anticipated world of reason and peace governed by autonomous reason, is generally regarded as an important contribution to the Enlightenment discussion of natural religion that anticipated the emergence of a bona fide scientific study of religions during the nineteenth century.[29] The consistency of Lessing's progressivist philosophy of religious history with the anti-sectarian theme of *Nathan der Weise* speaks for itself. On the other hand, while Blake, as a staunch opponent of Enlightenment philosophy, could engrave together with *All Religions are One* another aphoristic print entitled *There is No Natural Religion*,[30] he did not remain untouched by certain developments in the inchoate field of comparative religion which the Enlightenment helped promote. In one place he alludes to Jacob Bryant's seminal but flawed *A New System; or, An Analysis of Ancient Mythology* (1774-76) to support his own assertions that "the antiquities of every Nation under Heaven, is [sic] no less sacred than that of the Jews," and that "all had originally one language, and one religion."[31] One thus suspects, with Ruth apRoberts, that such speculations by Blake had some connection with the then current school of pseudo-scientific "Mythography" (satirized a century later in George Eliot's depiction of Mr. Casaubon's effort to establish "the key to all the mythologies"), which construed non-Judeo-Christian religions as corruptions of the one primal divine revelation and all languages as derivations from the original Hebrew abandoned at Babel.[32]

---

[29] See, e.g., the allusions to Lessing in Mircea Eliade's chronological survey, "The 'History of Religion' as a Branch of Knowledge," in *The Sacred and the Profane: The Nature of Religion*, trans. Willard R. Trask (New York: Harcourt Brace Jovanovich, 1959), p. 228; and Jan de Vries, *Perspectives in the History of Religions*, trans. Kees W. Bolle (1967; reprint, Berkeley: University of California Press, 1977), p. 43.

[30] Blake, *Complete Poetry and Prose*, p. 2.

[31] Blake, *A Descriptive Catalogue of Pictures, Poetical and Historical Inventions* (London, 1809), pp. 43-44, in *Complete Poetry and Prose*, pp. 529-51, quote on p. 543. See also Frye, *Fearful Symmetry*, p. 173.

[32] Ruth apRoberts, *The Ancient Dialect: Thomas Carlyle and Comparative Religion* (Berkeley and Los Angeles: University of California Press, 1988), p. 2.

It is significant that the same poet-prophet who proclaimed the oneness of all religions was, as Frye points out, among the first European idealists able to connect his own tradition of thought with the *Bhagavad Gita* ("the Geeta").[33] Charles Wilkens's recent English translation (1785) of that sacred Indian text had helped arouse interest in Hindu philosophy in the same way that Sir Edwin Arnold's poem *The Light of Asia* (1879) would later attract popular attention to Buddhism. Brought about by the contributions of such seminal translators and scholars of comparative philology and mythology as Sir William Jones toward the end of the eighteenth century and Max Müller a century later, the emergence of the history of religions as an independent discipline during the nineteenth century was matched by an increased interest in "Oriental" religions, whose influence on certain European Romantics, the American Transcendentalists, and numerous writers, poets, and thinkers of the Victorian period is well documented.[34]

One indirect offshoot of this developing attraction to Eastern religions was the recurrence of the theme of the ultimate unity of religions, bequeathed by Blake, in works by three of the most celebrated poets writing in English during the second half of the nineteenth century: Alfred Tennyson and Robert Browning in England and Walt Whitman in America. Two key examples of this theme crop up in a pair of poems by Tennyson and Browning that appeared at midcentury. In Tennyson's elegy *In Memoriam A.H.H.*, written between 1833 and 1850 and published anonymously the latter year (when he was named poet laureate), the opening section (dated 1849) addresses the "Son of God" as follows:

> Our little systems have their day;
>> They have their day and cease to be:
>> They are but broken lights of thee,
> And thou, O Lord, art more than they.
>> [Stanza 5][35]

---

[33] See Blake, *Descriptive Catalogue* (1809), p. 59, and in *Complete Poetry and Prose*, p. 548.

[34] See, e.g., A. Leslie Willson, *A Mythical Image: The Ideal of India in German Romanticism* (Durham, N.C.: Duke University Press, 1964); Carl T. Jackson, *The Oriental Religions and American Thought: Nineteenth-Century Explorations* (Westport, Conn.: Greenwood, 1981), which closes with a chapter on the Parliament of Religions (chap. 13, pp. 243-61).

[35] Alfred Lord Tennyson, *The Works of Tennyson*, 9 vols., Eversley edition, annotated by Alfred Lord Tennyson, ed. Hallam Lord Tennyson. (London: Macmillan, 1907-08), 3:40.

That same year Browning, a friend of Tennyson, published his own lengthy two-part poem *Christmas-Eve and Easter-Day* (1850), whose first part, composed in narrative form, acknowledges the fallibility of sectarian religion as a medium of divine truth. Discerning "A value for religion's self, / A carelessness about the sects of it," the poet thinks to himself:

> ["]Let me enjoy my own conviction,
>   Not watch my neighbour's faith with fretfulness,
> Still spying there some dereliction
>   Of truth, perversity, forgetfulness!
> Better a mild indifferentism,
>   Teaching that both our faiths (though duller
> His shine through a dull spirit's prism)
> Originally had one colour!
> Better pursue a pilgrimage
> Through ancient and through modern times
> To many peoples, various climes,
> Where I may see saint, savage, sage
> Fuse their respective creeds in one
> Before the general Father's throne!"
>   [Section 19, lines 1144-57][36]

In accordance with each other, *In Memoriam* and *Christmas-Eve* conceive of a God who is "more" than religious "systems," and before whom all "creeds" may be fused "in one." During the year after these two poems appeared, Walt Whitman across the Atlantic began work on his monumental *Leaves of Grass*, which would contain yet another variation on the "all religions are one" theme. When its first edition appeared four years later (1855), consisting of twelve untitled poems, the first and longest of them—later entitled "Song of Myself"—issued the following proclamation: "Of every hue and caste am I, of every rank and religion, / A farmer, mechanic, artist, gentleman, sailor, quaker, / Prisoner, fancy-man, rowdy, lawyer, physician, priest."[37] No less than Tennyson and Browning, Whitman looks beyond denominational distinctions to suggest that all religions are one; the difference is that, rather than imagine them as subordinate to God, or as being unified before God, Whitman subsumes them all ("every rank and religion") within the "am I" of his singer, who, as an embodiment

---

[36] Robert Browning, *The Complete Works of Robert Browning, with Variant Readings and Annotations*, general ed. Roma A. King, Jr., 5 vols. (Athens: Ohio University Press, 1969-81), 5:89-90.

[37] Walt Whitman, sec. 16 of "Song of Myself," in *Complete Poetry and Prose by Walt Whitman*, ed. James E. Miller, Jr. (Boston: Houghton Mifflin, 1959), p. 36.

of the spirit of American democracy, combines all humanity, from the farmer to the priest, within himself.

Of these three poets, the one who later developed most fully his vision of the unity of religious faiths underlying sectarian differences was Tennyson, especially in his poem "Akbar's Dream" (1892), composed the year of his death. From *In Memoriam* on, Tennyson had held that "the essential feelings of religion subsist in the utmost diversity of forms," that "different language does not always imply different opinions, nor different opinions any difference in *real* faith."[38] Finding now a remarkable paradigm for religious tolerance in the great Mogul emperor, who, dissatisfied with his own Muslim faith, evolved a new eclectic religion by which he aspired to integrate all creeds, castes, and peoples, Tennyson has his Akbar yearn

> To wreathe a crown not only for the king
> But in due time for every Mussulmân,
> Brahmin, and Buddhist, Christian, and Parsee,
> Thro' all the warring world of Hindustan.[39]

Regarding God, Akbar asserts:

> He knows Himself, men nor themselves nor Him,
> For every splinter'd fraction of a sect
> Will clamour "*I* am on the Perfect Way,
> All else is to perdition."

Aware of "how the living pulse of Alla [sic] beats / Thro' all His world," and how this assures that

> There is light in all,
> And light, with more or less of shade, in all
> Man-modes of worship;...

Akbar pits himself against the narrow-minded Ulama, who "sitting on green sofas contemplate / The torment of the damn'd" and "blurt / Their furious formalisms":

> I hate the rancour of their castes and creeds,
> I let men worship as they will, I reap
> No revenue from the field of unbelief.
> I cull from every faith and race the best
> And bravest soul for counsellor and friend.

---

[38] Quoted in his son's Introduction to the notes for *In Memoriam*, in Tennyson, *Works*, 3:208. Compare 3:209, 209 n.1.

[39] All quotations of this poem will be drawn from Tennyson, *Works*, 7:139-48, for which the poet's notes appear on 7:149-53.

The poem culminates with the emperor's account of his recent dream of realizing a religious reverence that would transcend all traditional sectarian bounds:

> I dream'd
> That stone by stone I rear'd a sacred fane,
> A temple, neither Pagod, Mosque, nor Church,
> But loftier, simpler, always open-door'd
> To every breath from heaven, and Truth and Peace
> And Love and Justice came and dwelt therein.

Although Tennyson, Browning, and Whitman all died before the Parliament of Religions was held (Browning in 1889, Tennyson and Whitman both in 1892), the former two were recognized as poetic anticipators of the parliament's ideal of interfaith harmony. Barrows closes his preface to the two-volume, 1,600-page proceedings from the parliament by remarking that Tennyson—"the English Laureate"—"had looked forward to the Parliament of Religions as the realization of a noble dream," which Barrows sums up by quoting a stanza from Tennyson's poem "The Golden Year."[40] Elsewhere, Barrows cites the passage quoted earlier from Tennyson's *In Memoriam* to illustrate the parliament's aim of changing "this many-colored radiance [of diverse religions] back into the white light of heavenly truth"; and later, after citing the last passage quoted above from "Akbar's Dream," which was evidently appended to the initial announcement the parliament committee had sent around the world to advertise the event, Barrows notes "how the Laureate, who regarded the proposal of a Parliament of Religions at Chicago as a noble idea, brooded much, in his last days, over the oneness of human need and spiritual aspiration after God."[41] Similarly, Max Müller, to illustrate his own remark about the parliament's literary pertinence, cites the passage quoted above from Browning as prefiguring the parliament's "vision" of the unity of the world's religions.[42]

In addition to Tennyson and, as we shall see, presumably Julia Ward Howe, at least one other prominent poet of the time had written

---

[40] The following portion of "The Golden Year" (ibid., 2:22-25) is paraphrased (without a citation of its source) by John Henry Barrows, "Preface," *WPR*, 1:ix:

> "Ah! when shall all men's good
> Be each man's rule, and Universal Peace
> Lie like a shaft of light across the land,
> And like a lane of beams athwart the sea,
> Thro' all the circle of the golden year."

[41] Barrows, "History," in *WPR*, 1:3-4, 11.
[42] See Müller's article in this volume.

to Barrows before the parliament to express approval of such a meeting. As reported by Barrows, the American poet John Greenleaf Whittier felt "in full sympathy" with the idea, which struck him as "an inspiration": "I can think of nothing more impressive than such an assemblage of the representatives of all the children of our Heavenly Father, convened to tell each other what witness he has given them of himself, what light he has afforded them in the awful mysteries of life and death."[43] Such openmindedness toward the thought of a truly "ecumenical" conference was not surprising, coming from a poet whose considerable body of religious poems, though mainly Christian in orientation, include a set of "Oriental Maxims" (paraphrases of Sanskrit translations) and "Hymns of the Brahmo Somaj."[44] As it happened, Whittier, like Tennyson and Whitman, died the year before the parliament.

We have now seen that the ideal of the unity of religions—"Akbar's Dream"—that was originally associated with the World's Parliament of Religions, had deep roots in Western literature. What remains to be considered is how that ideal actually fared at the parliament.

3.

What is expressible in literature, by virtue of its "power of detachment," is not necessarily realizable in life. This truism, whose recognition is as old as Aristotle's distinction between poetry and history, was substantiated by the fate which the ideal of a rapprochement of religions met at the 1893 Parliament of Religions, an event that was drawn into explicit associations with such dreams of religious unity as those informing the legends of the councils of Aśoka and Akbar, the Pentecost, and the parable of the rings. While Joseph Kitagawa rightly credits Barrows and his colleagues with "initiating what we call today the 'dialogue among various religions,' in which each religious claim for ultimacy is acknowledged,"[45] one could hardly argue that the parliament's Christian promoters attributed equal weight to any of the non-Christian claims.

To be sure, in addition to quoting "Akbar's Dream," Barrows was capable of saying that "religion, like the white light of Heaven, has been broken into many-colored fragments by the prisms of men. One of the objects of the Parliament of Religions has been to change this

---

[43] Quoted by Barrows, "History," in *WPR*, 1:11-12.

[44] John Greenleaf Whittier, *The Complete Poetical Works of John Greenleaf Whittier*, Cambridge ed. (Boston: Houghton, Mifflin, 1894), pp. 461, 465.

[45] Quoted from Kitagawa's lecture in this volume.

many-colored radiance back into the white light of heavenly truth."[46] Accordingly, over the parliament's duration, some twenty of its speakers voiced earnest hopes for the religious union of all mankind.[47] On the opening day, one of these speakers, Anagārika Dharmapāla (David Hewivitarne, 1864-1933) of Ceylon (today Sri Lanka), general secretary of the Mahābodhi Society of Calcutta, heralded the parliament as "the re-echo" of the Pāṭaliputra council twenty-four centuries earlier, predicting that "the name of Dr. Barrows will shine forth as the American Asoka."[48] Eight days later, the Indian Hindu Swami Vivekananda (1863-1902), a disciple of the mystic Sri Ramakrishna (1836-86), cast the parliament in an even more inclusive light: "Asoka's council was a council of the Buddhist faith. Akbar's, though more to the purpose, was only a parlor-meeting. It was reserved for America to call, to proclaim to all quarters of the globe that the Lord is in every religion."[49] This sentiment might seem in keeping with the spirit in which the Reform rabbi Kaufman Kohler of New York City had invoked Lessing's parable of the three rings on the parliament's third day: "Either all the rings are genuine and have the magic power of love, or the father himself is a fraud."[50] However, in making that bid for toleration, Kaufman—like Lessing—had referred exclusively to Judaism, Christianity and Islam, the three monotheistic faiths "Based on the bible." Barrows, for his own part, had an even more exclusive concern. While he always kept in mind that the parliament's scope encompassed the religions of the east as well as of the west, he clearly meant to suggest Christianity's completion of the other faiths when he compared the impression the parliament left on those who attended it to "what happened at Jerusalem on the day of Pentecost,"[51] the miraculous event which (as Christians view it) effectively reversed the dispersive consequence of Babel. Ironically,

---

[46] Barrows, "History," in *WPR*, 1:3.

[47] See John Henry Barrows, "Introduction to the Parliament Papers," in *WPR*, 1:242-46.

[48] Dharmapāla, in an untitled speech, quoted by Barrows, "History," in *WPR*, 1:95, 96.

[49] Vivekananda, "Hinduism," in *WPR*, 2:977.

[50] Kaufman Kohler, "Human Brotherhood as Taught by the Religions Based on the Bible," in *WPR*, 1:373.

[51] Barrows, "Review and Summary," in *WPR*, 2:1566. Barrows goes on to cite Dr. Frederick A. Noble's claim: "There were hours when it seemed as though the Divine Spirit was about to descend upon the people in a great Pentecostal outpouring. Never did Christ seem so large and precious to me, never did Christian faith seem so necessary to humanity and so sure to prevail as when the Parliament of Religions closed" (ibid.).

such hints at the notion of Christ's "fulfillment" of other religions insured that the parliament would ultimately reinforce the condition of Babel's aftermath; by the time the parliament ended, Vivekananda and any of the other Eastern representatives who had attended the parliament in the hope of breaking down barriers between their own religions and Christianity must have heard enough from Barrows and his Christian colleagues to suffer a rude awakening from Akbar's dream.[52]

Much has been written about the sensation caused at the religion parliament by Vivekananda, Dharmapāla, and Shaku Sōen (1859-1919), the abbot of the Zen Temple of Engakuji. These three relatively young men were, in Kitagawa's words, "modern Asian religious reformers" who had come to Chicago "not only because they all subscribed to the principle of interreligious understanding and cooperation, but also because they saw in the parliament an opportunity which they had never had: a platform from which to address the whole world," and thus a chance to realize "their audacious dream of reversing the tide of history and beginning the Easternization of the West."[53] In their addresses to the parliament, each of these three "pious adventurers"[54] in his own way pleaded for inter-religious harmony, suggesting that a unifying truth lies behind all religions, despite their sectarian differences. Thus, on the parliament's sixteenth day, Shaku observed: "Not only Buddha alone, but Jesus Christ, as well as Confucius, taught about universal love and fraternity," the implication being that "all beings on [sic] the universe are in the bosom of truth."[55] That same day Dharmapāla, who had already depicted Buddhism as a "synthetic religion" promulgated by its founder almost six hundred years before the birth of Christ,[56] devoted a whole speech to "Points of Resemblance and Difference between

---

[52] For an unfavorable critique of the missionary agenda of the parliament's Christian promoters see Clay Lancaster, *The Incredible World's Parliament of Religions at the Chicago Columbian Exposition of 1893: A Comparative and Critical Study* (Fontwell, U.K.: Centaur, 1987).

[53] Quoted from Kitagawa's lecture in this volume.

[54] Joseph M. Kitagawa has introduced this phrase to describe a specific type of religious leader, specifically "those who left their familiar surroundings for uncharted foreign lands for the propagation of the faith or in search of truth" ("Kawaguchi Ekai: A Pious Adventurer and Tibet," in *Reflections on Tibetan Culture*, ed. L. Epstein and Sr. Sherburne [Lewiston, N.Y.: Mellen, 1990], pp. 279-94, quote on p. 279).

[55] Shaku Sōen (Shaku Soyen), "Arbitration Instead of War," in *WPR*, 2:1285.

[56] See Dharmapāla's speech from the parliament's eighth day, "The World's Debt to Buddha," in *WPR*, 2:862-80.

Buddhism and Christianity," quoting ten passages from the Gospels as "Buddhist teachings as given in the words of Jesus," and citing R. C. Dutt's observation that Buddhism and Christianity have so much in common in their moral teachings and precepts that "some connection between the two systems of religion has long been suspected."[57] But it had been Vivekananda in his speech on "Hinduism" on the ninth day, who had elaborated most fully his own notion, derived from the teachings of Ramakrishna, that "the Lord is in every religion." According to Vivekananda, who would become internationally famous for his teaching of his "Universal Gospel" during the remaining nine years of his life after the parliament, "Every religion is only an evolving [of] a God out of the material man; and the same God is the inspirer of all of them." He went on:

> The Hindu might have failed to carry out all his plans, but if there is to be ever a universal religion, it must be one which would hold no location in place or time, which would be infinite like the God it would preach, whose sun shines upon the followers of Krishna or Christ; saints or sinners alike; which would not be the Brahman or Buddhist, Christian or Mohammedan, but the sum total of all these, and still have infinite space for development; which in its catholicity would embrace in its infinite arms and formulate a place for every human being, from the lowest groveling man who is scarcely removed in intellectuality from the brute, to the highest mind, towering almost above humanity, and who makes society stand in awe and doubt his human nature.[58]

How captivating these words were to many Americans in the audience, especially to those already influenced by the residual strains of early nineteenth-century New England transcendentalism (with its "Yankee Hindoo" dimension), is indicated by the reiteration of Vivekananda's central idea of the divinity of the human being in the short speech of the American poet Julia Ward Howe, "What is Religion?" which she presented at the parliament on its penultimate day. The only famous literary figure to speak there, Howe defined religion as "the aspiration, the pursuit of the divine in the human," clearly echoing Vivekananda's phrase, "an evolving [of] a God out of the material man." In her conclusion, Howe comes close to repeating another of the Vedāntist's key notions, that of the emanation of the truths of all religions from one God: "From this Parliament let some valorous, new, strong, and courageous influence go forth, and let us

---

[57] Dharmapāla, "Points of Resemblance and Difference between Buddhism and Christianity," in *WPR*, 2:1289, 1290.
[58] Vivekananda, "Hinduism," in *WPR*, 2:977.

have here an agreement of all faiths for one good end, for one good thing—really for the glory of God, really for the sake of humanity from all that is low and animal and unworthy and undivine."[59] (Compare this with Vivekananda's phrase above, "from the lowest groveling man.")

The overwhelmingly positive reception which the speeches of Shaku, Dharmapāla, and especially Vivekananda met at the parliament unsettled its Christian promoters, whose stance toward other religions was best summed up by a statement by Lyman Abbott, the pastor of Plymouth Congregational Church—quoted favorably in Barrows's own summary remarks—that "the difference between Christianity and the other religions is that we have something that they have not. We have the Christ, the revelation of God, the ideal Man, the loving and suffering Saviour."[60] A man intensely interested in the study of comparative religion, particularly the work of Müller, Barrows conceived of the parliament's meaning in terms of three concentric circles, with the Christian assembly embodying its center; the American religious assembly, including Jews, comprising the next circle; and the religions of the world making up the outer circle, among which Christianity was one of a plurality of faiths "competing for the conquest of mankind."[61] While Barrows considered these three circles at the parliament to be united in a common spiritual quest, he wrongly assumed that most people would agree with the statement of Theodore Thornton Munger, pastor of the United Church of New Haven, that "the Parliament shows that the world moves, and on the whole moves Christward."[62] As Barrows made clear, "The idea of evolving a cosmic or universal faith out of the Parliament was not present in the minds of its chief promoters. They believe that the elements of such a religion are already contained in the Christian ideal and the Christian Scriptures."[63]

There can be little doubt that Barrows intended this as a direct response to Vivekananda's Vedāntic advocacy of a universal religion, which had attracted so much popular attention at the parliament. Elsewhere, after quoting the Hindu's plea for "religious unity" on the

---

[59] Julia Ward Howe, "What is Religion?" in *WPR*, 2:1251.

[60] Barrows, "Review and Summary," in *WPR*, 2:1574. Abbott elaborated upon this point in his speech on the parliament's fourth day, "Religion Essentially Characteristic of Humanity," in *WPR*, 1:494-501, see 500-01.

[61] See in this volume the lecture by Kitagawa.

[62] Quoted by Barrows, "Review and Summary," in *WPR*, 2:1575.

[63] Barrows, "Review and Summary," in *WPR*, 2:1572.

basis of an assimilation of the truth claims of all religions, Barrows remarks somewhat nastily: "Swami Vivekananda was always heard with interest by the Parliament, but very little approval was shown to some of the sentiments expressed in his closing address"[64]—an assertion contradicted by the documented public reaction.[65] The effort by Barrows and some of his Christian colleagues to use the parliament as a means for proving the supremacy of their own faith effectually disintegrated any illusions that Akbar's dream might be realized there. Barrows's expressed theory that all other religions would be "fulfilled" in Christianity backfired; as Kitagawa points out, Vivekananda, Dharmapāla, and Shaku Sōen promptly appropriated this formula for themselves and reversed the Christian claim, developing "fulfillment" theories from their own faith perspectives.[66] Not surprisingly, Barrows's associations with those three men were ridden with bitter tensions in the years following the parliament.[67]

Notwithstanding Barrows's opposition to the pursuit of a universal religion, Max Müller would later observe that many people of different faiths prior to the parliament "had been thinking about a universal religion, or at least about a union of the different religions, resting on a recognition of the truths shared in common by all of them," so that "it would have been possible, even at Chicago, to draw up a small number of articles of faith...to which all who were present could have honestly subscribed."[68] Interestingly, this speculation by the most important late-nineteenth-century pioneer of *Religionswissenschaft* would have struck one of that same century's greatest literary artists and seekers of a universal religion as overly optimistic. When the French clergyman and professor Gaston Charles Bonét-Maury, who had spoken at the 1893 parliament, later invited Leo Tolstoy to participate in the Congress of Religions which was to

---

[64] Barrows, "History," in *WPR*, 1:171.

[65] See Marie Louise Burke, *Swami Vivekananda in America: New Discoveries* (1958; 2d, rev. ed., Calcutta: Advaita Ashrama, 1966), pp. 91-94.

[66] See Kitagawa's lecture in this volume.

[67] According to Sailendra Nath Dhar, Barrows sought actively to bring down Vivekananda in public estimation following the parliament (*A Comprehensive Biography of Swami Vivekananda*, 2 vols. [Madras: Vivekananda Prakashan Kendra, 1975], 2:939-47). Regarding the 1896 "controversy on Buddhism" that began with a disagreement between Barrows and Shaku Sōen and later involved F.F. Ellinwood (who supported Barrows) and Dharmapāla (who supported Sōen), see Larry A. Fader, "Zen in the West: Historical and Philosophical Implications of the 1893 Chicago World's Parliament of Religions," *The Eastern Buddhist* 15 (1982): 128-29.

[68] Quoted from Müller's article in this volume.

convene in Paris in 1900, the celebrated novelist wrote back, arguing that such congresses were not only useless, but even detrimental:

> The idea of the Congress is to unite the religions by external means—while according to the idea of Religion, that is, the one universal Religion, unification can only take place from within; that is to say that debates and talks by various representatives of different religions cannot in any way help in uniting men in their relationship with God (rather, they produce the opposite effect), and the only way this union can be achieved is by sincere study by every individual of his relationship with the world, the Infinite, God.[69]

These remarks encapsulate a crucial, paradoxical lesson of Chicago's religion parliament: for all its justly applauded success at bringing together representatives of different faiths from around the world and providing them a congenial atmosphere in which to share their views and beliefs, the parliament ultimately failed to overcome their sectarian distinctions and thereby proved an inadequate forum in which to realize the truly pluralist vision bequeathed by "Akbar's Dream." It is appropriate that the inherent inadequacy of *any* congress to fulfill such a dream should be noted by Tolstoy, whom, as we saw earlier, Frye singled out as his primary exemplar of the literary "power of detachment." From Frye's eminently humanist perspective, any literary text, not to mention literature as a whole, can afford readers opportunities to suspend beliefs as well as disbelief, and to engage in the freedom of detachment (an ideal dramatically dishonored by today's cursers of Salman Rushdie). Unlike literature thus understood, any congress or parliament worthy of the name, religious or otherwise, must be a bastion of commitments.

---

[69] L. N. Tolstoy, letter of November 23, 1896, in his *Polnoe Sobranie Sochinenii* (Complete Collected Works), 90 vols. (Moscow: Gosudarstvennoe Izdatelstvo Khudozhestvennoi Literatury, 1935-58), 69:198; quoted by Luigi Stendardo, *Leo Tolstoy and the Bahá'í Faith*, trans. Jeremy Fox (Oxford: Ronald, 1985), p. 25.

REDISCOVERING WOMEN'S VOICES AT THE WORLD'S PARLIAMENT OF RELIGIONS

Ursula King

The significance of the 1893 World's Parliament of Religions is widely celebrated and its impact on the development of the interfaith movement and the study of world religions is recognized more clearly than ever before. With the centenary of the parliament the historiography and critical discussion of the original event have gained more momentum over the last few years than was the case in earlier decades. We must not forget that the earlier suggestion to organize another parliament in 1900 was not taken up, and that a second "Parliament of Religion," held in Chicago in 1933 to coincide with another World's Fair, has mostly been forgotten and made little impact except for the founding of the World Fellowship of Faiths.

Until recently the 1893 parliament was little known outside specialized scholarly and religious circles. My own initial acquaintance with the parliament occurred in India where the event is always mentioned in connection with Swami Vivekananda and the tremendous impact he made in America. His importance is so much overemphasized that one almost gains the impression that he was the only Indian delegate at the parliament, whereas there were more than ten, and half of them gave opening and closing addresses apart from plenary papers. The parliament was an event on a very large scale, even by today's standards, but information about it has always been very selectively presented. Our lively contemporary interest in the event is directly linked to the current growth in interfaith activities which make us recognize the parliament—the first large gathering of members from different faith communities around the globe—as a historical landmark and challenge. In spite of much of its Victorian rhetoric many of the issues raised then still concern us today. The parliament challenges us to ask how far we have come in interfaith relations since then, and in which direction the interfaith movement will have to move creatively forward into another century ahead.

As a woman scholar I cannot write about the interfaith movement simply in general terms, but have to take into account the critical category of gender which provides an important variable in all contemporary scholarly inquiry. Given the patriarchal framework of institutional religion, it is perhaps not surprising that most religious leaders and representatives of interfaith dialogue are men, and that at many official interfaith gatherings women are conspicuously absent while being much involved at the grassroots level. Male participants were also the main actors at the World's Parliament of Religions of 1893, but women also actively participated, though in much smaller numbers. The gender politics of knowledge and scholarship are such that so far little attention has been paid to the women present at the parliament. We have heard little about their voices. This is not only scholarly neglect but also indicative of the marginality and invisibility of women in the contemporary interfaith movement.

I would like to rediscover and draw attention to the voices of women who spoke a hundred years ago at the World Parliament of Religions in Chicago. What did their participation mean then, and what does it mean for us today? What contribution did they make? And how clearly do their voices still speak to us today?

To reconstruct and recover what the women participants contributed to the parliament is no easy task because of the relative paucity of sources, the difficulty of access to them, and the summarized versions in which John Henry Barrows published most of the original speeches. My reflections cannot be anything but preliminary. Much further research will be needed to gain a comprehensive picture of the participation of women at the 1893 event. As a beginning to the study of this much-neglected aspect of the parliament I shall present (1) a general overview of women's presence, participation and representation, then (2) consider some individual contributions and (3) finish with some concluding reflections.

1. Women at the World's Parliament of Religions: An Overview

Contemporary works dealing with the 1893 parliament give us little information on the contributions of women to the event. For example, the history of "The World's Parliament of Religions" given in Marcus

Braybrooke's *Pilgrimage of Hope: One Hundred Years of Global Interfaith Dialogue*[1] contains no reference to women participants at all. *The Dawn of Religious Pluralism: Voices from the World's Parliament of Religions, 1893*, edited by Richard Hughes Seager,[2] which is said to be "inclusive of the many different voices that gained expression in the first global, ecumenical assembly in world history,"[3] includes the text of four women's speeches—those of Julia Ward Howe, Annis F.F. Eastman, Frances E. Willard, and Fannie Barrier Williams—and lists nineteen addresses given by women under the relevant religious traditions in the Appendix without providing any other information on the participation of women. In the following discussion I have based my analysis primarily on the data found in John Henry Barrows, *The World's Parliament of Religions*, 2 volumes,[4] supplemented by information from other sources.

Early in his first volume Barrows mentions the important organizational contribution made by Rev. Dr. Augusta Chapin, D.D., from the Universalist Church who, with the help of Lady Henry Somerset from England and Miss Frances E. Willard (both active in the Women's Christian Temperance Union), led the Woman's Committee on Religious Congresses and "secured the presence and participation of some of the most distinguished women of our time."[5] Ordained in 1863, Chapin was reportedly the first woman to receive a D.D. and was chosen to give a welcome address on behalf of women at the opening session of the parliament.[6] This is one of twenty-four

---

[1] London: SCM Press, 1992.

[2] Published in association with the Council for a Parliament of the World's Religions (La Salle, Ill.: Open Court, 1993); cited hereafter as *DRP*.

[3] Ibid., p. 2.

[4] Cited throughout as *WPR*.

[5] John Henry Barrows, "History," in *WPR*, 1:38. Barrows later refers to Chapin as "Chairman [sic!] of the Women's Committee of Organization" (1:81).

[6] Seager's stated rule of omitting from his list of "major" speakers "people who appeared on the floor and made brief statements on the opening and closing days" ("Appendix,"*DRP*, p. 477) explains why Chapin has not been listed in *DRP* as a participant at the parliament; however, given her importance, as well as this recorded address and her closing speech, her absence on the list seems misleading insofar as it ipso facto renders invisible her significant presence at and contribution to the parliament. Chapin's importance at the parliament is highlighted by the fact that her full-page photo is the first of any woman in *WPR*, 1:55 (followed by that of Mrs. Charles H. Henrotin in *WPR*, 1:63), and that among the eighty-one "Biographical Notes" provided at the end of Barrows's second volume, Chapin's details are given (and those of two other women, Anna G. Spencer and Mrs. Celia Parker Woolley). The note in *WPR*, 2:1585 reads: "CHAPIN, REV. AUGUSTA J., D.D., pastor at Oak Park Universalist Church;

welcoming speeches listed by Barrows,[7] who summarized the text, emphasizing women's share in the parliament. Among other statements Chapin is reported to have made is the following: "A hundred years ago the world was not ready for this Parliament. Fifty years ago it could not have been convened, and had it been called but a simple generation ago one-half of the religious world could not have been directly represented." She continued:

> Woman could not have had a part in it in her own right for two reasons: one that her presence would not have been thought of or tolerated, and the other was that she herself was still too weak, too timid and too unschooled to avail herself of such an opportunity had it been offered....Now the doors are thrown open in our own and many other lands. Women are becoming masters of the languages in which the great sacred literatures of the world are written. They are winning the highest honors that the universities have to bestow, and already in the field of Religion hundreds have been ordained and thousands are freely speaking and teaching this new gospel of freedom and gentleness that has come to bless mankind.[8]

There was not only this one woman speaker at the opening of the parliament, but three women sat on the platform among the male delegates: Miss Jeanne Sorabji, an Indian Christian from Bombay;[9] Mrs. Potter Palmer, president of the Board of Lady Managers of the World's Columbian Exposition; and Mrs. Charles H. Henrotin, vice-president of the Woman's Branch of the World Congress Auxiliary, who is quoted to have said: "That the experiment of an equal presentation of men and women in a Parliament of Religions has not been a failure, I think can be proved by the part taken by the women who have had the honor to be called to participate in this great gathering."[10]

Equal presentation may have been the aim, but it remained far from being realized. From our contemporary perspective it is perhaps less surprising that there was no equal number of women present; more important is that a hundred years ago already so many highly

---

studied at Olivet College and University of Michigan; ordained 1863; first woman to receive D.D.; lecturer on English literature for the University of Chicago." As indicated by Barrows, "History," in *WPR*, 1:146, Chapin chaired the evening session of the fifteenth day of the parliament—yet another indication of her standing among the participants.

[7] See "Table of Contents," *WPR*, 1:xv.

[8] Augusta J. Chapin, untitled opening-day speech, quoted by Barrows, "History," in *WPR*, 1:82.

[9] Seager includes her in his long list of delegates from Protestantism without assigning a denominational affiliation to her ("Appendix," *DRP*, p. 490).

[10] Quoted beneath the photo-portrait of Mrs. Charles H. Henrotin in *WPR*, 1:63.

qualified women were official delegates at the parliament and gave plenary addresses. They were present in higher numbers than found at some conferences today. In a brief reference to the women's voices at the parliament Seager says in his Introduction to *The Dawn of Religious Pluralism*: "The Parliament was hailed as a breakthrough for women in religion, but under close examination most Protestant women on the floor were from the liberal religious traditions, either Universalists or Unitarians. Several Jewish women who subsequently rose to prominence in their community presented papers, but there were no female delegates, in or out of orders, in the Catholic delegation."[11]

At the close of the parliament Miss Susan B. Anthony and Dr. Sarah Hackett Stevenson were among the delegates on the platform, and of the eleven speeches given during the final session three were by women: by Mrs. Charles H. Henrotin, by Augusta Chapin, who had already spoken at the opening session, and by Julia Ward Howe, the well-known Unitarian pacifist who received a tremendous response when she addressed the audience briefly.

Who were these women speakers, and what percentage of delegates did they represent? It is unfortunately impossible to give a definite answer to this question; only an approximate one can be found because of the discrepancies between different sources. If one counts all the addresses listed under "The Parliament Papers" in Barrows's two volumes, one arrives at 172 papers to which can be added the eighteen papers listed under the "Scientific Section." This gives a total of 190 papers of which nineteen were given by women, that is to say, ten percent.[12]

For the record I shall list here the names of the nineteen women speakers and the titles of their papers in the order given in the two volumes of Barrows's *The World's Parliament of Religions*:

---

[11] *DRP*, p. 7.

[12] If one bases one's calculation on a total of 172 papers, the percentage is higher still, as it is also if one takes into account some of the women's papers given to parallel congresses. Seager has based his selection on "representative texts drawn from some 194 papers" ("Preface,"*DRP*, p. 2), but in his "Appendix," 202 contributions are listed; see *DRP*, pp. 477-92. Of those nineteen are by women; they included Mary Baker Eddy who did not give a plenary address, but not Eliza R. Sunderland who did. If one adds to the nineteen officially-given papers listed in Barrows's "Table of Contents" (which I have reproduced in my essay) the contributions by Augusta Chapin and Mary Baker Eddy, one arrives at a total of twenty-one women speakers.

Volume 1:

Mrs. Lydia Fuller Dickinson, "The Divine Basis of the Cooperation of Men and Women"

Mrs. Laura Ormiston Chant, "The Real Religion of To-Day"[13]

Mrs. Eliza R. Sunderland, Ph.D., "Serious Study of All Religions"[14]

Miss Josephine Lazarus, "The Outlook of Judaism"[15]

Rev. Annis F.F. Eastman, "The Influence of Religion on Women"[16]

Rev. Marion Murdock, "A New Testament Woman"

Volume 2:

Lady Henry Somerset, "Letter"

Rev. Ida C. Hultin, "The Essential Oneness of Ethical Ideas among all Men"

Rev. Anna G. Spencer, "Religion and the Erring and Criminal Classes"

Miss Jeanne Sorabji, "Women of India"

Miss Henrietta Szold, "What has Judaism done for Women?"

Rev. Olympia Brown, "Crime and its Remedy"

Alice C. Fletcher, "The Religion of the North American Indian"

Mrs. Fannie Barrier Williams, "What can Religion further do to advance the Condition of the American Negro?"[17]

Rev. Antoinette Brown Blackwell, "Woman and the Pulpit"

Miss F.E. Willard, "A White Life for Two"[18]

Mrs. Elizabeth Cady Stanton, "The Worship of God in Man"

Mrs. Julia Ward Howe, "What is Religion?"[19]

Mrs. Celia Parker Woolley, "The World's Religious Debt to America"

It would require more time, space and research than available at present to consider the individual contributions of all these women. I shall restrict my discussion to only four in the second part of my paper. But before I come to that, it is worth pointing out that the overriding concerns of the Women's Movement of the late nineteenth century are reflected in several of the addresses: the decisive importance of the women's suffrage movement, women in education and in the churches,

---

[13] Chant also contributed a poem on "The World's Parliament," included in *NHP*, pp. 811-12 and reprinted in *DRP*, pp. 455-56.

[14] It is difficult to explain why this is not listed in Seager, *DRP*. Sunderland's paper is reprinted in the present volume.

[15] In *WPR*, 1:705-15, reprinted in *DRP*, pp. 234-44.

[16] In *NHP*, pp. 345-50, reprinted in *DRP*, pp. 80-87.

[17] In *NHP*, pp. 631-36, reprinted in *DRP*, pp. 142-50.

[18] In *WPR*, 2:1230-34, reprinted in *DRP*, pp. 88-92.

[19] This is the title listed in Barrows's "Table of Contents." The summary of her actual contribution in *WPR*, 2:1250-51 is entitled "What is, and What is not Religion?" Seager, *DRP*, pp. 75-78 reprints her address from *NHP*, pp. 764-66 under "Possible Results of the Parliament." Julia Ward Howe took issue with her preceding speaker, Professor W.C. Wilkinson who had spoken on "The Attitude of Christianity Toward Other Religions." She argued that the parliament should take a stand against manifestations of violence in religion, and that religion should dissociate itself from sexual discrimination for "surely nothing is religion which puts one sex above another....Any religion which sacrifices women to the brutality of men is no religion" (*NHP*, p. 766, reprinted in *DRP*, p. 77).

burning social issues, the temperance movement, the influence and importance of religion and its study.

More information about women's further participation comes from the "Denominational Congresses" held parallel to the World's Parliament. Barrows lists thirty-three such congresses by names as well as "Other Congresses." The Jewish Congress specifically mentions in brackets "Inc. JEWISH WOMEN."[20] Several of the women who gave plenary addresses also spoke at these denominational congresses. For example, Rev. Marion Murdock addressed the Unitarian Congress when a separate women's meeting was organized on the theme of "Woman's Theological Emancipation." Four different speakers dealt with this topic from the perspective of Judaism, Universalism, Unitarianism and the Free Religious Association. How frustrating it is that we do not have their texts![21] Other contributions to parallel congresses included a paper by Mary Baker Eddy to the Christian Science Congress read in her absence, and Annie Besant's participation in the Theosophical Congress.

Of the greatest interest among the parallel congresses is "The Woman's Congregational Congress" which was organized under the theme "The Summons of the Coming Century to the Women of To-day." Regrettably Barrows has only summarized the six sessions of this Congress in a mere two and a half pages which mention over thirty women's names and over twenty papers, one of which was given by Rev. Annis F.F. Eastman, also one of the plenary speakers. Another contribution was made by Miss Jane Addams who lectured on "The Home and Labor Problem" whereas other participants presented papers on the "Modern Pilgrim Woman," on the "trials, firmness, constancy and heroism of the Pilgrim mothers," the "Scope of Woman's Work in the Churches," the work of the "church-mother," "Woman and the Bible" and similar topics. Of particular interest are the references to "The Work of the Indians on the Frontier" and to the paper "Among Indians and Negroes at Home" and to another one, "A Bit of History Concerning the Higher Education of Women," presented by Miss Harriet N. Haskell, principal of the Monticello Ladies' Seminary.[22]

---

[20] From "Table of Contents," *WPR*, 2:816.

[21] See John Henry Barrows, "The Denominational Congresses," in *WPR*, 2:1526.

[22] All references are to Barrows, "The Denominational Congresses," in *WPR*, 2:1434-36.

Given the summary presentation of papers by Barrows, it is difficult to capture the full sound of all the voices that spoke at the World's Parliament, whether female or male, but it is doubly difficult to hear the women's voices and discover their full significance and impact. As so often in other cases, they have only been marginally recorded and remain partially or even wholly muted.

Only the briefest of testimonies from the women themselves have been preserved. Mrs. Charles H. Henrotin who gave so much service to the parliament, said at its closing session: "The place which woman has taken in the Parliament of Religion and in the denominational congresses is one of such great importance that it is entitled to your careful attention." She went on:

> As day by day the Parliament has presented the result of the preliminary work of two years, it may have appeared to you an easy thing to put into motion the forces of which this evening is a crowning achievement but to bring about this result hundreds of men and women have labored. There are sixteen committees of women in the various departments represented in the Parliament of Religions and denominational congresses, with a total membership of 174.[23]

Here a larger number of actively involved women is mentioned than anywhere else, but most of these women will forever remain unknown. In terms of visual representation it is worth mentioning that the many illustrations in Barrows's two volumes, dealing as much with sacred sites as with parliament delegates, included photographs of twenty-four women. For the record I also include a list of names here as these photographs provide additional documentary evidence of women's presence at the parliament. In Barrows's first volume we find photographs of Rev. Augusta J. Chapin, D.D., Mrs. Charles H. Henrotin, Eliza R. Sunderland, Mrs. Laura Ormiston Chant, Lady Henry Somerset. In Barrows's second volume: Rev. Marian (sic) Murdock, Rev. Ida C. Hultin, Rev. Anna G. Spencer, Miss Alice C. Fletcher, Rev. Olympia Brown, Mrs. Fannie B. Williams, Rev. Antoinette B. Blackwell, Miss Frances E. Willard, Mrs. Julia Ward Howe, Mrs. Celia Parker Woolley, Mary B.G. Eddy, Eliz. P. Bond, Emma R. Flitcraft, Miss Jeanne Sorabji, Mrs. Besant, Mercie Thirds, Elizabeth Cady Stanton, Susan B. Anthony, Mrs. Potter Palmer. (The names are cited as given in Barrows's lists of illustrations.[24])

---

[23] Mrs. Charles H. Henrotin, untitled closing address, in *WPR*, 1:178.

[24] *WPR*, 1:xi-xiv; 2:807-09. The photos of these women appear on 1:55, 63, 475, 595, 755; 2:821, 965, 1029, 1091 (two of them), 1147 (two of them), 1231, 1245, 1267, 1431, 1459 (two of them), 1469, 1519 (two of them), 1525, 1533, 1567. The spelling of

Some of these women are well known from other contexts and have been much written about, yet little has ever been said about their contribution to the World's Parliament of Religions. Ideally one would need to examine each of these women in turn, but at present I can only consider the contribution of four different figures.

2. *Four Women's Voices at the World's Parliament of Religions*

I have chosen to discuss four women plenary speakers: an ordained Christian woman, an Indian woman, a Jewish woman, and an American woman scholar. The first is Rev. Antoinette Brown Blackwell (1825-1921), who contributed a paper on "Woman and the Pulpit," which in her absence was read out on the thirteenth day of the parliament by Rev. Dr. Augusta Chapin. Although only summarized in a mere two pages by Barrows, it is a paper worth commenting on because of its author and topic. Blackwell, described by Seager as a Universalist and by others as a Unitarian, became in 1853 the first woman ever to be ordained. She had been the first theology student at Oberlin College and was ordained at the age of twenty-eight in an "orthodox Congregational Church," according to her own account.[25] She got married in 1855 and carried out her ministry for many years, combining it with marriage and the upbringing of six daughters. Forty years after her own ordination Blackwell reflects in her paper on the Christian ministry of women and refers to "the opposition still felt by very excellent persons to the presence and the wise, helpful teaching of capable women in the Christian pulpit."[26] Yet she feels that the arguments against women preaching have been answered long ago, that women's good work is "familiar and appreciated" and "that the sex of the worker is not a bar to good work."[27] Women of her time are taking an increasing share in education and enter almost every field of work. In fact, the Parliament of Religions itself is evidence "that

---

Rev. Murdock's first name is inconsistent in *WPR*: it is spelled "Marian" in at least two places (2:807, 821), but given as "Marion" in the "Table of Contents" (1:xxiv) and with her paper (1:796). Mrs. Potter Palmer's full-page photo (2:1567) carries the following quotation from Barrows's "Preface" (1:vii-viii): "The gracious lady, who is so worthy of her place in the fore front of this gathering of the nations, has said that, as Columbus discovered America, the Columbian Exposition discovered woman. These volumes will show many of the jewels of thought and self-sacrifice which she has contributed to the golden treasury of history."

[25] Antoinette Brown Blackwell, "Woman and the Pulpit," in *WPR*, 2: 1149.

[26] Ibid., p. 1148.

[27] Ibid.

narrow conservatism is rapidly decreasing, and that our conception of the religious pulpit must widen until it can take in all faiths, all tongues which strive to enforce the living spirit of love to God and man."[28]

It is not sexual divisions but choice and capacity which should determine whether women take up work in the church. She asks quite rightly: "Was there ever a reason why capable women should not have continued to be expounders of the highest truth to which their era could attain"[29] as they had been in earlier ages? She describes how her own ordination happened in quite a pragmatic fashion: after she had already worked as a woman pastor in a Congregational Church for six or eight months, a church council was called and it decided to ordain her, thus regularizing the work she was doing. This is a good example of how decisive changes are often brought about empirically and then subsequently legitimized, just as happened this century with the first ordination of women in the Episcopalian Church.

Blackwell's paper also provides some simple statistics by telling us that after her own ordination two other women were ordained in 1859 by the Adventists, and in 1863 two more women were ordained by the Universalist Church. In fact, after the first three women had been ordained between 1850 and 1860, five more were ordained between 1860 and 1870, thirty to forty between 1870 and 1880, and "more than two hundred have received ordination from many denominations" between 1880 and 1890.[30] It has been estimated that when Antoinette Blackwell died, there were more than three thousand women ministers in the United States.[31] Blackwell also points out that many capable women working as preachers and pastors did not seek ordination; yet the world needs more women in the pulpit, for once women will have abandoned "the ingrained habit of unconscious imitation," they will become "indispensable to the religious evolution of the human race."[32] One would have liked to see this point more fully developed as the question of women's part in the development of religion and spirituality is today, under quite different circumstances, much debated.

---

[28] Ibid.

[29] Ibid., p. 1149.

[30] Ibid., p. 1150.

[31] Elizabeth Deen, *Great Women of Faith* (London: Independent Press, 1959), p. 396.

[32] Blackwell, "Woman and the Pulpit," in *WPR*, 2:1150.

It is quite remarkable, though, that out of the nineteen women who gave plenary addresses at the World's Parliament of Religions—or the twenty women, if one counts the opening and closing speeches given by Augusta Chapin—seven were ordained Christian ministers: Antoinette Blackwell, Unitarian; Olympia Brown, Universalist; Augusta Chapin, Universalist; Annis Eastman, Unitarian; Ida Hultin, Unitarian; Marion Murdock, Unitarian; Anna Garlin Spencer, Nondenominational. These affiliations are significant for it was in liberal Protestant groups and churches that women were first able to preach and get ordained. Without a liberal theology such a development is not possible, as has been convincingly argued by Rosemary Ruether,[33] but in spite of recent theological developments the ordination of women is still not possible in the Roman Catholic and Orthodox Churches. A hundred years after the World's Parliament of Religions many Christian women can still not carry out a full Christian ministry. Mrs. Henrotin's farewell address at the parliament was overoptimistic when she said: "It is too soon to prognosticate woman's future in the churches. Hitherto she has been not the thinker, the formulator of creeds, but the silent worker. That day has passed. It remains for her to take her rightful position in the active government of the church, and to the question, if men will accord that position to her, my experience and that of the Chairman of the Women's committees warrants us in answering an emphatic yes. Her future in the Western churches is in her own hands, and the men of the Eastern churches will be emboldened by the example of the Western to return to their country, and bid our sisters of those distant lands to go and do likewise."[34]

If we look at a second contribution, that of Jeanne Sorabji of Bombay on "Women of India," a regrettably brief summary of just over one page tells us something of the impact of the Women's Movement on Indian women from a privileged social background. We learn from Barrows that Miss Sorabji was a Christian convert from Parsi background, but I have no other information on her at present. She was the only woman among the eleven Indian delegates of the parliament who made it her special concern to speak about recent changes among Indian women. These were largely due to the opening

---

[33] See Rosemary Radford Ruether, "The Preacher and the Priest: Two Typologies of Ministry and the Ordination of Women," in C.F. Parvey, ed., *Ordination of Women in Ecumenical Perspective* (Geneva: World Council of Churches, 1980), pp. 67-73.

[34] Henrotin, closing address, in *WPR*, 1:178.

of schools and colleges which had mainly Christian women as principals (she also mentions one Christian of Parsi background). She briefly refers to several Indian women with distinguished educational achievements including the well-known Pandita Ramabai, renowned for her Sanskrit learning, who also converted to Christianity. Today her writings are attracting new attention among contemporary Indian feminists, especially because of her criticism of traditional Hindu attitudes toward women.

Sorabji defends the traditional seclusion of Indian women who, in her view, do not live in ignorance but only in seclusion from the outside world. She knows that Indian women have been actively involved in human affairs and even been "at the head of battles, guiding their men with word and look of command."[35] The summary of her speech finishes with the prophetic utterance: "My countrywomen will soon be spoken of as the greatest scientists, artists, mathematicians and preachers of the world."[36]

That word could have been spoken by Swami Vivekananda who precisely wanted this for the women of his country, especially after he had experienced the impact of the Women's Movement during his stay in the United States. He wanted women to be educated and to be educators themselves; above all he wanted them to be preachers of spirituality. But it took more than another half century before a parallel women's wing to the Ramakrishna Math and Mission could be founded—the Śāradā Devī Math which came into existence in 1954.[37] Members of this small women's Hindu religious order are found in different parts of India and abroad today, and the practice and preaching of spirituality together with social and educational work are their special vocation. Another women's movement of Indian origin, but now of global diffusion, concerned with the development of spirituality are the Brahma Kumaris. Their male founder taught earlier this century that women will be the primary spiritual teachers and perform a major role in effecting world change. It came as no surprise that the Brahma Kumaris World Spiritual Organization, to

---

[35] Jeanne Sorabji, "Women of India," in *WPR*, 2:1038. This paper was given on the eleventh day of the parliament.

[36] Ibid.

[37] I have discussed the wider context and historical background of its development in my paper "The Effect of Social Change on Religious Self-Understanding: Women Ascetics in Modern Hinduism," in K. Ballhatchet and D. Taylor, eds., *Changing South Asia: Religion and Society* (Hong Kong: Asian Research Service for London SOAS Centre of South Asian Studies, 1984), pp. 69-83.

quote their full name, organized a workshop on "Women, Spirituality and Leadership" to be held at the 1993 Parliament of the World's Religions in Chicago.

After discussing two contributions by women dealing *with* women as their main focus, I shall now consider briefly two further contributions concerned with other issues.

Miss Josephine Lazarus from New York contributed a paper on "The Outlook of Judaism" which in her absence was read out by a Mrs. Max Leopold on the sixth day of the parliament. Of particular interest is the way in which her paper wrestles with the question of Jewish identity long before the existence of the modern state of Israel where this issue is today much debated. She speaks of the Mosaic code as the moral ideal of the Hebrews, divinely sanctioned and ordained, and of ancient Jerusalem as the stronghold and sanctuary for national and religious life. Yet she also maintains that the "true greatness of Israel was never to consist in outward greatness, nor in the materializing of any of its ideas, either in the religious or the secular life, but wholly in the inner impulse and activity, the spiritual impetus."[38] The Jews are a nation which has always been the "God-intoxicated" race, "intent upon the problem of understanding him and his ways with them, his rulings of their destiny."[39] "Their God was a God whom the people could understand,"[40] a God working upon earth, a God of justice and mercy who mingles in human affairs. If the prophets were the highlights of Judaism, Miss Lazarus judges the Talmud and rabbinical thinking as being responsible for Judaism having lost its power to expand and its claim to become a universal religion. Instead it remained "the prerogative of a peculiar people,"[41] a people subject to long tragedy ever since the Christian era began to dawn for Israel with fire and sword.

She writes with pathos about Jewish martyrdom of eighteen centuries, "the long tragedy that has not ended yet," a passage which sounds almost prophetic when read from a post-Holocaust perspective:

> Jerusalem was besieged, the temple fired, the Holy Mount in flames, and a million people perished....Death in every form, by flood, by fire, and with every torture that could be conceived, left a track of blood through history,

---

[38] Josephine Lazarus, "The Outlook of Judaism," in *WPR*, 1:708. This paper is reprinted in *DRP*, pp. 234-44.
[39] Lazarus, "The Outlook of Judaism," in *WPR*, 1:709.
[40] Ibid.
[41] Ibid., p. 710.

the crucified of the nations. Strangers and wanderers in every age, and every land, calling no man friend, and no spot home. Withal the ignominy of the Ghetto, a living death. Dark, pitiable, ignoble destiny! Magnificent, heroic, unconquerable destiny, luminous with self-sacrifice, unwritten heroism, devotion to an ideal, a cause believed in, and a name held sacred![42]

Lazarus speaks positively of the changes since the French Revolution when ghetto gates were thrown open and Jews entered the modern world. But spiritual and secular life have grown apart since then so that the Jews of her time, whether liberal, progressive or humanitarian, are described as having lost sight of spiritual horizons and as lacking the larger vision of the Hebrew prophets. She also warns of the large rise in anti-Semitism, signs of which are found in every country, though the problem is seen as most acute "in barbarous Russia, liberal France and philosophic Germany."[43]

What answer have Jews for themselves and for the world "in this, the trial-hour of our faith, the crucial test of Judaism?"[44] What is the meaning of the Jewish exodus from Russia and Poland? Are these Jews the last of that "weary pilgrimage through the centuries"?[45] No concrete political solution is offered here. Rather what is suggested is the renewal of Judaism as a spiritual force with a special mission in spiritual fellowship with other believers: "John, Paul, Jesus himself, we can claim them all for our own. We do not want 'missions' to convert us. We cannot become Presbyterians, Episcopalians, members of any dividing sect....Christians as well as Jews need the larger unity that shall embrace them all, the unity of spirit, not of doctrine."[46] It is out of the heart of materialistic civilization that "the cry of the spirit hungering for its food" has come to which Jews and Christians alike have to answer by worshipping God who is Spirit "in the ever-growing, ever-deepening love and knowledge of his truth and its showing forth to men."[47] She finishes with the call to "make known the faith that is in you" and to show its fruits.[48]

Miss Lazarus's paper has much to say which can still speak to contemporary Jewish self-understanding. While some expressions appear dated, they nonetheless raise issues which are central to Jewish

---

[42] Ibid.
[43] Ibid., p. 712.
[44] Ibid.
[45] Ibid., p. 714.
[46] Ibid.
[47] Ibid., p. 715.
[48] Ibid.

debates and to those of Jewish-Christian dialogue. As in other papers delivered at the parliament there is also the call for spiritual renewal grounded in the conviction that it cannot come about without members of different faiths, or in this case especially Jews and Christians, developing deeper understanding of and closer collaboration with each other.

The last woman speaker to be considered is Alice C. Fletcher who gave a paper on "The Religion of the North American Indians"[49] on the twelfth day of the parliament. Seager lists this anthropologist from Harvard University as one among eight "Noted Scholars,"[50] the only woman included in his list. But contrary to this information it must be mentioned that Fletcher was not the only woman scholar lecturing at the parliament, for there were also Eliza R. Sunderland from Ann Arbor[51] who lectured on the fifth day on "Serious Study of All Religions," and Augusta Chapin, described as a lecturer on English literature from the University of Chicago,[52] who gave opening and closing addresses, as already mentioned.

As for the topic of Fletcher's paper, Diana Eck has pointed out that "no late-twentieth-century Parliament would conceive of having an anthropologist speak for the native peoples of America."[53] Like some other groups Native Americans did not participate in the parliament, but when Seager writes that Native American religions were represented by only "one brief, highly general paper presented by an academic anthropologist in the Parliament's scientific section,"[54] this is strictly speaking inaccurate. Fletcher's paper is clearly listed under the plenary "Parliament Papers" on the twelfth day,[55] whereas she is not officially listed under the "Scientific Section"[56] although she repeated the same paper in this section where she also seems to have been the only woman speaker.

---

[49] A brief summary is given in *WPR*, 2:1078-79; a longer text is found in *NHP*, pp. 584-87.

[50] *DRP*, p. 481. Fletcher's scholarship is documented by thirty-five entries under her name in *The National Union of Congress Catalog Pre-1956 Imprints*, vol. 175.

[51] Her name is not mentioned anywhere in *DRP*.

[52] See n. 6 above.

[53] Diana L. Eck, "Foreword" to *DRP*, p. xviii.

[54] "General Introuction,"*DRP*, pp. 6-7.

[55] See *WPR*, 2:812. There are also two papers in "The Woman's Congregational Congress" which refer to North American Indians: "The Work of the Indians on the Frontier," by Mary C. Collins, and "Among Indians and Negroes at Home," by Alice W. Bacon; see Barrows, "The Denominational Congresses," in *WPR*, 2:1435.

[56] See "Table of Contents," *WPR*, 2:815.

Her paper takes up four pages in *Neely's History of the Parliament of Religions,* and although admittedly speaking of North American Indians in very general, inclusive terms, it makes a number of noteworthy points, especially when looked at from a contemporary perspective. The author is well aware of the limitations of her paper, which she says cannot do justice to the variety of tribes, languages and cultures found among the North American Indians. But she emphasizes the startling fact that "in this so-called new world"[57]—a world which was much praised and glorified beyond any other at the parliament—a living culture of great antiquity can be studied and much can be learned from it. Some kind of consensus about Indians' beliefs can be obtained "from a careful study of the myths of the people, of their ceremonies, their superstitions, and their various customs."[58] The Indian feeling concerning God, as Fletcher puts it, "seems to indicate a power, mysterious, unknowable, unnamable, that animates all nature."[59] She explains how from this great mysterious source of life the flow of life pours into "the concrete forms which make up this world, as the sun, moon, and the wind, the water, the earth, and the thunder, the birds, the animals, and the fruits of the earth."[60] With our contemporary ecological interest and the growing awareness of the sacredness of all life this passage is of particular interest to us today.

There are other references too: to the North American Indian vision quest, the virtue of peace inculcated through numerous rituals, but especially through the sacred pipe ceremony, the belief in immortality, and the ethics of hospitality: "The richest man was not he who possessed the most, but he who had given away the most."[61] This lofty ideal is called into question, though, when she comments that this "deeply rooted principle of giving is a great obstacle in the way of civilizing the Indians, as civilization depends so largely upon the accumulation of property."[62] One hundred years later we are more skeptical because we recognize the lack of wisdom and the danger inherent in this long-cherished assumption of linking civilization with property.

---

[57] Alice C. Fletcher, "The Religion of the North American Indians," in *NHP,* p. 584.

[58] Ibid., p. 585.

[59] Ibid.

[60] Ibid.

[61] Ibid., p. 587.

[62] Ibid.

We are also not the first to comment on the absence of the North American Indian voice at the parliament. Fletcher concluded her paper with the critical comment: "Upon this platform have been gathered men from every race of the Eastern world, but the race that for centuries was the sole possessor of this Western continent has not been represented. No American Indian has told us how his people have sought after God through the dim ages of the past. He is not here, but can not his sacred symbol serve its ancient office once more and bring him and us together in the bonds of peace and brotherhood?"[63]

The answer to this, as to other questions raised by women's voices at the World's Parliament of Religions, is still outstanding. What can one conclude then from the contributions of these distinguished women who spoke with such assurance and hope at the first interfaith gathering a century ago?

3. Concluding Reflections

To promote peace and the spirit of human brotherhood among people of diverse faiths were some of the explicit objectives of the World's Parliament whose participants met under the motto "Have we not all one Father? Has not one God created us?" suggested by the chief rabbi of the British Empire, Dr. H. Adler. The overriding mood of the parliament was triumphant, imperial and assertive of the achievements of the "New World," a mood one also senses in many of the women's speeches as well as those of the men. But there were also strong voices of dissent, expressing disagreement with the prevailing mood by offering self-critical reflections on global inequalities and injustices.

Women were present at the parliament in their own right and they spoke their own voice, grounded in their own experience. They spoke clearly, competently and critically, contributing important insights and challenging some of the dominant views of their time. Listening carefully to the voices presented in this essay—the voices of Antoinette Brown Blackwell, Jeanne Sorabji, Josephine Lazarus, and Alice Fletcher—we still feel addressed by their words and share their concerns as women and as human beings.

The historical and spiritual significance of the powerful dynamic of the Women's Movement was well expressed in Lydia Fuller Dickinson's speech on "The Divine Basis of the Coöperation of Men and Women" in which she said: "The Woman Movement means in the

---

[63] Ibid.

Divine Providence 'the hard-earned release of the feminine in human nature from bondage to the masculine.' It means the leadership henceforth in human affairs of truth no longer divorced from, but one with, love. It is the last battle ground of Freedom and Slavery. We are in the dawn of a new and final dispensation....Many forms of slavery have disappeared; but we have also failed. Other forms remain to be dealt with in the new spirit of the New Age. Man has failed as an exponent of wisdom, women of love." Furthermore, stated Dickinson, "We are still measurably ignorant of the nature of woman in women, of her real capacities, inclinations, and powers, nor shall we know these until women are free to express them in accordance with their own ideas, and not as hitherto, in accordance with man's ideas of them."[64]

As this passage shows, many of the attitudes and aims of the women at the parliament connect with ours, in spite of much of the strident, confident rhetoric of their age and the clear limitations of their discourse. Our sisters then had not yet perceived the extent of the powers of patriarchy and the all-pervasiveness of androcentric thought forms and exclusive language. Their struggles pioneered many of the struggles we are still facing today, as women and men, and yet their efforts, largely applauded by themselves, remained mostly unrecognized and were belittled. Indicative of this is a press report on the opening of the parliament in the *Daily Inter Ocean* describing the different religious representatives from East and West, followed by the comment: "The fair sex were there, too, and they were not neglected. But sisterhood in such a gathering was superfluous. The air was full of brotherhood, and it was of a generic kind, such as fits both sexes."[65]

---

[64] Lydia Fuller Dickinson, "The Divine Basis of the Coöperation of Men and Women," in *WPR*, 1:506, 507.

[65] Quoted from the excerpt from the *Daily Inter Ocean*, September 12, 1893, as reprinted in *DRP*, p. 31. Among the many voices of women connected with the parliament one must not forget those of women journalists reporting on the speeches in the press. C.T. Jackson mentions in connection with reports on eastern religions Florence E. Winslow writing for *Christian Thought* and Lucy Monroe for *The Critic*; see his chapter on "The Parliament of Religions: The Closing of One Era and the Opening of Another" in C.T. Jackson, *The Oriental Religions and American Thought* (Westport, Conn.: Greenwood, 1981), pp. 242-60. [Nor should those women who composed poems inspired by the parliament be forgotten. In addition to the poem written *for* the Parliament of Religions by Laura Ormiston Chant (n. 13 above) and read out there by Barrows, at least two other poems were composed by women *about* the parliament and published in its aftermath; see my Introduction to the present volume (Ed.).]

Such generic inclusion has usually meant in practice that women are excluded or simply disregarded. That was less the case at the parliament itself, as many of the quotations have shown, than in its historiography and the subsequent development of the global interfaith movement which it initiated.

In the women present at the parliament we discover a great vision of strength sustained by a strong belief in the independence and power of women. They believed in women's power because they lived it. A hundred years later we can feel affirmed and empowered by the strength of their convictions and the nature of their achievements. And yet their forecasts regarding matters of gender were far too optimistic because "one-half of the religious world," as Augusta Chapin expressed it, still does not enjoy equal participation and representation in religion.

Personally, I take away one strong message from the women speakers at the World's Parliament of Religions: women must be given an equal share in contributing according to their full capacity in all areas of religion and spirituality. The current patriarchal structures of religious institutions do not permit this yet, but women of all faiths are striving to bring about a transformation which could be of great spiritual significance for the future of humankind. It is particularly in the area of personal and global spirituality that contemporary women are making many new connections or rediscovering ancient ones which provide great sources of inspiration and empowerment. But women also need public visibility and official recognition. To give women greater recognition and visibility, the World Council of Churches called in 1988 for a "Decade of the Churches in Solidarity with Women." Following this example and celebrating the centenary of so many women taking part in the 1893 parliament, I would like to suggest to the 1993 Parliament of the World's Religions to encourage all religions to give more space and recognition to women's voices by calling publicly for a global "Decade of Religions in Solidarity with Women." This is my most ardent wish in reflecting on the voices of our sisters one hundred years ago. It would also be the most befitting way of acknowledging and celebrating their contribution to the great interfaith event of that time.

NOTES ON THE AUTHORS

※※※※

Authors of the papers of parts I and the articles of part II:

Note: Indication is given at the end of the profiles of those authors whose lives and works are treated in Louis Henry Jordan, *Comparative Religion: Its Genesis and Growth* (New York: Charles Scribner's Sons, 1905); Jacques Waardenburg, *Classical Approaches to the Study of Religion: Aims, Methods and Theories of Research*, 2 vols. (vol. 1: Introduction and Anthology; vol. 2: Bibliography) (The Hague: Mouton, 1973-74); and *The Encyclopedia of Religion*, 16 vols., ed. Mircea Eliade (New York: Macmillan, 1987). More space below is devoted to Sunderland than to the other authors because the one substantial source on her life is not easily accessible to most readers.

John Henry Barrows (1847-1902), Presbyterian minister, lecturer, and organizer and chairman of the World's Parliament of Religions, was a graduate of Olivet College, Michigan (1867). He later studied at Yale, Union and Andover Theological Seminaries, and at Göttingen, Germany, receiving his D.D. at Lake Forest University. He served as pastor at Lawrence and Boston, Massachusetts, for fourteen years, before becoming pastor of the First Presbyterian Church in Chicago. After the 1893 parliament, he popularized his research as lecturer in India and Japan on the Christian religion (1896-97); as lecturer at Oberlin College, Ohio; as Ely Lecturer at Union Theological Seminary, New York (1898); and as Haskell Lecturer on comparative religion at the University of Chicago. In 1899 he became president of Oberlin College.

Aside from *WPR*, the books he authored included *Seven Lectures on the Credibility of the Gospel Histories* [cover title: *The Gospels are True Histories*] (Boston: D. Lothrop, 1891); *I Believe in God the Father Almighty* (Chicago: F.H. Revell, 1892); *The Life of Henry Ward Beecher: The Shakespeare of the Pulpit* (New York: Funk and Wagnalls, 1893); *Christianity the World-Religion*, Lectures delivered in India and Japan (Chicago: A.C. McClurg, 1897); *A World Pilgrimage* (Chicago: McClurg, 1897); and *The Christian Conquest of Asia* (New York: Scribner, 1899).

The most complete account of his life is by his daughter, Mary Eleanor Barrows, *John Henry Barrows: A Memoir* (Chicago: Fleming H. Revell, 1904). See also Jordan, *Genesis*, esp. pp. 465-66.

Charles Joseph de Harlez (1832-99), philologist, historian of religions, and Roman Catholic prelate (from 1881), was a specialist in the Avestan texts and the religions and culture of China. The founder and rector of Justus Lipsius College, University of Louvain (1868), he served there as professor of Oriental languages, and of Chinese and Barbaric (sic) languages and literature (as his profile in *WPR*, 2:1586 puts it). He was a member of the Royal Academy of Belgium and director of the Orientalist review *La Muséon*. As the author of a French translation (1875) of the Avesta, he published a number of philological and exegetical studies of the Avestan texts, as well as numerous other studies of the Zoroastrian religion, and of Chinese religion, philosophy, languages, literature, and history.

Friedrich Max Müller (1823-1900), German-born linguist, philologist (specializing in Sanskrit), scholar of comparative religion, and professor at Oxford University, was the son of Wilhelm Müller, a celebrated German poet. He studied philosophy, linguistics, and languages at Leipzig, Berlin, and Paris universities, and later went to London, before moving to Oxford in 1848, where he stayed for the rest of his life. He is credited as one of the founders of the "science of religion" (*Religionswissenschaft*).

Müller's bibliography is remarkably extensive. Aside from his numerous translations of classic Sanskrit texts, his writings on German classics and poetry and on the Indian religious traditions, and his editing of the *Sacred Books of the East*, 50 vols. (Oxford: Clarendon, 1879-1910), his most important works on comparative religion and mythology included "Comparative Mythology" in *Oxford Essays*

(London: J.W. Parker and Son, 1855-58); *Chips from a German Workshop*, 4 vols. (London: Longmans, Green, 1867-75); *Introduction to the Science of Religion*, Lectures at the Royal Institution (London: Longmans, Green, 1873); *Lectures on the Origin and Growth of Religion, as Illustrated by the Religions of India*, Hibbert Lectures at Westminster Abbey, 1878 (1879; rev. ed., London: Longmans, Green, 1882); *Natural Religion*, Gifford Lectures, 1888 (London, 1889); *Physical Religion*, Gifford Lectures, 1890 (London: Longmans, Green, 1891); *Anthropological Religion*, Gifford Lectures, 1891 (London: Longmans, Green, 1892); *Theosophy; or Psychological Religion*, Gifford Lectures, 1892 (1893; new ed., London: Longmans, Green, 1895); and *Contributions to the Science of Mythology*, 2 vols. (London: Longmans, Green, 1897).

Max Müller's *My Autobiography. A Fragment*, edited by W.G. Max Müller, was published posthumously in London by Longmans, Green, 1901. On his life and works see also Jordan, *Genesis*, esp. pp. 169-77, 521-23, 552-54; Waardenburg, *Classical Approaches*, 1:13-17, 85-95; 2:184-88; *Encyclopedia of Religion*, ed. Eliade, s.v. "Müller, F. Max," 10:153-54, whose bibliography gives reference to five biographies.

Albert Réville (1826-1906), French Protestant minister and historian of religions, is considered one of the "founders" of comparative religion, comparable to—although not as influential as—Müller and Tiele. His ministries in Luneray (1848) and Rotterdam (1851-73) and his early critical studies of the Gospel of Matthew and of the dogma of Christ's divinity are said to have established him as the head of Protestant "liberalism" based on "science." In 1880 he was named the first occupant of the chair in the history of religions in the Collège de France. He was father of Jean Réville.

His most significant works include *Essais de critique religieuse* (1860; Paris: J. Cherbuliez, 1869); *Manuel d'histoire comparée de la philosophie et de la religion* (1861); *Prolégomènes de l'histoire des religions*, 3d ed. (Paris: Fischbacher, 1881); *Les religions des peuples non-civilisés* (Paris: Fischbacher, 1883); *Lectures on the Origin and Growth of Religion, as Illustrated by the native Religions of Mexico and Peru*, trans. Philip H. Wicksteed, Hibbert Lectures, 1884 (London: Williams and Norgate, 1884); and *Jésus de Nazareth*, 2 vols. (1897; 2d ed., Paris: Fischbacher, 1906).

He is discussed briefly in Jordan, *Genesis*, esp. pp. 188-89. For a bibliography of his works and references to extended studies of his life and works see Waardenburg, *Classical Approaches*, 2:241-42.

Jean Réville (1854-1908), Protestant pastor at Montbélier and, later, chaplain at the Lycée Henri IV at Paris, was the son of Albert Réville. The editor of *Revue de l'Histoire des Religions*, considered then the foremost journal of its kind in the world, he became professor at the École des Hautes Études (beginning in 1885) and on the faculty of theology at the University of Paris. His writings include *Le Logos d'après Philon d'Alexandrie* (Geneva: Ramboz and Schuchardt, 1877) and *La Religion à Rome sous les Sévères* (Paris: E. Leroux, 1886).

Passing references are made to him in Jordan, *Genesis*, pp. 447-48, 601.

Merwin-Marie Fitz Porter Snell (1863-?), Roman Catholic scholar and advocate of the "science of religion," was secretary of Bishop John Keane at Catholic University in Washington D.C. He served as assistant to the chairman of the 1893 Parliament of Religions, John Henry Barrows, and presided over the parliament's "Scientific Section." A contributor to American and European periodicals, Snell also collaborated with European specialists in the inauguration of the *Oriental Review* (1893). He was author of *Hints on the Study of the Sacred Books* (Baltimore: J. Murphy, 1887); a "list of books useful to students of the Catholic Religion" entitled *One Hundred Theses on the Foundations of Human Knowledge* (Washington, D.C.: published by the author, 1891); and *The Liturgical Languages and their Uses* (n.p., n.d.)

Eliza Read Sunderland (1839-1910), writer, lecturer, preacher (though not ordained), and activist for the advancement of women, was born in Huntsville, Illinois, where she grew up in a log cabin on a farm. Inspired by her reading of the Life of Mary Lyon, she attended Mount Holyoke Seminary in Massachusetts, where she graduated in 1865. She subsequently taught Latin, English literature, and history at the High School of Aurora, Illinois, where she was named principal in 1868, becoming probably the first woman principal of a high school in the United States.

After her marriage in 1871 to Jabez Thomas Sunderland (1842-1936), the noted Baptist-turned-Unitarian minister, she lived with him where he held pastorates: Milwaukee, Wisconsin, 1871-72; Northfield,

Massachusetts, 1872-76; Chicago, Illinois, 1876-78; Ann Arbor, Michigan, 1878-98; Oakland, California, 1898-99; Toronto, Canada 1900-06; Hartford, Connecticut, 1906-10. A high school teacher during her Chicago and Ann Arbor years, she also earned a Ph.D. from the University of Michigan (1892), writing her dissertation on "The Relation of the Philosophy of Kant to that of Hegel." In addition, she was associate editor of the *Illinois Social Science Journal* (1878); president of the Women's Western Unitarian Conference (1882-87); and director of the National Society for the Advancement of Women (1885-95). At the World's Parliament of Religions and the Columbian Exposition's Woman's Congress, she represented Unitarian Women of America. Her parliament speech (included in this volume) was by contemporary accounts one of the best-received addresses of the whole congress. Although almost an hour in length, and reportedly delivered without a note, her lecture was printed in full in *The Chicago Tribune*, which assessed it as follows:

> Three thousand people in the Hall of Columbus stood up and cheered and applauded the remarkable address of Mrs. Eliza R. Sunderland. Hers was the clearest and most eloquent voice in all the great parliament of religions yesterday. She spoke on 'Comparative Religions,' and she showed such clearness and force of expression, that the audience hailed her as easily the orator of the day.
>
> (Quoted by Jabez Thomas Sunderland, *Eliza Read Sunderland: A Brief Sketch of her Life. Memorial Addresses* [n.p., 1912], p. 13.)

Rev. John C. Kimball is reported to have said after the parliament that Eliza Sunderland's address "impressed the men from the Orient more than any other utterance of the great gathering; evidently, too, all the more surprising them because coming from a woman" (paraphrased by J.T. Sunderland, *Brief Sketch*, p. 13).

She was co-author, with Jabez T. Sunderland, of *James Martineau and his Greatest Book*, a centennial tribute (Toronto: W. Tyrrell, 1905). She also authored several pamphlets, and various addresses and articles in magazines and newspapers. In his *Brief Sketch*, Jabez Sunderland identifies his wife's *Heroes and Heroism* (a pamphlet published in Chicago, 1882, 1884) and *Stories from Genesis* (1890?) as her "best known" writings. The former text, but not the latter, is included among the writings listed under her name in *The National Union Pre-1956 Imprints*, vol. 576.

The only substantial account of her life is her husband's *Brief Sketch* cited above.

Cornelius Petrus Tiele (1830-1902), Dutch historian of religions, began as a Remonstrant minister (1853-73). After studying the Avestan language, Akkadian, and Egyptian, he took his Th.D. from the University of Leiden in 1872. He taught the history of religions as a professor at the Remonstrants' seminary in Leiden from 1873 until 1877. He was then named to the new chair in the history of religions and philosophy of religion on the faculty of theology at the University of Leiden, a post he held until 1900.

Like Müller, Tiele is one of the recognized pioneers of the "science of religion." His major works in English translation are *Outlines of the History of Religion, to the Spread of Universal Religions*, trans. J. Estlin Carpenter (London: Trübner, 1877); *History of the Egyptian Religion*, trans. James Ballingal, 2d ed. (Boston: Houghton, Mifflin, 1882); and *Elements of the Science of Religion*, 2 vols., Gifford Lectures, 1896, 1898 (Edinburgh: W. Blackwood and Sons, 1897-99).

For more on his life and works see Jordan, *Genesis*, esp. pp. 180-84; Waardenburg, *Classical Approaches*, esp. 1:14-15, 96; 2:282-86; *Encyclopedia of Religion*, s.v., "Tiele, C.P.," 14:507-08.

Contributors to Part III:

Tessa Bartholomeusz, who received her Ph.D. in Buddhist Studies from the University of Virginia in 1991, has taught in the Department of Oriental Languages at the University of Virginia, and in the Department of Religious Studies at Indiana University, Indianapolis. She is at present an assistant professor of Religious Studies at Florida State University. She has published articles on women in Buddhism, and her book, *Women Under the Bo Tree: Buddhist Nuns in Sri Lanka*, is forthcoming from Cambridge University Press. Her present research focuses on religious identity in Sri Lanka, especially the impact of nationalism on minority communities, including the Burghers.

James Edward Ketelaar, a graduate of Kalamazoo College (1978), took his M.A. (1981) and Ph.D. (1986) at the University of Chicago. He is currently assistant professor of Japanese History, with a focus on early modern Japan, at Stanford University. A past winner of a Fulbright (1984-85) and a Charlotte Newcombe dissertation fellowship (1985-86), he has been named a Whittier Fellow at the Stanford Humanities Center (1992-93), and also won the Hans Rosenhaupt Memorial

Award for his study *Of Heretics and Martyrs in Meiji Japan: Buddhism and Its Persecution* (Princeton, N.J.: Princeton University Press, 1990), from which his contribution to the present volume is reprinted. He is currently working on a book on the conceptions and colonization of Japan's northern frontier.

Ursula King, who currently heads the Department of Theology and Religious Studies at the University of Bristol, is the author and editor of numerous volumes, including three that focus specifically on women's issues in religion, theology, and spirituality. She is president of the British Association for the Study of Religions, one of the vice-presidents of the World Congress of Faiths, and fellow of the Royal Society for the Encouragement of Arts, Manufactures and Commerce (FRSA) in London. Her latest book is *Women and Spirituality: Voices of Protest and Promise*, published this year by Penn State University Press.

The late *Joseph Mitsuo Kitagawa*, historian of religions and Episcopal priest, was born in Osaka, Japan in 1915. He received his Bungakushi (B.A.) degree from Rikkyo University in 1937. He came to the United States in 1941 to study theology at the Church Divinity School of the Pacific, but his theological education was interrupted when he was consigned to a detention camp by the Government at the outbreak of World War II. He was interned for three and a half years in three different camps (two in New Mexico, one in Idaho), being ordained while at the second of these, the Army Internment Camp at Lordsburg, New Mexico. After the war, he attended Seabury Western Theological Seminary, receiving his Bachelor of Divinity degree there in 1946. The following year he entered the University of Chicago Divinity School, where he concentrated his studies in the area of the history of religions under Professor Joachim Wach. He wrote his dissertation on "Kōbō Daishi and Shingon Buddhism," for which he received his Doctor of Philosophy degree in 1951. That same year Kitagawa joined the faculty of the Divinity School. There, he took the lead in carrying on the scholarly tradition of his mentor, Wach, after the latter's death (1955), and later served a remarkably innovative and productive ten years as dean (1970-80). He continued teaching at the Divinity School through his retirement in 1985, remaining there as professor emeritus until his death in the fall of 1992.

With Mircea Eliade and Charles H. Long, Kitagawa was a founding editor in 1961 of the international journal *History of Religions*.

He also taught as visiting professor at many universities and colleges, and gave major lectures around the world, including the Joachim Wach Memorial Lecture at the University of Marburg, the American Council of Learned Societies Lectures in History of Religions, the Charles Wesley Brashares Lectures on the History of Religions at Northwestern University, and the Charles Strong Memorial Lectures in Comparative Religions in Australia. In addition to his four books cited in notes 71 and 150 of the Introduction to the present volume, Kitagawa authored *Religions of the East* (1960; enlarged edition, Philadelphia: Westminster, 1968), *Religion in Japanese History* (New York: Columbia University Press, 1966), *Spiritual Liberation and Human Freedom in Contemporary Asia* (New York: Peter Lang, 1990), and edited or co-edited numerous other volumes, including English translations of works by Wach.

Kitagawa offered interesting reflections on his life and works in his Introduction to *Spiritual Liberation and Human Freedom*, pp. 1-18.

Martin E. Marty is the Fairfax M. Cone Distinguished Service Professor of the History of Modern Christianity at the University of Chicago, where he teaches in the Divinity School, the History Department, and the Committee on the History of Culture. The past president of the American Academy of Religion, the American Society of Church History, and the American Catholic Historical Association, he is author of numerous books on American religion and has published the first two of a four volume work, *Modern American Religion,* published by the University of Chicago Press. Volume I: *The Irony of It All: 1893-1919* (1986) begins with reference to the World's Parliament of Religions, from which the passage in this book is excerpted.

Sunrit Mullick, a descendant of Debendranath Tagore's son Hemendranath, received his B. Com. in 1978, from St. Xavier's College, Calcutta; his M.A. in Comparative Religion in 1984, from Visva-Bharati University, Santiniketan; and his D. Ministry in 1988, from Meadville/Lombard Theological School (University of Chicago). His doctoral dissertation, "Protap Chunder Mozoomdar in America: Missionary of a New Dispensation," researches and documents the nineteenth-century Brāhmo Samāj leader's three visits to the United States in 1883, 1893, 1900, and examines the relevance of his message for contemporary Unitarian Universalism. After completing his doctorate in 1988, Sunrit Mullick returned to India to begin a ministry with Brāhmo Samāj and Unitarian congregations as director of Project India, a program supported by the Unitarian Universalist Association, Boston.

Richard Hughes Seager received his Ph.D. and A.M. in the Study of Religion from Harvard University; his M.T.S. in History of Religion, from Harvard Divinity School; his B.A. in Modern History from University of Wisconsin-Madison. He has taught at the University of North Carolina at Chapel Hill, Harvard Divinity School, Weston School of Theology, and Harvard University. He is the editor of *The Dawn of Religious Pluralism: Voices from the World's Parliament of Religions*, an anthology of addresses published by Open Court this year, and is currently completing an interpretation of the East-West encounter at the 1893 parliament which is under contract to Indiana University Press.

INDEX

�જ૪ૹૹ